The Monk and the Book

The Monk and the Book

Jerome and the Making of
Christian Scholarship

MEGAN HALE WILLIAMS

The University of Chicago Press

CHICAGO AND LONDON

MEGAN HALE WILLIAMS is assistant professor of history
at San Francisco State University and, with Anthony Grafton,
coauthor of *Christianity and the Transformation of the Book:
Origen, Eusebius, and the Library of Caesarea.*

The University of Chicago Press, Chicago 60637
The University of Chicago Press, Ltd., London
© 2006 by The University of Chicago
All rights reserved. Published 2006
Printed in the United States of America
15 14 13 12 11 10 09 08 07 06   5 4 3 2 1

ISBN-13 (cloth): 978-0-226-89900-8
ISBN-10 (cloth): 0-226-89900-4

Library of Congress Cataloging-in-Publication Data

Williams, Megan Hale, 1969–
The monk and the book : Jerome and the making of
Christian scholarship / Megan Hale Williams.
      p.   cm.
Includes bibliographical references and index.
ISBN-13: 978-0-226-89900-8 (cloth : alk. paper)
ISBN-10: 0-226-89900-4 (cloth : alk. paper)
1. Jerome, Saint, d. 419 or 20.   I. Title.
BR65.J476W55 2006
270.2092—dc22
                              2006012416

Contents

Illustrations

Acknowledgments

MANY people—colleagues, friends and family—have contributed to making this book possible. I would like to thank the members of my dissertation committee at Princeton University, who supervised the research on which the book is almost entirely based: Peter Brown, John Gager, Anthony Grafton, Martha Himmelfarb, Robert Kaster, Elaine Pagels, and Ruth Webb. Peter Brown and Anthony Grafton deserve special thanks, for the intensity of their involvement with the project and for their continuing engagement with it long after the dissertation stage was past. Without them, it would have been neither conceived nor brought to fruition. James O'Donnell and Carole Straw also read the dissertation and gave valuable suggestions for revision. Among my peers, Adam Becker, Nathaniel Levtow, Grant Parker, and Annette Reed deserve thanks for professional and personal support at many points. A special debt of gratitude is due to Maya Jasanoff, who read the entire manuscript at a crucial stage and gave invaluable editorial comments, as well as much encouragement. My colleagues at the University of Montana, especially Paul Dietrich and Stewart Justman, deserve my thanks not only for their advice and encouragement at the final stages of this project but especially for the warm welcome they extended to me. I would also like to thank the anonymous readers for the University of Chicago Press, two of whom commented repeatedly on revised versions of the manuscript. Much of what is worthy in the book is due to my mentors and colleagues; errors and other deficiencies are, of course, mine alone.

Further thanks are due to the Center for Advanced Judaic Studies at the University of Pennsylvania and its director, David Ruderman; to the Michigan Society of Fellows and its chair, James Boyd White; and to the Department of Near Eastern Studies of the University of Michigan and two successive chairs of that department, Alexander Knysh and Gary Beckman. These institutions and their presiding genii provided congenial circumstances under which the revisions to the dissertation were undertaken in 2001–4. The librarians at the Center for Advanced Judaic Studies—in particular Judith Leifer; Beau Case, Classics librarian at the University of Michigan; and the inter-library loan staff of the University of Montana's Mansfield Library—all have my lasting gratitude.

Work that was eventually incorporated into this book was presented at Duke University; the Center for Advanced Judaic Studies; the Philadelphia Seminar on Christian Origins; and in the Fellows' colloquium of the Michigan Society of Fellows. Many thanks to my hosts and to the audiences at all of these venues for their hospitality and for helpful comments and criticisms.

Special thanks go to my editor, Alan Thomas, of the University of Chicago Press, for his early and sustained interest in this project.

I would also like to thank Kyla Dunn, Catherine Magid, Ted Sichelman, and Elsa, Graham, and Ronald Williams for everything they have done. The support of my friends and family have made it possible for me to bear the burden that this book has been for me over the past several years.

Abbreviations

CCSL	Corpus Christianorum Series Latina. Turnhout: Brepols, 1953–.
CSEL	Corpus Scriptorum Ecclesiasticorum Latinorum. Vienna, 1866–1957.
IH	*iuxta Hebraeos*
LCL	Loeb Classical Library
GCS	Die griechischen christlichen Schriftsteller der ersten [drei] Jahrhunderte
MT	Masoretic Text
OLD	*Oxford Latin Dictionary*. Oxford: Clarendon Press, 1968–82
PG	Patrologia Graeca. Edited by J.-P. Migne Paris, 1844–64.
PL	Patrologia Latina. Edited by J.-P. Migne Paris, 1844–64.
PLRE	*Prosopography of the Later Roman Empire*. 2 vols. Cambridge: Cambridge University Press, 1970–.

Quotations from Jerome's works are taken from the best available current editions, whose orthography is followed without alteration. This is true also of Greek words inserted into Jerome's Latin text: where the editors have supplied accents and other diacritical marks, these have been included, whereas they have been omitted where absent from the published texts. All translations are my own, except where otherwise noted.

INTRODUCTION

———— ✳ ————

IN THE fifteenth century, a standard iconography of Saint Jerome emerged, taking two distinct forms.[1] Two of Albrecht Dürer's most famous prints exemplify the alternatives. The more familiar iconographic type portrays Jerome as a scholar (fig. 1). Dürer's Jerome sits in his study, bent over a book. In the foreground, a small dog is curled up asleep, serving as a visual indication of the silence of the scholar's workroom. Jerome's traditional lion—a figment of the twelfth-century *Golden Legend* of Jacobus de Voragine—is also asleep, though his eyes remain slightly open, the left seeming to peer at the viewer. Medieval science credited to the lion the ability to sleep with its eyes open.[2] Though the saint wears the garb of a Roman cardinal, a traditional attribute,[3] his distinctive hat hangs on the wall above him, suggesting that he has left behind the tumult of ecclesiastical politics for the moment and reinforcing the impression of domesticity conveyed by the postures of the animals and the orderly arrangement of the room, with its spare yet luxurious furnishings.

The alternative image depicts Jerome as a penitent ascetic in a harsh, rocky landscape (fig. 2). The saint kneels in three-quarter view, his gaze again turned away from the viewer. His attributes are those of a desert hermit. He is naked to the waist, only his lower body covered by a length of drapery, and he holds a stone with which he is about to beat his breast.

1. Rice, *Jerome*, 76ff., 104ff., describes the fifteenth-century evolution of Jerome's iconography.

2. Rice, *Jerome*, 41.

3. Rice, *Jerome*, 35–37.

1

FIGURE 1. Albrecht Dürer (1471–1528), *Jerome in his study*. 1514.
Fondazione Magnani Rocca, Corte di Mamiano, Italy. Scala / Art Resource, NY.

FIGURE 2. Albrecht Dürer (1471–1528), *Jerome in the wilderness*.
Foto Marburg / Art Resource, NY.

The prominence of his well-muscled trunk in the image reminds us that his ascetic regimen used the body as a means to train the soul. The lion, again, occupies the very foreground. In this image, however, instead of resting with eyes almost closed, it crouches tensely, glaring out of the page.

The contrast between the peace of the scholar's study and the torment of the repentant hermit at prayer is sharp, despite the restraint with which Dürer portrays the saint's agony in the latter of the two etchings. The contrast is driven home not only by the traits of the saint himself but also by his physical setting. One figure is seated, indoors, fully clothed, his attention directed toward his book. His workroom is a model of bourgeois order.[4] The other kneels on the bare earth, his body exposed to the elements, his expression pained, his mind focused inward in recollection of his sins. The dramatic landscape, with its jagged rocks and spiky pine trees, contrasts with the solid horizontality of the scholar's study. The man-made interior could not be more distinct from wild nature, in both visual and moral terms.

The two different versions of Saint Jerome canonized in the Renaissance iconographic tradition reflect a fundamental problem that the saint presents for those who attempt to understand his life and legacy. The ways of life of the scholar and of the Christian ascetic are not readily seen together, much less brought together in practice. The monastic ideal emphasizes the virtues of poverty, chastity, and humility. This is particularly so for the cenobitic monastery, where the monks hold their property and keep their rule in common. Although scholarship too can readily be conceived of in ascetic terms, its values are at odds with those of the monastery.

While the scholar may be chaste, his activities characteristically require an expensive infrastructure: a library, a workplace — some fifteenth-century images of Jerome show him seated in a *studiolo* that would have been the envy of a North Italian prince — and the means of disseminating his work, whether in print or through the labor of a staff of copyists. Scholarship thereby violates the monastic norm of poverty. Furthermore, the scholar by his very assumption of that identity asserts his authority. In particular, biblical criticism, the establishment of the text of scripture and its explication, implies the interpreter's authority over the sacred word. Such an assertion

4. Other versions of this iconographic type represent Jerome as an aristocratic cardinal, for example the painting by Antonello Da Messina in the National Gallery in London. Dürer also depicted Jerome as a hermit in his cave surrounded by books, in a woodcut of 1512. The image is reproduced in E. Panofsky, *Albrecht Dürer*, 2 vols., 2nd ed. (Princeton, 1945), 2:40, no. 333 (Rice, *Jerome*, 106, citing Panofsky in n. 72).

of authority sharply differentiates the exegete from the monk in terms of their relation to the text. The traditional monastic reading practice of the *lectio divina,* already well developed by the fathers of the Egyptian desert, aimed at submission to the Word embodied in the scriptures, not at the exercise of critical judgment over it. Exegesis can readily be seen as threatening to violate the norm of humility.

On several levels, then, Jerome presents an enduring challenge to his interpreters and to his cultural heirs. Not only did he have the audacity to fuse the identities of scholar and monk: he went so far as to represent textual scholarship at the highest level as itself a form of *askesis,* of spiritual "training," appropriate for a cenobite. This book aims to address that challenge by interpreting Jerome's career as a biblical scholar and Christian writer within its immediate historical context, in the last decades of the fourth and the first decades of the fifth centuries. Jerome himself, seen through the lens of his own writings, will be the focus of attention. Taking advantage of progress in the historiography of the period, and of innovations in the history of scholarship in general, I will propose new interpretations of Jerome's scholarship that promise to remove enduring obstacles to understanding this major figure in the Western tradition.

*

Jerome lived through a time of immense change for the Roman world. Two long-term developments converged in the period under discussion to create a new Roman culture. A trend toward centralization and rule by decree that had begun in the political crisis of the mid-third century reached its first peak under Diocletian and the Tetrarchy at the end of that century. The same tendency continued to unfold during the next century, completely changing the structure of the Roman elite and its relation to both the central government and the mass of the population. Simultaneously, Christianization—begun under Constantine, but proceeding with new intensity under Theodosius I and his successors—reshaped the elite from the inside out.

Imperial rule, from Augustus through the end of the second century, was a rather decentralized affair. Much legislation was driven not by the emperor's own initiatives but by requests from the periphery. Emperors who lacked the bureaucratic apparatus to rule their far-flung dominions more directly depended on local elites to administer justice and collect taxes. During the third century, the internal dynamics of imperial government had driven a slow shift away from this model, toward a new emphasis on imperial power and policy. Already in the third century the importance of provincial cities and, especially, of their elites was on the decline. No longer could civic elites, in particular the hereditary *curia* or city councils, effectively mediate imperial power. Curial status, once a privilege, became a burden. The extension of Roman citizenship to all inhabitants of the empire under Caracalla in the 230s, the reorganization of the provinces under Diocletian around 290, and an ongoing reshuffling of the armies all contributed to, and reflected, the new tendency.[5]

Administratively, the first Christian emperor, Constantine, continued his pagan predecessors' policies, but his religious policy brought further changes in its wake. Under Constantine and his successors in the mid-fourth century, the decline of the urban elites in favor of a new administrative and military class accelerated. At the same time, the hierarchy of the Christian church began to take on the contours of an alternative civic leadership. Already, Constantine had entrusted important civic functions to Christian bishops. These duties, and the informal influence that accompanied them, were only to expand over the course of the century. The old urban elites did not entirely disappear, but their values and their relations to imperial administration and to other major institutions were transformed. A new culture—late Roman and Christian—emerged.

Since at least the early second century of our era, the elites of the Roman empire had shared a literary culture, and an educational system, whose roots lay far back in the late Republic and the Hellenistic kingdoms. The school curriculum was based on a narrow canon of literary texts. Students learned to regard the literary tradition as a continuum, whether it spanned the centuries from Homer to Demosthenes or the decades that separated Cicero from Seneca, and to feel a profound sense of continuity with this unitary past. Educated men situated themselves in a relationship of atemporal closeness to their illustrious precursors, whose works they adopted as models both for written and spoken self-expression and for the conduct of the virtuous life. Their schooling distinguished the ruling class of late antiquity from their less educated peers by instilling stereotypical patterns of spoken and written expression that served as passports to careers as advocates and bureaucrats.

Contemporary prescriptive texts divided literary education into three phases: the *ludus litterarius,* the humble school of letters; the school of the *grammaticus,* where students moved from basic literacy skills to the study of

---

5. For this picture of the political and administrative development of the Roman empire, see fundamentally Millar, *Emperor,* supplemented by Ando, *Imperial Ideology.*

literature; and the rhetorician's school, where young men mastered advanced exercises in composition, with an emphasis on improvisation. In reality, the three stages tended to run together, and only in major cities was the full curriculum even available. Schooling in basic literacy was available almost everywhere, and to children from virtually any background if they could be spared from work. Grammatical schooling was available in many small towns, but the demands placed on the pupils might be much lower there than in a larger center. Rhetoricians, finally, tended to cluster in a few cities, either great capitals or traditional centers of learning.[6]

Formal schooling began with the *grammaticus* or grammarian, who taught reading, writing, and the language itself—"grammar" in the modern sense. He introduced students to the basic elements of literary study, including the vocabulary of the poets and the history, geography and mythology necessary to understand them.[7] The texts studied did not include prose authors: poetry was considered more appropriate for the young. The archaism of the curriculum led to the rise of an extensive commentary literature, which extended the preoccupations of the *grammaticus*—mythography, geography, and an obsession with rare words and grammatical oddities—to a more serious intellectual level. Grammatical education culminated with the *progymnasmata*, a series of increasingly complex exercises in composition.[8]

Boys from elite backgrounds attended a rhetorician's school beginning in their mid- to late teens. There, these privileged young men read the canonical orators and learned to produce and present sample speeches, called

6. The classic study of ancient Greek and Roman education is Marrou, *History of Education;* more recent work has modified many of his interpretations, although the overall reconstruction of the educational system remains much the same: see Morgan, *Literate Education,* Cribiore, *Gymnastics,* and, for a study of the educational papyri as sources for grammatical study, Cribiore, *Writing.* On the stages of education and the organization of schools, see Marrou, *History of Education,* 358–59; Morgan, *Literate Education,* 50–89; Cribiore, *Gymnastics,* 36–44.

7. On Latin grammatical education, see Marrou, *History of Education,* 369–80; Bonner, *Education,* 47–64, 189–276. On the status of the grammarian, see Kaster, *Guardians,* and Bonner, *Education,* 146–62. Morgan, *Literate Education,* 163–89, gives some attention to the study of "grammar" in the modern sense, while Cribiore, *Gymnastics,* 185–219, deals with the *grammatika* as found in the school papyri.

8. Greek manuals of *progymnasmata:* second century CE, Theon and Aelius [Donatus], *Progymnasmata,* ed. Michel Patillon and Giancarlo Bolognesi (Paris: Belles Lettres, 1997), and Hermogenes, *Opera;* fourth century, Aphthonius, *Aphthonii Progymnasmata.* Translations are available in Kennedy and Spengel, *Progymnasmata.* Libanius left an impressive corpus of examples, covering each type of *progymnasma:* see Libanius, *Opera,* vol. 8. For *progymnasmata* in the school papyri, see Cribiore, *Gymnastics,* 220–44.

declamations, in imitation of their models.[9] Declamation was the practice of presenting artificial speeches before a school audience, often on fantastic, even bizarre topics. The declaimer's art attracted great attention, among both the rhetorically schooled and the public at large. Rhetorical education also used the *progymnasmata,* so that the two different schools overlapped to a considerable extent. Indeed, throughout the curriculum students returned repeatedly to the same texts and the same types of exercise, which they repeated with increasing degrees of sophistication.[10]

The canonical texts were pressed into serving different purposes at different stages. Homer or Virgil could function as a primer for boys learning to read, as a source of moral examples and mythological and geographical trivia a few years later, and finally as a mine of well-turned phrases to be deployed by the declaimer at crucial turns in his argument. Boys in grammatical school were taught to avoid solecism and barbarism, and to eschew neologisms and expressions typical of everyday spoken language in favor of a consciously archaic diction. Examples from canonical works were used to teach moral lessons. Later, intensive study of the canonical orators and the production of sample discourses on stock themes produced an effect of assimilation of both word and thought to the models of the tradition. The result was a cohort of young men whose every word and gesture set them apart from their inferiors, and bound them to each other, as members of a cultured elite.[11]

The changes in the structure of Roman society that took place from the mid-third through the fourth centuries were accompanied by more subtle shifts in elite culture. Peter Brown, in *The Making of Late Antiquity,* describes the transformation as a passage "from an age of equipoise to an age of ambition," from a society where the paradigmatic social relation for the elite was that of competition for prestige among equals to one where centralized power imposed itself with scarcely veiled brutality.[12] For the urban elites of the age of the Antonines, participation in a common literary culture had

9. On the development of Latin rhetorical education, Marrou, *History of Education,* 381–87; Bonner, *Education,* 65–75, 75–111. Grammarians versus rhetoricians: Marrou, *History of Education,* 378–79.

10. That the same canonical texts were studied repeatedly at different points in the curriculum, producing the effect described in the next paragraph, is a central observation of Cribiore, *Gymnastics.*

11. On rhetorical education as a means of producing embodied signs of social distinction, see Gleason, *Making Men.* On the importance of shared literary culture in binding together the elites that ruled the far-flung Roman empire, see Brown, *Power and Persuasion.*

12. Brown, *Late Antiquity,* 34.

been one of the characteristics that delineated their social milieu. The competitive nature of that culture had provided an important outlet for the agonistic energies that drove the machine of urban society and at the same time threatened to burst out of it.

The fourth century was far more suspicious of competition, even among near equals within the urban elites. The stakes had been raised, the game was being played in deadly earnest. Rhetoric was now a device directed not at one's peers, but primarily at the emperor himself, an emperor become newly distant and majestic. Cultivated speech, in this context, could serve to mollify an enraged potentate, or to sway him to be well disposed. The two roles, of competition among peers and appeal to the higher power, had co-existed already in the second century. In the fourth century, the latter came greatly to outweigh the former.

At the same time that the changed political order placed traditional elite culture in new contexts, Christianization subjected it to a new kind of scrutiny. The question of the value of Greek and Latin literature for Christians was by no means new in the second half of the fourth century. Traditional education focused unrelentingly on a canon of classical literature in which pagan gods appeared on every page. Its aims were shaped by an agonistic society in which elite males competed in public for prestige, civic standing, and the rewards these brought. Not only was rhetorical culture competitive, selfish, and potentially coercive, but it sanctioned a level of duplicity that sat poorly with Christian emphases on simplicity and truth. On many levels, the culture of the literate elite had been fundamentally at odds with Christianity from the moment of their first encounter.

But as the fourth century gave rise to a Christian ruling class, the problem was posed with new urgency. Fourth-century Christian writers express a profound suspicion of rhetorical culture and, more broadly, of literary cultivation in any form. To some extent, this suspicion rested on the pagan content of classical literature. But it did not end there. Augustine lays out the problem in characteristically explicit terms in his *De doctrina christiana*. His ideal of *caritas,* and the transparent honesty it demanded, were profoundly at odds with rhetorical culture. Rhetoric, by its very nature as a form of persuasion with the potential to make the worse cause seem the better, had been portrayed as a form of coercion—if not violence—since the days of Gorgias in the fifth century BCE. As such, it was a treacherous weapon for a Christian bishop to wield.

As an alternative to the *rhetor* as intercessor before emperors, Christianity in the fourth century put forward the holy man. The holy man's power to intercede rested on his status as one who chose to remain outside of the elite and its struggle for precedence — indeed, in many cases, physically outside the city itself, even outside of civilization. Because his radical asceticism stood as concrete and undeniable proof of his disinterestedness, the holy man could be regarded by all sides to a dispute as a neutral broker. He had nothing to gain, because he had already lost everything — voluntarily. Extreme forms of Christian *askesis*, therefore, produced figures who came from the humblest of backgrounds, yet could compete for the social roles previously monopolized by the educated, whether they were philosophers, sophists, or bishops. One who could combine the prestige of the two traditions, it might seem, would wield all the more power. Ascetic renunciation of the quest for power might tame the disturbingly self-centered aspects of rhetorical culture.

Christian asceticism by the fourth century had already a long history. In the first century CE, Jews and those messianic Jewish sectaries who followed the crucified Jesus of Nazareth had assembled in ascetic conventicles. We know of one such group, outside Alexandria, from the Jewish author Philo. In Syria in the second century, Christians had advocated and practiced *enkrasis* or "restraint," abstaining from sex, from food, and from participation in the larger society, in the attempt to prepare for the imminent reign of God. Even as third-century emperors produced martyrs in increasing numbers, Christian ascetics retreated to the deserts of Egypt to seek the "white martyrdom" of renunciation. By the early fourth century, ascetics in the East had pioneered several forms of monastic organization, from the solitary life of the hermit, supervised only by a spiritual father, to the cenobitic (from the Greek *koinos bios* or "common life") model instituted by Pachomius, an Egyptian peasant, in upper Egypt. News of the heroism of the desert fathers quickly spread throughout the empire and even beyond, attracting imitators wherever it went. By the late fourth century, asceticism had become a powerful social force — in the form of both the communities of monks it fostered, and the holy men who emerged from their ranks.

The classical tradition of literary scholarship had its profoundly ascetic aspects. Like philosophy, rhetorical and literary activities could be represented in terms of exercise or *askesis*, as forms of training that could eventually bring about a profound transformation of the person. This was true for ancient literary education, which aimed at instilling specific moral dispositions, at creating a particular kind of person, at least as much as it served to transmit to the new generation a body of skills and information. It was also true for the uses to which adult men who were products of this educational system put literature in their daily lives. Furthermore, literary pursuits could readily be figured in terms of the renunciation of other activities, and therefore in terms of restraint or renunciation *tout court*. From Seneca to Tacitus, Apuleius, and Augustine (to draw only on the Latin part of the empire), we find examples of the literary life described as a turning away from the combative, dangerous, and all-too-corrupt world of the city to a purer, more austere, less self-interested condition, set apart from both the pursuit of power and the struggle to survive.[13]

Yet the *otium*, or leisure, of the aristocrat on his south Italian estate was a far cry from the harsh existence of the desert fathers in Egypt and Syria. Michel Foucault, influenced by the work of the historian of philosophy Pierre Hadot, describes the *askesis* of the elite male of the classical Greek and Roman world as the expression of an ethic of care of the self.[14] His thesis was taken up by Peter Brown, who in the first chapter of *The Body and Society* describes vividly the austerity that this ethic could imply.[15] Yet the ascetic training these men practiced was directed toward a larger goal. The well-bred male of the ancient Mediterranean world learned self-control so that he could control others. His *askesis,* both in boyhood and for the rest of his life, created and sustained the dispositions that would allow him to exercise command, whether over women, slaves, or free men in positions of social subordination.

The *askesis* of the monks, on the other hand, was based on a fundamentally different ethic: one of self-mortification rather than self-care. Specific examples seem to argue against this description. Anthony, the founder of the Egyptian eremitic tradition, ate only bread and water brought to him every six months by a nameless supporter, yet according to Athanasius his body was still strong and healthy even in advanced age.[16] Pachomius's monks adhered to a severe regimen of prayer, work and fasting, which nevertheless

---

13. Seneca: e.g. *De tranquillitate animi;* Tacitus: *Dialogus de oratoribus.* On asceticism in the second-century empire, see Francis, *Subversive Virtue.* In his *Apology,* Apuleius describes the physical effects of his devotion to rhetorical studies at the expense of all other pursuits in sharply ascetic terms. Augustine, in his Cassiciacum dialogues, presents an ideal of Christian asceticism as learned *otium,* a retreat to a country estate where theological concerns can be the central preoccupation of a group of elite Christians. On the tradition of representing the literary life as a withdrawal from politics and the city, see André, *Otium,* covering the earlier period; Madec, *Saint Augustin,* 45–52, for Augustine; also Harries, *Sidonius,* 103–24.

14. Foucault, *Care of the Self;* Hadot and Davidson, *Philosophy.* On the asceticism of second-century elites and philosophers, see also Francis, *Subversive Virtue.* Some fourth-century Christian ascetics, notably Augustine, were strongly influenced by third-century, especially Neoplatonic, models.

15. Brown, *Body and Society,* 5–32.

16. *Life of Anthony,* 93.

allowed for considerable relaxation in the case of the elderly, the ill, and the very young.[17] Simeon, who in the early fifth century ascended a pillar in the hinterland of Antioch, makes a stronger argument for monastic *askesis* as self-mortification. His standing posture, maintained for decades, caused his flesh literally to rot on his bones.[18] Such extremism might allow his model to be dismissed too easily, but its very marginality is what makes it most useful in defining an ideal type.

As the work of Foucault and Brown has shown, Christian *askesis* both appropriated and transformed practices and language already well developed in the classical tradition. The goal of the Christian ascetic, like that of the classical philosopher, was to perfect the self. The context in which that perfection would be realized, however, was not rulership in this world but salvation in the next. Monks did not aspire to be philosopher-kings. Instead, they held humility and obedience as cardinal virtues. Nor did they learn to obey in order that they might command. Rather, they practiced submission to a spiritual father, or to a monastic superior, as a way of breaking down the human will so that it could submit fully to the commandments of God. In the context of this other-worldly orientation, self-mortification became, paradoxically, a path to self-perfection. The ethic of care of the self was a way of life directed toward the city of men; that of self-mortification toward the city of God. One had to die to this world in order to live in the next.

Reflecting the centrality of the grammatical and sophistic traditions to second-century Roman culture, Christian commentary on scripture emerged early on and quickly developed into a substantial corpus. The first Christian commentary that we know of was written by the Gnostic teacher Heracleon in about 140. In the late second and early third centuries, biblical exegesis blossomed among Christians of all kinds. Very little of their work survives. We have commentaries on several books of the Bible by Hippolytus, perhaps a bishop of Rome in the late second century; the *Stromateis,* a collection of notes on many problems, including exegetical issues, by Clement, a Christian teacher at Alexandria in the same period; and a substantial corpus of

---

17. Pachomian rule: for translation see Veilleux, *Pachomian koinonia,* 2:145–67; for discussion see Rousseau, *Pachomius;* for rigorous regimen see Elm, *Virgins,* 283–89, 96–98; for care of the sick, young, and old, see Veilleux, *Pachomian koinonia* 2, precepts 40–43 (pp. 151–52).

18. Theodoret, *History,* XXVI, 23: Simeon developed an ulcer in his foot from standing; the anonymous Syriac life of Simeon, 48–54, says that maggots inhabited Simeon's wounds, which gave off a terrible stench.

exegesis, in the form of homilies and commentaries, from the pen of Origen, who wrote at Alexandria and at Caesarea in Palestine in the first half of the third century. In the fourth century, as the church became a mainstream institution and benefited from imperial patronage, exegetical writings exploded. For the entire period, the evidence suggests that lost exegetical works vastly outnumber those that survive.

The practice of commentary was important in every area of learned culture in antiquity. Commentaries may date back as far as the origins of written literature. By the Roman period, exegetical texts had proliferated, not only on literary works but on philosophical and technical treatises as well. Some modern scholars have gone so far as to see the commentary as the typical genre of late antiquity, a belated culture whose creativity could express itself only as an appendage of the greatness of the past. It is probably truer to say that ancient learning was always already belated, that commentary was, in some sense, the typical mode of ancient thought almost from the beginning. But certainly, by Jerome's day, the territory was well occupied.

Christian biblical exegesis found its greatest exponent early on, in the person of Origen (185–253).[19] What we know of Origen's life comes from the work of the fourth-century Christian historian, Eusebius, who revered him and went to great lengths to preserve his memory. Eusebius tells us that Origen was born at Alexandria, to Christian parents. Origen received an excellent education in both Greek literature and philosophy. After his father's death in a persecution, he had to work as a *grammaticus,* or teacher of literature, to support his mother and younger siblings. From a precocious age, he was sought out by other Christians as a teacher and spiritual guide. Eventually he gave up his secular career to become a full-time instructor of Christian doctrine and biblical exegesis. His followers at Alexandria included wealthy and highly educated Christians, some of whom became his patrons. Origen's prominence, and his independent ways, led him to clash with the bishop of Alexandria. In 234 he accepted the invitation of the bishops of Caesarea and Jerusalem to relocate to Palestine, where he spent the rest of his life.

Throughout his mature years, Origen maintained an incredible pace of literary productivity, writing or dictating hundreds of works in a variety of genres. His *On First Principles* was the first work of Christian systematic theology. Above all, he produced a vast body of interpretation of both the Old and the New Testaments. His exegesis took several forms: *scholia,* or notes,

---

19. There is some debate over the exact dates of Origen's birth and death, but these dates reflect the general consensus; see most recently Trigg, *Origen,* for the underlying data.

on many books; homilies preached to congregations and collected for publication; and his great *tomoi,* or commentaries—lengthy, discursive, and excruciatingly detailed expositions of biblical texts, which expounded their meaning on many levels.

Origen's biblical interpretation drew upon a wide range of models from the Greek literary culture of his day, many of which had already been appropriated by earlier Christians. Greek readers had long regarded literary texts as rich in meaning, pregnant with learned arcana, technical information, moral exempla, and even mystical philosophy. Homer, in particular, was regarded as an all-knowing sage. Greek teachers and commentators first had to contend with basic difficulties that literary, and also philosophical, texts presented. Whether their author was Homer, Aeschylus, Demosthenes, or Plato, the classical texts' diction was archaic, their concerns those of worlds remote from the high Roman empire. Obscure language, lost dialects, geographic, mythological, and historical references all required elucidation. Then too, the texts themselves were unreliable. Manuscript transmission leads inevitably to variation. Scholars developed methods to adjudicate between different readings and to determine whether a given line of Homer was truly the poet's or not. Finally, the reverence accorded to the poets led to the view that their works contained meanings beyond those that lay on the surface. Ancient Mediterranean culture revered the past, and regarded innovation with suspicion. Doctrines whose origins could be traced to the earliest ages of mankind, or at least to a long-dead Golden Age, had much greater prestige. Allegorical reading was the tool that made Homer into a philosopher and conferred upon his readers' worldviews the sanction of antiquity.

Little of Origen's massive exegetical oeuvre survives, but there is enough to make clear that he took up all of these methods in turn. He went to great lengths to establish the correctness of the texts he worked on. He mined the work of earlier Christian writers, and of the Jewish authors Philo and Josephus as well, to reconstruct the historical context of biblical stories. He even consulted with living Jews, and used the Hebrew texts and Greek translations that they preserved to help attain a correct text of the Old Testament and to clarify its historical reference. But his great love was allegory, which he used to derive moral lessons and spiritual teaching from both the Old Testament and the New. The events of biblical history were real for Origen, their chronicle of God's saving interventions in the past crucial to salvation today. But even more important was the spiritual message that each story concealed. For Origen, the Bible overflowed with meaning, its inspired texts purposely crafted to provide for the needs of each reader, whether his level of intellectual and spiritual development left him hungering for factual information, moral teachings, or mystical wisdom. Origen was both a scholar and a philosopher. As such, he was convinced that his philosophical beliefs found their greatest expression in the object of his scholarship, the Bible.

As well as being an exegete, Origen was an ascetic. Indeed, his way of life combined the two roles inextricably, making his literary labors into a form of *askesis*. But Origen's asceticism was not fashioned after a monastic pattern. In his day, no such model existed. Rather, his career—both as a writer and as an ascetic—was little different from that of a contemporary philosopher, such as Plotinus. Indeed, the only surviving contemporary testimony to Origen's activity describes him simply as a philosopher. This is *In Praise of Origen* by his student Gregory, who became bishop of Pontus and whose miracles earned him the sobriquet *Thaumaturgus* or "wonder-worker." The challenge that Origen faced was not that of fusing scholarship with the life of a Christian monk, but that of fusing the life of a philosopher—whose calling naturally included asceticism—with Christianity. Even the disgust for sexuality that reputedly led him to castrate himself as a teenager can be understood in a philosophical as well as a Christian context.[20]

Revered in his own lifetime, patronized by the rich, protected by bishops, consulted by an empress, and persecuted almost to death as an old man, Origen became a legend after his death. His legacy was assured by Pamphilus, a wealthy presbyter of Berytus who settled in Caesarea in the late third century and devoted himself to building a Christian library, whose centerpiece was an exhaustive collection of Origen's works. Pamphilus himself perished in the persecution of the first decade of the fourth century, but his protégé Eusebius survived to become bishop of Caesarea and a major beneficiary of Constantine's imperial patronage. Eusebius inherited Pamphilus's library and, having added to it considerably, passed it on to his successors in the see of Caesarea.

*

Jerome was born almost a hundred years after Origen's death, into a very different world. The empire had been Christian for decades, and the Christianization of its elite was well underway. Born about 347, Jerome was the son of Christian parents of some standing in a small town in Dalmatia or Pannonia in the northwestern Balkans.[21] His hometown, Stridon, was suf-

---

20. This argument is developed more fully, with supporting documentation, in Grafton and Williams, *Christianity*, chapter 1.

21. For the controversy surrounding the date of Jerome's birth, see the Appendix, section 1.

ficiently obscure that scholars cannot locate it today. All we know of his life
before he moved to Antioch in 368, at the age of thirty-one or so, is what can
be gleaned from his own later writings, which often reflect literary conven-
tion—and Jerome's self-conception—more than specific realities. But if secure details are few, a clear outline nevertheless emerges.

Jerome's upbringing was very much the standard one for a young elite
male of his day. It was unusual only insofar as his parents obtained for him
an education rather above their own status. Provincial notables from a small
town, they sent him to school with the sons of Roman senators. He learned
his letters at home in Stridon, then began his grammatical studies at Aquileia, at the head of the Adriatic, at that time the great city of the region. From
Aquileia he went on to Rome, where he studied with the most famous Latin
grammarian of the day, Donatus. He refers to reading the commentaries of
the grammarians on a range of both poets and prose writers while he was a
boy, which suggests that Donatus's pupils pursued their literary studies to
an advanced level.[22] We do not know the name of Jerome's teacher of rhetoric, but his many references to his rhetorical schooling make clear that it
adhered to the conventional pattern, with its emphasis on declamation.[23] At
the age of fifty or so, he recalled vividly the terror that had gripped him as a
young boy when he had to face an audience and recite a prepared declamation.[24] In another context he allows us to glimpse him going with his friends
to hear the performances of famous advocates in the law courts of the Roman forum.[25] Presumably his parents hoped that he would pursue a career
that would yield a return on their investment in his education.

When he was about twenty, in apparent obedience to his parents' expec-
tations, Jerome traveled to Trier in northern Gaul. At the time, the city was
the capital of the emperor Valentinian. Jerome's childhood friend Bonosus,
also from his Dalmatian hometown of Stridon, accompanied him. The two

---

22. *Puto quod puer legeris Aspri in Vergilium ac Sallustium commentarios, Vulcatii in orationes
Ciceronis, Victorini in dialogos eius, et in Terentii comoedias praeceptoris mei Donati, aeque in Ver-
gilium, et aliorum in alios, Plautum uidelicet, Lucretium, Flaccum, Persium atque Lucanum* (*Contra
Ruf.* 1.16).

23. Jerome uses the terms *declamatio* or *declamatiunculus* in the context of such a contrast in the
following passages: *Comm. in Esaiam* 8, praef.; *Comm. in Hiezech.* 8, praef., 12.40; *Comm. in
Osee* 1.2, 3.10; *Comm. in Soph.* 3; *Comm. in Gal.* 3.427; *Altercat. Lucif. et Orth.* 4.165; *Contra Vigil.*
3.356; *Dialog. contra Pelag.* 3.5; letters 36.14, 52.4, 57.54. Other terms used in the same sense
include *controversia* and *oratio.*

24. *Contra Ruf.* 1.30.

25. *Comm. in Gal.* 2.11.

probably hoped to take service in the imperial administration, as many of their peers would have done.[26] Instead, they developed a serious interest in Christian asceticism, and in Jerome's case in Christian literature: later, Jerome mentions having copied several Christian works in his own hand during his stay at Trier.[27]

After a brief stay in the western capital, Jerome and Bonosus left for Aquileia. There they were drawn into a loosely defined ascetic coterie, made up of both well-connected locals and several men from Aquileia and other northern Adriatic cities who had been Jerome's schoolmates at Rome. The city's future bishop Chromatius and his family may have formed the nucleus of the group. The others included Rufinus, a native of Concordia near Aquileia, and Heliodorus, from Altinum on the gulf of Venice, both of whom had studied at Rome with Jerome and Bonosus.[28] For unknown reasons, the group at Aquileia broke up within three years of Jerome's arrival.[29] In 368, he left Italy and traveled to the east, where he settled for the next decade in Antioch and its environs.[30]

Jerome was thus the product of a very specific set of circumstances, whose particulars can only be partially documented. We know that his education was of the very highest quality, the best the Latin-speaking world could offer. His works reveal that he became a past master of the language and the intellectual repertoire that such an education sought to instill. He developed a Latin style of great purity and force, and an immense dexterity in deploying literary allusions and developing stock themes in new ways. But despite this success, his background would have made him an outsider in some respects to elite Roman culture. His origins were provincial and obscure,

---

26. For the date of Jerome's move to Trier, see the Appendix, section 2, and Kelly, *Jerome*, 26-27. In letter 3.5, Jerome describes his move to Trier with Bonosus, and relates that there the two began to take an interest in asceticism. For the opportunities that Valentinian's court offered to ambitious young men, see Matthews, *Western Aristocracies*, 32-55.

27. Letter 5.2.

28. Kelly, *Jerome*, 19; Cavallera, *Saint Jérôme*, 1:14, n.1; Jerome, *Comm. in Obad.* prol. On Jerome's years at Aquileia, see Rebenich, *Hieronymus*, 42-51; Kelly, *Jerome*, 30-35; Cavallera, *Saint Jérôme*, 19-24. Several of Jerome's letters written from Antioch and the desert between 372 and 379 are addressed to North Italian and Dalmatian ascetics and to former members of the "circle" at Aquileia: letter 3 (Rufinus); letter 7 (Chromatius, Jovinus, and Eusebius); letter 8 (Niceas, a subdeacon and future bishop of Aquileia); letter 9 (Chrysogonus, a monk at Aquileia); letter 10 (Paul of Concordia), sent with the *Vita Pauli;* letter 11 (the virgins at Emona); letter 14 (Heliodorus).

29. Kelly, *Jerome*, 33-35.

30. Rebenich, *Hieronymus*, 76-85; Kelly, *Jerome*, 36-45; Cavallera, *Saint Jérôme*, 24-29.

his family's resources far more modest than those of many of his school-fellows.[31] Expected to take advantage of his education to make his way in the world, he soon sought to escape it. Perhaps this should not be surprising. The alacrity with which he abandoned Trier and the emperor's court, and even Aquileia, for a remote Greek-speaking metropolis and its desert hinter-lands has suggested to many interpreters that even as a young man, Jerome was already alienated from the society for which he had been groomed.

Jerome's youth and education deserve so much attention because they are crucial to understanding the rest of his career. Throughout his adult life, Je-rome traded on his literary skills and their association with a particular elite milieu to attract attention, to persuade his readers, and to legitimate his own works and ideas. At the same time, he repeatedly claimed to have repudiated his past. This apparent contradiction, and much else in Jerome's oeuvre, can be understood only in the context of the nature of late Roman elite educa-tion and literary culture, and of fourth-century Christian reactions to it. These reactions included both suspicion and criticism, and the reappropri-ation of literary culture in new contexts, often those created by the power vacuum left by decline of traditional urban elites. These two tendencies could be opposed to each other, or—as in Jerome's case—brought together in a complex mixture. The end result was that traditional elite culture was not abandoned but transformed, transposed from its existing context in the Mediterranean city into new and sometimes startling social and institu-tional settings.

Despite the evident relevance of social context to an understanding of intellectual and cultural transformations like those that took place in the late Roman world, historians of the scholarship of that period as of others long interpreted their subject matter in isolation from other phenomena. The first modern approaches to the study of learning in the ancient world focused on the propositional content of ancient works on grammar, rheto-ric, and textual interpretation. Scholars evaluated the axioms they extracted

---

31. In his letter 66, Jerome mentions the sale of the patrimony that he and his brother Paulinian had inherited from their parents: *compulsi sumus fratrem Paulinianum ad patriam mittere, ut semirutas villulas, quae barbarorum effugerunt manus, et parentum communium cineres venderet, ne coeptum sanctorum ministerium deserentes risum maledicis et aemulis praebeamus,* "I was com-pelled to send my brother Paulinian to our homeland, to sell the half-ruined little country houses that had escaped the hands of the barbarians, along with the ashes of our common ancestors, so that we might not provide naysayers and the envious with an occasion for mockery by aban-doning the service of the saints that we had already begun." The brothers' parental estates had suffered from barbarian invasions in the western Balkans, leaving little to sell. The description implies that, even before the invasion, those estates had been relatively modest.

from ancient texts in terms of a timeless standard of truth, against which technical innovations from various periods could be measured with equal validity.[32] Social and institutional change might speed or hinder progress in the world of scholarship, but its essential trajectory was immutable: from a state of ignorance to one of knowledge.

More recent work, influenced by innovations in the history of science as well as in literary studies, has eschewed teleological narratives of "progress" and the evaluative comparisons between ancient and modern learning that inevitably accompany them. Instead, scholars such as Peter Brown, Robert Kaster, and Richard Lim have placed ancient grammar, rhetoric, and literary culture in their social context, where they formed part of the apparatus of power by which a narrow elite dominated the late imperial Mediterranean.[33] Even the more recent scholarship, however, often remains content to expose the social roles of learning in antiquity, without attending to the material conditions under which it operated. We come to understand the stakes that ancient elites held in their literary culture, but not what that culture was like as an activity or as a way of life.

In formulating a new approach to the history of scholarship in late antiquity, I have drawn inspiration from several sources. The sociology of Pierre Bourdieu has been particularly important, especially his early work in *Outline of a Theory of Practice*. There, Bourdieu develops the concepts of *habitus*, symbolic capital, and strategy. Put simply, Bourdieu's *habitus* is an enduring set of dispositions that incline an individual to act in stereotyped and predictable ways. The *habitus*, for Bourdieu, is the primary bearer of culture. It is inculcated in each of us in youth, through informal socialization and formal education. In any society, *habitus* varies from one individual to another; yet a class or other social group will display a coherent set of dispositions that together form a collective *habitus*.[34]

Bourdieu defines symbolic capital as power accumulated and stored not as wealth, social ties, or tools of physical domination, but through the acquisition of traits particular to the *habitus* of an elite. Significantly, education, which produces a particular set of personal dispositions, allows elites to transform money and standing into symbolic capital. Because the edu-

---

32. The classic example of this approach is Pfeiffer, *Classical Scholarship*.

33. Brown, *Power and Persuasion;* Kaster, *Guardians;* Lim, *Public Disputation.* Kaster, *Guardians,* 158ff., in his discussion of Pompeius, comes close to an analysis of the grammarian's practice, but the object is always to determine his "mindset" (161).

34. Bourdieu, *Outline,* 72–96 and passim.

cated impress their contemporaries as superior men, they are accorded deference as if in recognition of merit.[35] Finally, Bourdieu's concept of strategy describes the ways that individuals schooled in the appropriate *habitus* spontaneously and without apparent reflection choose culturally appropriate courses of action. He uses the metaphor of a "feel for the game" to describe how successful actors unselfconsciously adjust their behavior to their social and cultural situation.[36] Together, these three concepts allow Bourdieu to describe social action as the product of individual agency, which nevertheless is constrained by cultural norms and social structure.

More recently, the French cultural historian Roger Chartier has called for a new cultural history, which would take "discourses as practices . . . not reading them only in order to ascertain the overall ideology that they contain but taking into account their mechanisms, their rhetorical apparatuses and their demonstrative strategies." Chartier argues that ideas, texts and the discourses in which they participate must be understood not merely as abstractions, but as activities carried out by specific groups and individuals in history, and shaped by their education, personal habits, and other traits.[37] Elsewhere, Chartier has demanded that historians attend to the materiality of discourse. Not only are discourses the activities of particular persons endowed with specific dispositions and placed in specific positions in society, but they are embodied in material forms—books, for example—and perpetuated by social relations and physical behavior. Any approach to the "order of discourse" demands an analysis of the material and social contexts in which discourse takes form, what Chartier calls the "order of books."[38]

Historians, both of Roman antiquity and of other periods—particularly the early modern era—have in recent decades paid increasing attention to questions of self-presentation and self-fashioning, to the creation and culti-

---

35. Gleason, *Making Men*, xxi.

36. Bourdieu, *Outline*, 3–9 and passim.

37. Chartier also writes, "To consider reading to be a concrete act requires holding any process of the construction of meaning (hence, of interpretation) as situated at the crossroads between readers endowed with specific competences, identified by their positions and their dispositions and characterized by their practice of reading, and texts whose meaning is always dependent on their particular discursive and formal mechanisms." Chartier, *Cultural History*, 10–12.

38. Chartier, *Order of Books*, ix: "Whether they are in manuscript or in print, books are objects whose forms . . . command the uses that can invest them and the appropriations to which they are susceptible. Works and discourses exist only when they become physical realities and are inscribed on the pages of a book [or] transmitted by a voice reading. . . . Understanding the principles that govern the 'order of discourse' supposes that the principles underlying the processes of production, communication, and reception of books (and other objects that bear writing) will also be deciphered in a rigorous manner."

vation of public, often literary, personae. Stephen Greenblatt, in his *Renaissance Self-Fashioning*, emphasizes the importance of self-presentation, and of the "fashioning" of a public self that then shapes the interpretation of one's words and actions.[39] What holds true for the early modern Englishmen he studied goes as well for the Romans, who were acutely aware of the necessity of constructing and maintaining a coherent and authoritative public persona. Maud Gleason's work on second-century rhetorical culture draws on Bourdieu, and also on Michel Foucault's work on the production of the self, to interpret sophistic culture, particularly the gendered aspects of sophistic performance. She emphasizes an understanding of "rhetoric as process," according to which rhetoric must be seen as a set of embodied practices if it is to be understood at all.[40]

Culture, then, is the work neither of rational actors nor of automata. Cultural agents need not be understood as consciously calculating their every move, and social constraints have a very real force, expressed in unthinking adaptation to situations. At the same time, innovation is always possible—though it must manipulate the terms of the existing cultural repertoire in order to be comprehensible. Within that context, the production and the reception of discourse can only be understood as material practices embodied in specific social relations and in specific acts of reading, writing, and transmission. The history of scholarship, therefore, cannot be described merely as a series of transformations of ideas, but must be analyzed in terms of the history of books, readers, and writers, of the people and things in which knowledge is embodied and by which it is shaped. Further, discourse entails not only the production of texts but the construction of literary personae that shape those texts' reception. Authors work to present themselves in ways that both take advantage of, and innovate within, preexisting assumptions about authority and legitimacy. But strategic self-fashioning need not imply explicit self-knowledge. The doublethink (or, in Bourdieu's terms, misrecognition) that strategy frequently demands is a natural, perhaps even a necessary, element of participation in culture.[41]

*

Studies of Jerome's scholarship have generally been shaped by older, more positivist approaches to the history of learning. His veneration as a saint has

39. Greenblatt, *Renaissance Self-Fashioning*, 1–9.

40. Gleason, *Making Men*, xix–xxix.

41. See Bourdieu and Johnson, *Field of Cultural Production*, 29–73, especially 48–49, and 74–111 on misrecognition as the price of entry into the "cultural field" in modern societies.

also shaped the reception of his work, even in modern times. Evaluations of his exegesis and philology have therefore tended to fall into two camps, the reverential and the iconoclastic. As a doctor of the Western Church and patron saint of scholars and churchmen, Jerome long held a position of real authority among Christian intellectuals. The desire to shore up that authority has inspired centuries of pious appreciations of his biblical scholarship. Since Erasmus, Jerome's standing, and the tendentiousness of his apologists, have also made him a target for increasingly vociferous debunkers. In particular, these latter have attempted to prove that Jerome's scholarship was weak, uncritical, and largely derivative. In some areas their success is undeniable. In others, their extreme skepticism has produced contradictory results. Neither the reverential nor the skeptical approach, however, has produced a coherent interpretation of Jerome's life and work.

My purpose is neither to defend Jerome as a scholar nor to expose his failings. I will therefore stand to one side of the tradition of scholarship on the topic. For the disagreements over whether particular elements of Jerome's scholarly method hold up to scrutiny have obscured what seem to me the most important issues. Whether they are for him or against him, scholars have tended to evaluate Jerome in terms of modern canons of honesty, thoroughness, and originality—standards that were unthinkable in Jerome's own day, which had its own norms for judging the scholarship that it produced. Jerome's statements about his methods have been interpreted not as part of his self-presentation, but as straightforward evidence for how he worked—or, on the other hand, as apparently irrational lies. Efforts to reconstruct his actual practice as a reader and a writer have centered not on the matters that were important to Jerome but on areas where he provides evidence for some question of interest to modern scholars.

This study begins by examining Jerome's earliest attempts to describe himself as a scholar and an adherent of Christian asceticism. It then proceeds to an analysis of the intellectual framework of his most important exegetical works, the commentaries on the Prophets. When these commentaries—particularly the early works on the Minor Prophets—are treated not as sources to be mined for exegetical material but as works in their own right, several new features of Jerome's intellectual project emerge. First of all, the way that Jerome composed his commentaries allowed him to make implicit claims to authority that did not conflict overtly with his status as a monk. Second, the contents of the commentaries demand attention to the relation between the texts Jerome produced and the infrastructure that supported his literary activities. I therefore move outward from the study of the commentaries themselves to examine the infrastructure of books and skilled assistants that allowed Jerome to produce these and other works. I argue that it was precisely in his representation of this infrastructure that Jerome did the primary work of redescribing biblical scholarship as an ascetic practice suitable for a monk—indeed, as the characteristic practice of his own unique brand of cenobitic monasticism. Finally, I consider Jerome's relation to his readers, as he constructed them in ideal form within his own texts, and as he sought to recruit them to support his scholarly activities, whether by their endorsement, their labor, or their patronage.

Throughout, I show that Jerome's work as a biblical scholar partook of, and helped to construct, a specifically late antique, and specifically Christian, culture of learning. This culture was not yet that of the monasteries of the medieval West, much less of the modern university, but was nevertheless a crucial step toward the institutionalization of knowledge as represented by both the monastery and the university.

———— ✳ ————

CHAPTER ONE

The Making of a Christian Writer

JEROME appears in the literary record as a young Latin ascetic resident in Antioch and its hinterland in the 370s. The letters he wrote during these years show a curious combination of burning enthusiasm for asceticism and self-conscious striving after literary effect. Jerome was both a passionate convert to the new models of Christian renunciation then emerging from the deserts of Egypt and Syria, and a proud product of the best education the Latin West could provide. There are signs that he felt some tension between these two cultures. The general impression, however, is one of harmony, if not of settled purpose. The young Jerome seems very much at ease in the field of Christian learning. His devotion to the scriptures is entirely compatible with a tendency to cite Horace whenever an opportunity presents itself. There is no evidence that the effort to define a persona as a Christian writer had, as yet, set Jerome at odds with his own Latin classical culture.

This view of Jerome's early years depends on overcoming the temptation to read back onto his first, hesitant essays as a writer the evidence of later, far more vivid and compelling self-descriptions.[1] In a letter written more than a decade after the events it purports to recount, Jerome portrays himself during his years in Syria as an ascetic tortured by his inability to live up

---

1. In questioning the usefulness of letter 22 for a reconstruction of Jerome's situation in Syria in the 370s, I depart from the vast majority of the scholarship, which tends rather to imagine that the very details of the dream must be accounted for in reconstructing Jerome's early years in the East. Thus Kelly, *Jerome*, for example, describes the luggage that Jerome must have taken with him when he set out for the East in 372 as voluminous, since he had to bring his library with him! By contrast, my skepticism receives a degree of support in the new commentary of Neil Adkin on letter 22, *Jerome on Virginity*.

to his own ideals. He first describes how, despite his intention to renounce the world and his success in abandoning not only his family but, "what was more difficult than all these, the habit of delicate food," he could not go without reading the Latin classics. The uncultured style of the prophets horrified him, and he returned again and again to his volumes of Plautus and Cicero.[2] In the story's climax, Jerome falls seriously ill. In his fevered state, he experiences a terrifying vision. "Seized in the spirit," he finds himself "hauled before the tribunal of the Judge."[3] Questioned as to his *condicio,* his legal status, he professes that he is a Christian. The terrifying figure who confronts him responds that he lies: he is no Christian but a "Ciceronian."[4] This "judge" orders Jerome scourged. Begging for mercy, the wretched young man throws himself to the ground. Bystanders intercede for him and a concession is granted: upon swearing an oath that he will never read secular literature again, he is released to return "to the upper world."[5] Those who stand grieving by his sickbed marvel to watch him open tear-filled eyes. His shoulders, he avers, long bore the marks of the beating he had received, although he had not moved from his bed. The account of this startling episode is telegraphic, leaving ambiguous the identity of the "judge" whom Jerome confronts, the location of the action, and even the status of the events recounted as dream or (miraculous) reality. Yet the narrative's power is undeniable.

But Jerome's writings from the 370s know nothing of this incident. Nor do they betray any trace of the tortured mentality of the ascetic unable to give up reading the classics that later letters would capture so vividly. Instead, not only did the young Jerome show no discontent with his Christian literary diet, but he seems to have seen no conflict in a regimen that juxtaposed such sustenance with non-Christian reading. At the same time, in writings elaborately adorned with classical allusions, he attempted to define for himself a persona as a Christian writer that explicitly depended on his excellent traditional education and his undeniable literary talents.

In the face of this evidence, it seems likely that the story of the dream is

---

2. Letter 22.30.

3. Letter 22.30: *Interim parabantur exsequiae et uitalis animae calor toto frigente iam corpore in solo tam tepente pectusculo palpitabat, cum subito raptus in spiritu ad tribunal iudicis pertrahor.* In this note and the two that follow, I give the text of the more ambiguous portions of the passage.

4. *Interrogatus condicionem Christianum me esse respondi: et ille, qui residebat, 'Mentiris,' ait, 'Ciceronianus es, non Christianus: "ubi thesaurus tuus, ibi et cor tuum."'*

5. *In haec sacramenti uerba dimissus reuertor ad superos.*

a fiction. At best, it may be a literary elaboration of an incident that had originally borne none of the heavy freight of meaning it later acquired.[6] The tale, and the language in which it is told, fit all too well with the mentality of the other letters Jerome wrote at the same time, and with the self-presentation that he developed in them.[7] Furthermore, the description of the dream is a tissue woven of literary allusions, especially to Virgil.[8] We ought, therefore, to read this narrative as a stylized reinterpretation of Jerome's younger self, governed by a sense of the incompatibility of Latin literary culture and Christian ascetic piety that he had not felt a decade or more earlier.

Another passage from a later letter has also been read back onto the period that Jerome spent in Syria in the 370s to produce an even more distorted effect. In 412, Jerome wrote that in his youth, while a hermit in the desert, he had begun to study Hebrew with a converted Jew who had become a monk. From the perspective of forty years later, he represents Hebrew study in terms of a sharp contrast with rhetorical culture, couched entirely in aesthetic terms. Hebrew is harsh and guttural, the antithesis of the literary pleasures of Quintilian, Cicero, Fronto, and Pliny, which had been his favored reading before his conversion to asceticism.[9]

But this calculated evocation of the revulsion produced by Hebrew study in the cultivated soul of a well-educated young man finds no resonance in anything Jerome wrote before he arrived in Rome in 382. There is no contemporary evidence that Jerome studied Hebrew, or any other Semitic language, while he was in Syria in the 370s. In a letter written from Constantinople in 381, he does refer to a teacher of Hebrew, but this man shares little

---

6. Whether the dream actually occurred as Jerome recounts it, and if so when, has been the subject of a lengthy debate. Antin, for example, in the bibliography at the beginning of CCSL 72 in 1959, listed eight items under the rubric "De somnio Hieronymi." Most of these authors, as well as more recent scholars, accept the dream as a historical reality, but there is no consensus as to its precise date and context. Cavallera (*Saint Jérôme*, 29–31), argued that the dream occurred at Antioch, before Jerome relocated to the desert. Kelly (*Jerome*, 41), accepts Cavallera's date and location. Rapisarda ("Ciceronianus es"), Thierry ("Date"), and Antin (*Recueil*) argue for a date during Jerome's stay in the desert. Contrary to the standard view, De Labriolle ("Songe") persuasively suggests that the dream was a self-serving fiction, invented for use in letter 22. His argument depends in part on an analysis of the literary construction of the account, which makes clear that it is far from a straightforward recollection of experience. De Labriolle supplies close parallels to the story Jerome tells from Plutarch (transmitted by Eusebius), Lucian, and Eusebius himself.

7. On this see also Adkin, "Gregory of Nazianzus."

8. De Labriolle, "Songe."

9. Letter 125.12.

with the one who figures in his much later, retrospective construction of his early career.[10] Just as we ought to be suspicious of the accuracy of the dream narrative's depiction of Jerome's anguished attempts to renounce secular literature, so too the representation of Hebrew study as the harsh remedy appropriate for the self-indulgent tastes instilled by that literature cannot be taken as a straightforward reflection of reality.

Rather than telling the story of Jerome's early life from the retrospective point of view he created in his later letters, then, this chapter will move forward from the evidence of Jerome's earliest writings, then build upon that foundation to analyze the self-presentation he developed at Rome in the 380s. The evidence reveals a transformation on two levels: at once in terms of social networks and in terms of intellectual horizons, from participation in an inward-looking circle of Latin-speaking ascetics to engagement in the intellectual life, and the high ecclesiastical politics, of the Greek East.

When he traveled to Antioch in late 373, Jerome's social ties were exclusively Latin; so were the books he read. From his early letters, we learn that he had been engaged in serious Christian study as early as about 368, when he was at Trier with his boyhood friend Bonosus. For the dozen or so years from that time until he traveled to Constantinople in 380, we have no direct, contemporary evidence that he studied Christian literature in Greek. In 382, Jerome returned to the West, as the protégé of prominent—or at least controversial—Greek bishops attending a church council. Immediately, he presented himself to Rome as the self-appointed ambassador to the West of Greek Christian learning. The transformation is striking, and its intermediate stages are difficult to trace.

The first person to bridge the gap that separated Jerome from the far more vital and contentious Christian culture of the Greek-speaking world was Evagrius of Antioch, his first patron. Through Evagrius, Jerome met other prominent ecclesiastics from Syria and Palestine: Paulinus, the ultra-Nicene bishop of Antioch; and, fatefully, Epiphanius of Salamis, whose truculence would incite the outbreak of the Origenist controversy in 393. Perhaps, too, Jerome studied with Apollinaris of Laodicea at Antioch and with Gregory of Nazianzus at Constantinople, as he would later claim: there is no compelling reason to disbelieve him.

But from the works that Jerome wrote in the early 380s we gain no explicit information about his exposure to the social world of Greek Christian

---

10. Letter 18A.15: *Audiui enim hoc in loco non paruam Hebraei mei disputationem.* Jerome then gives a lengthy account of "his Jew's" exegesis of Isaiah 6:8.

learning, or about his ties to the Nicene Church of the East. Those to whom he addressed his letters and his other writings remained exclusively Latin. What changes, instead, are the range of his own reading and the terms of his self-presentation. Whatever Jerome did and whomever he met at Constantinople, he made a fateful encounter there—with the literary legacy of Origen. It was under Origen's banner that he began, at Rome, to advance a new model for Christian scholarship as an ascetic practice, and to invoke the authority of the Hebrew text of scripture.

A LATIN LITERARY LIFE IN THE EAST

Late in the year 373, Jerome arrived in Antioch, the metropolis of Syria, after an arduous journey from the West. There, he spent much of the next seven years as the guest of the prominent—not to say notorious—priest and littérateur Evagrius, whom he had met in Italy.[11] His life in Evagrius's household was broken only by a stint of no more than eighteen months as a hermit in the arid hinterlands of Antioch, in 375 and early 376.[12] Jerome produced no major literary or scholarly works in Syria. What he did write, however, makes clear that he was a young man of great ambition as well as substantial literary gifts. In his surviving letters and other brief works, we see him casting about for ways to combine the new kinds of Christian asceticism, then arousing so much enthusiasm, with modes of literary production typical of late antique elites; to be both a desert hermit and, in a phrase that Henri-Irenée Marrou, in an earlier era of scholarship, famously applied to Augustine, a *lettré de la décadence*. Needless to say, he was not wholly successful.

---

11. PLRE Evagrius 6. Evagrius was the son of an Antiochene curial family of middling wealth and standing; they descended from a third-century general, likely a Latin, who defeated the Palmyrene Zenobia under emperor Aurelian. Evagrius led a checkered career in government and the church. He was a protégé of Libanius and obtained two official posts, but he was dismissed from the second, flogged, and forced to pay a fine. His name was later cleared, but he was left impoverished. He seems to have converted to Christianity and accepted the priesthood in the wake of these reverses. He traveled to Illyricum in 363 with the returning Nicene bishop Eusebius of Vercelli, and there became involved with other Western bishops, including Damasus of Rome. After his return to Antioch around 371, he became a partisan of Bishop Paulinus, one of three who quarreled over the see during the last decades of the fourth century. On Evagrius's involvement with Paulinus and the schism of Antioch, see later in this chapter; see also Cavallera, *Schisme;* Rebenich, *Hieronymus*, 58–61.

12. As to the time of Jerome's move to the desert, the only certainty is that he did so after the death of Evagrius's friend Innocentius, the dedicatee of Jerome's letter 1, who died in mid-374 (Kelly, *Jerome*, 33 n. 43). For a chronology of Jerome's years in Syria, see the Appendix, section 3.

Jerome's letters—some from the 370s, others much later—provide only scattered and allusive evidence for the reasons he moved to the East in 373. He had perhaps been drawn to the ascetic movement as early as his stay in Trier in the 360s. Leaving Trier, he moved to Aquileia, where he became part of a loose association of ascetics. The group included Jerome's friend from Stridon, Bonosus; his schoolmates from Rome, Rufinus and Heliodorus; and several local clergy and wealthy lay Christians, including the city's future bishop, Chromatius, and his family. But after less than two years, the ascetic circle at Aquileia fragmented. Bonosus became a hermit on an uninhabited Adriatic island.[13] Many of the others departed for the East. Jerome's schoolmate Rufinus traveled to Egypt where he sat at the feet of the desert monks and studied with the learned Didymus the Blind, successor to Clement and Origen as the foremost Christian teacher at Alexandria.[14]

In moving from Aquileia to Antioch, Jerome made the transition from a wealthy provincial center to one of the four great *metropoleis,* the "mother cities" of the Mediterranean. Antioch was notorious for its wealth, for the sophisticated tastes of its populace, and for the arrogance and luxury of its elites. But the move had another, perhaps even more important, dimension. At Aquileia, Christian asceticism was in its earliest stages. Antioch was at the center of a region in which the most stringent forms of Christian renunciation had been pioneered and had reached a high level of development. The city itself lay on the banks of the Orontes river, in the center of a fertile plain. Its wealthiest suburb, Daphne, was famous as a resort where cooling springs provided refreshment even in the hottest months of the Syrian summer. Beyond the city, the terrain rises rapidly into rugged mountains and highlands—rich agricultural land and miles of olive groves, dramatically interspersed with harsh, stony desert.

In the caves and on the summits of the rocky hills of north Syria, hermits had long pursued forms of renunciation as extreme as any practiced in the Egyptian desert. As in Egypt, where the sharp demarcation between desert and farmland created by the unique ecology of the Nile valley meant that monastic *anachoresis* might not in fact remove an aspiring hermit very far from his native village, so in the region around Antioch the hermits often remained close either to the city itself or to its numerous nearby settlements, some of them major cities themselves. But in Syria the mixture of stony mountainsides with rich farmland was far less orderly than in the valley of

13. For Bonosus as a hermit in the Adriatic, see letters 3.4–5 and 7.3.

14. For Rufinus in the East, see letter 3.

the Nile. Relations between hermit and village or town, too, seem to have been more varied. Such is the picture, for example, that we glean from Theodoret of Cyrrhus's *History of the Monks of Syria*, which chronicles the careers of heroic hermits stationed in the hinterlands of Theodoret's hometown, a city not far from Antioch.[15]

This picture of Antioch and its region may help to make sense of the pattern of Jerome's life in the 370s after his move to Syria. His relocation was clearly motivated by a desire to be closer to the Eastern roots of the ascetic movement that had become the focus of his life. But it was only after several years, and then rather briefly, that he experimented with a life of extreme ascetic renunciation as a desert hermit. His attraction seems to have been more to the ascetic idea than to the ascetic life, if indeed he had any clear sense of what he was seeking in moving to the East. The years Jerome spent in and near Antioch in the 370s were a period of experimentation, even confusion. The poignant terms in which he wrote home, begging for letters from the friends he had left behind, suggest that he was a bit lost—a Latin at sea in a far more sophisticated and more treacherous Greek world. Perhaps only the connection to Evagrius, and through him to the controversies that divided Christian Antioch throughout the fourth century, gave Jerome any sense of purpose at all. By moving to the East, he had undertaken a quest for a life of Christian purpose, guided by the most stringent ideals. For a variety of reasons he was repeatedly diverted from his course.[16]

Yet the years in Antioch were of great importance for Jerome's later career. By placing himself under Evagrius's protection, Jerome enmeshed himself in the complex politics of the Antiochene see. Evagrius had translated Athanasius's *Life of Anthony*, the pioneering work of ascetic propaganda, into Latin with great success. He was also an adherent (and the eventual successor) of the ultra-Nicene Paulinus, one of three contenders for the episcopacy of Antioch in the 370s. The association with Evagrius, therefore, embroiled

---

15. Theodoret, *Philotheos historia*.

16. The scholarship on Jerome's earliest works has suffered from a tendency to read his intensely literary and rhetorical writings as if they were direct evidence for his psychology. Not only is the spirit of crisis that is expressed in the story of the dream read back onto Jerome's brief spell as a desert hermit, but the letters that he wrote at the time are taken too literally. In particular, Jerome's repeated contrasts between the ascetic virtue of his friends and his own miserable failings as a monk have been taken as evidence for his inability to live up to his own ascetic ideals. Kelly, *Jerome*, is a particularly problematic example of this tendency. It has now been recognized that these early essays in ascetic propaganda are elaborate literary constructions, their content drawing on biblical themes, their antithetical structure modeled on passages from Tertullian and Cyprian: see Vogüé, *Histoire littéraire*, 1:105-37.

Jerome in one of the nastiest squabbles of a century of Christian controversy, and linked him to some of its less appealing players, notably the intransigent Epiphanius of Salamis.[17]

It is difficult to give a straightforward narrative of Jerome's years in Syria. Many of the letters he wrote during the period are impossible to date within it; it is equally clear that most of his contemporary correspondence is lost. But the surviving letters from the 370s do support a general picture of Jerome's activities and his social contacts. His circle of correspondence was exclusively Latin: the only Greek to whom his letters refer is the bilingual Evagrius.[18] We have one letter—a rather contentious one—that Jerome wrote to a family member at this time.[19] His other surviving letters reveal the many ties that still connected him to friends in Aquileia and its hinterland, some of them known from boyhood, others acquaintances gained during his years there in the early 370s. Jerome also wrote to other Westerners who had traveled to the East: not only his old friend Rufinus, but a new acquaintance, Florentinus, a wealthy Latin established at Jerusalem, whom Jerome knew exclusively by letter.[20] Already Jerome's world was one of elective affinities, held together by common ascetic ideals that linked men and women of varying social statuses across a broad swath of the Mediterranean world. In such a milieu, letters took on an intense symbolic significance. They were tokens of affiliation, not merely vehicles for information. Hence the passion with which Jerome beseeched his friends in Italy to write to him, and the care that he put into crafting his letters to them—even those whose content consists of little more than a request for a letter in return.[21]

17. Alongside the misleading psychological interpretation of Jerome's letters that has distorted our impressions of the earliest phase of his career, there has been a failure to appreciate the impact of the controversy at Antioch in the 370s on Jerome's life, then and for decades afterwards. This failure in the scholarship is probably best laid at the door of Cavallera, *Saint Jérôme,* following his own earlier work in *Schisme,* where his bias toward the Meletian party, combined with instinctive reverence for both Jerome and "Pope" Damasus, render his account of Jerome's involvement in the schism almost incomprehensible.

18. For the chronology of Jerome's letters written during his years in Syria, see the Appendix, section 3.

19. Letter 13, to his maternal aunt Castorina.

20. Letters 4 and 5 were addressed to Florentinus; letter 4.1 refers to Heliodorus as the link between Jerome and Florentinus.

21. Captured with lapidary precision by Vogüé, *Histoire littéraire,* 1:107: "L'ermite du désert de Syrie ne renoncera pas à ses habitudes de Latin lettré, pour lequel correspondre élégamment avec des amis est un besoin."

Jerome's earliest surviving work, letter 1, was addressed to Evagrius's friend Innocentius before his sudden death in 374.[22] Its aim, quite transparently, was to burnish the glory of Jerome's new patron, Evagrius. Addressing himself to Innocentius was a clever ploy: Jerome seems to have used this device to allow him to praise Evagrius more fulsomely that he could have done in a work dedicated directly to his patron. Furthermore, the work itself was entirely gratuitous. As far as we can discern, Jerome had met Innocentius through Evagrius. Yet it must have been Evagrius himself who had informed Jerome of the events narrated in the letter. Surely, the story was no news to Innocentius. Rather than being in any sense a vehicle for information, then, letter 1 was produced in order to create and afffirm a set of relationships — though the text itself betrays little sign of this function.

The letter tells the fantastic, even lurid, story of a woman of Vercelli, in northern Italy, who had been falsely accused of adultery. Maintaining her innocence and calling God to witness, the unfortunate woman held out against the most savage torture. The man accused with her confessed and was put to death; the woman was condemned despite her denials. But a miracle spared her from the executioner's sword. Her body, apparently dead, was carried off to a monastery, where she recovered from her ordeal and remained in hiding, disguised as a man. Although she had survived, she was still under condemnation. At this point Evagrius enters the story. Meeting the woman in secret and hearing her sorry tale, he seeks an audience with the emperor and gains a pardon for her. The letter's content, with its gruesome details of judicial torture, its heroine's false death and escape in male dress, and its theme of chaste Christian virtue prevailing against the hasty condemnation of a hostile provincial administrator, mixes the genres of martyrology and the ancient novel in an unholy brew.

Evagrius, it would appear, received the tribute with pleasure, for Jerome seems to have settled in happily at Antioch. When his desire for a more intensely ascetic way of life led him out into the city's desert hinterland, Evagrius forwarded his mail, linking the would-be hermit with his far-flung network of correspondents. Writing to Rufinus perhaps a year later, Jerome described Evagrius as an intimate friend. But his appeal to the conventions

---

22. Letter 1 was addressed to Innocentius, who died in 374 (Kelly, *Jerome*, 33 n. 43), and written at Antioch, since letter 3.3 to Rufinus (written to tell him of the deaths of Innocentius and of Melania's slave Hylas) shows that Jerome was still there at the time of Innocentius's death.

of late Roman *amicitia,* with its elaborate language of friendship between equals, should not blind us to the power differential within the relationship or to its likely patronal dynamics.[23]

Not only letters but books too circulated widely among Jerome's acquaintances. In a letter to Florentinus, his new epistolary acquaintance at Jerusalem, Jerome makes a number of literary requests. Several relate to books his friend Rufinus had brought with him from the West. These include the commentaries of Reticius of Autun on the Song of Songs, of which Jerome sought a copy; a volume of Tertullian that Rufinus had borrowed from the aged ascetic Paul of Concordia before he left Italy (Paul had written *to Jerome* to demand its return); and, finally, Hilary of Poitiers' commentary on the Psalms and his *De synodis,* which Rufinus had also borrowed, this time from Jerome, who had copied them in his own hand at Trier more than a decade before and now wanted them for himself. On a separate sheet, now lost, Jerome listed other works, asking Florentinus to have them copied for him. In return, he offered to make a copy for Florentinus of any book he had that his correspondent could not obtain at Jerusalem.[24] In another letter, Jerome requests books from Paul of Concordia himself: the Italian hermit must have been quite a bibliophile.[25]

Clearly, these two letters are but a selection from what must have been an active correspondence on literary topics. Their contents give a striking impression of the role that books played in Jerome's early life as a Christian ascetic. Books, in this world, were at least as mobile as persons, traveling great distances and linking men who had never met. Their circulation provided a material correlate to the social ties that bound like-minded readers across the entire expanse of the Mediterranean world. Participation in this network of literary exchange required access to resources. Even in the desert outside Antioch, we find our own hermit well equipped for scholarly pursuits. Not only does he brag about the riches of his library, but he even refers to certain "protégés, who practice the scribal arts," whose services al-

---

23. On Evagrius as Jerome's patron, see Rebenich, *Hieronymus,* 52–75: "Unter den frühen *patroni* des Hieronymus ist Evagrius der bedeutendste" (p. 52). On inequality within relationships of literary and cultural patronage, masked by the language of affectionate friendship, see Saller, *Personal Patronage,* 7, 11–15, and Saller, "Martial on Patronage." Against the idea that the wealthy friends of poets served as their patrons, see White, *"Amicitia,"* and White, *Promised Verse.* In Jerome's case, I find Saller's model more helpful.

24. Letter 5.2: *scripsit mihi et quidam de patria supra dicti fratris Rufini Paulus senex Tertulliani suum codicem apud eum esse, quem uehementer repoposcit.*

25. Letter 10.3, discussed below.

low him to offer copies of his books to new acquaintances.[26] The network also held out opportunities: Jerome could hope to inject his own writings into the channels that conveyed other Christian works to eager audiences. As we have seen, a longer, more ambitious letter could attract the sustained support of a patron; at the same time, the acceptance of a work by its dedicatee marked the recipient's approval of its content and helped to ensure its circulation.

To judge from the books that Jerome mentions in these letters, his intellectual life during his years in Syria was exclusively and explicitly Christian. Far from showing anxiety about his reading, he refers complacently to Christian literature as "the pearl of the Gospel," and "the nourishment of the Christian soul."[27] His self-confidence was so great that his program of Christian learning could include the works of pagans and heretics.[28] Thus he asks Paul of Concordia for copies of the history of Aurelius Victor, a pagan and an opponent of Christianity, and of the letters of the third-century schismatic Novatian, without fear for his own faith or orthodoxy.[29] Despite the inclusiveness of Jerome's reading, however, it did not extend to works in Greek, much less any other language. Jerome's later claims to have studied with Greek teachers at Antioch and to have learned Hebrew in the desert find no reflection in the writings of the 370s. Rather the opposite, it would seem: in a letter to friends back in Aquileia, Jerome complains that in the desert "one must either speak a barbarous half-speech, or remain silent." However difficult silence may have been, Jerome seems unlikely to have taken great interest in learning the *barbarus semisermo* of the natives.[30]

In the context of this network of learned Christians scattered across the Mediterranean from Italy to Egypt, what must have set Jerome apart, at the age of twenty-five or thirty, was his superlative command of literary Latin. Even the most ephemeral among the surviving letters that he wrote from Syria—and many of them are no more than notes, mostly written to his

---

26. Letter 5.2: *alumnos, qui antiquariae arte seruiant.* On these *alumni*, see Vogüé, *Histoire littéraire,* 1:110.

27. Letter 10.3: *margaritam de euangelio;* letter 5.2: *Nosti hoc esse Christianae animae pabulum, si in lege domine meditetur die ac nocte.*

28. Vogüé, *Histoire littéraire,* 1:109–11.

29. Letter 10.5.

30. Letter 7.2: *Hic enim aut barbarus semisermo discendus est aut tacendum est.* There is a long-standing difficulty over the text of this passage. Hilberg, the editor of the authoritative CSEL edition of the letters, printed *seni sermo* against the evidence of all the manuscript authorities, in what appears to be an overzealous application of the principle of *lectio difficilior.*

friends in Italy to complain that they had failed to write to him—are alive with vivid, imagistic turns of phrase. Furthermore, the young Jerome was practiced at the art of adorning his texts with literary *sententiae* and with allusions to earlier authors. He cites the classical poets with an abandon that reveals none of the anxiety about the literary canon described in letter 22, which tells the story of his dream. He constantly quotes or alludes to Horace, Terence, Virgil, and Cicero, who would remain reliable sources of embellishment for the rest of his life.[31] But in these early letters, he also refers to writers whom he never mentioned after his move to Constantinople in 380: the poets Turpilius, Lucilius and Florus, for example.[32] Jerome's confidence as a Christian reader, sure of his ability to extract what was of value from pagan and heretical works, is matched by his assurance as a writer.

This assurance is on full display in Jerome's letter 10 to Paul of Concordia. Here, Jerome indulges his facility for rhetorical elaboration, while playfully distancing himself from his own skill. The letter opens with an improvisation on the theme of old age, whose material is biblical but whose language, style, and range of allusion is heavily classicizing. Concluding this baroque tour-de-force, Jerome steps neatly outside it. Adopting the persona of his addressee, he writes, "Why, you ask, this starting point so remote and so far-fetched that one might well employ against us the Horatian jest, 'He begins the story of the Trojan War from Leda's twin eggs'?" Such grandeur, he answers himself, is fitting for the praise of his centenarian addressee, which he proceeds to develop in another rhetorical passage. Again, he doubles back upon himself, with a quotation from Cicero criticizing the frivolity of the flattering Greeks. Finally, he comes to the substance of the letter: he offers, in exchange for copies of certain books he wants, the dedication of his *Life of Paul the First Hermit,* of which he remarks, "I have worked very hard to bring down the level of my discourse to that of simpler folk. But, I know not how, even if it is full of water, 'the bottle preserves the aroma of what filled it when it was first used.'" The closing phrase is a reference to Horace's first epistle. In each section of this letter, Jerome displays his literary facility, then makes a show of disclaiming it—in terms which are, in each instance, themselves drawn from the literary canon. At the same

31. Hagendahl, *Latin Fathers,* 100–107; he remarks that "in the dream, Jerome was accused of being a Ciceronian, not a Christian. Not a few reminiscences of Cicero resound in the letters written shortly afterwards" (p. 103).

32. Turpilius appears in letter 8.1; Lucilius in 7.5; and Florus in 4.1, 5.1, and *Vita Pauli* 4 (Hagendahl, *Latin fathers,* 102–5).

time, he offers up a work of his own as currency in a network of literary patronage and exchange analogous to the one in which Horace famously participated, albeit in this case a Christian and ascetic one.

The letter's reference to Cicero invokes the institution of literary patronage in its crudest form. Jerome writes of those "most learned among the Greeks," dismissed by Cicero for their "ingenious levity and studied frivolity," who accepted payment from their kings in return for writing their praises. Jokingly, Jerome demands that Paul reward him for his praise—but the currency in which he will be paid is books, not money, a reward appropriate for a Christian monk.[33] Jerome's irony implies that in fact he does not produce panegyrics in return for patronage. But we have seen from letter 1 that he was far from being above such arrangements. Furthermore, despite the contrast Jerome draws, in his dedicatory epistle to Paul of Concordia, between the manner of the *Life of Paul the First Hermit* and that of his letter to Innocentius, the two works share many traits. Stylistic similarities are far easier to detect than differences. On the level of content, too, the resemblance is acute. Both texts attempt to redeploy the literary charisma of the martyr—complete with miraculous plot twists and lurid scenes of torture—within new kinds of narrative, appropriate to a Christian empire that no longer produced new martyrs.

The *Life of Paul* opens with an account of the persecutions under Decius. Jerome manages to cram into this brief prelude the stories of two Christian martyrs who suffered in Egypt in particularly sensational circumstances. The first, having held out against every form of torture available to Roman justice, was finally smeared with honey and left bound and naked in the sun, to be tormented by flies. The second, having proved his courage, too, against the usual cruelties, was also tied down naked—on a featherbed, in the midst of a fragrant garden. There, the lewd caresses of a wanton whore overcame the firmness of his resolve. Mounting the martyred youth, the woman began to rape him. In desperation, he bit off his tongue and spat it in her face, "thus overcoming pleasure by pain," as Jerome notes with satisfaction.[34]

These graphic scenes, narrated in a prose that combines epigrammatic concision with feverish intensity, provide a wholly gratuitous introduction to the account of Paul's retreat into the fastnesses of the Eastern Desert of

33. Letter 10.3: *Doctissimi quique Graecorum, de quibus pro Flacco agens luculente Tullius ait: "ingenita leuitas et erudita uanitas," regum suorum uel principum laudes accepta mercede dicebant,* etc.

34. PL 23 *Vita Pauli* 3.

Egypt, between the Nile and the Red Sea. Only the fact that Paul left the settled world behind in order to avoid the horrors of persecution justifies their presence. Jerome goes on to recount that Paul, having renounced his inheritance and adopted an ascetic way of life, retreated farther and farther into the desert, until finally he immured himself in an abandoned quarry, where he remained for the rest of his life.[35]

At this point, the attentive reader notes significant parallels between the early careers of Paul and of Anthony, as depicted by Athanasius and by Evagrius, in his translation of Athanasius's *Life*. Both protagonists gave up inheritances; both had sisters whom they consigned to the care of others; both withdrew only gradually from the settled lands. But Jerome's Paul, as what follows in the text makes painfully clear, not only preceded Anthony but outdid him. For Anthony becomes a character in the narrative: tempted to congratulate himself for being the greatest monk in Egypt, he dreams by night of one greater than himself, and sets out the next day to find him. Guided by mythological creatures, he journeys deep into the wilderness, where at last he discovers Paul in his fastness. The two confer; Anthony departs; a year later he returns, only to find Paul dead. Anthony realizes that he was inspired to find the old man so that the solitary Paul could be given a proper burial, and recognizes in him his own predecessor and superior.[36]

Jerome's attempt in the *Life of Paul* to combine elements of the martyrology and the novel, as in letter 1, with the new genre of ascetic hagiography, strikes a modern critic as ultimately unsuccessful—despite the popularity it achieved in its day and for centuries after. Its juxtaposition of satyrs, centaurs, martyrs, and monks is jarring and sensationalistic. Furthermore, its language shows little sign of catering to the *simpliciores*, as Jerome had promised in his dedicatory letter. Rather, like letter 1, the *Life of Paul* combines tightly compressed syntax, the strategic deployment of rare and even poetic words, and allusions to canonical literary texts, to produce a highly spiced prose style that is ultimately as indigestible as the bizarre and artificial plot.[37]

In its use of the figure of Anthony, moreover, the *Life of Paul* places Jerome's literary activities in a curious relation to those of his patron Evagrius. The Antiochene priest's translation of Athanasius's *Life of Anthony* enjoyed

35. PL 23 *Vita Pauli* 4.

36. PL 23 *Vita Pauli* 7–16.

37. On the *Life of Paul*, its style, its relation to the *Life of Anthony*, its reception, and its author's likely intentions in writing it, see Vogüé, *Histoire littéraire*, 1:184. I differ from Vogüé only in that I see the work as more peculiar, and as more of an implicit challenge to Evagrius, than he does.

an immediate and long-lasting success. Among Latin readers—people like Jerome and his circle at Aquileia—it exerted a powerful influence in favor of Eastern-style monasticism. By incorporating Anthony into his text, and explicitly placing him in a subordinate relation to "his" hermit, Paul, Jerome aimed at his patron's literary success, implicitly claiming preeminence for himself as he openly did for the subject of his narrative. The contrast to letter 1, where Evagrius was the object of Jerome's adulation, is striking. Having recruited Evagrius as a sort of literary and ascetic surrogate father, Jerome now symbolically attacks him. Such ambivalent relations with the figures whose example served to legitimate his literary productions were to be typical of Jerome throughout his career, culminating in his thoroughly conflicted attitude toward the great Origen.

Despite the playful literary provocation of the *Life of Paul,* Jerome's relationship to Evagrius remained warm for decades. At Antioch in the 370s, the connection pulled Jerome irresistibly into the controversy over the Antiochene episcopate. The quarrel dated back to the ordination of the ultra-Nicene bishop Paulinus by the Western exile Lucifer of Cagliari in 362, during the confusion caused by the pagan emperor Julian's recall of quarreling bishops exiled under his predecessor, Constantius.[38] Since then, Paulinus's small congregation had fought a running battle for legitimacy against the supporters of another Nicene or quasi-Nicene bishop, Meletius. Evagrius's old friend Basil of Caesarea was a long-time supporter of Meletius. To his dismay, when Evagrius returned to the East in 373, he aligned himself with Paulinus and against Meletius.[39]

Jerome's writings reflect little of this controversy. We know that it affected him only from the final letters that he wrote from the Syrian desert. In 375, Jerome addressed a desperate plea to bishop Damasus at Rome, asking him to pronounce on a theological difficulty. Jerome complained of harassment by violent monks, adherents of Paulinus's rival Meletius. They insisted that he subscribe to a doctrine of "three hypostases" in the Trinity, which he believed concealed their secret Arian tendencies. In his letter, Je-

---

38. Cavallera, *Schisme.*

39. Evagrius's alignment with Paulinus disappointed his onetime friend Basil of Caesarea, a supporter of Meletius: see Basil, letter 156. The tone of the letter is very cold, but only a few sentences give any insight into what had divided the two men. Basil writes, "Our most beloved son Dorotheus, our deacon, caused us sorrow when he informed me about your Piety, that you refused to take part with him in his religious service. And yet such were not the matters which were discussed by you and me . . . " (Basil, *Letters,* 2:389–401). As a guest of Evagrius Jerome probably found himself in Paulinus's party from his arrival at Antioch.

rome metaphorically casts himself at Damasus's feet, declaring his willingness to accept any creed the Roman bishop sanctions—though his language strongly hints that he expects his addressee to repudiate Meletius and his followers.[40] He concludes this first appeal by instructing his addressee that, since he himself is immured in an obscure corner of the Syrian desert, the bishop may direct his reply to his old acquaintance Evagrius at Antioch.[41] If Jerome did not write on Evagrius's urging, surely he had his approval. When he received no response, Jerome wrote a second letter, repeating the pleas of the first in even more desperate terms.[42]

No reply from the Roman bishop to his former parishioner is preserved; however, Damasus wrote to Paulinus in summer 376, implicitly approving his episcopacy by addressing him as the sole orthodox bishop of Antioch.[43] What persuaded Damasus to do so remains obscure.[44] By this time, Jerome had probably abandoned the desert, the Meletian monks having made life there too uncomfortable, and returned to Antioch, where he spent the next four years.[45] This was not an uneventful period for the Antiochene Church, and Jerome was in the thick of it. In 376, the prospects for Paulinus and his adherents must have looked good. Not only did Damasus write in encouraging terms, but Epiphanius of Salamis visited Antioch that same summer and chose to enter into communion with Paulinus rather than Meletius.[46]

---

40. In letter 15.5 Jerome implies that he does not expect his addressee to endorse the doctrine of the "three hypostases" put forward (as he claims) by, among others, the party of Meletius (whom he refers to as the *campenses*): *simul etiam, cui apud Antiochiam debeam communicare, significes, quia Campenses, cum Tarsensibus hereticis copulantur, nihil aliud ambiunt, quam ut auctoritate communionis uestrae fulti tres hypostases cum antiquo sensu praedicent.* Kelly (*Jerome*, 57), who writes that Jerome in these letters had refused to decide between the rivals, does not seem to take account of this language.

41. Letter 15.5: *et ne forte obscuritas, in quo dego, loci fallat baiulos litterarum, ad Euagrium presbyterum, quem optime nosti, dignare scripta transmittere.*

42. Letter 16.2: *Meletius, Vitalis atque Paulinus tibi haerere se dicunt . . . mihi litteris tuis, apud quem in Syria debeam communicare, significes.*

43. Damasus, letter 3: PL 13, 356 f. and PL 56, 684–86. For the date of this letter see Kelly, *Jerome*, 57–58. On Damasus's career, see Rade, *Damasus*. See also Basil of Caesarea, letters 214 and 216, both to Damasus.

44. For chronological issues related to the letters to and from Damasus, see the Appendix, section 5.

45. For a discussion of the date of Jerome's departure from the desert, see the Appendix, section 5. I see his stay there as rather shorter, and therefore probably less important, than it has traditionally been depicted.

46. On Epiphanius's relations with Paulinus in 376, see Cavallera, *Schisme*, 195–96. In agreement with my belief that Jerome probably met Epiphanius while at Antioch in the 370s, and my estimate of the significance of this connection, see Rebenich, *Hieronymus*, 106–7.

Some time after his return from the desert, perhaps in the wake of these favorable developments, Jerome was ordained a priest by Paulinus.[47] This action would have given an important institutional dimension to Jerome's connection with the ultra-Nicene party, since from then until 382 he was a priest of Paulinus's clergy.[48]

The next few years, however, did not go so well for the Paulinians. In 377, the Arianizing emperor Valens revoked an edict of exile against the Nicene bishops of the Eastern cities, which had forced Meletius (but not Paulinus) out of the churches of Antioch. When the edict was rescinded, the Meletians seem to have fought for, and won, control of the city's basilicas. Likely the monks who had harassed Jerome in the desert played their usual role as shock troops for their bishop in the street fighting that would have accompanied Meletius's return.[49] But the aftermath of Valens's death in the battle of Adrianople in 378 must also have promised opportunities for the embattled Paulinians: the new emperor, Theodosius, was a devout adherent of the Nicene faith.[50] In late 380, probably to attend the council convened by Theodosius to resolve the problems caused by Valens's anti-Nicene edict and its revocation, Jerome set out for the Eastern capital.[51]

BROADENING HORIZONS

Theodosius I was the first Christian Roman emperor to pursue an aggressive policy of repression against those who deviated from his own religious beliefs, although Valens's policy in favor of anti-Nicene bishops had set the stage for Theodosius's actions. Under Theodosius, both pagans and heretical Christians were hounded, their places of worship confiscated or destroyed. These measures were enforced both directly by imperial troops, and indirectly by orthodox mobs, composed largely of monks, whose vio-

47. For Jerome's ordination by Paulinus, see Cavallera, *Saint Jérôme*, 1:55–56, citing *Contra Ioh. Hier.* XLI (PL 23, B–C). See also the discussion in Rebenich, *Hieronymus*, 98, and the Appendix, section 3.

48. Nautin, "Excommunication," explains many details of Jerome's career over the following several decades in terms of the consequences of Jerome's continued status as a priest of the clergy of Antioch. This position seems exaggerated.

49. Cavallera, *Schisme*, 211–16, with the caveats of Spoerl, "Schism."

50. Matthews, *Western Aristocracies*, 101–45.

51. Adkin, "Gregory of Nazianzus," 13 with n. 2, points out that Jerome never states why he went to Constantinople. He cites E. D. Hunt, in a review of Kelly, *Jerome*, appearing in *Journal of Religious Studies* 67 (1977): 169, as explaining Jerome's move in "political terms." As I argue in the next section, Jerome probably went to Constantinople to attend the first Council of Constantinople as a supporter of Paulinus of Antioch, since he was a member of his clergy at the time.

lent outbursts the emperor refused to control. Theodosius's religious policy involved both the use of force against disapproved factions, and active intervention in support of those whom the emperor deemed orthodox. Thus Theodosius, within a few days of his official entry into Constantinople in November 380, removed the non-Nicene bishop of Constantinople and replaced him with the leader of the tiny Nicene congregation there, Gregory of Nazianzus. Having set matters right in that city and issued laws expressing his will to the rest of the empire in no uncertain terms, Theodosius soon convened a general council at Constantinople.[52]

While the emperor vigorously enforced his official religious policy, he and other members of his court privately sponsored religious foundations and individuals that reflected their enthusiasms. Many of Theodosius's courtiers took a strong interest in Eastern-style asceticism. They built monasteries on their estates and installed hermits and entire cenobitic communities. They also brought many relics to Constantinople, constructing new churches in the city and on their suburban estates to house them. These pious Spanish nobles, together with others from the far western provinces, became frequent pilgrims to the Holy Land and visitors to the Egyptian fathers.[53]

It seems very likely that Jerome went to Constantinople with Paulinus of Antioch, as part of the faction that hoped to see Paulinus installed securely as bishop of the city by authority of the council.[54] The court of Theodosius was a milieu where Jerome might have felt quite at home, were it not for the unfavorable outcome of the council from the point of view of Paulinus's party. Unfortunately, we have no contemporary documents that reflect whether, or how, Jerome was involved in the messy business of assigning the see of Antioch to one of the two Nicene contenders. It is improbable that the young Jerome, now in his early thirties, was more than a highly partisan bystander. But the tumultuous events of 381 undeniably affected him: for when he left for Rome in summer 382, he traveled in the company of the defeated (though not discouraged) Paulinus, and his staunch supporter Epiphanius of Salamis.[55]

---

52. Matthews, *Western Aristocracies*, 123–25.

53. Matthews, *Western Aristocracies*, 127–45.

54. See Cavallera, *Schisme*, 219ff. for the purpose and timing of the council. The dates of Jerome's stay in Constantinople have been much disputed: for details, see the Appendix, section 4.

55. See Jerome, letter 127.7, to Principia on the death of Marcella. Describing his arrival at Rome in 382, Jerome writes, *Denique cum et me Romam cum sanctis Pontificibus, Paulino et Epiphanio.* For the context of the Council of Rome, see Cavallera, *Schisme*.

At the same time that he maintained his existing contacts with Eastern bishops in the circle of Paulinus of Antioch, Jerome made important new acquaintances during the year and a half he spent at Constantinople. Two Latins, Vincentius and Dexter, were perhaps typical of those who had been drawn to the Eastern capital in the wake of the Spanish emperor Theodosius. We are aware of Jerome's relations with them because he dedicated works to them. Vincentius we know only through Jerome's references to him. He was the dedicatee of the two major works that Jerome produced at Constantinople, and became Jerome's lifelong companion, following him to Rome in 382 and then to Bethlehem in 385.[56] Jerome mentions in one of his dedications to Vincentius that his friend "supplied" the scribal labor that allowed Jerome to dictate as he translated. The phrasing is ambiguous: it could mean that Vincentius paid for a hired *notarius,* that he lent Jerome one of his slaves, or even that Vincentius, trained in shorthand, served as the scribe himself. These alternatives, of course, would imply a different social position for Vincentius and a different relation between the two men: patronage on the one hand, collaboration on the other.[57]

We have more sources of information for the career of Nummius Aemilianus Dexter, whom Jerome may have met at Constantinople in the early 380s. He was a Spanish aristocrat who became a prominent member of Theodosius's administration. Ten years later, after Jerome had settled in Palestine, he dedicated his *On Famous Men* to Dexter. The two men do not seem to have overlapped in any location other than Constantinople. By the time of the dedication of *On Famous Men,* Dexter had returned to Spain after resigning his proconsulship in Asia. If he and Jerome had met at all, it must have been during the early 380s.[58] That would mean that Jerome's connection with Dexter was a durable one, suggesting that the young ascetic had made a strongly positive impression on at least one highly placed member of Theodosius's court.

56. Dedications: to Vincentius, in *Praef. in Hom. Orig. in Hiezech.;* to Vincentius and Gallienus, in *Praef. in Eus. Chr.* Other references to Vincentius appear in letter 66.3 and letter 88; *Contra Ioh. Hier.* 41; *Contra Ruf.* 3.22, 24.

57. In *Praef. in Hom. Orig. in Hiezech.* Jerome writes: *ea lege, quae tibi saepe constitui, ut ego vocem praebeam, tu notarium.*

58. PLRE Dexter 3. Proconsul Asiae 379–87, CRP (East) 387, PPO Italiae 395, office mentioned by Jerome *Contra Ruf.* 2.23. As proconsul of Asia, Dexter may not have been at court in 380, but if Jerome's claims to a connection with Gregory were totally false, it seems unlikely that he would advance them repeatedly in a work dedicated to someone who probably had at least met Gregory himself. Jerome's relations with Dexter are discussed by Matthews, *Western Aristocracies,* 111; Rebenich, *Hieronymus,* 126, 198, 214f., 23, 93.

In later writings, Jerome proudly claimed a close acquaintance with Gregory of Nazianzus during Gregory's tenure as bishop of Constantinople.[59] He refers to the Cappadocian as *praeceptor meus*, "my teacher," and describes his sessions of instruction in biblical exegesis with Gregory as occasions for friendly banter.[60] Such a relationship would have represented a significant broadening of Jerome's social world in comparison to his situation in Syria. Jerome's claim to intimacy with Gregory has been challenged.[61] For a number of reasons, however, his assertions should not be entirely discounted. In 379, Gregory was still the leader of a tiny splinter congregation. His appointment to the episcopacy of Constantinople by Theodosius in 380 was not to be long-lived.[62] His prestige as bishop of Constantinople was not what his immense posthumous reputation would make it. Gaining access to his inner circle, therefore, may have been rather less difficult than it seems in retrospect. Perhaps, too, Jerome's connection with Evagrius of Antioch helped him to make contact with Gregory. Evagrius's relationship with Gregory's intimate friend, Basil of Caesarea, was long-standing, if strained by this time. Gregory's own behavior during the succession of councils that attempted to resolve the question of the Antiochene see in the early 380s suggests that he may have been open to persuasion from the Paulinian side of the schism.[63] Finally, when Jerome boasts of his close relations to Gregory in *On Famous Men* in 392, he does so in a work dedicated, as we have just noted, to Dexter, who had probably been in Constantinople during Gregory's episcopacy and might well have known if Jerome were lying. Gre-

---

59. Gregory appears in Jerome's works at *De vir. ill.* 113, 117, 120, 128; *Adv. Iov.* 1.13; *Contra Ruf.* 1.13, 30; *Comm. in Ephes.* 5.32; *Comm. in Esaiam* 6.1; letters 50.1, 52.8, 70.4.

60. *Praeceptor meus* of Gregory: Kelly (*Jerome*, p. 70 n. 8) cites *De vir. ill.* 117; *Adv. Iov.* 1.13; *Contra Ruf.* 1.13, 30; *Comm. in epist. ad Ephes.* 5.32; *Comm. in Esaiam* 6.1; letters 50.1, 52.8; friendly banter, letter 52.8.

61. Adkin, "Gregory of Nazianzus," questions the plausibility of Jerome's descriptions of his relationship with Gregory of Nazianzus. Adkin shows that Jerome's references to Gregory are not nearly as unambiguously positive as apologetically inclined scholars have tended to admit, and that there is little sign of Gregory's influence on Jerome's own work.

62. Gallay, *Vie de Saint Grégoire;* on his episcopate at Constantinople, see Meredith, *Cappadocians,* 39–42; Matthews, *Western Aristocracies,* 122–26.

63. Evagrius's relations with Basil may have remained chilly for six or seven years after the latter's frosty letter 156; note, however, that Gregory of Nazianzus himself was not always agreeable to Basil's machinations and the role he was expected to play in them, and that Gregory came out in support of Paulinus at the Council of Constantinople in 381. For the relevant data, see Cavallera, *Schisme.* Cavallera's interpretations, however, are rendered unreliable by his unwillingness to acknowledge the possibility of conflict between Basil and Gregory.

gory's influence, furthermore, can help to explain the novel direction that Jerome took in the literary works he produced at Constantinople. The Cappadocians—Gregory Nazianzen, Basil, and Basil's younger brother, Gregory of Nyssa—were among the great fourth-century exponents of Origen. It is more than plausible that it was under Nazianzen's influence that Jerome discovered the Alexandrian master.[64]

Despite these tantalizing suggestions, however, very little can be said with assurance about Jerome's social world at Constantinople. What is certain is that there he began to present himself in a new light, as an exponent of Greek Christian learning, in particular that of Origen and of Origen's devotee Eusebius of Caesarea. Jerome carried out two substantial scholarly projects during his brief stay in the Eastern capital. The first and most impressive was the translation, adaptation, and extension of Eusebius's *Chronological Canons,* the comprehensive chronological tables that had been the primary innovation of Eusebius's *Chronicle.* The second was the translation of a series of Origen's own homilies on the prophets. Finally, two short letters on the interpretation of Isaiah, written at Constantinople but dedicated to Damasus of Rome, represent Jerome's first tentative essays in the creation of an independent exegetical persona. Their content largely paraphrases Origen's exegesis. Yet Jerome not only presented the readings he proposed as his own, but even asserted his independence by openly criticizing an interpretation of the master's.[65]

In the prefaces to the translations he made at Constantinople, Jerome developed new ways of representing his literary activity that revolved explicitly around his relation to Greek texts and to Origen's example. On the one hand, he proposed a program of creating Latin Christian culture modeled on the figure of Cicero. The works of Origen and Eusebius would play an analogous role to the Greek philosophical works that Cicero translated and adapted. On the other hand, Jerome also put forward Origen himself as a model of Christian culture. The two figures, Cicero and Origen, stand for

64. Kelly, *Jerome,* 76, argues that Jerome simply must have known of Origen before he came to Constantinople. But the dominance of Latin writers (many of whom Jerome later derides as poor imitators of Origen) in the letters earlier than 380 is quite striking, as is the enthusiasm with which Jerome embraces Origen in the works written after that date. Furthermore, Apollinaris of Laodicea, with whom Jerome claims to have studied at Antioch in the late 370s, would not have been an enthusiast of Origen's. We may safely conclude that if Jerome knew of Origen before he came to Constantinople, he did not hold him in the same regard that he later did.

65. For the dependence of Jerome's letters 18A and 18B on Origen's exegesis, see Jay, *Exégèse,* 63–64.

quite different literary and cultural modes. Cicero is the paradigm of rhetorical culture, while Origen is presented as its opposite. Both of Jerome's new versions of himself—as Christian Cicero, or as Latin Origen—imply a new level of seriousness and ambition.

The prologue to the translation of Eusebius's *Chronological Canons* places striking emphasis on the question of literary style, a strange preoccupation for the preface to a work composed almost entirely of tables of names and numbers. Yet Jerome chooses this opportunity to dilate on the problems of conveying style in a translation. His tone is weighty and rhetorical, his own literary gifts ostentatiously on display. First, he invokes Cicero as a paradigm of the translator's art:

> It was the ancient custom of learned men, that for the sake of mental exercise they would render Greek books into the Latin language and, which is the more difficult, translate the poetry of illustrious men with the added requirement of representing the meter. Whence too our Tully translated entire books of Plato word for word, and when he had published a Roman version of Aratus in hexameters, he amused himself with the *Oeconomica* of Xenophon.[66]

For Cicero, as Jerome would have it, translation was a recreation, a form of erudite play. Challenging or even dangerous play, to be sure: perhaps only a Cicero could find mental refreshment in translating Plato, Aratus, or Xenophon from Greek into Latin.

But Cicero's own eloquence is disrupted, sometimes occluded, when his prose becomes a vehicle for the work of others: as Jerome puts it, in Cicero's translation of Xenophon's *Oeconomica*, "the golden river of his eloquence is often held back by rough and turbulent obstacles, so that one who did not know that it was a translation would not believe that these were Cicero's words."[67] Jerome implies that Cicero's characteristic style is recognizable, a reflection of his identity. Translation threatens to muddy, if not to deform, a writer's literary persona. For the moment, that threat is held at bay by the language of recreation and athletic training, which figures translation as subordinate to the real business of the literary man. But we ought to take note of this passage's implication that to translate might mean to be

---

66. *Praef. in Eus. Chr.* 1: *Vetus iste disertorum mos fuit, ut exercendi ingenii causa graecos libros latino sermone absoluerent et, quod plus in se difficultatis habet, poemata inlustrium uirorum addita metri necessitate transferrent. Unde et noster Tullius Platonis integros libros ad uerbum interpretatus est et cum Aratum iam romanum hexametris uersibus edidisset, in Xenofontis Oeconomico lusit.*

67. *Praef. in Eus. Chr.* 1: *ita saepe aureum illud flumen eloquentiae quibusdam scabris et turbulentis obicibus retardatur, ut, qui interpretata nesciunt, a Cicerone dicta non credant.*

transformed, perhaps to mar or to mortify a carefully cultivated personal style.

In the next section of the preface, Jerome moves from the technical difficulty of transferring an author's style intact into another language to consider the literary quality of the Hebrew scriptures. He emphatically assures his readers that the stylistic excellence of the Hebrew scriptures, in the original, at least equals that of canonical Greek and Latin authors. Christian readers, he claims, are misled into thinking that their scriptures are crude in comparison to the literary classics. Not only do the translations distort the aesthetic qualities of the originals, but worse, "even learned men are unaware that they are translated from the Hebrew, so that seeing the surface, not the substance, they are horrified by what is, as it were, the sordid garment of the language, rather than discovering the beautiful body hidden within it." He goes on to compare various biblical books explicitly, and favorably, with the work of Horace and Pindar.[68] By attributing to the Hebrew Bible the literary merit of a classic, Jerome constitutes it as a proper object of literary investigation. At the same time, he opens up the possibility that such an engagement with a barbarian literature might involve entanglement in the "sordid," an experience potentially "horrifying" to a cultivated sensibility.

The opening paragraphs of the preface to the *Chronicon* reflect powerful but unarticulated beliefs about literary style, social status, and the possibility of a Christian culture based on the Bible. Running beneath the surface is a deep anxiety over the issue of literary self-fashioning in a cultural field defined by competing canons. Style, Jerome assumes, is an essential element of literary value. Those who judge the Hebrew scriptures on the basis of the style of the translations recoil in distaste, failing to appreciate the beauties

68. *Praef. in Eus. Chr.* 2: *difficultatem rei etiam diuinorum uoluminum instrumenta testentur, quae a septuaginta interpretibus edita non eundem saporem in Graeco sermone custodiunt. Quam ob rem Aquila et Symmachus et Theodotio incitati diuersum paene opus in eodem opere prodiderunt, alio nitente uerbum de uerbo exprimere, alio sensum potius sequi, tertio non multum a ueteribus discrepare. Quinta autem et sexta et septima editio, licet quibus censeantur auctoribus ignoretur, tamen ita probabilem sui diuersitatem tenent, ut auctoritatem sine nominibus meruerint. Inde adeo uenit, ut sacrae litterae minus comptae et sonantes uideantur, quod diserti homines interpretatas eas de Hebraeo nescientes, dum superficiem, non medullam inspiciunt, ante quasi uestem orationis sordidam perhorrescant quam pulchrum intrinsecus rerum corpus inueniant. Denique quid psalterio canorius, quod in morem nostri Flacci et Graeci Pindari nunc iambo currit, nunc alcaico personat, nunc sapfico tumet, nunc senipede ingreditur? Quid Deuteronomii et Esaiae cantico pulchrius, quid Solomone grauius, quid perfectius Iob? Quae omnia hexametris et pentametris uersibus, ut Iosephus et Origenes scribunt, apud suos composita decurrunt. Haec cum Graece legimus, aliud quiddam sonant, cum Latine, penitus non haerent.*

of the original. This problem of the literary quality of the scriptures had to be addressed as part of any project of creating Christian literary culture in the fourth century. To readers shaped by the grammatical and rhetorical schools, the biblical writings seemed crude, simple, the work of uneducated authors—in short, inappropriate fare for members of the elite.[69] The Christian canon could not be used as a model for self-fashioning in the same way that Cicero, Horace, and Virgil had been for centuries. If Christian writers were to model themselves after their own canonical authors, a revaluation of what counted as excellence in literary style would be required. The danger was that such a revaluation would reduce the power of literary style to express, and to create, social distinction. Jerome was clearly conscious of a tension between the Ciceronian ideal of eloquence and the creation of a Christian literary persona grounded in the authority of scripture, but he had yet to define that tension in terms that would allow him to propose a solution to it.

In the preface to his translation of Origen's homilies on Ezekiel, Jerome develops an alternative model for his literary activities: the figure of Origen himself. Again, the vocabulary of style plays an important role. Jerome relates that when he translated Origen's homilies on Jeremiah and Ezekiel, his "greatest concern was that the translation should maintain that man's peculiar idiom, and the simplicity of his speech, which alone is proper for churchmen." He goes on to describe the style of the translation in terms that are crucial to his own self-presentation as a translator, and indeed as a writer: "In this task I disdained every splendor of the rhetorical art—for I wish to be praised for the thing itself, not for mere words."[70] He explicitly contrasts the "splendors" of the rhetorician's art with the style appropriate for a Christian writer, characterized by simplicity and a concern for the thing itself, not for the form of its presentation. In his letter to Paul of Concordia a few years earlier, Jerome had described his efforts to simplify his style as undertaken for the benefit of the *simpliciores*, leaving open the possibility that rhetorical elaboration might be appropriate for other audiences.[71]

---

69. On Jerome's attitude toward the style of the scriptures in its broader cultural context, see Meershoek, *Latin biblique*, 4–30.

70. *Praef. in Hom. Orig. in Hiezech.*, PL 25, p. 691: *Itaque post quattuordecim homilias in Hieremiam, quas iam pridem confuso ordine interpretatus sum, et has quattuordecim in Ezechielem per interualla dictaui, id magnopere curans, ut idioma supradicti viri* [sc. Origen] *et simplicitatem sermonis, quae sola ecclesiis prodest, etiam translatio conservaret omni rhetoricae artis splendore contempto—res quippe uolumus, non uerba laudari.*

71. Letter 10.3.

Here he presents the simple style as the only one proper for a man of the church. That style is associated with Origen's own *idioma*, his personal vocabulary and mode of expression: literary production, again, is figured as a natural expression of the individual's character. Furthermore, Jerome melds his description of Origen's literary persona with a statement of his own aims as translator. Origen had mastered a style suitable for a man of the church. Jerome as his translator patterns his own style on Origen's.

The models of Origen and Cicero conflict with each other. To imagine the creation of Christian culture as Ciceronian is to remain within the sphere of the cultivated aristocracy. To imitate Origen — at least as Jerome describes him — is to step outside it. The two men's literary styles are the focus of the contrast Jerome sets up between them. Where Cicero's eloquence flows like a river of gold, Origen's style rejects rhetorical splendor. Origen's Christian simplicity is appropriate to an ecclesiastical setting quite separate from the aristocracy and its literary diversions. Behind the difference between the two styles, deeper conflicts can be discerned: between the power of worldly elites and that of ecclesiastical officeholders; between *askesis* as aristocratic self-cultivation and *askesis* as Christian self-mortification. Jerome's prefaces from the period at Constantinople implicitly raise these issues but cannot confront them directly. Given his investment in the culture of the elite and its importance for his own nascent literary persona, Jerome's difficulties here are unsurprising. In the next phase of his career, he would come to a new and stark formulation of the opposition between classical and Christian culture, one that would demand at least the appearance of choosing one side over the other.

A TROUBLESOME PRIEST

Leaving Constantinople after the defeat of the Paulinians at the council of 381, Jerome spent the next three years at Rome. As a young, enterprising, and eloquent priest with a reputation for vigorous asceticism, he quickly became a favorite among certain elements of the city's Christian elite. He left only when he was driven out, in the late summer of 385, by the controversy that his intransigent advocacy of asceticism and virginity, and his association with a number of prominent female ascetics, had evoked. The period that he spent at Rome was one of extraordinary activity and intellectual ferment.[72] During these years, Jerome developed a depiction of Christian learn-

---

72. On the milieu that Jerome entered at Rome, see Curran, *Pagan city*, 260–320.

ing as a form of ascetic piety, and of the new figure of the Christian scholar as professed ascetic, that included several new features. He represented rhetorical and literary culture as sensual indulgence, using elaborate metaphors to equate books and reading with food and eating. He described both the Christian Bible and the Hebrew original of its Old Testament as coarse and unappealing to a refined literary sensibility. Through the figure of Origen, he portrayed the intellectual activity of the Christian scholar as a form of incessant labor. He cast his Hebrew studies as a deliberate mortification of the aesthetic sense developed through literary education. In sum, he equated the effects of biblical scholarship on the speech and deportment of the ascetic Christian scholar with those of fasting, vigils, and the avoidance of baths on his body.

When Jerome arrived in Rome, it was as a priest in the suite of Paulinus of Antioch, who had come in answer to a summons from Ambrose of Milan. Neither Ambrose nor Damasus was pleased with the outcome of the turbulent series of synods at Constantinople. The majority of the Eastern bishops refused their invitation to a council at Rome, but Paulinus had nothing to lose. His loyal supporter, Epiphanius of Salamis, traveled with him.[73] On reaching the Western capital, Jerome quickly formed a close relationship with bishop Damasus. He soon appeared by Damasus's side, serving him as a sort of confidential secretary during the council of Rome and remaining with him after the council ended. Scholars have questioned whether Jerome's relations with Damasus were actually so intimate. But the traditional idea that Jerome was a trusted member of Damasus's clergy and the beneficiary of Damasus's literary patronage is supported not only by the two men's preserved correspondence and Jerome's later writings but also by convincing external evidence. And after all, Jerome came to Rome as part of a small but prestigious Eastern delegation, made up of bishops who had long been Damasus's correspondents and allies. By 382, furthermore, Jerome had been a priest for about six years, so that his clerical identity would have been firmly established. His later protestations, after he had become a monk in Bethlehem, that he at that time refused to act as a priest are beside the point. For a Latin priest serving a Greek bishop to be assimilated into Damasus's clergy would not have seemed unnatural.

Damasus continued to rely on his articulate new assistant to draft his correspondence after the council had dispersed. As Jerome put it in a letter he wrote immediately after Damasus's death in 385, and just before his own departure from Rome, "my speech was the mouth of Damasus of blessed

---

73. On the council of Rome, see Cavallera, *Schisme*, 245–62.

memory."[74] In 409, Jerome described the role he had played at Rome in more prosaic terms: "I assisted Bishop Damasus of Rome in the ecclesiastical archives, and wrote responses to the inquiries of synods of both East and West."[75] Damasus also put a number of exegetical questions to Jerome, in formal letters that he addressed to his protégé even while the latter served him as a secretary. Presumably the two men also conferred regularly in person, as their preserved correspondence implies.[76] Finally, toward the end of his stay at Rome, Jerome began to revise the Old Latin version of the New Testament from the Greek originals. He attributed to Damasus the initial impetus behind this undertaking, and dedicated his version of the Gospels to the Roman bishop after his death.[77]

External evidence, from an anecdote recounted years later by Rufinus of Aquileia, confirms and adds detail to the impression given by Jerome's direct references to his relations with Damasus. Rufinus describes an occasion when Damasus instructed an unnamed individual described as "a friend of his who was a priest, a most learned man, who in his customary role took care of this task for him," to draw up a statement of faith to which those accused of Apollinarianism would have to subscribe.[78] The wily Apollinarians, in Rufinus's account, duped the unnamed priest. In a rejoinder to this veiled attack, Jerome identifies himself as the man in question.[79] Combining the

---

74. Letter 45.3: *beatae memoriae Damasi os meus sermo erat,* cited by Rebenich, *Hieronymus,* 144.

75. Letter 123.9: *ante annos plurimos, cum in chartis ecclesiasticis iuuarem Damasum, Romae urbis episcopum, et orientis atque occidentis synodicis consultationibus responderem,* cited by Rebenich, *Hieronymus,* 144.

76. Letters 19 (Damasus to Jerome) and 20 (Jerome to Damasus), on the meaning of the word "hosanna"; letter 21 (Jerome to Damasus), on the prodigal son; letter 35 (Damasus to Jerome) and 36 (Jerome to Damasus), on five exegetical questions. For the dating and authenticity of this correspondence, see the Appendix, section 5.

77. *Praef. in Euangelio, Biblia sacra* 1515–16: *Beato papae Damaso Hieronymus. nouum opus facere me cogis ex uetere.*

78. Rufinus, *De adulteratione libris Origenis,* 13: *amico suo presbytero, uiro disertissimo, qui hoc illi ex more negotium procurabat,* cited in Vessey, "Forging," 498. This evidence comes from a polemical work written after the outbreak of the bitter controversy over Origenism in the 390s. Rufinus was at this point engaged in an attack on Jerome in which he used every means to hand to discredit his former friend; what he says of Jerome, therefore, owes nothing to the latter's attempts at self-promotion.

79. In his *Contra Ruf.* 2.20 Jerome writes, *et sub nomine cuiusdam amici Damasi, Romanae urbis episcopi, ego petar, cui ille ecclesiasticas epistulas dictandas credidit* ("and under the name of some friend of Damasus, the bishop of Rome, I am attacked, to whom that man entrusted the task of dictating ecclesiastical letters"). Jerome thus identifies himself as the nameless priest whose involvement in the controversy with the Apollinarians Rufinus had recounted. For this argument, see Vessey, "Forging."

two passages, we gain a clear picture of Jerome as Damasus's assistant, conducting research in the ecclesiastical archives and drafting documents that would appear over the bishop's signature.

The correspondence between Jerome and Damasus must be interpreted in the context of Jerome's services to the bishop. Rather than taking the place of frequent face-to-face contact, their letters, like many in late antiquity, were written with an audience beyond the correspondents in mind. The two writers' primary purpose was to advertise the nature of their relationship and to make public its intellectual fruit. Damasus wrote to Jerome with certain exegetical questions that he wished his secretary to address. He would have done so not because he was unable to make such a request of his protégé in person, but in order to publicly and formally proclaim his patronage of Jerome's work. Such a letter may have functioned analogously to a letter of recommendation, providing Jerome with a credential that he could display before others. Not only Damasus's standing as bishop of Rome but also his unquestioned orthodoxy in Trinitarian matters would have enhanced this endorsement. In return, Jerome offered the first fruits of his Greek and Hebrew studies to the Roman bishop, whose cultural prestige would have been augmented by his patronage of such a brilliant young priest. Jerome, of course, had more to gain from the relationship. But he also offered a far more substantial gift, in the form of his literary productions as well as his services as secretary. Damasus, by virtue of his standing at the pinnacle of the Latin Christian world, needed little from one such as Jerome. Equally, however, it cost him little to dispense his patronage, and thus implicitly to certify Jerome's orthodoxy.

Along with Damasus, Jerome acquired other new patrons during his stay in Rome. He became intimate with several female ascetics of senatorial family and wealth. These women included Marcella, a widow who had turned her aristocratic household on the Aventine into a monastic community, and Paula, also a widow, whose daughters joined her in her renunciation. We know nothing of Marcella in the 380s except the little that can be gleaned from Jerome's letters. She seems to have been a woman of considerable learning, whose ascetic practice was well established. Jerome addressed an impressive dossier of letters to her while he lived at Rome. The subject matter and concerns of these letters overlap substantially with the smaller collection addressed to Damasus.[80] Paula was a younger widow who had en-

---

80. PLRE I, "Marcella 2," 542, compiles the information that Jerome's writings provide for Marcella; letters 23–32, 34, 37–38, 40–45 purport to have been addressed to her at Rome; on the relationship, as well as the correspondence, during Jerome's years at Rome, see Vessey, "Je-

thusiastically adopted a severe ascetic regimen based on Eastern models. Jerome was a primary advocate of these practices at Rome, and he became a close associate of Paula's. When he was driven from Rome in 385, it was largely as a result of his relations with her. He may have met her through her connection with a friend from his school days, the senator Pammachius, who was the husband of Paula's daughter Paulina.[81]

Jerome's preserved correspondence with Marcella from this period, and the smaller number of letters to Paula and Eustochium, again would not have substituted for face-to-face contact. Instead, the letters served to publicize the alliance between these prominent female ascetics and their younger male protégé, as Jerome must be considered with respect to these senatorial ladies. Their worldly standing, and in the case of Marcella her experience in asceticism, outweighed Jerome's by far. Even in writing to Eustochium, a young woman and a virgin, Jerome refers to his addressee as *domina*, the feminine form of *dominus*, meaning "lord" or "master."[82] The use of this term acknowledges Eustochium's role as patron, while trading upon her social standing to establish Jerome's own position of authority as a Christian writer who can claim to prescribe for his fellow ascetics. Compared to his relationship to Bishop Damasus, Jerome's relations with his female patrons would have been less unequal. His status as a male and a priest would have partly balanced their wealth and their aristocratic descent. But it seems likely that at Rome, at least, Jerome was the subordinate partner in these relationships as well.

As his Roman letters reveal, until his flight in 385, Jerome thought of himself as a priest, albeit one dedicated to a strictly ascetic life.[83] His literary activities and his relations with female ascetics took place in the context of his role as a member of the clergy of Damasus, bishop of Rome. His ability to articulate a convincing program for Christian learning played an im-

---

rome's Origen"; Rebenich, *Hieronymus*, 154–70; Kelly, *Jerome*, 91–96; Cavallera, *Saint Jérôme*, 1:84–88.

81. See PLRE I, "Paula 1," 674; Jerome, letter 108, gives the most detail on Paula's family and background. See also Rebenich, *Hieronymus*, 154–70, 81–92; Kelly, *Jerome*, 96–99; Cavallera, *Saint Jérôme*, 1:88–91.

82. Letter 22.26: *mi Eustochia, filia, domina, conserua, germana—aliud enim aetatis, aliud meriti, illud religionis, hoc caritatis est nomen* ("my Eustochium, daughter, lady, fellow servant, sister—the first title refers to your age, the second to your rank, the third to your religious vocation, and the last to my affection for you").

83. See letter 22.28. Male monks at Rome play almost no role in the taxonomy of ascetics (real and false) that letter 22 presents. After briefly criticizing two men who seem to have been monks, Jerome moves on to lampoon priests who profess asceticism as an excuse to gain access to women. The monks whom he discusses in paragraphs 32ff. are all explicitly described as Egyptian.

portant role in gaining his patrons' support. As I suggested in the case of Damasus, Jerome's writings were the only currency he had to spend in his exchanges with persons of greater wealth and influence. Once bishops and aristocrats accepted his writings and publicized their interest in his studies, Jerome's work became valuable. But for his writings to achieve acceptance, Jerome had to find means of legitimating them that would appeal to his patrons and to readers in their circles. His search for a foundation for his authority as a writer thus took on renewed urgency.

It was in his letter 22 to Eustochium, in which he set forth a program for the life of the Christian virgin, that Jerome recounted the famous dream described already at the beginning of this chapter. The story of the dream contains several of the most prominent components of his cultural program.[84] Jerome describes his pitiful state as an ascetic who nevertheless could not refrain from reading the classic poets and orators, then recounts the bizarre vision that finally broke him of the habit. The highly colored rhetoric of the passage represents classical literature as a sensual indulgence, which is contrasted with the coarse and unappealing Christian scriptures.

> Let me recount for you my own sad story. Many years ago, when I had abandoned my home, my relatives, my sister, my brother, and, what was more difficult than all these, the habit of delicate food, for the sake of the kingdom of heaven, and set out for Jerusalem to enter the service, I was still unable to abandon my library, which I had collected at Rome with so much effort and toil. Therefore, wretch that I was, I read Tully while I fasted. After repeated nighttime vigils, after the tears that the memory of my former sins drew forth from the depths of my entrails, I took up Plautus. If, when I returned to my senses, I began to read the prophet again, the crude language horrified me.[85]

---

84. There is a scholarly controversy over the chronology of Jerome's Roman letters, on which see the Appendix, section 5. Out of the letters conventionally assigned to the years at Rome, two—letters 22 and 39—can be dated without question to that period, and therefore provide our surest evidence for the initial articulation of Jerome's attempt to fuse learning with Christian *askesis*. Kelly, *Jerome*, 100, dates letter 22 ca. 384; Cavallera, *Saint Jérôme*, 2 : 24, dates it to the spring of 384. The date of letter 39 is fixed by Blesilla's death in December 384; 39.3 refers to Blesilla's baptism four months earlier, implying that her death was still very recent: see Kelly, *Jerome*, 110–11. Cavallera, *Saint Jérôme*, 2 : 22–23, specifies a date for letter 39 between December 9 and December 11, 384.

85. Letter 22.30: *Referam tibi meae infelicitatis historiam. Cum ante annos plurimos domo, parentibus, sorore, cognatis et, quod his difficilius est, consuetudine lautioris cibi propter caelorum me regna castrassem et Hierosolymam militaturus pergerem, bybliotheca, quam mihi Romae summo studio ac labore confeceram, carere non poteram. Itaque miser ego lecturus Tullium ieiunabam. Post noctium crebras uigilias, post lacrimas, quas mihi praeteritorum recordatio peccatorum ex imis uisceribus eruebat, Plautus sumebatur in manibus. Si quando in memet reuersus prophetam legere coepissem, sermo horrebat incultus.*

As in the prefaces to the translations he made at Constantinople, Cicero and Plautus on the one hand, and the Christian scriptures on the other, are characterized in terms of their literary styles. But Jerome's evaluation of the style of biblical literature here is strikingly different than in the preface to the translation of the *Chronicon*. There, Jerome argued that the style of the biblical authors was equal to that of Greek and Latin poets. Here, he describes his horror in the face of their uncultivated language. The preface to the *Chronicon* had presaged this reaction, suggesting that a poor translation might leave the reader "horrified" by the "sordid outer garment" of the scriptures. But here the emphasis has shifted radically, so that rather than being a covering to be stripped away, revealing the true beauty of the Bible's poetic language, the style of the biblical texts now holds out a valuable opportunity for self-mortification.

The connection between reading and eating that runs through the entire passage deserves emphasis. Jerome frequently links biblical study to fasting as forms of self-mortification. Here he confides that the most difficult habit to renounce, besides reading secular literature, was eating delicate food. Athough as a hermit he fasted, he nevertheless went on reading Cicero. By implication, the effect of biblical study on a cultivated literary sensibility is equated with the effect of fasting on a body previously accustomed to a rich diet. Christian reading—or at least Bible reading—is a form of *askesis* specifically adapted to the highly cultivated monk. In effect, Jerome's self-castigation is a form of self-promotion. Only one whose sensitivities had been developed by elite education, he implies, could have suffered in precisely this way from the typical regimen of a desert hermit. Jerome's refinement makes his austerities all the more impressive.

Further elements of Jerome's program of ascetic scholarship emerge clearly in letter 39, which he wrote to his patroness Paula on the death of her daughter Blesilla, elder sister of Eustochium. Blesilla had been a young widow only recently converted to asceticism under Jerome's influence. Her death aroused great anger among those who found Jerome's advocacy of a particularly rigorous form of renunciation extremist and his relations with aristocratic female ascetics suspect. In his eulogy for her, Jerome catalogues Blesilla's intellectual attainments, especially her mastery of languages. The letter served not only to console Paula for her loss but to defend Jerome's positions and his relationship with Paula and her family. Given this double purpose, we must be prepared to interpret Jerome's description of Blesilla as a statement of his own self-conception, as well as an idealized portrait of a specific young woman.

One passage stands out for its direct relevance to Jerome's cultural program.[86] Jerome describes not only Blesilla herself but his addressee, her mother Paula, as students of Hebrew. Origen was the model for this undertaking, a model whom Blesilla, at least, not only imitated but surpassed in her assiduity and intelligence. Blesilla mastered Hebrew with astounding rapidity and was also fluent in both Greek and Latin, an accomplishment that made her, on the model of Jerome himself, a *femina trilinguis*.[87] Jerome uses his eulogy of Blesilla as an opportunity to develop a portrait of the ideal ascetic. That ideal includes intellectual activities, among which the study of Greek and Hebrew appear prominently. Further, this program of study is explicitly connected to the model of Origen. Jerome's inclusion of such traits in the death-portrait of a young woman who had recently renounced the world under his influence strongly suggests that at the time he wrote this letter, he already saw his own project of ascetic learning in similar terms.

Other letters yield a richer, more detailed impression of Jerome's developing literary persona and its grounding both in the example of Origen and in the authority of the Hebrew tradition. In Jerome's correspondence with Paula, Marcella, and Damasus, Origen takes on new attributes, and the portrayal of Hebrew study as inherently ascetic comes into sharper focus. Origen's ascetic lifestyle made up part of the personal charisma that gave his writings authority. Jerome, whose knowledge of Greek and of Greek Christian biblical scholarship gave him access to Origen's full literary corpus, could thus set himself above those Latin exegetes who ignored Origen or used his work inappropriately. He could also take advantage of the eagerness of Western audiences for translations of Origen's writings.[88] But Jerome

---

86. Letter 39.1: *Quis sine singultibus transeat orandi instantiam, nitorem linguae, memoriae tenacitatem, acumen ingenii? Si graece audisses loquentem, latine eam nescire iurasses; si in romanum sonum lingua se uerterat, nihil omnino peregrinus sermo redolebat. Iam uero, quod in Origene illo Graecia tota miratur, in paucis non dico mensibus, sed diebus ita hebraeae linguae uicerat difficultates, ut in edis-cendis canendisque psalmis cum matre contenderet* ("Who could mention without sobs the eagerness of her prayers, the purity of her speech, the tenacity of her memory, the acuity of her thought? If you had heard her speaking Greek, you would have sworn she knew no Latin; if her tongue returned to Roman sounds, her speech betrayed no foreign taint. Indeed, she accomplished what in Origen was a marvel to all Greece: she so conquered the challenges of the Hebrew language, in the span of a few—not months—but days, that she rivaled her mother in memorizing and chanting the Psalms").

87. Melania the Younger, in her *Vita*, is similarly described as equally fluent in Latin and Greek, to the point that she had no foreign accent in either language (Gerontius, *Melania the Younger*, 46). Of course Melania lived in the East for years, and may have learned her Greek there, but it is by no means impossible that Blesilla had studied Greek at Rome.

88. See, for example, Jerome's prefaces to his to translations of Origen's Homilies on Ezekiel (ca. 380–81), on the Song of Songs (ca. 384), and on Luke (ca. 389); see also Augustine, letter 28.2,

based his authority as a writer not only on Origen's works but also on his own capacity to imitate and even surpass Origen, through direct access to the Hebrew text of the Bible and to Jewish learning. He developed an elaborate vocabulary describing the Hebrew text and the learning of the Jews who possessed it as a wellspring of truth, differentiated sharply from the muddy rivulets of opinion transmitted by the Greek and Latin translations of the scriptures and the traditions of commentary in those languages.

Jerome's letter 33, addressed to Paula, contains his most famous description of Origen. The central theme of the letter is Origen's immense productivity. This trait gives Jerome the excuse to introduce a catalogue of Origen's works. Origen's labors as a writer are compared to those of the most productive exponents of the Greek and Latin scholarly traditions, Didymus Chalcenterus and Varro: Origen excelled them both. Through the ordering and arrangement of the items in his catalogue, Jerome implies that Origen's primary field of activity was exegesis of the scriptures. The essence of Christian scholarship, Jerome seems to say, is commentary on the Bible. This activity can be conceived of as ascetic inasmuch as it involves the exegete in constant, strenuous labor.[89]

In comparing Origen to two of the greatest figures of the Greek and Latin grammatical traditions, Jerome implicitly represents the Christian Bible as literature. Both the intensity of the grammarian's focus on the canonical texts, and his methodology as a critic, depended on the assumption that the text under study exemplified an ideal of literary excellence. Those works that conformed to this ideal were set apart from other writings, given a special status that made them worthy not only of scholarly study but, even more importantly, of inclusion in the school curriculum. That status was predicated on a number of qualities. Most prominent in many ancient discussions was the style of the canonical authors. Their mastery of language set their writings apart from the mass of inferior work. The grammarian's art largely focused on the assessment of a writer's characteristic style; the evaluation of variants was based on their conformity to that style. Origen, according to Eusebius, had been a grammarian before he became a Christian teacher, and continued to teach Greek literature for some time after he began his second

---

urging him to continue his translations of Greek commentators and especially Origen (ca. 394 – 95, i.e. after the initial outbreak of controversy in the East; see Cavallera, *Saint Jérôme*, 2 : 48).

89. For this characterization of Origen as portrayed in letter 33, I follow Vessey, "Jerome's Origen," who writes that the letter's emphasis "is on productivity, single-minded engagement with the Bible, and sheer hard work."

career. In Jerome's version, Origen's biblical exegesis becomes a form of Christian *grammatikē*.

The style of the Bible, however, was not equal to that of the classics. We already know that Jerome made much of how he suffered from the inferiority of the Christian writings in this regard. The model of the grammarian, therefore, had to be strained to the breaking point to apply to Origen's study of the Bible as Jerome portrayed it. For the elite milieu that fostered classical literary scholarship was radically different from the Christian ascetic world in which Jerome sought to situate biblical exegesis. The *askesis* of the elite male of the ancient world was shaped by the ethic of care of the self. Devotion to literature was but one element of constant effort toward self-perfection. The ideals of the desert fathers were different. The perfection of the self they sought was to be found not in the forum of the ancient city, nor even in the *otium* of an aristocratic estate, but beyond the boundaries of human society, whether in the isolation of the desert or in the world to come. While he remained entombed in a body of flesh, the Christian ascetic aimed not at the care of the self but at its radical refashioning. Jerome could therefore place immersion in the crude diction of the scriptures at the center of his ascetic program. The Bible was literature in the sense that it was a text that could be used to produce a certain kind of self, just as literary education used Virgil and Cicero. The selves it shaped, however, promised to be quite different.

In a passage of his letter 43 to Marcella, Jerome further develops his portrayal of Origen's scholarship as unending labor. In this letter, the tight focus on the great man himself opens out to a picture that places Origen's efforts in their social and material context.

> Ambrose, who provided the parchment, money, and shorthand secretaries that allowed Adamantius, our Chalcenterus, to produce his innumerable books, reported in a letter that he wrote him from Athens that never in his presence had Origen taken a meal without a reading, nor did he ever go to sleep without one of the brothers' reading aloud something from the sacred writings, and he comported himself thus night and day, so that reading took the place of prayer and prayer of reading.[90]

90. Letter 43.1: *Ambrosius, quo chartas, sumptus, notarios ministrante tam innumerabiles libros uere Adamantius et noster χαλκέντερος explicauit, in quadam epistula, quam ad eundem de Athenis scripserat, refert numquam se cibos Origene praesente sine lectione sumpsisse, numquam uenisse somnum, nisi e fratribus aliquis sacris litteris personaret, hoc diebus egisse uel noctibus, ut et lectio orationem susciperet et oratio lectionem.*

Origen's routine combines study and prayer in an unrelenting focus on the Bible.[91] The passage gives us an intimate portrait of the great man. Jerome invites us to watch Origen at his meals, even preparing for bed. Origen is constantly surrounded by a crowd of assistants. Shorthand secretaries, the "brothers" who read to him, and his patron Ambrose were all needed to make his immense productivity possible. This picture of the author as the center of a collaborative undertaking contrasts with the one given in letter 33, where Origen stands in impressive isolation, ranged only against his literary rivals.

Jerome's presentation of Origen as supported by a whole circle of assistants, as well as the patron who pays for them, is worth pausing over. Clearly, this vignette was a thinly veiled hint aimed at Jerome's own patrons. Just as Origen served as a model for Jerome, so he implies that Ambrose might serve as a model for Marcella (and presumably for others who supported Jerome's work). Jerome even applies to Marcella the epithet *ergōdiō-kitēs*, "slave-driver," used playfully by Origen to refer to Ambrose.[92] But the scene of Origen at his labors also acknowledges the immense expense involved in Origen's—or Jerome's—way of life. Thus Jerome's Origen is frankly dependent on his wealthy patron. Without Ambrose, his characteristic form of asceticism would be impossible.[93] In a later era, when the fathers of the Egyptian desert held a powerful appeal, a mode of renunciation so obviously tied to an aristocratic fortune—or patron—might seem incongruous. The Jerome who could so brazenly hint that he needed money was a priest and a prominent member of the Roman clergy, who probably expected that one day he would become a bishop. His status at Rome was secured by his position within a well-established institutional structure that commanded abundant resources. After 385, when he became a mere monk, Jerome's reputation for intellectual integrity would have been more sharply threatened by the imputation of financial dependence on powerful patrons.

Alongside his portrait of Origen as an exemplary figure, whose works

---

91. Vessey, "Jerome's Origen," 141, cites this passage, commenting that "Jerome's Origen is indefatigable, reading and writing uremittingly in the service of religion. Those close to him are both subject to his regimen and partly responsible for its maintenance." He adds that the letter presents Origen as a exemplar of "an ascetic lifestyle in which Christian *writing* was associated with the canonical alteration of *lectio* and *oratio* in a ceaseless round" (142).

92. Letter 28.1, cited in Vessey, "Jerome's Origen."

93. On the costliness of Origen's scholarship, the importance of Ambrose's financial support, and the parallels to this situation among Greek philosophers throughout the Roman period, see Grafton and Williams, *Christianity*, chapter 1.

and way of life conferred legitimacy on the literary productions of his imitators, Jerome developed a vocabulary to describe the Hebrew text of the Bible, and Jewish biblical learning in general, as sources of authority. At the same time, he used striking metaphorical language to represent the study of Hebrew as inherently ascetic. His central metaphor was the image of a spring or fountain of truth. The earliest appearance of this comparison is perhaps in letter 20, which he probably wrote to Damasus during his first year at Rome.[94] Neither there nor in any other work he wrote before 386 did Jerome use the phrase *Hebraica veritas*, "the Hebrew truth," which was to be so common in his later writing. But the conception that phrase would later designate is fully expressed in letter 20.[95] Jerome's Latin predecessors, he notes, were misled in their attempts to interpret both Testaments by their ignorance of the Hebrew language. Jerome, however, has access to that very font from which the evangelists drew, the truth hidden in the Hebrew text.[96] This notion that the writers of the New Testament—especially Paul and Matthew—knew Hebrew and used their knowledge in ways analogous to Jerome's own scholarly method was to remain part of his representation of Hebrew study, and would lead Jerome into some strange byways in years to come. In letter 20, it already functions to broaden the scope of Jerome's expertise: the relevance of Hebrew learning is not restricted to the Old Testament, but extends even to the New.

Not only is the study of Hebrew essential to sound biblical exegesis, but it is an inherently ascetic activity. In portraying his study of Hebrew as itself a form of asceticism, Jerome employs the same metaphorical equation of reading with eating that appears in letter 22. A passage from letter 29 to Marcella contains a particularly vivid example of this language.[97] Jerome

---

94. Letter 20.1–2: *Multi super hoc sermone [osanna filio David] diuersa finxerunt . . . Restat ergo ut, omissis opinionum riuulis, ad ipsum fontem unde ab euangelistis sumptum est, recurramus. Nam quomodo illud neque in Graecis neque in Latinis codicibus possumus inuenire: "ut conpleretur id quod dictum est per prophetas: quoniam Nazareus uocabitur," et illud: "ex Aegypto uocaui filium meum," ita et nunc ex hebraeis codicibus veritas exprimenda est.* Note Jerome's juxtaposition of the language of the font or wellspring of truth with the authority of the Hebrew text.

95. Cavallera, *Saint Jérôme*, 2 : 26. On the early emergence of the concept, if not the vocabulary, of the *Hebraica veritas*, see chapter 2 below and Kamesar, *Jerome*, 42.

96. The Hebrew text cited by Jerome in transliteration in letter 20.2ff. presents serious problems; however, a combination of plausible textual variants with a certain imprecision on Jerome's part can account for the marked discrepancy between the Masoretic text of the psalm and the text Jerome cites. The implication is that Jerome at this point in time did not fully control the Hebrew text, although he did have some access to it, perhaps with the help of a Jewish teacher.

97. Letter 29.1: *Denique heri famosissima quaestione proposita postulasti ut quid sentirem statim rescriberem; quasi uero pharisaeorum teneam cathedram ut, quotienscumque de uerbis Hebraicis*

represents himself as an authority on Jewish matters, recognized by all and invited to judge disputes among his circle. The Hebrew sources, as Jerome characterizes them, are no luxurious dishes fit for dainty palates: they are "no soft foods—savoring of pastry, prepared according to Apicius—and without any fragrance of the learned men of this temporal world." The reference to Apicius, the famous Roman cookbook writer, evokes literary as well as material gastronomy. The vivid culinary metaphor, thus enriched, allows Jerome to represent classical learning as an almost physical indulgence. Unlike the canonical orators, Hebrew is a fit study for the austere Christian ascetic. Furthermore, there is slippage between the literary qualities (or lack thereof) of the Hebrew Bible and of Jerome's own letter. He who writes about the sacred scriptures has no more need of the eloquence of Cicero or Demosthenes than did the authors of the biblical texts themselves.

This passage stands in sharp contrast to the passages from the preface to the translation of Eusebius's *Chronicon* discussed above, which invoke Cicero as a model for the Christian translator and praise the literary quality of the Hebrew original. Jerome's depiction of the Hebrew has evolved in a new direction. Jerome now opposes his Hebrew studies to rhetorical education and its stock texts in stark terms. This opposition and its extension into an ascetic precept reflect the same logic seen in the description of Jerome's dream in letter 22. Because the Bible was written in a debased literary style, the study of scripture was an act of self-mortification for a reader shaped by immersion in the texts of the traditional literary curriculum.

A passage from the conclusion of letter 29 extends even farther the presentation of Hebrew study as an ascetic activity. Not only has Jerome mortified his cultivated literary sensibilities, but he has marred his own speech: "As for myself, as you know, restricted to the reading of the Hebrew language, my Latin has rusted away, to such an extent that when I speak, a certain harsh, un-Latin sibilance intrudes." [98] This conceit represents Hebrew studies as almost physically dangerous. To read in late antiquity was, in general, to read out loud. This practice took on further significance for men trained in the literary tradition. Not only did schooling begin with learning to read aloud, but ancient prescriptive writers recommended both declama-

---

iurgium est, ego arbiter et litis sequester exposcar. Non sunt suaues epulae, quae non et placentam redo-
leant, quas non condit Apicius, in quibus nihil de magistrorum huius temporis iure suffumat. Sed quia
uector et internuntius sermonis nostri redire festinat, rem grandem celerius dicto quam debeo, licet de
scripturis sanctis disputanti non tam necessaria sint uerba quam sensus, quia si eloquentiam quaerimus
Demosthenes legendus aut Tullius est, si sacramenta diuina nostri codices, qui de Hebraeo in Latinum
non bene resonant peruidendi.

98. Letter 29.7.

tion and reading as forms of physical training for adults. The mild stimulation provided by the careful exercise of the voice could be particularly useful to the elite male as he strove to maintain the vocal and physical deportment that proclaimed his status to all he encountered. The notion that one could internalize the values, and the style, of the canonical writers by immersion in their work takes on an almost comic literalism in the medical writers' prescription of the reading of specific authors as curatives for specific ailments.[99]

If there had been any reality to Jerome's assertion that he had lost his correct accent under the influence of a barbarian tongue, the implications would have been profound. If its effects were as advertised, ascetic self-mortification in this form could have had the same kind of public-display value as another favorite of Jerome's, the complete avoidance of bathing. It is unlikely that this claim was intended to be taken seriously. But the rather unreal quality of the passage just cited only reinforces the point that Hebrew was useful to Jerome as a way of representing his scholarly activities as self-mortifying, and of using the ideology of asceticism to counter the imperatives of rhetorical culture.

99. For the culture of declamation and its connections with medicine, see Gleason, *Making Men*, chapters 4 and 5. For Latin authors on declamation and physical health, see Gleason, *Making Men*, 103–21. All the writers she mentions (Cicero, Seneca the Elder and the Younger, Quintilian, and the author of the *Rhetorica ad Herennium*) would have been familiar to Jerome and his audience from their schooling. On Hebrew as a "barbarian" language in Jerome, see the passage cited from letter 7.2 in n. 30, letter 20.5, and *Praef. in Eus. Chr.*

CHAPTER TWO

——— ✳ ———

Experiments in Exegesis

IN THE summer heat of August 385, Jerome found himself forced to flee Rome, his detractors nipping at his heels. He had made a number of influential enemies during his last two years at Rome, and when his patron Damasus died, he was no longer safe in the Western capital. Traveling via Cyprus with a small group of male companions, he enjoyed the hospitality of Bishop Epiphanius of Salamis, whom he had first met when he journeyed to the Council of Rome in Paulinus's train in 382. He visited Evagrius and Paulinus at Antioch; there he rejoined his patroness Paula, who had traveled to the East separately with her daughter Eustochium. The group reached Jerusalem in midwinter.[1] It was some months before the three Latins settled on Bethlehem as their new home, in the summer of 386; the construction of the monastic complex there, which Paula's fortune was to underwrite, was not complete until 389. In the interim, they found time for a short trip to Egypt, where they went to see the desert fathers. At Alexandria, Jerome spent a few weeks sitting at the feet of Didymus, the great blind

---

1. Cavallera, *Saint Jérôme* 1:123–28; *Contra Ruf.* 3.22.2: *mense autem augusto, flantibus etesiis, cum sancto Vincentio presbytero et adulescente fratre et aliis monachis qui nunc Hierosolymae commorantur, nauim in Romano portu securus ascendi, maxima me sanctorum frequentia prosequente. ueni regium, in Scyllaeo litore paululum steti, ubi ueteres didici fabulas, et praecipitem pellacis Vlixi cursum, et Sirenarum cantica, et insatiabilem Charybdis uoraginem. cumque mihi accolae illius loci multa narrarent darentque consilium ut non ad Protei columnas, sed ad Ionae portum nauigarem—illum enim fugientium et turbatorum, securi hominis esse cursum—, malui per Maleas et Cycladas Cyprum pergere; ubi susceptus a uenerabili episcopo Epiphanio, cuius tu testimonio gloriaris, ueni Antiochiam, ubi fruitus sum communione pontificis confessorisque Paulini, et deductus ab eo, media hieme et grauissimo frigore, intraui Hierosolymam.*

exegete and theologian. He and Paula also toured Palestine, visiting sites mentioned in both Old and New Testaments with Jewish guides.[2]

A strong thematic continuity between Jerome's Roman correspondence and what he wrote after he settled in the East obscures the significance of the relocation for his social role. Jerome's much later protestations that he had never wanted to be anything more than a monk should not be taken at face value. A contemporary letter, written in the immediate aftermath of the conflict, reveals that when Damasus died, Jerome and his supporters had entertained the idea that the Roman bishop's brilliant young secretary might succeed him in his see.[3] Perhaps Jerome was never a serious candidate for the Roman episcopate. Still, despite his unpopularity in some circles, his prickly personality, and his relative poverty, it is hard to imagine that if the educated and energetic Jerome had remained in the West, he would not have been drafted to fill some bishopric or other. Qualified personnel were in demand in the growing church administrative hierarchy. His relocation to the East, however, excluded him from any formal career in the church as long as he remained there. The defeat of the Paulinian party at Antioch meant that whatever hope Jerome, as a Latin, might once have had of finding a place in the ecclesiastical power structure there was closed off. He had therefore to find a role for himself that was compatible with the standing of a mere monk, rather than that of an ascetic priest or bishop. For someone of Jerome's undeniable ambition, this would prove a challenge—but a fruitful one. In meeting the demands of his situation after 385, Jerome created a new and influential model for the Christian literary career, founded on a new approach to biblical exegesis.

Despite the rigors of his journey to the East and the disappointment of his hopes for promotion within the Roman Church, Jerome was already hard at work on several literary projects in 386. During the next six years, he produced a substantial but disparate collection of scholarly works. On one level, these mark a succession of false starts. In 386 he began a series of commentaries on Paul's letters, which never extended beyond the treatments of Galatians, Ephesians, Titus, and Philemon written during that first summer.[4] About the same time, the preface to a hagiographic work, the *Life of*

2. Preface to the translation of Chronicles from the Septuagint: *unde et nobis curae fuit cum eruditissimis Hebreorum hunc laborem subire, ut circuiremus prouinciam quam uniuersae Christi ecclesiae sonant*. Letter 108.8-13 describes Paula's travels after her relocation to the East in 385: presumably Jerome accompanied her.

3. Letter 45.3; Kelly, *Jerome*, 90, 111.

4. Traditionally, the Pauline commentaries were dated to the late 380s; I have accepted, with some caution, Pierre Nautin's arguments for redating them to the period immediately after Je-

Malchus the Captive Monk, promised that this brief, novelistic narrative was only a preparatory exercise for the far more ambitious undertaking of a history of the church. The latter never materialized.[5] A few years later, in the early 390s, Jerome translated several books of the Hebrew Bible from a critical recension of the Septuagint, but abandoned the project before it was half-finished.[6] During the same period, he wrote his *Hebrew Questions on Genesis*, which he explicitly advertised as only the first in a series of *Hebrew Questions* on the entire Bible. No further installments appeared.[7]

At the very end of this period, Jerome began work on the two projects that would eventually form his enduring legacy. He began his translation of the Bible *iuxta Hebraeos*, "according to the Hebrews"—now largely incorporated into the Latin Vulgate—in about 391. It was completed only in 405.[8] This translation, which Jerome claimed he had made from the original Hebrew text, was received with skepticism by many of his contemporaries.[9] Over time, however, its prestige rose, to the point that by the seventh century Jerome's versions of the Hebrew Scriptures had largely overcome the

---

rome's move to Palestine. For a full discussion of the issue, see the Appendix, section 6. Kelly, *Jerome*, 149 with n. 55, cites *Comm. in Philemon* 1 (*PL* 26:746), as implying that Jerome intended at one point to comment on all of Paul's letters.

5. On the date of the *Vita Malchi*, see Cavallera, *Saint Jérôme*, 2:27. For the reference to the project of a church history, see the preface to the *Vita Malchi*: *ego, qui diu tacui (silere quippe me fecit cui meus sermo supplicium est), prius exerceri cupio in paruo opere et ueluti quandam rubiginem linguae abstergere, ut uenire possim ad historiam latiorem. scribere enim disposui . . . ab aduentu saluatoris usque ad nostram aetatem—id est, ab apostolis usque ad huius temporis fecem—quomodo et per quos Christi Ecclesia nata sit et adulta, persecutionibus creuerit, martyriis coronata sit, et postquam ad Christianos principes uenerit, potentia quidem et diuitiis maior sed uirtutibus minor facta sit.*

6. On the dating of the translations from the Septuagint, see Cavallera, *Saint Jérôme*, 2:28. On these translations, see Kelly, *Jerome*, 158–59. Against Kelly's view, see Kamesar, *Jerome*, 49–58, who argues that the abandonment of the translation from the Septuagint did not signal a "conversion" from the Septuagint to the Hebrew. As will be apparent from my remarks below, I share Kamesar's belief that Jerome did not radically change his estimate of the authority of the Hebrew around 390–91, but I interpret the decision to begin the translation *iuxta Hebraeos* in rather different terms than he does. Prefaces survive for the following books translated from the Septuagint: Job, Proverbs, Ecclesiastes, Song of Songs, Psalms, and Chronicles. Whether Jerome ever made any further translations is uncertain. The commentaries on the Minor Prophets present a nearly complete Latin text of many of the Minor Prophets from the Septuagint, suggesting that Jerome might have translated at least the Minor Prophets as well, though he could also have translated while he was dictating the commentaries.

7. *Quaest. Heb. in Gen*, pref. l.22: *libris hebraicarum quaestionum, quos in omnem scripturam sanctam disposui scribere.*

8. Cavallera, *Saint Jérôme*, 1:290–91; Jay, "Datation."

9. E.g. Augustine, letter 28.2, urged Jerome to stick with his original project of translating from the Septuagint rather than working directly from the Hebrew.

Old Latin text used in the late antique church. The new Latin Bible of the early Middle Ages incorporated an Old Testament made up of Jerome's translations *iuxta Hebraeos*, with the exception of the Psalms, where an earlier translation he had made on the basis of a critical recension of the Greek was preferred. Its New Testament used his translations of the Gospels, made at Rome for Damasus, together with anonymous retranslations of the rest of the canon. This mixed translation was finally enshrined as the Bible of the Catholic Church at the Council of Trent in 1546.[10] The first translations in the series, made in 391 and 392, included new versions of the Psalms and the book of Job, which Jerome had previously translated from the Septuagint, and of the Prophets and the books of Samuel and Kings, which were fresh territory.

The greatest achievement of Jerome's career as a biblical scholar was his commentaries on the Hebrew Prophets. No other patristic writer, either in Greek or in Latin, came close to equaling the comprehensiveness of Jerome's exegesis of the Prophets. He began the project in 392, writing on five of the Minor Prophets; the final commentary, on Jeremiah, was left half-finished at his death in 419. In the commentaries on the Minor Prophets, Jerome adopted a novel and rigorous approach to the Hebrew scriptures. Although his commentaries were written over the course of fifteen years, they adhere to a consistent intellectual framework, whose internal logic I will analyze in detail in chapter 3. That logic grew organically out of the intellectual experiments of Jerome's early years at Bethlehem. Both the false starts and the more ultimately successful essays in biblical scholarship produced during the crucial years from 386 to 392 made possible the innovation of the commentaries on the Prophets. During these years, Jerome began to replace the rather overblown rhetoric of the Roman correspondence with concrete achievement, in the process defining a new approach to biblical scholarship and a new social role for the monk as exegete.

As Jerome's scholarly method matured, he became more and more willing to distance himself from his Greek sources and to emphasize his independent access to Jewish materials. In turn, in order to represent his use of Hebrew and Jewish exegesis as a radical innovation, Jerome had to play down the central role of Jewish learning in Origen's own biblical scholarship—although he could not erase the connection completely, for Origen's example provided crucial legitimation for Jerome's engagement with a tra-

10. For the wide acceptance of the Vulgate in the West by the seventh century, see Loewe, "Medieval History," 110ff.; for the canonization of the Vulgate at Trent, see Crehan, "Bible," 203ff.

dition regarded by most Christians with suspicion, if not hostility. At the same time, Jerome's mature commentaries continue to acknowledge, even to advertise, their indebtedness to Greek Christian allegorical exegesis. Jerome moved, over perhaps five to seven years, from an almost abject deference to Origen as ultimate authority, to a far more ambivalent relation to him both as a valued but problematic source and a necessary but insufficient model.

THE BIBLE IN JEWISH AND CHRISTIAN ANTIQUITY

The first Christian scripture was a Jewish Bible: the Greek translation of the Hebrew scriptures known as the Septuagint or, more correctly, the Old Greek version. The name Septuagint, "seventy" in Latin, derived from the legend that conferred upon this translation its special prestige. It referred to seventy Jewish elders who had reportedly been commissioned by King Ptolemy II of Egypt to translate the sacred books of their people for inclusion in his new library at Alexandria. Miraculously, although the translators labored in isolation in seventy cells on the harbor island of Pharos, they all produced identical versions, down to the very last letter. In its original, Jewish form, the tale of the identical translations produced in isolation applied only to the Pentateuch. The name, however, came to designate a collection of translations that encompassed all the texts now included in the Hebrew Bible, and several others as well. On the basis of the legend of the seventy translators, the Greek versions included in the Christian biblical canon were considered inspired in their own right, their authority independent of any notional Hebrew original.[11] In fact, the Old Greek Bible is the opposite of what the legend implies. The text that became the basis for the Old Testament of the Christian Church in late antiquity was a heterogeneous collection translated over the course of several centuries. Furthermore, it reflects an original that was not a fixed point but an object in motion. But for Jerome's contemporaries, the Greek Old Testament was itself an authoritative text, and his appeal to the Hebrew seemed counterintuitive at best, heretical at worst.[12]

---

11. The earliest version of the legend appears in the *Letter of Aristeas,* composed at Alexandria perhaps at the beginning of the second century BCE. Thereafter it spread widely, appearing in Aristobulus (a fragment preserved by Eusebius, in the *Praeparatio Evangelica,* 13.12.2), Philo (*Vita Moysis* 2.5), and Josephus (*Antiquities* 1, pref.), and in numerous Christian authors, from Justin and Irenaeus to Augustine and John Chrysostom.

12. On the history of the Greek version of the Hebrew Scriptures, Swete et al., *Introduction,* remains basic; for an overview of more recent research, see Jellicoe, *Septuagint.*

The Hebrew scriptures include literary traditions whose origins may lie as early as the tenth century BCE. In their present form, however, the texts collected in the canon date to the period from the sixth through second centuries BCE. Many texts whose core is early continued to receive editorial editions well into the Hellenistic period. The canon is not a unitary whole. Rather, its several components reflect the history of its development. The earliest part of the canon, the Torah or "law" of Moses, is the same in both the Jewish and Christian Bibles. These five books were probably canonized early in the Persian period, in the fifth or even the sixth century BCE. The development of the rest of the canon was more complex.

The Jewish canon is made up of three major divisions. The first is the Torah. The second is known as Neviim, Hebrew for "prophets." It is subdivided into Former Prophets and Latter Prophets. The Former Prophets are historical books, which together form a continuous account of the history of the Israelites from the entry into their land until the destruction of the first temple. They include Joshua, Judges, 1 and 2 Samuel, and 1 and 2 Kings. The Latter Prophets are the "prophets" as such: Isaiah, Jeremiah, Ezekiel, and the twelve Minor Prophets, which in the Hebrew canon count as a single book. The third major division is Ketuvim, or "writings," which comprises all the other books in the Hebrew canon, including Daniel. Among the Jews of Palestine, at least, this canon existed in something like its present form by the end of the first century CE.[13] However, the canon was not fixed, nor its authority universally accepted, for several more centuries, with the consequence that the Hebrew *text* (as opposed to the number and order of the books) of today's Jewish scriptures is a product of late antiquity.[14]

The Christian Old Testament canon is organized in a very different way. The first division of the Christian Old Testament comprises a history of Israel from creation to the rebuilding of the Temple, stretching from Genesis through Nehemiah. It thus includes the Jewish divisions of Torah and Former Prophets, with additions from the Writings. As in the Jewish Bible, the

---

13. A description of the biblical canon corresponding in overall shape to that of the modern Jewish Bible is first attested in Josephus, *Against Apion* 1.38–42. Earlier references which presuppose something like the threefold division of the books in the modern Jewish canon appear in the *Wisdom of Sirach* (*Ecclesiasticus*), particularly in the preface to the Greek version written by its translator, and in the *Letter of Aristeas*. The latter, however, seems to regard only the five books of Moses as "scripture." For further information on the complex history of the canon of the Jewish scriptures (and of the Christian Old Testament), see Beckwith, *Old Testament Canon;* Blenkinsopp, *Prophecy and Canon.*

14. For an overview of the history of the text of the Hebrew Bible, with a discussion of the history of the canon, see Tov, *Textual Criticism.*

Pentateuch is still followed by the narratives of Joshua and Judges, but the little book of Ruth interrupts the flow of the account, coming in before the double books of Samuel and Kings, which in the Septuagint are called 1–4 Kingdoms. There follow the books of Chronicles, Esther, Ezra, and Nehemiah, which in the Jewish Bible are classed among the Writings, but here serve to carry forward the historical account of Genesis–2 Kings into the period after the Babylonian exile. The next division of the Christian canon includes a number of poetic books that among the Jews are assigned to the third division, the Writings. Here, these books are not only placed at a different point in the canon but arranged in a completely different order. Finally, the Christian Old Testament closes with what Christians call the Prophets, which largely correspond in content, but not in arrangement, to the Latter Prophets of the Jewish Bible. The Christian version of the Prophets begins with Isaiah, Jeremiah, and Ezekiel, but then adds Daniel, which Jews class among the Writings. It ends with the twelve Minor Prophets. The Prophets, in the Christian sense of the term, become the bridge between Old and New Testaments.

This order is common to the Septuagint, Jerome's Latin translation, and modern Christian Old Testaments. However, the Septuagint varies somewhat from the familiar arrangement of modern Protestant Bibles. It inserts a number of extra books in the second and third divisions. In the second division, Tobit and Judith follow Nehemiah, while 1–4 Maccabees follow Esther. The third division adds the Wisdom of Solomon, Ecclesiasticus (Sirach), and the Prayer of Manasseh after the Song of Songs, which is the final book of this portion of the Protestant canon. Furthermore, the Septuagint versions of two books, Esther and Daniel, include substantial passages not present in other versions, which today are generally printed among the Apocrypha. Jerome's translation eliminated all of these "extra" books because they were not canonical among the Jews he knew.[15]

The two canons reflect the divergent histories of the Jewish Bible in its original language and in Greek. The process of translating the Jewish scriptures into Greek began before the latest books of the Hebrew Bible had even been written, and long before the fixation of the Jewish canon. Translation thus took place in parallel with canonization, sometimes following it, sometimes preceding it. At no time before late antiquity was there a precisely defined scriptural canon among either Jews or Christians, one that had both

15. On the Septuagint canon, see Swete et al., *Introduction*. A number of important articles on the history of the various Scriptural canons in Hebrew and Greek appear in Mulder and Sysling, *Mikra*, and Saebo, *Hebrew Bible*.

a set list of books in a definite order and a fixed text. The complexity of the process of translation had three important consequences. First was the variation in the shape of the two canons that has just been described. Second, methods of translation differed between different divisions of the canon and between different books. Some of the translations are very close to the originals, while others are more in the nature of adaptations. It seems that the translators of books already considered canonical at the time of translation felt constrained to follow the originals faithfully, while the translators of less authoritative books—usually those more recently composed—freely adapted their base texts to produce what are essentially new Greek works. Third, in every book, the Old Greek text often diverges, on the level of individual words and phrases, from the Hebrew text current among the Jews in late antiquity. This third observation requires further consideration, as it is of immense importance for understanding the history of the biblical text and, therefore, for text-critical method.

Our oldest biblical manuscripts come from the roll books found at Qumran in the Judean desert, the so-called Dead Sea Scrolls, whose discovery in the 1940s added immensely to our knowledge of the text of the Hebrew scriptures in antiquity. The manuscripts from Qumran make clear that in the third through first centuries BCE, a variety of texts were in circulation for each book of the Bible, including the Pentateuch. Among biblical manuscripts of this period, scholars distinguish at least three major text-forms, none of which can be reduced to a mere corruption or development of one of the others. There seems to have been no effort to fix the text before the first century BCE at the earliest. Between about 100 BCE and 100 CE, Hebrew biblical manuscripts—found at Qumran and at other sites in the Judean desert—begin to display a more homogeneous text, one which resembles in many respects the text that was eventually canonized among the Jews by the fourth century. Before the discovery of these ancient biblical scrolls, the oldest known copies of the Hebrew scriptures in their original language dated to the tenth century. By that time, the text had long been fixed, its form a result of the activities of the late antique and early medieval Jewish scholars known as the Masoretes. The scrolls thus provide unique evidence for the state of the text of the Hebrew scriptures during the period when the first Greek biblical translations were made.[16]

16. The fundamental analysis of the Qumran evidence and its relevance for the history of the text of the Hebrew Bible is Cross and Talmon, *Qumran*. For a concise and accessible summary, with a useful history of the scholarship, see Talmon, "Old Testament Text."

It is highly unlikely that, as legend would have it, the Old Greek Torah—the Septuagint properly so-called—was translated for the library of Ptolemy II. But this translation probably was made in Alexandria in the early Hellenistic period, perhaps even during that king's reign, in the mid-third century BCE. Its text differs at many points from the Masoretic Hebrew, the text as canonized by the Masoretes and transmitted by the Jews through the Middle Ages. Scholars had long conjectured that the divergences between the Septuagint and the Masoretic text reflected the Septuagint's use of a different Hebrew base text. The discoveries in the Judean desert confirmed that such a text had existed, and revealed that it, along with the text-form now referred to as "proto-Masoretic," were only two of the several text-forms in circulation in Jewish Palestine during the Hellenistic period. At the time when the Septuagint was translated, there had been no effort as yet to eliminate textual variation. It is no surprise, therefore, that the Hebrew text chosen as the basis for what became the canonical Greek translation differs from the text that was canonized centuries later as the authoritative Hebrew scriptures.

What this means, for our purposes, is that the Greek Christian biblical text of Jerome's day was in no sense a translation of the Hebrew text in use among contemporary Jews. The seemingly commonsense notion that in order to establish a correct text of the Hebrew scriptures, one ought to turn to the language in which they were composed, becomes a choice not between original and copy but between two independent textual traditions, each with its own history. Although modern textual critics of the Hebrew Bible are far from according the Septuagint the inspired status it enjoyed among Jerome's Christian contemporaries, they hold it in much higher esteem than did Jerome. Jerome's privileging of the Hebrew text used by the Jews, together with its attendant traditions of interpretation, as the ultimate sources of biblical truth was by no means a simple recognition of scientific fact. Rather, it was an idiosyncratic insight, which allowed Jerome to construct for himself a unique position as an authority on the scriptures.

Christian textual criticism of the Old Testament before Jerome's lifetime is difficult to reconstruct, since so much of what earlier commentators wrote is lost. It is clear, however, that the educated Christians of antiquity regarded their Greek Old Testament as an independent body of literature in its own right. When they sought to preserve and to improve the text of their Bibles, they worked within the Greek tradition, employing the tools created by the scholars of Hellenistic Alexandria for the study of the canonical works of Greek literature. They sought out old manuscripts and collated them against each other. They judged variants in terms of the context in which they appeared and the style of the various biblical writers.

Furthermore, educated Christians who were aware that the original language of the Bible was Hebrew rather than Greek, and that the Hebrew versions possessed by their Jewish contemporaries differed from their own Greek copies, tended not to explain these variations in terms of deficiencies in the translation. Instead, they accused the Jews of willfully corrupting their own biblical texts in order to refute Christian apologetic arguments based on the shared scriptures of the two communities. Jewish rejection of the Septuagint was for most Christians an argument in favor of its accuracy. Christians in antiquity had no trouble believing that the Jews, who had denied Christ, were capable of altering their Bibles to support tendentious interpretations.[17] Christian biblical scholars, therefore—with the exception of Origen and some of his followers—did not turn to the Hebrew original.

But even Origen, for all his interest in the Hebrew text and Jewish traditions of interpretation, seems to have had only limited knowledge of Hebrew. His biblical philology, therefore, also made use of a series of later Greek translations, made by Jews and Jewish Christians after the rise of Christianity. These translations had been created to replace the Septuagint, appropriated by the new sect's Gentile wing. Because they had been written centuries after the Septuagint, they came to be known as the *recentiores,* or "more recent" translations. Despite their potentially suspicious provenance, the *recentiores* were the backbone of Origen's criticism of the text of the Hebrew scriptures. Their importance was conveyed graphically by their place in Origen's massive text-critical tool, the Hexapla, literally "sixfold" in Greek. This multicolumn parallel Bible juxtaposed the Septuagint to the Hebrew text and to several other Greek versions. Origen seems to have used the Hexapla in preparing a recension of the Greek Old Testament. This recension used asterisks and obeli—the critical signs developed by the Alexandrian grammarians—to mark those places where the Septuagint contained material absent from the Hebrew, and where Origen had supplied material lacking in the church's Bible from the Greek version of Theodotion, one of the *recentiores.* It is difficult to determine the goals of Origen's text-critical

---

17. For references to Christian literature, and the concept in general, see Simon, "Bible in Earliest Controversies," 54. Kraft, "Christian Transmission," lists sources for the belief in deliberate alteration of the Jewish Greek scriptures among both Jews and Christians. On Jewish belief in the deliberate alteration of the Hebrew scriptures, see Gordis, *Kethib-Qere;* McCarthy, *Tiqqune sopherim.*

work. The most widely accepted recent proposal argues that he hoped to reconstruct the original text of the Septuagint, but in the absence of new discoveries, certainty seems impossible.[18]

Whatever their original purpose, the tools for textual research that Origen created—the Hexapla and the recension based upon it—survived for centuries in the library at Caesarea, lending themselves to new uses. Later Christian writers frequently borrowed Jewish readings and interpretations from Origen's work on the Hebrew scriptures. Eusebius of Caesarea, active at the end of the third century and in the first decades of the fourth, is perhaps the best-documented example. In his surviving commentaries on Isaiah and Psalms, Eusebius drew heavily on Origen's philological and exegetical legacy. In particular, Eusebius's commentaries often adduce variant readings from the *recentiores*. He surely had access to the original codices of the Hexapla preserved in the episcopal library of his own see.[19] Copies of some or all of the materials compiled in the Hexapla also circulated independently among third- and fourth-century Christians with a serious interest in the scriptures. By Jerome's time, an interest in the *recentiores* was almost fashionable for those who hoped to present themselves as biblical scholars, even among Latins.[20] Origen's example, and his works both exegetical and technical, exerted a powerful influence on Jerome's predecessors and contemporaries.

THE AUTHORITY OF ORIGEN

A number of the works that Jerome wrote in his first years at Bethlehem, and the prefaces and other programmatic statements that advertise and justify them, show him wrestling with Origen, experimenting with different ways of positioning himself and of appropriating Origen's scholarly legacy. Over the course of four or five years, from about 386 to 390 or 391, we can observe Jerome adopting a variety of stances with respect to his predecessor, from the deferential to the defiant. Often, his self-descriptions are wildly at odds with the reality of how he worked. Especially in some of the later pref-

18. On Origen's textual criticism of the Hebrew Bible, see Williams and Grafton, *Christianity*, chapter 2, with references.

19. On Eusebius's use of Origen and the *recentiores*, see Jay, *L'exégèse*, 110; Barthélemy, "Eusèbe," 63–66; Kamesar, *Jerome*, 37.

20. For example, Jerome claims that Rufinus possessed copies of the *recentiores* (Jerome, *Contra Ruf.* 2.34).

aces from this period, he represented translations and compilations from Greek sources as wholly or partly original works, so that the reader is misled as to the sources of Jerome's learning. Always, the tendency is toward an increasing emphasis on his knowledge of Hebrew and on access to Jewish sources, even when that requires serious misrepresentation.

Origen, as Jerome had portrayed him in his Roman letters, provided a comprehensive pattern for the life and work of the Christian ascetic as exegete.[21] Origen's example therefore presented both an opportunity and a problem. On the one hand, the precedents set by Origen helped to legitimate Jerome's approach to exegesis, especially his interest in Jewish biblical learning. On the other hand, so long as Jerome justified his scholarly approach by reference to Origen, he could present himself only as a translator, or at best a continuator, of his Greek predecessor's work. In order to become a biblical scholar in his own right, rather than a mere conduit for Origen's learning, Jerome had to develop an approach to scripture that he could call his own. This involved not only innovations in text-critical and exegetical method but also the portrayal of the authority of the Hebrew tradition as distinct from Origen's legacy—despite Jerome's continued reliance on the textual methods and tools that Origen had devised.

The preface to one of the first works he wrote after settling in Bethlehem, the commentary on Galatians of the summer of 386, provides the strongest example of Jerome's use of extreme deference to Origen to legitimate his own exegesis. In this preface, Jerome contrasts his own work with the inadequate efforts of an earlier Latin commentator on Paul, Marius Victorinus. He condemns Victorinus for his ignorance of the scriptures, rejecting his rhetorical brilliance as irrelevant to biblical exegesis. But instead of following up his criticisms of his Latin predecessor with the statement of his own qualifications that he has led his reader to expect, Jerome parades his humility by claiming to have relied entirely on Origen:

> What then, am I stupid or foolhardy, that I should promise what [Victorinus] could not accomplish? By no means. Rather, I have improved upon him, in my judgment, only in that being more cautious and more fearful—since I am aware how feeble my own abilities are—I have followed Origen's commentary.[22]

---

21. On Jerome's portrait of Origen, see Opelt, "Origene"; Vessey, "Jerome's Origen"; and chapter 1 above.

22. *Quid igitur, ego stultus aut temerarius, qui id pollicear quod ille non potuit? Minime. Quin potius in eo, ut mihi uideor, cautior atque timidior, quod imbecillitatem uirium mearum sentiens, Origenis Commentarios sum secutus.*

Without Origen's works as sources, Jerome claims, his own limited skills would be far from sufficient to the daunting task before him. As we shall see, these self-deprecating words do not tell the whole story. Yet the pose of humility before Origen's authority that Jerome assumes here is noteworthy, if only because it contrasts so sharply with the tone he was to take in works written just a few years later.

Jerome's self-abasement in the preface to the commentary on Galatians is already somewhat undermined by the content of the work itself. While it probably did depend very heavily on Origen's exegesis of Galatians,[23] the close relationship between his commentary and Origen's did not preclude Jerome from an occasional display of independence. In particular, he sometimes introduces references to his own researches among the Jews, whom he represents as a source of exegetical information distinct from his use of Origen. For similar passages in some of Jerome's other works, parallels with Origen's surviving commentaries (among other evidence) suggest that Jerome translated verbatim Origen's descriptions of his contacts with Jewish scholars. Jerome thus made it appear that he had himself carried out research that was actually done by his predecessor. Origen's work on the relevant passages of Galatians does not survive to confirm or deny this possibility, but it may well be that Jerome did the same thing here. If so, these passages only reinforce the impression that Jerome felt he had something to gain from boasting of his personal contacts with learned Jews.[24]

In one particularly interesting passage of his commentary on Galatians, Jerome not only claims to have done extensive research on the Hebrew text of the Bible, but presents his own method of interpretation as a reflection of the apostle's mode of composition. In book 2 of the commentary, Jerome discusses Paul's use of a verse from Deuteronomy in Galatians 3:10. This citation from the Hebrew scriptures provides him with the opportunity to introduce not only the evidence of the *recentiores* and the Hebrew original, but even a reading taken from a manuscript of the Samaritan Pentateuch, which he claims to have examined personally. His methodology, which he describes

---

23. None of the sources Jerome cites in the preface to the *Comm. in Gal.* survive, even in substantial fragments; however, we have strong evidence that Jerome used Origen very heavily in his *Comm. in Ephes.*: see Bammel, "Pauluskommentare"; Layton, "Origen's Pauline Exegesis," 373–411. The primary evidence comes from the accusations of Rufinus, *Apol.* It is probably safe to assume, therefore, that Jerome relied on Origen to a similar degree in *Comm. in Gal.*, where he acknowledges his debt to Origen so explicitly.

24. Bardy, "Maîtres hébreux," 145–64, followed by others; this issue is taken up in detail in the notes to chapter 6 below.

as his customary procedure, is similar to that which he would later apply to the text of the Hebrew scriptures. He begins his comment on Galatians 3:10, in which Paul cites Deuteronomy 27:26, by remarking, "My habit is, whenever the Apostle quotes something from the Old Testament, to return to the original books, and to examine diligently how the words are written in the original context." [25] He then adduces the entire verse of Deuteronomy as it appears in the Greek versions of the Septuagint, Aquila, Symmachus, and Theodotion. Paul's text does not correspond exactly to any of the Greek versions. Jerome explains that the apostle intended to cite the text not verbatim but according to the sense.

However, as Jerome goes on to note, one of the divergences among the different versions of Deuteronomy is especially problematic. Paul's citation reads, crucially, "Cursed are *all* who do not remain *in all* that is written." [26] Only the Septuagint supports the repeated "all," *omnis* in the Latin. Neither the Hebrew nor any of the *recentiores* includes either occurrence. Yet the presence of the word, especially in the phrase *in omnibus quae scripta sunt*, "in all that is written," was central to later Christian use of Paul's text to support both Christian rejection of the law and condemnation of Jewish observance. Jerome must therefore ask, "whether the Seventy translators added 'every man,' and 'in all,' or whether it read thus in the old Hebrew, and later was deleted by the Jews." [27] He concludes that the Jews had corrupted the text deliberately. For Paul himself must have been aware of the importance of the double *omnis* to his own argument, yet he could only be imagined to have cited the text accurately from the original. As Jerome observes, "The apostle was a man familiar with Hebrew, and most learned in the law, and would never have put forward [a citation] if it were not present in the Hebrew scrolls." [28] Jerome therefore makes of Paul's Hebrew learning an exegetical, indeed a text-critical, principle. Given that Paul himself must have been familiar with the Hebrew text, his quotation cannot have deviated from it. This reasoning also recruits the apostle in support of Jerome's own philological axioms. It assumes, and thereby reinforces, the basic idea that the

25. *Comm. in Gal.*, PL 26, col.383, l.3ff.: *Hunc morem habeo, ut quotiescunque ab apostolis de Veteri Instrumento aliquid sumitur, recurram ad originales libros, et diligenter inspiciam, quomodo in suis locis scripta sint.*

26. *Maledictus omnis qui non permanserint in omnibus quae scripta sunt . . .* (emphasis added in translation).

27. *utrum Septuaginta interpretes addiderint, "omnis homo," et, "in omnibus," an in ueteri Hebraico ita fuerit, et postea a Iudaeis deletum sit.*

28. *Apostolus vir Hebraeae peritiae, et in lege doctissimus, nunquam protulisset nisi in Hebraeis uoluminibus haberetur.*

Hebrew original is the ultimate authority—even when that text fails to support a reading of immense significance for Christian polemic against Jews. In such a case, the Hebrew remains authoritative, even if one must therefore acknowledge that it may be corrupt.

Jerome goes on to clinch the argument by advancing evidence from his own textual researches in support of the conjecture he has proposed: "When I was studying a Samaritan Hebrew scroll, I found that the word 'kol,' which means 'every,' or 'to every,' was written in the text, and it agreed with the Seventy translators."[29] Manuscripts of the Samaritan Pentateuch support the variant that Jerome cites.[30] Perhaps he did examine a Samaritan Torah scroll. But we need not assume as much. It could well have been Origen who had seen the Samaritan scroll, while Jerome simply copied his reference to it, as he did in other cases.[31] In either case, within the commentary itself, the citation of the Samaritan scroll shifts the emphasis decisively to Jerome's own authority as a critic of the biblical text. Not only the authority of Origen but even that of Paul himself recedes into the background. Jerome, through his diligence and his access to exotica such as a manuscript of the Samaritan Pentateuch, becomes the arbiter of textual truth.

In the commentary on Galatians, a slavish display of devotion to Origen's legacy coexists with the claim that Jerome's own Jewish researches confer upon him independent authority over the biblical text. The juxtaposition of these contrasting modes of legitimating his activities within a single text shows that they were more conceptually than chronologically distinct. The commentary's internal contradictions nevertheless seem typical of this early point in Jerome's efforts to develop a coherent research program and to fit his self-descriptions to it. The spate of scholarship that began to flow at the end of the 380s continues to display a varied degree of dependence on Greek writers, both on the level of representation and on that of methodological reality. But the range of options shifts somewhat. Jerome expresses a new arrogance in relation to his Greek predecessors in the prefaces to works like the commentary on Ecclesiastes and the translations of the Hebrew Bible from the Septuagint. Even as the tone of his self-descriptions shifts, he con-

---

29. *Samaritanorum Hebraea uolumina relegens, inueni kol, quod interpretatur omnis, siue omnibus, scriptum esse, et cum Septuaginta Interpretibus concordare.*

30. The Samaritan Pentateuch to Deut. 26 : 27 presents several variants from the Masoretic text (Gall, *Pentateuch der Samaritaner*), which include the insertion of *kol* at the points where Jerome claims to have found it.

31. It was Jerome's tendency to copy his sources' references to their own researches as if they were his own: for an example of this habit, see chapter 4 below on Jerome's Jewish teachers.

tinues to produce mere translations or compilations alongside works of real innovation.

The changing tone of Jerome's self-descriptions comes across very clearly when we compare the preface to a translation of Origen that he made late in this period to those of the prefaces to the translations made at Constantinople in 380 and 381.[32] In 392 or early 393,[33] at the behest of Paula and Eustochium, Jerome rendered into Latin Origen's thirty-nine homilies on the gospel of Luke. A decade earlier, he had described translation as an erudite recreation, a form of exercise for a learned man's linguistic faculties. In the preface to this new translation, however, he expresses a marked distaste for the undertaking, which he calls "a most unpleasant task, a sort of torment, as Tullius said, to write according to another's taste and not one's own."[34] The reference to Cicero is the same as in the earlier preface; its use, however, is quite different. Instead of being a form of exercise, or even play, translation has become a nasty chore.

When Jerome translated Origen's homilies on Luke, Ambrose of Milan had recently published a commentary on the same gospel. This work drew heavily on Origen, but did not credit him. In the fracas that followed Damasus's death in 385, Ambrose seems to have taken the side of Jerome's persecutors. The preface to Jerome's translation of Origen's homilies on Luke contains a veiled attack on another exegete who has borrowed earlier writers' materials without acknowledging his debts. Evidently, Jerome held a grudge against the bishop of Milan and made the translation in an attempt to embarrass him. If this little project had not provided him with the opportunity to take a stab at his far more powerful exegetical competitor, Jerome implies, he would have refused to undertake it, whatever his patronesses' demands.[35]

Two other translations, *On Hebrew Names* and *On Hebrew Places,* allowed

32. *Praef. in Eus. Chron.: unde et noster Tullius Platonis integros libros ad uerbum interpretatus est et cum Aratum iam Romanum hexametris uersibus edidisset, in Xenofontis Oeconomico lusit. in quo opere ita saepe aureum illud flumen eloquentiae quibusdam scabris et turbulentis obicibus retardatur, ut, qui interpretata nesciunt, a Cicerone dicta non credant. difficile est enim alienas lineas insequentem non alicubi excedere, arduum, ut quae in alia lingua bene dicta sunt eundem decorem in translatione conseruent.*

33. For this dating, see the Appendix, section 6.

34. *petistis, ut . . . triginta et nouem Adamantii nostri in Lucam omelias, sicut in Graeco habentur, interpreter—molestam rem et tormento similem alieno, ut ait Tullius, stomacho et non suo scribere; quam tamen idcirco nunc faciam, quia sublimiora non poscitis.*

35. For Ambrose as Jerome's target in these prefaces, see Rufinus, *Apol.* 2.22-25; Kelly, *Jerome,* 142-44.

Jerome to display a greater degree of critical distance from his Greek sources. *On Hebrew Places* is a fairly straightforward version of Eusebius's original. Nevertheless, its preface asserts Jerome's independent status as an expert on the material. He claims that he is not merely a translator but in some sense the author of a new work, since he has removed what he thought was unworthy and has made numerous alterations to the original.[36] In the preface to *On Hebrew Names*, Jerome goes even farther: he explains that the manuscript copies of the original that he had amassed in preparing to make the translation contained several forms of the text, which were often seriously corrupt. His own access to the Hebrew text, therefore, was an important qualification for the undertaking, for he could evaluate the Greek onomastic tradition from a position of independent expertise.[37] Yet *On Hebrew Names* itself shows only a shallow and erratic application of Jerome's knowledge of Hebrew. Incomprehensibly, he reproduces the text's extensive catalogue of "Hebrew" etymologies for New Testament names, even as he repeatedly acknowledges that these attempts to derive Greek and even Latin proper names from Hebrew roots have no basis in linguistic reality. The result is a strange hybrid of philological fact and speculative etymological fantasy, producing an oddly self-undermining effect: Jerome cites pages of etymologies only to dismiss them as clearly fallacious, but without substituting correct interpretations of his own.[38]

At the same time that Jerome provided the Latin world with translations of Greek technical works, he had also begun to translate the Hebrew scriptures from Origen's critical recension of the Septuagint.[39] These translations

36. In the preface to the *De situ et nomin.*, Jerome writes: *semel enim et in temporum libro praefatus sum, me uel interpretem esse uel noui operis conditorem.*

37. In the preface to the *De nomin.*, Jerome writes: *Itaque hortatu fratrum Lupuli et Valeriani, qui me putant aliquid in Hebraeae linguae notitia profecisse, et rei ipsius utilitate conmotus, singula per ordinem scripturarum uolumina percucurri, et uetus aedificium noua cura instaurans, fecisse me reor quod a Graecis quoque adpetendum sit.* For the dating of this work, see the Appendix, section 6.

38. Examples of this abound in the *De nomin.*, e.g. 142.1.24ff.: *Andreas decus in statione uel respondens pabulo. Sed hoc uiolentum. Melius autem est, ut secundum graecam etymologiam ἀπὸ τοῦ ἀνδρός, hoc est a uiro, uirilis adpelletur. . . . Alexander auferens angustiam tenebrarum. Sed hoc uiolentum. . . . Exceptis paucis nominibus omnia paene ex C littera uiolenter interpretata sunt. . . . Erastus frater meus uidens. Satis absurde uocabulum figuratum. . . . Omnia paene ex L littera uiolenter usurpata sunt. . . . Mesopotamia eleuata uocatione quadam. Sed melius a graeco etymologiam possidet, quod duobus fluuiis Eufrate ambiatur et Tigri. . . . Haec omnia graeca nomina uel latina quam uiolenter secundum linguam hebraicam interpretata sint, perspicuum puto esse lectori.*

39. Jerome attributes the recension to Origen: see the passages cited in the next note. There is scholarly controversy over whether Origen actually prepared such a recension or not. What is important here, however, is not the origins of the recension that Jerome used, but its nature and existence as of the 380s, and the fact that he claimed, in these passages, to have prepared it himself.

according to the Septuagint or *iuxta LXX* present a curious paradox. They show Jerome at his most derivative, yet their prefaces represent them as independent scholarly works. In later references to the translations *iuxta LXX*, Jerome frankly attributes the Greek recension he used to Origen. He credits Origen with inserting the critical signs that marked places where the text varied quantitatively from the Hebrew original, and with supplementing the Septuagint with material from the translation of Theodotion where the Septuagint omitted passages that appeared in the Hebrew.[40] But in the prefaces that Jerome wrote for the versions *iuxta LXX* at the time he made them, he explicitly claims to have compared the Greek and Hebrew texts himself and to have inserted the asterisks and obeli that marked their divergences.[41]

The irony here is sharp: precisely in advertising those works where he was most dependent on Origen's biblical philology, Jerome promoted himself as wholly independent of his Greek predecessor and model, to the point that no reference to him appears in these prefaces. Furthermore, he describes in vivid circumstantial detail the studies with learned Jews that had enabled him to carry out this philological task.[42] The alternative to the explicit admission of dependence on Origen's example and on his works, at

---

40. To cite only the examples from the first group of translations made in the early 390s, in *Prol. in Iob de Hebr. interp.* (*Biblia sacra*, 731) we find: *omnia ueteris instrumenti uolumina Origenes obelis asteriscisque distinxerit, quos uel additos uel de Theodotione sumptos translationi antiquae inseruit.* And in *Prol. in Chronicis de Heb. interp.* (*Biblia sacra*, 546) we find: *et certe Origenes non solum exempla conposuit quattuor editionum e regione singula uerba describens, ut unus dissentiens statim ceteris inter se consentientibus arguatur, sed, quod maioris audaciae est, in editione Septuaginta Theodotionis editionem miscuit, asteriscis designans quae minus fuerint, et uirgulis quae ex superfluo uideantur adposita.* See also *Prol. in Pentateucham de Heb. interp.* (*Biblia sacra*, 3 – 4).

41. None of the prefaces to the translations from the Septuagint mentions Origen, although they all explain the use of asterisks and obeli. The preface to the translation of the Solomonic books makes abundant use of the first person: *reddidi, correxi, feci.* Perhaps the strongest example comes from the preface to the translation of the Psalms from the Septuagint: *unde consueta praefatione commoneo tam uos quibus forte labor iste desudat, quam eos qui exemplaria istiusmodi habere uoluerint, ut quae diligenter* emendaui, *cum cura et diligentia transcribantur. notet sibi unusquisque uel iacentem lineam uel signa radiantia, id est uel obelos uel asteriscos, et ubicumque uirgulam uiderit praecedentem, ab ea usque ad duo puncta quae inpressimus sciat in Septuaginta translatoribus plus haberi; ubi autem stellae similitudinem perspexerit, de Hebraeis uoluminibus additum nouerit, aeque usque ad duo puncta, iuxta Theodotionis dumtaxat editionem qui simplicitate sermonis a septuaginta interpretibus non discordat* (emphasis added). The impersonal constructions do not mitigate the implication that Jerome's "emendation" involved the insertion of critical signs and the addition of passages from Theodotion.

42. Preface to the translation of Chronicles *iuxta LXX: denique cum a me nuper litteris flagitassetis, ut uobis Paralipomenon Latino sermone transferrem, de Tiberiade legis quondam auctorem, qui apud Hebreos admirationi habebatur, adsumpsi, et contuli cum eo a uertice, ut aiunt, usque ad extremum unguem, et sic confirmatus ausus sum facere quod iubebatis.*

this point in Jerome's career, was to put forward his own personal authority as underwritten by his consultations with Jews and his knowledge of their languages. That he felt the need to do so precisely in the prefaces to those works in which he depended most directly on Origen underlines the tension between the two sources of authority by which he legitimated his special brand of Latin biblical scholarship.

THE INVENTION OF THE *HEBRAICA VERITAS*

Already in his Roman correspondence, Jerome had represented himself as an exponent of the biblical learning of the Jews. This was a novel and compelling claim in the Latin world and, indeed, among Greek Christians as well. However, a dependence on Jewish learning laid him open to the charge of Judaizing heresy. Even the claim that the Hebrew text was a privileged source of biblical truth aroused the suspicions of many of Jerome's readers.[43] The Septuagint, after all, was the authoritative Bible of the church in both East and West, and strong historical and theological arguments supported its continued centrality. For the rest of his career, Jerome remained vulnerable to the charge of irreverence toward the Christian scriptures.[44] Yet his concept of the *Hebraica veritas*, which he came to place at the center of his self-presentation as an authoritative translator and exegete, encompassed not only a broad range of Jewish learning but most of the philological legacy of his Greek Christian sources as well. Rather than emphasizing that his Greek predecessors had already done much of the dirty work of making Jewish materials available for use by Christian exegetes, Jerome minimized their role in his own access to those materials. In examining the works that most strongly exemplify Jerome's independent scholarship based on Hebrew sources, we will see that it was crucial for him to emphasize direct access to the Hebrew and to Jewish interpretation in order to establish for himself an authority independent of his Greek Christian sources.

The commentary on Ecclesiastes, probably composed in 388,[45] uses a

---

43. For an attempt to discredit Jerome's studies with Jewish teachers, see Rufinus, *Apol.* 2.12, who reviles Jerome's claim to rely on a Jewish teacher: *Ignosce mihi pro hoc quod malui ante inperitus et indoctus audire, quam Barrabae discipulus dici. Proposito etenim Christo simul et Barabba, ego quasi inperitus Christum elegi; tu, ut uideo, cum illis clamas, qui dicunt: Non hunc sed Barraban.*

44. See for example *Comm. in Abacuc* 2.3.14–16 discussed below; prefaces to the translations *iuxta Hebraeos; Contra Ruf.* 2.24, 2.35; letter 112 to Augustine.

45. For the dating of this commentary, see the Appendix, section 6.

philological method presaged in the passage of the commentary on Galatians already examined. Jerome's approach to the text relies on the *recentiores* to assist in interpreting the Hebrew, which in turn is treated as the ultimate source of textual authority. For the first time, Jerome applies this methodology to an entire book of the Hebrew Bible. The text of Jerome's lemma—the version of Ecclesiastes that he uses as the basis for his commentary—is neither an Old Latin text nor a translation of the Septuagint. Instead, it is a hybrid, sometimes following the Hebrew original closely, sometimes more or less reliant on one of the earlier Greek translations.[46] Within the commentary, Jerome cites the *recentiores* extensively to clarify difficult passages,[47] and repeatedly invokes Jewish learning, which he claims to have obtained directly from native informants.[48]

The preface to the commentary advertises this novel approach in terms that make very clear that Jerome's sense of his own legitimacy as a scholar is at stake:

> I have followed no-one's authority [*nullius auctoritatem secutus sum*]; but in translating from the Hebrew, I have tried to follow the custom of the Seventy translators, at least in those points in which they do not differ greatly from the Hebrews. Sometimes I have made reference to Aquila and Symmachus and Theodotion, in such a manner as not to deter the reader by too much novelty, nor on the other hand do I neglect the source of truth against my own conscience and pursue the rivulets of opinion.[49]

Nullius auctoritatem secutus sum: this is strong language, and deserves to be interpreted as such. On one level, Jerome's words are probably a realistic description of the commentary's philological methods: he based his study of the text on the Hebrew original rather than on any of the Greek translations. But the language of the preface suggests more than this. The authority that Jerome has not followed is not merely that of the *recentiores*. More impor-

---

46. Cavallera, *Saint Jérôme*, 1:136.

47. Forty-five separate passages of *Comm. in Eccles.* cite the *recentiores* by name; 35 of these mention Symmachus, 12 Aquila, 12 Theodotion.

48. Twenty passages in *Comm. in Eccles.* explicitly attribute material to a Jewish informant or source.

49. *nullius auctoritatem secutus sum; sed de hebraeo transferens, magis me septuaginta interpretum consuetudini coaptaui, in his dumtaxat, quae non multum ab Hebraicis discrepabant. Interdum Aquilae quoque et Symmachi et Theodotionis recordatus sum, ut nec nouitate nimia lectoris studium deterrerem, nec rursum contra conscientiam meam, fonte ueritatis omisso, opinionum riuuli consectarer* (Preface to the *Comm. in Eccles.*, CCSL 72, p. 249, ll. 12–18).

tantly, it is Origen's authority that Jerome rejects. Origen goes unmentioned in the preface, although Jerome probably used his exegesis of Ecclesiastes as a source, and certainly drew his philological methods from him. It was Origen, after all, who had recognized the usefulness of the *recentiores* for a critical philology of the Old Testament. Without his example and the philological tools he had created, Jerome might never have been aware of these Jewish Greek versions. The irony deepens when one considers that Jerome likely had access to the *recentiores* through Origen's Hexapla, the great sixfold parallel Bible in which their versions were set alongside the Hebrew original and the Septuagint translation. Indeed, the commentary on Ecclesiastes repeatedly represents Jerome at work in the library of Caesarea, checking references in the original Hexapla. Yet in this preface, Origen's example plays no part in Jerome's self-presentation. It is as if he had never existed.

A few years later, while he was making the translations of the *On Hebrew Names* and *On Hebrew Places,* Jerome also began to prepare what he was to characterize as an *opus novum,* exemplifying an approach to the Hebrew scriptures hitherto unknown to either Greek- or Latin-speaking Christians. This was his *Hebrew Questions on Genesis,* which finally appeared in 392. Adam Kamesar's comprehensive study has established that it was indeed a work of great originality. Kamesar documents in detail Jerome's independence from and critical attitude toward the biblical philology of his Greek Christian predecessors, including Origen and Eusebius.[50] The work is a collection of etymologies and solutions to other philological problems. Kamesar shows that this material is based on an independent use of the *recentiores* to support close study of the Hebrew original,[51] and on an extensive assimilation of Jewish exegetical traditions.[52] He attributes to Jerome a coherent approach to the biblical text which he terms his "rabbinic-*recentiores* philology," that is, reliance on a combination of Jewish exegesis and the translations of Aquila, Symmachus, and Theodotion as compiled in the Hexapla, all of which helped Jerome to access the Hebrew original.[53]

The preface to the *Hebrew Questions on Genesis,* unlike that of the commentary on Ecclesiastes, invokes the example and legacy of Origen as well as the authority of Jewish biblical scholarship to legitimate Jerome's work.

---

50. Kamesar, *Jerome,* 97–175.

51. Kamesar, *Jerome,* 70–72 et passim.

52. Kamesar, *Jerome,* 176–91.

53. Kamesar, *Jerome,* 191.

The work's title describes its purpose: to clarify problems in the text and interpretation of Genesis on the basis of the Hebrew original. The preface states as much in unambiguous terms:

> Our purpose therefore will be either to refute the errors of those who suspect that the Hebrew books are unreliable, or to restore by means of their authority the errors that can be seen to abound in the Greek and Latin codices, and in addition to explain by recourse to their native tongue the etymologies of things, names and places, which are unintelligible in our language.[54]

Jerome bases his authority as a critic of the biblical text on his access to Hebrew manuscripts. He justifies this approach, however, by means of Origen's example. Jerome faces criticism from ignorant or even ill-intentioned attackers. His great predecessor had aroused their ire all the more when in his commentaries he turned to the Hebrew text to elucidate difficulties. Jerome deploys Origen's authority with a combination of self-deprecation and defiance:

> But concerning Adamantius [i.e., Origen] I am silent, whose name (if it be permitted to compare the small with the great) is even more hated than my own name: for while in his homilies, which he addressed to the common people, he followed the common edition, in his Tomes, that is in his serious scholarship, he is overcome by the Hebrew truth and while surrounded by his own troops he occasionally seeks the assistance of a foreign language. I say only this: that I would prefer to have his knowledge of the scriptures even if accompanied by the hatred his name incurs.[55]

Despite his opening assertion, Jerome is far from silent on the subject of Origen here. The passage is a volatile mixture of the exaggerated self-abasement of the preface to the commentary on Galatians with the arrogance of the prefaces to the translations from Origen's recension of the Septuagint. Jerome defers elaborately to his famous predecessor, yet he bases his authority not on his use of Origen's work but on his own access to the He-

---

54. *studii ergo nostri erit uel eorum, qui de libris Hebraicis uaria suspicantur, errores refellere uel ea, quae in Latinis et Graecis codicibus scatere uidentur, auctoritati suae reddere, etymologias quoque rerum, nominum atque regionum, quae in nostro sermone non resonant, uernaculae linguae explanare ratione* (Preface to the *Quaest. Heb. in Gen.*, CCSL 72:1-2).

55. *de Adamantio autem sileo, cuius nomen (si parua licet conponere magnis) meo nomine inuidiosius est, quod, cum in homiliis suis, quas ad uulgum loquitur, communem editionem sequatur, in tomis, id est in disputatione maiori, Hebraica ueritate superatus et suorum circumdatus agminibus, interdum linguae peregrinae quaerit auxilia. hoc unum dico, quod uellem cum inuidia nominis eius habere etiam scientiam scripturarum* (Preface to the *Quaest. Heb. in Gen.*, cont., 72:2).

brew text. His deference is not to Origen as a source, as in the commentary on Galatians, but to Origen as a model. Rather than disclaiming any scriptural expertise, as he did in 386, he expresses the wish that his own learning could be as great as Origen's: the difference is telling. By now, Jerome had developed a substantial profile as an exegete, in terms of both real contributions to scriptural knowledge and his self-presentation as an independent authority. He was no longer the neophyte he had been when he wrote his first biblical commentaries six years earlier.

While completing the *Hebrew Questions on Genesis*, Jerome began to translate the Hebrew Bible from the original.[56] The translations *iuxta Hebraeos* contrast sharply with the versions based on Origen's recension of the Septuagint that Jerome had made just a few years earlier, both in their methodology and in the ways that their prefaces present them. The new translations were products of the same philological approach that shaped the *Hebrew Questions on Genesis*, which drew on a combination of the Hebrew text itself, rabbinic sources, and the *recentiores*. Jerome used the *recentiores* to clarify difficult passages, to supply translations for *hapax legomena*, and so on; his translations reveal this inasmuch as they often echo one or more of the earlier versions.[57] Yet although he often followed the earlier translators' ver-

---

56. Whether Jerome's translation was actually based on the Hebrew itself or primarily or exclusively on the *recentiores* or other Greek authorities has been a topic of sustained controversy since the origins of critical study of Jerome's biblical scholarship. Two detailed studies of Jerome's translation technique that appeared in the second half of the twentieth century came to diametrically opposed conclusions. Kedar, "Vulgate," concluded that while Jerome used the *recentiores*, he translated directly from the Hebrew and drew extensively upon rabbinic exegesis. His position seems to me the most convincing, for reasons that I specify in the notes below. Estin, *Psautiers*, studied Jerome's three translations of the Psalter, comparing the final version, made at Bethlehem in the early 390s, with the remnants of the versions of Aquila, Symmachus, and Theodotion. She concluded that Jerome's version *iuxta Hebraeos* was no more based on the Hebrew itself than were his earlier translations, which revised the Old Latin Psalter to reflect the emendations of Origen's recension. Instead, Jerome had translated from the *recentiores*, in particular Aquila and Symmachus. However, Estin did not compare Jerome's translation with the Hebrew, and provided no explanation for the criterion that guided Jerome's choices as he drew alternately on various Greek authorities. The logical flaws in her study, and her failure to examine the Hebrew or to study Jerome's use of rabbinic tradition, which she freely admitted she was unqualified to do, vitiate her results. Useful summaries of the two scholars' research appear in Estin, "Traductions," and Kedar, "Latin Translations"; unfortunately, neither seems to be aware of the other's work. Numerous other authors have addressed the broader issue of Jerome's knowledge of Hebrew; Rebenich, "Vir Trilinguis," provides a helpful summary of the debate.

57. Estin succeeds in showing that Jerome often translates in agreement with one or the other of the *recentiores*. However, since her unit of analysis is the single word, and she does not compare Jerome's text to the Hebrew itself, she is unable to prove that Jerome depended on the *recentiores* rather than the Hebrew as his primary criterion.

sions of a single word or phrase, he never adhered to any one of them for even an entire sentence. Instead, his own reading of the Hebrew was the criterion by which he chose from among their interpretations.[58] Furthermore, he incorporates numerous rabbinic exegeses into his translation.[59] He must have worked with a range of texts before him: the Hebrew, the *recentiores*, the Septuagint, and the Old Latin, and perhaps a number of Greek commentaries as well. At the same time, he consulted a Jewish teacher. From him Jerome gleaned insight into the correct reading of the Hebrew text, including both linguistic and exegetical information.[60]

The prefaces to the translations *iuxta Hebraeos* were among Jerome's most influential and characteristic attempts at legitimating his scholarly undertaking. They contrast in several important respects with earlier descriptions and justifications of his mode of translating. In the preface to the commentary on Ecclesiastes, although Jerome had opened by asserting that he followed no authority in making the translation that served as the basis for his commentary, he immediately went on to acknowledge that he had retained the wording of the Septuagint wherever possible, and to invoke the *recentiores* as important elements of his approach to the text. In the prefaces to

58. For this evaluation, see Kedar, "Vulgate." See also his 1990 article "Latin Translations": "Much has been made of Jerome's dependence on these [i.e. the *recentiores*], especially on Symmachus. However, such [an] impression of dependence prevails only as long as we look for points of contact between the Vg and any particular source. The moment we survey the overall picture, his relative independence becomes apparent: He never agrees with one of his informants for more than a short clause. In other words, Jerome made use of the works of his predecessors in a way a modern scholar has recourse to a concordance, a dictionary, a grammar and scholarly commentaries. This, of course, also applies to the information he gathered from his Jewish instructors. The final decision rests with Jerome and he reaches it having weighed the evidence" (323, with references in n. 48).

59. On Jerome's use of traditions found in the Midrash and Targum in his translation, see Kedar, "Vulgate," 62: "Reading the Vulgate, one comes across innumerable instances where Jerome's rendition reflects midrashic interpretation or a comprehension that is paralleled by the Targum or the Jewish commentators of the Middle Ages. I adduce a small number of examples out of the many I have encountered while researching the Vulgate." He gives seven examples from Isaiah 25–33 alone (p. 63).

60. Kedar, "Vulgate," 70, describes Jerome's methods: "In surveying the factors that had influence on Jerome's manner of translating, we conclude that the information that he himself gives us as to his translation procedure is essentially correct: in the preface to his commentary on the Book of Ecclesiastes, Jerome states that he first turned to the Hebrew text, and discerned its meaning. He then compared his results with the Rabbinical interpretation. After, Jerome considered the Septuagint and used it whenever it did not stray from the original, consulted the later Greek translators, especially Symmachus, and finally tried to leave intact as much of the Old Latin version as possible. The welding of this vast amount of information into one smooth Latin version was Jerome's own and unique work."

the translations from Origen's recension of the Septuagint, on the contrary, Jerome admitted of no Christian predecessors. Instead, he based his authority exclusively on his studies with Jewish teachers. The prefaces to the versions *iuxta Hebraeos* present a much more complex picture than either of these earlier cases. Jerome invokes the full spectrum of available authorities. Origen, the *recentiores*, and his Jewish teachers all put in an appearance. Yet he asserts his independence passionately. The translations, he claims, are wholly his own creation. His predecessors, whether Jewish or Christian, serve as models for his scholarly undertakings, who legitimate what many considered to be a display of irreverence toward the Christian Bible. They do not serve in any real sense as sources of information.

The prefaces to the translations *iuxta Hebraeos* appeal to the *recentiores* not as authorities for the meaning of the biblical text but as examples for his own work. He places himself on or above their level, even claiming that his translations are superior to theirs. In the preface to his translation of the Psalms *iuxta Hebraeos*, dedicated to the monk Sophronius, a native speaker of Greek and a resident of Jerome's monastery at Bethlehem, Jerome claims that Sophronius asked him for a translation of the Psalms as a successor, or perhaps a replacement, to the versions of Aquila, Symmachus, and Theodotion.[61] Given that Jerome's preface, despite the conceit of the personal dedication, is transparently addressed to a larger reading public, one should not

---

61. Estin, "Traductions," 80, asserts that in the preface to this translation Jerome identified "the Hebrews" with the *recentiores*. She writes: "'Les Hébreux' ce sont, d'après la préface de Jérôme à cette traduction, Aquila, Symmachus, et Théodotion. Notons immédiatement ce pluriel, qui représente *la* 'vérité hébraïque.'" (emphasis in original) This interpretation wholly misrepresents the passage in question, which reads: *studiosissime postulasti ut post Aquilam, Symmachum et Theodotionem nouam editionem Latino sermone transferrem. . . . certe confidenter dicam et multos huius operis testes citabo, me nihil dumtaxat scientem de Hebraica ueritate mutasse. sicubi ergo editio mea a ueteribus discreparit, interroga quemlibet Hebraeorum et liquido peruidebis me ab aemulis frustra lacerari* ("you most zealously requested that after Aquila, Symmachus, and Theodotion, I translate a new edition into the Latin language. . . . Certainly I may say confidently, and I will cite many witnesses of this work, that I never knowingly altered anything from the Hebrew truth. Therefore, wherever my edition differs from the older ones, question whomever you like among the Hebrews and you will clearly perceive that I am being attacked in vain by the envious") (*Praef. in Psalmos de Heb. interp.*, *Biblia Sacra*, 768). Estin has read Jerome's phrase *post Aquilam, Symmachum et Theodotionem*, where *post* has a temporal sense, as if it meant "according to," a sense which the Latin preposition cannot have (OLD: *post* 1: "after"; *post* 2: "behind" with related meanings). Farther along in the same preface, Jerome anticipates that his readers will be disturbed by the difference between his translation and the older versions (plural), and urges them to consult the Jews so as to determine whether the new version is an accurate representation of the *Hebraica veritas*—surely a pointless operation if that phrase referred to the Greek versions of the *recentiores*!

overemphasize the fact that Sophronius was a Greek who could read the *recentiores* for himself if he chose. Yet in *On Famous Men*, perhaps two years later, Jerome referred to Sophronius's intention of translating his versions *iuxta Hebraeos* into Greek. Clearly, therefore, he was capable of imagining his work as a replacement for the *recentiores* in every sense, even for readers who had access to the originals.[62]

In the preface to his translation of Job *iuxta Hebraeos*, Jerome not only asserts that his translation stands on a par with the *recentiores* but uses this equivalence to argue for the legitimacy of his undertaking and to refute the suggestion that he showed irreverence toward the Septuagint by translating directly from the Hebrew. He points out that Aquila was a Jew and that Symmachus and Theodotion were Jewish-Christian heretics. Yet their translations had been accepted by the Greek Church, to the extent that Origen had included them in his Hexapla, and he and other Greek commentators had incorporated their versions in their exegesis.[63] Unlike the *recentiores*, Jerome was a good Christian. His translations, therefore, ought to be all the more welcome in the church.[64] This argument implies that Jerome's work as a translator was fully parallel to the work of the *recentiores*, and therefore that they legitimate his efforts by serving not as sources—as in the preface to the commentary on Ecclesiastes—but as models.[65] Furthermore, Origen now serves not as a source for Jerome's biblical criticism, nor even as a model for him, but as an example for his readers. As Origen accepted the *recentiores*, so Jerome's Latin audience ought to accept his new translations. In this con-

---

62. *De vir. ill.* 134; in *Contra Ruf.* 2.24 Jerome claims that Sophronius did translate the entire version *iuxta Hebraeos* into Greek, and it was a success.

63. *cogor per singulos scripturae diuinae libros aduersariorum respondere maledictis, qui interpretationem meam reprehensionem Septuaginta interpretum criminantur, quasi non et apud Graecos Aquila, Symmachus et Theodotion uel uerbum e uerbo, uel sensum de sensu, uel ex utroque commixtum et medie temperatum genus translationis expresserint, et omnia ueteris instrumenti uolumina Origenes obelis asteriscisque distinxerit, quos uel additos uel de Theodotione sumptos translationi antiquae inseruit, probans defuisse quod additum est* (*Prol. in Iob de Heb. interp.*, *Biblia Sacra*, 731-2).

64. *quod si apud Graecos, post Septuaginta editionem, iam Christi Euangelio coruscante, Iudaeus Aquila, et Symmachus ac Theodotion iudaizantes heretici sunt recepti, qui multa mysteria Saluatoris subdola interpretatione celarunt et tamen in* εξαπλοις *habentur apud ecclesias et explanantur ab ecclesiasticis uiris, quanto magis ego Christianus, de parentibus Christianis et uexillum crucis in mea fronte portans, cuius studium fuit omissa repetere, deprauata corrigere et sacramenta ecclesiae puro et fideli aperire sermone, uel a fastidiosis uel a malignis lectoribus non debeo reprobari?* (*Prol. in Iob de Heb. interp.*, *Biblia Sacra*, 732).

65. On Jerome's representation of the *recentiores* as models for his own translations in this preface, see Kamesar, *Jerome*, 68–70. His interpretation of the argument of the preface is very similar to my own, though we differ in our views of the larger context of the argument.

text it is no wonder that Jerome can again acknowledge the importance of Origen's philological contributions by referring explicitly to his use of the *recentiores* and even to the Hexapla. Jerome's predecessor can no longer pose any threat to his independence.

The most striking assertion of Jerome's intellectual paternity appears in the famous *prologus galeatus,* the "helmeted preface" that introduced Jerome's translations of the books of Samuel and Kings:

> Read first, therefore, my Samuel and my Kings; mine, I say, mine: for whatever by repeated translation and careful emendation we have learned and possess, is ours. . . . I know of no way in which I have altered anything whatsoever from the Hebrew truth.[66]

Jerome's work admits of no outside influences. He himself, on the basis of his own efforts, legitimates this new text of the Bible. His authority as a translator rests solely on his access to the *Hebraica veritas,* the "Hebrew truth." On first inspection, the implications of this phrase seem rather limited: the only factors involved in the production of the translation are the Hebrew text and Jerome's own intellect. Yet as a careful reading of this text and others makes clear, the concept of the *Hebraica veritas* was far more elastic, and more inclusive, than modern scholars have generally appreciated. For its reference extends far beyond the text of the Bible to include a whole range of Jewish materials—and not only Jewish materials, but a great deal of the biblical philology of Origen and his successors as well. In order to assess the full implications of Jerome's claim in this preface that he deviated in no respect from the *Hebraica veritas,* we must describe in more detail the range of materials that Jerome associated with the learning of the Hebrews.

In the letters he wrote at Rome, Jerome began to describe his approach to biblical interpretation using the image of the *fons veritatis,* which he opposed to the *rivuli opinionum.* Access to the "wellspring of truth"—the Hebrew text and the learning of the Jews—was what distinguished Jerome's scriptural learning from that of other Latin exegetes, who were limited to the "rivulets of opinion," the Greek and Latin translations and the scholarly traditions that used them. For Jerome always associated the image of the source or spring with Jewish learning and the Hebrew text, even before the phrase *Hebraica veritas* became part of his vocabulary. In his later work,

---

66. *lege ergo primum Samuhel et Malachim meum; meum, inquam, meum: quicquid enim crebrius uertendo et emendando sollicitius et didicimus et tenemus, nostrum est . . . mihi omnino conscius non sim mutasse me quippiam de Hebraica ueritate. (Prol. in Regum, Biblia Sacra,* 365).

where it is common, the phrase itself almost always refers to the Hebrew text of the Bible as transmitted among the Jews.[67]

The image of the source, however, and the sphere of Jewish learning that Jerome considered authoritative had far wider implications. Nor have these entirely escaped notice. Adam Kamesar suggested that the phrase *Hebraica veritas* might include the full range of what he termed Jerome's "rabbinic-recentiores philology."[68] Both conceptually and in practice, Jerome's biblical scholarship brought together a disparate assortment of material, which he represented as the biblical learning of the Jews. This material included not only information he obtained directly from Jewish informants but also what he had gotten second-hand from Greek writers like Origen and Eusebius. The significance of Jerome's invocations of the *Hebraica veritas* can best be understood in terms of this whole body of erudition, which goes far beyond the Hebrew text itself.

The prologue to the translation of Samuel and Kings *iuxta Hebraeos,* where the term *Hebraica veritas* plays such a pivotal role, provides a fascinating example of Jerome's interest in a broad range of Jewish matters. Most of the prologue is taken up with a discussion of the Jewish canon of the scriptures. Jerome lists the books of the Jewish canon, describing its order and divisions, giving the Hebrew names of the books, and finally listing those books rejected by the Jews as noncanonical. The list is prefaced by a numerological explanation of the correspondences between the twenty-two letters of the Hebrew alphabet and the twenty-two books of the Hebrew scriptures according to the Jewish canon. But this is no mere digression into exotica: the Jewish canon was an integral element of Jerome's conception of the *Hebraica veritas,* despite its numerous divergences from the canon of the Greek Bible used in the church. Indeed, Jerome's adoption of the Hebrew text used by the Jews as authoritative suggested that he had elevated the Jewish canon into a standard for the Latin Church.

Jerome makes his adherence to the Hebrew canon explicit in several cases. Not only did he purge variant readings, and lengthy passages, which did not find support in the Jewish Bible: he is famous for having rejected entire books as noncanonical because they did not exist in Hebrew. The texts eliminated included the Wisdom of Solomon, Judith, Tobit, Ecclesiasticus

---

67. The phrase appears over a hundred times, mostly in Jerome's exegetical works; only four instances, all cited below, unquestionably refer to something other than, or beyond, the Hebrew text itself.

68. Kamesar, *Jerome,* 80–81.

(also known as Sirach), and Baruch.[69] But he went beyond this, stigmatizing even those texts, like 1 Maccabees, which existed in Hebrew but were excluded from the canon of the Jews. It was the authority of the Jews, not the Hebrew language alone, that served as Jerome's criterion of canonicity.[70] He also adopted important elements of the organization of the Jewish canon. For example, in his translation of the twelve Minor Prophets he presented them in the order in which they appeared in Jewish manuscripts, rather than the very different order of the Greek Bible of the church. Furthermore, he repeatedly uses the phrase *Hebraica veritas* to designate the order of the Minor Prophets in the Jewish Bible.[71] The term is therefore explicitly used to refer to an aspect of the canon, as well as the text, of the Jewish scriptures.

But the special expertise in biblical scholarship that Jerome attributed to the Jews extended well beyond even beyond this broadened understanding of the *Hebraica veritas*. For Jerome came to assign to the Jews authority not only over the canon and text of the Hebrew scriptures but also over important aspects of its interpretation. In the next chapter, I turn to his commentaries on the Prophets. There, two of the primary senses of scripture under discussion are the literal interpretation, which usually means textual criticism, and the historical interpretation, which has a rather broad meaning. Jerome subsumes them both under a single interpretation *iuxta Hebraeos,* "according to the Hebrews." Everything that he learned from, or attributed to, Jewish sources is therefore brought together under one inclusive rubric.

On occasion, Jerome went so far as to apply explicitly the language of the *Hebraica veritas* to exegetical material that was clearly interpretative, not textual. In the preface to his historical commentary on the ten visions of Isaiah, written for Amabilis in 397, he uses the term to refer to everything that is not part of the Greek Christian exegetical tradition:

69. For Jerome's rejection of Wisdom of Solomon, Judith, Tobit, and Ecclesiastes, see prologue to Samuel and Kings *iuxta Hebraeos;* Baruch, *Comm. in Hier.* book 1, pref.

70. In the prologue to Samuel and Kings *iuxta Hebraeos,* Jerome writes: *igitur Sapientia, quae uulgo Salomonis inscribitur, et Iesu filii Sirach liber et Iudith et Tobias et Pastor non sunt in canone. Macchabeorum primum librum Hebraicum repperi, secundus Graecus est. (Biblia Sacra,* 365).

71. *non idem ordo est duodecim prophetarum apud Hebraeos, qui et apud nos. unde secundum id quod ibi* [i.e., among the Hebrews] *legitur, hic quoque dispositi sunt. (Prologus duodecim prophetarum, Biblia sacra,* 1374). For further confirmation that the *Hebraica veritas* includes the order of the books, see *Comm. in Ioelem,* prol., 1: *non idem ordo est duodecim Prophetarum apud Septuaginta interpretes, qui in Hebraica ueritate retinetur.* See also *In Michaeam,* prol., 1: *Michaeas, in quem nunc commentarios dictare cupio, in ordine duodecim Prophetarum, secundum Septuaginta interpretes tertius est, secundum Hebraicam ueritatem sextus, et sequitur Ionam prophetam, qui succedit Abdiae, atque ita fit ut tertius sit Amos, et Ioel secundus post Osee, qui apud omnes primus est.*

With what intensity, reverend father Amabilis, did you beseech me in your letters to explain for you by means of a historical exposition the ten visions, which
are the most obscure parts of Isaiah, and to do so leaving aside the works of our
own commentators, who, following a variety of opinions, have produced many
volumes, so that I should provide you with the Hebrew truth.[72]

Again, in the commentary on Zechariah of 406, he associates the image of
the Hebrew as source of truth with the entire Jewish interpretative tradition
rather than with the Hebrew text alone. In introducing an explanation of
the veiled historical reference of one of the prophet's mysterious visions, he
writes:

We are compelled therefore to return to the Hebrews, and to seek the knowledge of truth rather from the wellspring than from the rivulets, especially since
[the passage is] not a prophecy concerning Christ, where they are wont to pre-
varicate, and to conceal the truth with lies, but rather continues the order of the
historical account that precedes and follows it.[73]

These passages suggest that wherever Jerome invokes the *Hebraica veritas* in
a context that does not limit the phrase to a narrowly textual meaning, we
ought to consider the possibility that he was thinking not of the Hebrew text
alone but of the entire arena of scriptural interpretation in which he believed the Jews to be specially expert.[74]

In reality, the scriptural expertise that Jerome attributed to the Jews included a great deal of material that he obtained from Greek Christian sources
rather than from Jewish informants. His rhetoric masks the distinction, as-

72. *Comm. in Esaiam* 5, pref., 15 (preface to the literal and historical commentary on the visions
of Isaiah written for Amabilis in 397): *Hucusque papa Amabilis . . . per litteras flagitabas ut tibi
decem uisiones quae in Esaia obscurissimae sunt, historica expositione dissererem et omissis nostrorum commentariis, qui uarias opiniones secuti multa uolumina condiderunt, hebraicam panderem
ueritatem.*

73. *Comm. in Zach.* 2.8.526: *cogimur igitur ad Hebraeos recurrere, et scientiae ueritatem de fonte
magis quam de riuulis quaerere, praesertim cum non prophetia aliqua de Christo, ubi tergiuersari
solent, et ueritatem celare mendacio, sed historiae ex praecedentibus et consequentibus ordo texatur.*
Cited in Kamesar, *Jerome*, 178, 82.

74. A further interesting example, though perhaps difficult to interpret: *uultum ieiunantis moysi
et iuxta hebraicam ueritatem, dei confabulatione cornutum* (*Adv. Iov.* 2.15). Jerome based his translation of the Hebrew word *keren* as "horned" rather than "shining" on a rabbinic tradition; see
Kedar, "Vulgate," 51–52. Referring to his own translation *iuxta Hebraeos*, he writes in letter 71.5–
6: *canonem hebraicae ueritatis excepto octateucho, quem nunc in manibus habeo, pueris tuis et notariis describendum dedi—septuaginta interpretum editionem et te habere non dubito—et ante annos
plurimos diligentissime emendatum studiosis tradidi.* On the Exodus passage, which presents difficulties to modern commentators, and the history of its translation, see Propp, "Skin."

similating the philological and historical contributions of his Greek predecessors to the sphere of Hebrew learning. The preface to Jerome's translation of Chronicles from Origen's recension of the Greek provides two telling examples of this phenomenon. First, Jerome advises his addressees, the Roman monks Domnio and Rogatianus, that just as the reader of the Greek historians will comprehend them better if he has seen Athens, or as an understanding of the third book of Virgil's Aeneid is deepened by the experience of traveling by sea from Troy to Ostia via the strait of Messina, so the reader of the Holy Scriptures can benefit from a firsthand knowledge of the cities, the topography, and the place-names of Judea. For that reason, Jerome informs them, he has made the effort to take a comprehensive tour of the country with learned Hebrews as his guides.[75] Farther along in the same preface, he warns his readers that the interpretation of Chronicles is made more difficult by the corruption in many Greek and Latin texts of the numerous Hebrew names in the book. Special expertise is required to decipher these names correctly and thereby to restore the inaccuracies that had crept into the Septuagint text in the course of its transmission.[76] Jerome connects this effort with his studies with a Jewish expert, "a former authority on the Law from Tiberias, who was held in admiration among the Jews."[77] He therefore presents both the topography of Palestine and the proper names that appear in the Bible as areas in which the authority of the Jews legitimizes his scholarship.

At the time that he made this translation, Jerome was also hard at work on his versions of the *On Hebrew Names* and the *On Hebrew Places*, Greek works written by Philo and Origen (or so Jerome believed), and by Eusebius of Caesarea, respectively. The spheres of knowledge involved in these two reference works and those evoked in the preface to the translation of Chron-

---

75. *quomodo Grecorum historias magis intellegunt qui Athenas uiderint, et tertium Vergilii librum qui Troade per Leucaten et Acroceraunia ad Siciliam et inde ad Ostia Tiberis nauigarint, ita sanctam scripturam lucidius intuebitur qui Iudaeam oculis contemplatus est et antiquarum urbium memorias locorumque uel eadem uocabula uel mutata cognouerit. unde et nobis curae fuit cum eruditissimis Hebreorum hunc laborem subire, ut circuiremus prouinciam quam uniuersae Christi ecclesiae sonant.*

76. *libere enim uobis loquor, ita et in Grecis et in Latinis codicibus hic nominum liber uitiosus est, ut non tam Hebrea quam barbara quaedam et Sarmatica nomina congesta arbitrandum sit. nec hoc Septuaginta interpretibus, qui Spiritu Sancto pleni ea quae uera fuerant transtulerunt, sed scriptorum culpae adscribendum, dum de inemendatis inemendata scriptitant, et saepe tria nomina, subtractis e medio syllabis, in unum uocabulum cogunt uel e regione unum nomen propter latitudinem suam in duo uel tria uocabula diuidunt. sed et ipsae appellationes non homines, ut plerique aestimant, sed urbes et regiones et saltus et prouincias sonant ...*

77. *de Tiberiade legis quondam auctorem, qui apud Hebreos admirationi habebatur.*

icles from the Septuagint are too similar for coincidence. Just as the translation introduced by this preface was far more directly dependent on Greek scholarship than Jerome admitted at the time, so the Jewish learning, gained on the spot in the Holy Land, which he describes as essential to his work on the text of the Bible, includes a significant element acquired at second hand from Greek sources. In his commentaries on the Prophets, he went on to include information that he owed to these two works within the interpretation *iuxta Hebraeos.*[78] Jerome's "Hebrew" learning, that is, extended to materials that had already been naturalized within the Christian tradition by their use among his Greek predecessors.

Perhaps the most telling example of Jerome's broadening the sphere of Hebrew learning to include material that he drew from Greek sources was his integration of the *recentiores* into his text-critical methodology as an element of the interpretation *iuxta Hebraeos.* He was able to do this, despite the probability that he drew his citations of the *recentiores* from Origen's Hexapla, preserved in the episcopal library at Caesarea, only by emphasizing that the translators themselves were Jews or quasi-Jews. He had already drawn this connection in the passage of the preface to the commentary on Ecclesiastes cited above. There, Jerome inserts their names immediately after a reference to his reliance on "the Hebrews," and describes his use of them in terms of recourse to the *fons veritatis,* as opposed to the *rivuli opinionum.* In the preface to his translation of Job *iuxta Hebraeos,* too, he stresses that the *recentiores* were either Jews or semi-Jewish heretics; the same language appears in the preface to his translation of Ezra, written more than a decade later. Even as he used the acceptance of these "Jewish" versions by Greek exegetes to argue for the legitimacy of his own translations, he drove home the point that the *recentiores* were foreign to the Greek Christian tradition, taken over by Origen from Jewish sources.

We have no letters written by Jerome during his first years at Bethlehem, and the works he did produce, while voluminous, provide little insight into aspects of his life beyond his scholarly activities. His productivity suggests that this was a peaceful period for Jerome, allowing him to do a great deal of serious scholarly work. At the same time, he established himself, through Paula's patronage, as a prominent figure among the Latin pilgrims and as-

---

78. The index to the CCSL edition of the commentaries on the Minor Prophets lists the references to the *Liber nominibus*: the list fills more than fifteen pages in small type. Fourteen passages from the *De situ et nominibus* are cited, one twice. The other commentaries on the Prophets present similar data.

cetics who gathered in and around Jerusalem to be near the holy sites. He must also have reestablished his relationship with his schoolfellow and former fellow ascetic at Aquileia, Rufinus, who had by this time taken up residence in a monastery on the Mount of Olives above Jerusalem, paid for by his aristocratic and extremely rich Roman patroness Melania the Elder. But we have no contemporary evidence for contact between the two monastic establishments.

Instead, Jerome's dedications from the years 386 to 392 are almost all to Paula and Eustochium, his patrons. A few works are dedicated to monks in his own monastery, including his brother Paulinian, who had joined Jerome at Bethlehem, and the Greek Sophronius. Another early preface mentions Epiphanius of Salamis. Only two works, the translation of Chronicles from the Greek and the translation of Kings from the Hebrew, were intended for recipients living in the West. Both are dedicated to the Roman monks Domnio and Rogatianus. Jerome's circle during these years seems to have been a small one, closely based on the group of Latins who had accompanied him to the East in 385. Certainly, Jerome expected his writings to reach an audience far beyond his dedicatees. The works he wrote during these years, however, give no evidence for the kind of broad, cosmopolitan connections among the Christian elite that he would develop later in his career.

Jerome's relative isolation, and the peace it seems to have brought, were to be broken in 393 by the eruption of the Origenist controversy, instigated by Jerome's old acquaintance Epiphanius of Salamis. Some of the passages discussed in this chapter already warn of the controversy's outbreak. In the preface to the *Hebrew Questions on Genesis,* Jerome claims that Origen's name is hated. Perhaps, by developing his concept of the *Hebraica veritas* into a basis for independent scholarly authority, Jerome was preparing to distance himself from Origen theologically as well as philologically. Whether fortuitously or not, by 393 Jerome had put himself in a position where he could argue with some persuasiveness that although he was an enthusiastic student of Origen's biblical exegesis, he had not swallowed the Greek master whole, and could therefore claim exemption from the charges of heresy that were soon to be leveled against his great predecessor.

CHAPTER THREE

Interpretation and the Construction of Jerome's Authority

JEROME'S commentaries on the Prophets, unlike many ancient commentaries, are neither mere crystallizations of oral teaching, nor collections of annotations parasitic on the texts they exegete, but freestanding works in their own right. In comparison to other biblical commentaries of their day, they are formal, compendious, and exhaustive. They seem designed to give Jerome's Latin audiences everything such readers might need in approaching the texts of the Prophets. Aiming at comprehensiveness, these commentaries take in a great mass of earlier material, which is presented as if it had been little altered. However, the manner in which Jerome arranges this material, and the relations of authority that he imposes upon it, are carefully structured. The tacit effect of this structure is to establish Jerome as the ultimate arbiter of biblical truth, while maintaining the appearance that his works are merely conduits for the views of earlier authorities. The cornerstone of the entire edifice, and the most impressive and original element of the commentaries, is Jerome's text-critical method, which is founded upon and serves to defend the absolute primacy of the *Hebraica veritas*.

Although the commentaries bear little sign of it, they were composed during a period of immense turmoil, both for Jerome and his immediate circle, and for the churches East and West. During the crisis that has come to be called the Origenist controversy, accusations and defenses, provocations and attempts at repression, flew back and forth in Palestine, Egypt, and Italy, between those who accused the Greek master of having taught heresy and those who refused to abjure his works. Jerome, whose entire literary career was founded on the prestige of Origen but who was bound by longstanding social ties to those who initiated the attack, was caught in the middle.

In 393, the same year that Jerome began work on his first commentaries on the Prophets, Epiphanius of Salamis visited Jerusalem, where he stirred up a controversy over the teachings of Origen. First, he seems to have sent a monk, Atarbius, to the monasteries of Jerome and Rufinus to demand that the two Latin expatriates sign a condemnation of Origenism. Jerome willingly did so; Rufinus refused and, according to Jerome, barred Atarbius and his party from his monastery by force.[1] From this point on, the rupture between the two childhood friends was to develop into open enmity. Epiphanius's next move was to challenge Bishop John of Jerusalem publicly. In a sermon delivered before the Jerusalem congregation during an important festival, Epiphanius inveighed against the heresy of the Origenists. He refrained from accusing his host of Origenism directly, but it seems from what followed that John knew himself to be Epiphanius's true target.

There were complex personal and theological agendas behind Epiphanius's intemperate behavior.[2] Among other factors, it may be possible to discern the lingering effects of the schism of Antioch. John was the designated successor of Cyril, who had been among the many supporters of Meletius. Epiphanius, of course, had been a longtime partisan of Paulinus. In 393, the schism at Antioch was not yet a dead issue. Certainly, Jerome's close connection with Epiphanius, which dated to the days when he had been a priest in Paulinus's clergy at Antioch, had a great deal to do with the position that Jerome was forced to take in the debate that ensued.[3]

In the short run, John was victorious over the meddling Epiphanius, to Jerome's immediate detriment. Jerome and his monks felt excluded from the churches of Jerusalem and Bethlehem by John's hostility. The irregular ordination of Jerome's brother Paulinian by Epiphanius at the latter's own Palestinian monastery in Besanduk, in the see of Eleutheropolis, may have been intended to give Jerome and his followers access to the sacraments. In the event, it led John to excommunicate the monks at Bethlehem.[4] Matters

---

1. Jerome, *Contra Ruf.* 3.33; Kelly, *Jerome*, 198–99.

2. The basic data for this phase of the controversy derive entirely from Jerome's polemical treatise of 397, *Contra Ioh. Hier.* 11–12. For discussions, see Cavallera, *Saint Jérôme;* Holl, *Aufsätze,* for the chronology, together with Kelly, *Jerome,* 198–207; Clark, *Origenist Controversy,* 86–104, exploring the theological context of Epiphanius's charges.

3. On Jerome's relations with Epiphanius, see chapter 1 above, and Rebenich, *Hieronymus,* 106–7; Clark, *Origenist Controversy,* 26–27, who does not, however, connect the link between the two men with their mutual ties to Paulinus of Antioch.

4. *Contra Ioh. Hier.* 41–43; Jerome, letter 82.8; Epiphanius, *apud* Jerome, letter 51; Cavallera, *Saint Jérôme;* Kelly, *Jerome,* 200–201. Nautin, "Excommunication," gives the most detailed

continued to worsen: in 395, John seems to have procured from the prefect of the East (also named Rufinus) an order of exile against Jerome and his monks. This decree was not executed, only because the prefect was killed shortly thereafter, slain by the returning soldiers of the Gothic general Gaïnas in November 395.[5]

Finally, in 396, John asked Theophilus, bishop of Alexandria, to mediate the dispute. According to Jerome, Theophilus entered the debate on the side of John.[6] In 397, however, he addressed a letter to the two parties, which seems to have been a sincere attempt to reconcile them. Jerome replied to Theophilus in respectful but inflexible terms, blaming John for the dispute and contrasting the reverence that the monks of Egypt exhibited toward their fatherly bishop with the scorn of the Palestinian monks for the overbearing John.[7] Theophilus's emissary visited Jerusalem, and a temporary peace ensued. Jerome was readmitted into communion by John, and he and Rufinus were publicly reconciled in the Church of the Resurrection in Jerusalem at Easter 397.[8] Soon afterward, Rufinus returned to Italy.

But the quarrel was far from over. In its next phase, Theophilus entered the lists on the side of the anti-Origenists, driving out of Egypt four well-known intellectual monks, the so-called Tall Brothers, whom he charged with Origenism. The Tall Brothers fled to Constantinople, where they were received favorably by the city's new bishop, John Chrysostom, who owed his appointment to Theophilus in the first place. Chrysostom's support of the Tall Brothers, among a complex sequence of other incidents, turned Theophilus against him. The Alexandrian bishop was instrumental in having his former protégé deposed temporarily in 403 and finally driven into exile in 404.[9]

---

account of the events of this first phase of the controversy, but in his typical dogmatic fashion he overemphasizes the importance of the canon of the Council of Nicea that forbade a priest to leave the diocese of his ordination, thus vitiating his interpretation of the affair.

5. Jerome, letter 82.10, to Theophilus of Alexandria against John of Jerusalem.

6. *Contra Ioh. Hier.* 37.10: *Scribit ergo ad episcopum Theophilum apologiam;* 37.41ff. of this work contains Jerome's charge that Isidore, the envoy of Theophilus, had been prejudiced in favor of John.

7. Jerome, letter 82.

8. Kelly, *Jerome,* 209, citing Jerome, *Contra Ruf.* 3.33. For the date, see Nautin, "Études de chronologie I," 213, and the Appendix, section 8.

9. Our primary sources for these events are Palladius, *Historia Lausiaca* and *Dialogue on the Life of John Chrysostom,* and the ecclesiastical histories of Socrates and Sozomen. The most recent biography of Chrysostom, which recounts his fall in detail, is Kelly, *Golden Mouth,* 191–249.

Meanwhile, Rufinus had settled in Italy, where he began to produce Latin translations of Origen's works. In 398, he translated the *Peri Archon,* Origen's great treatise in speculative theology. In his preface, Rufinus invokes Jerome—without naming him—as authority for the project. The translation excited a great deal of controversy in the Western capital, and caused Jerome's friends there to write to him in consternation. Jerome soon replied to their request by preparing a literal translation of the work, emphasizing its most controversial aspects, which Rufinus had deliberately elided. Together with the translation, he sent letters to Rome explaining what he was doing and justifying his own orthodoxy, in terms that amounted to an attack on Rufinus.[10]

In 400, Theophilus of Alexandria convened a synod, which anathematized Origen's works. Rufinus, in 401, composed an *Apology* against Jerome, in which he accused Jerome of plagiarizing Origen, and used that charge among many others to denigrate Jerome and to defend his own integrity and orthodoxy. Jerome took the charges seriously enough that he began to reply even before Rufinus's work had reached him in Palestine. He produced two books of his own *Apology* before he had seen his opponent's work. These were followed by a third, which addressed Rufinus's specific charges in even more detail. At this point, Rufinus dropped out of the contest, at least as far as we can tell from his preserved writings. He continued to translate Origen, among other Greek writers, for the next ten years, until his death in the summer of 411 in Sicily, where he had fled the invasion of Alaric and the Goths. But he wrote no further controversial works. Jerome, on the other hand, never forgave his old friend, and continued to take satirical jabs at him long after he was dead.

This brief outline of the main events in the controversy during the 390s and early 400s cannot begin to do justice to its complexity. The bitterness on both sides reflected what each had at stake in terms of both theological commitments and temporal power. Elizabeth Clark has shown that the theology of Evagrius Ponticus, diffused among the monks of the Egyptian desert in the second half of the fourth century, was central to the Origenists' position. On the other side, Jerome and his partisans were motivated by the desire to establish not only the resurrection of the flesh but also the persistence of the hierarchy of virgins, ascetics, and laypersons in the resurrection.[11] Clark diagnoses Jerome's own opposition to Origenism as "lukewarm": his polemics were driven more by a desire to protect his own

---

10. Jerome, letter 84.

11. Clark, *Origenist Controversy.*

position, and to attack those who had attacked him, than by a determination to stamp out Origenist speculation. Clark estimates that Jerome's own comprehension of the subtleties of fourth-century Origenist thought was weak, at best. By contrast, it was in the Egyptian desert that Origenist theology reached its fullest development. That theology's best-informed and most violent opponents were men who were in a position to exert control over the desert monks.[12]

Here, a more holistic appreciation of Jerome's activities at the time of the controversy — one that takes into account the time and energy he devoted to biblical scholarship, as well as to polemics, during these years — can illuminate a further aspect of the struggle over Origenism. One of the key stakes in the Origenist controversy was the right of monks to be intellectuals, or of intellectuals to remain monks, outside the sphere of recruitment into the episcopal clergy of the great cities and therefore potentially beyond theological control. Both Jerome and Rufinus were monks, and both were men of learning (though Rufinus did not become an author until the Origenist controversy was entering its second phase). It was against both of them that Epiphanius's first challenge was directed. Later, when Theophilus decided to oppose rather than to tolerate Origenist views, he attacked the monks of Cellia and Nitria, driving them out of their cells and singling out their intellectual leaders, in particular the Tall Brothers, for special persecution. For whatever reason, John of Jerusalem had not dared to take such violent measures against Jerome a few years earlier, but he did succeed in enforcing a ban of excommunication that set Jerome and all the inhabitants of his monastery outside the bounds of the church. The entire controversy was a series of confused struggles in which bishops attempted to bring monks under their control, and monks — especially learned, articulate, well-connected monks — sought to assert their independence.

The prestige of many desert monks rested on their simplicity: they were men of no previous social status who achieved charismatic authority through their way of life and the dispositions it produced. Either as groups or as individuals, such men were already idealized in the literature of monasticism in the fourth century[13] and would gain real power in the

---

12. Clark, *Origenist Controversy*, 85–158 ("The Charges against Origenism"), discusses the anti-Origenist activities of Epiphanius, Theophilus, Jerome, and Shenute of Atripe. Her characterization of Jerome's position appears on 150.

13. Rubenson, *Letters of St. Anthony*, compares in detail the portrayal of Anthony in Athanasius's *Life* with the figure who can be reconstructed from Anthony's own letters. Rubenson emphasizes the contrast between the illiterate, uneducated, inarticulate Coptic monk portrayed in some passages of the *Life* and canonized in the later sayings attributed to Anthony in the various collec-

fifth.[14] On the other hand, there were also highly educated men, many with philosophical as well as rhetorical training, who were attracted to the monastic way of life. How were they to be incorporated into social milieux that had emerged from peasant movements? Could they be transformed into men of equal simplicity to their peasant brethren?[15] Or would they become intellectual leaders in the monastic movement? Origen's thought was obviously a rich philosophical resource for monks inclined to speculation about the theological aspects of their experience: hence his importance for Evagrius Ponticus. At the same time, Origen was himself a model, as we have already seen, for the scholar as committed ascetic. But could he be retained as a model for the monk?

In different ways, Rufinus and Jerome were both Origenist monks. Their split over Origen's theological orthodoxy reflected different approaches to the problem of how to be a literary man—an intellectual—and at the same time a monk. Rufinus adopted, seemingly without discomfort, the stunningly anti-intellectual language of the traditional episcopal representation of the monk.[16] Jerome's monastic rhetoric, as we will see in chapter 7, refused to give up the ideal of a fusion of asceticism and learning in one person.

JEROME'S EXEGESIS AND THE ANCIENT COMMENTARY

In the first book of his *Apology against Rufinus,* Jerome defended himself against Rufinus's charge that his commentary on Ephesians had plagiarized Origen. Rather than denying that he had used Origen as a source, Jerome tried to shift the terms of the debate. Claiming the grammatical commentators on the Latin literary classics as his authority, he articulated a theory of commentary that made compiling earlier exegetical texts a virtue rather

---

tions of the *Sayings of the Desert Fathers,* with the philosophical, even Platonist, writer, steeped in Origen's works, who emerges from the letters. On Athanasius and the monks more generally, see Brakke, *Athanasius,* especially 80-142, 201-66.

14. For an example of the independent power of monks, see their role in the controversy over the Theotokos at Constantinople in the 450s, described by Holum, *Theodosian Empresses,* 166, 200-201.

15. For material that reflects this side of the dilemma, see the sayings of Arsenius, in Ward, *Sayings,* s.v.

16. For example, many of Rufinus's additions to the *Ecclesiastical History* of Eusebius display a ferocious anti-intellectualism, which represents learning as the sole property of heretics and pagans. There, Rufinus echoes the polemic of the Cappadocians against Aetius and Eunomius, as well as more generalized depictions of the powerful simplicity of the desert fathers, which stemmed ultimately from the *Life of Anthony.*

than a failing. The passage is worth citing at length, as it will remain important for much that is to come:

> In my commentary on Paul's letter to the Ephesians, I followed the work of Origen, Didymus, and Apollinaris, who certainly hold contrary opinions, in order that I not lose the truth of my faith. What is the task of commentaries? They explain the words of another, they make manifest in plain speech what is written obscurely, they repeat the opinions of many authorities, and they say: "Some explain this passage thus, others intepret it thus, and by these citations and this method they attempt to confirm their interpretation and opinion," so that the prudent reader, when he has read the various interpretations and has learned which of the many are to be approved or rejected, will judge which is more true and, like a good money-changer, will reject the false coinage. Now is he to be held responsible for all these different interpretations, contradictory among themselves, who lays forth in one work what he has learned concerning the arguments of many? I think that when you were a boy you read Asper on Virgil and Sallust, Vulcatius on the orations of Cicero, Victorinus on his dialogues, and my teacher Donatus on Terence and Virgil, and other commentators on other authors, for example Plautus, Lucretius, Horace, Persius, and Lucan. Attack their interpretations because they have not followed a single explanation, and have instead on each passage enumerated their own views and those of others.[17]

The commentator's task, as Jerome describes it, is to compile the opinions of earlier authorities without prejudice. The commentary serves to explain the words of the text, to paraphrase in clear language what the author had expressed obscurely, and to summarize the opinions of the many earlier commentators who had interpreted the text in a variety of ways. By its very nature, the commentary includes contradictory opinions within a single text. The author of the commentary takes no responsibility for these opinions: he simply channels them. The crucial task of evaluating the various

---

17. *Contra Ruf.* 1:16: *Ego in commentariis ad Ephesios sic Origenem et Didymum et Apollinarem secutus sum, qui certe contraria inter se habent dogmata, ut fidei meae non amitterem ueritatem. Commentarii quid operis habent? Alterius dicta edisserunt, quae obscure scripta sunt plano sermone manifestant, multorum sententias replicant, et dicunt: Hunc locum quidam sic edisserunt, alii sic interpretantur, illi sensum suum et intellegentiam his testimoniis et hac nituntur ratione firmare, ut prudens lector, cum diuersas explanationes legerit et multorum uel probanda uel improbanda didicerit, iudicet quid uerius sit et, quasi bonus trapezita, adulterinae monetae pecuniam reprobet. Num diuersae interpretationis et contrariorum inter se sensuum tenebitur reus, qui in uno opere quod edisserit, expositiones posuerit plurimorum? Puto quod puer legeris Aspri in Vergilium ac Sallustium commentarios, Vulcatii in orationes Ciceronis, Victorini in dialogos eius, et in Terentii comoedias praeceptoris mei Donati, aeque in Vergilium, et aliorum in alios, Plautum uidelicet, Lucretium, Flaccum, Persium atque Lucanum. Argue interpretes eorum quare non unam explanationem secuti sint, et in eadem re quid uel sibi uel aliis uideatur enumerent.*

opinions presented by the commentator, "and like a good money-changer, rejecting the false coinage," is assigned to the reader, not to the commentator himself.[18]

Jerome's programmatic statements imply certain claims about the Latin grammatical commentaries he lists. First, the commentary includes a paraphrase of the text followed by explanations of one kind or another. Jerome's language implies that these explanations include the interpretation of rare words and difficult expressions—material we know to have been typical of the grammatical tradition. Furthermore, the commentary adheres to specific citational practices. Jerome does not state explicitly that individual authorities are cited by name, but his description strongly suggests that their views are somehow differentiated from each other.

This depiction of ideal commentarial practice raises a number of concrete issues regarding the nature of the ancient commentary. Does Jerome's description correspond to what we know from other sources about commentaries in antiquity? What form did the commentary in antiquity take, and what did it deal with? When and how did commentaries and other exegetical materials first come into existence? Who were their primary audiences? Were these readers likely to be equal to the demands that Jerome places on his *prudens lector* in the passage just cited? What were ancient Christian commentaries like, and what was their relation to commentary traditions that had developed in other contexts? All of these questions will need to be answered before we can examine Jerome's own commentaries in detail, and before we can relate his practice as a commentator to his self-presentation.

Ancient writers produced hundreds of commentaries on authoritative works of all kinds: literary, religious, philosophical, and technical. Exegesis itself goes back almost as far as written literature, at least in the Greek tradition.[19] The composition of separate commentaries probably began in the Hellenistic period, perhaps in the milieu of the Museum and its library at Alexandria. The first commentaries likely dealt with literary texts, but commentaries on other kinds of writings soon followed. From the third century BCE until the end of antiquity, commentary literatures of various kinds proliferated.[20] The vast Byzantine lexicon called the Suda refers to hundreds of

18. For further discussion of this saying, an unwritten teaching attributed to Jesus, see chapter 7 below.

19. Pfeiffer, *Classical Scholarship*, claims that Homer glosses his own meaning and believes that the rhapsodes were exegetes. According to Janko, "Physicist," 67–68, the Derveni papyrus argued for the necessity of the allegorical interpretation of myth.

20. For a conspectus of this literature, see Pfeiffer, *Classical Scholarship*.

commentaries on everything from the works of Plato to technical treatises in grammar and rhetoric.

Almost none of this vast body of material survives in its original form. For example, of the several thousand commentaries on literary works attributed to the Alexandrian grammarians of the Hellenistic and early Roman period, only one survives: a commentary of Didymus Chalcenterus on Demosthenes' Philippics preserved on a papyrus.[21] The Latin world also produced a vast body of commentaries on literary and other works; here too, very little survives. The only surviving Latin grammatical commentary is the work of Servius on Virgil, which probably dates to the beginning of the fifth century. Servius, like Jerome, was a pupil of the great Donatus, whose own commentary on Virgil, unfortunately, is represented only by fragments.[22] We have scant evidence, therefore, for the form and arrangement of ancient commentaries.

From what little does survive, scholars tend to conclude that ancient commentaries usually occupied separate books, rather than being written in the margins of the text of the author under interpretation. The exception is the presence of *scholia minora*, brief interpretative marginalia, in certain literary papyri. These scholia, however, generally seem to be written ad hoc rather than to reflect a preexisting arrangement.[23] The medieval book, in which elaborate, formal scholia are arrayed about a text that occupies only a small part of the page, was impossible in antiquity. Not only was such an arrangement incompatible with the roll book that was standard until at least the early fourth century, but it demanded developments in codex technology that occurred later still. The earliest surviving Latin manuscripts that incorporate text and commentary into a predetermined *mise en page* date to the ninth century.[24] In Jerome's day, then, the commentary as such took the form of a separate book from that containing the text commented on.

The Hellenistic philologists devised a series of critical signs to link text and commentary. These signs—the asterisk, obelus, and others—were inserted in specially prepared copies of the texts on which they commented, drawing attention to textual difficulties and indicating that a discussion would be found in the accompanying commentary. If the commentaries

21. *Didymus in Demosthenem commenta,* ed. Lionel Pearson and Susan Stephens (Stuttgart: Teubner, 1983).

22. Kaster, *Guardians,* 169ff.

23. On annotated papyri, see McNamee, "Marginalia" and *Sigla*. An edition of grammatical commentaries from the papyri is forthcoming and may shed further light on this difficult issue.

24. Holtz, "Manuscrits latins."

themselves contained a text of the work under exegesis, it was usually partial, supplying only enough to indicate to a reader already familiar with the text where to find each passage as it came up. Later commentaries continued to assume that the reader had a text of the work under comment before him, or perhaps that he had committed it to memory. Furthermore, the unit of exegesis in grammatical commentaries was generally very brief, a word or at most a phrase.[25]

For the content of ancient grammatical and literary commentaries we have far more information than for their form. Both the medieval scholia and the papyri transmit abundant grammatical and literary comments on Greek and Latin literary texts. Indeed, the volume of material is so great that no real synthesis has yet been attempted.[26] The outlines of the picture, however, are clear. Paraphrase, the discussion of textual problems, and the explanation of archaic or poetic language, rare words, and abstruse references, were the stock in trade of commentaries on literary works, and formed the basis of the commentary tradition in other fields as well. Commentaries also dealt with the historical background to the texts they discussed. The commentary of Didymus on Demosthenes' *Philippics,* for example, explains at some length the background of events against which the orations were delivered. Finally, some commentaries presented allegorical interpretations, philosophical or religious reflections on the deeper meaning of the text. Such interpretations were often occasioned by problematic passages—those, for example, that seemed to represent the gods in a disrespectful light.

As the example of the scholia suggests, exegetical literature, by its very nature, lent itself to fragmentation and rearrangement. The commentary by definition is a text organized in terms of another text. Each comment is potentially autonomous, its meaning dependent in principle not on the other comments, which make up the commentary as a whole, but on its relation to the text under exegesis. So long as this relation remains clear, a single comment can be detached from its original context and can circulate independently, being reused by other commentators and taken up in a variety of contexts.

---

25. For example, Servius, who cites single words and brief phrases: see Kaster, *Guardians,* 177–93 for a number of examples, with discussion.

26. Recent years have seen some progress toward both a comprehensive collection of the evidence for commentary in antiquity, and a more sophisticated interpretation of that evidence: see especially Geerlings and Schulze, *Kommentar;* and selected articles in Most, *Editing texts,* and Gibson and Kraus, *Classical Commentary,* which is primarily concerned with modern commentaries on ancient works but also contains several articles with substantial discussions of ancient commentaries in various fields.

The nebulous boundaries of the individual commentary as a discrete literary work were further weakened by the commentary's position on the boundary between oral and written culture. This claim may seem at first glance perverse: for what text could be more "written" than one that depends on another text for its raison d'être? Yet in ancient manuscript sources the commentary was never far removed from live, oral exegesis as carried on in the grammarian's classroom or the philosophical circle. In antiquity, far more than we as products of a culture of print literacy can readily imagine, reading took place not only out loud but in groups or even in public. In such a context, the lines separating the formal written commentary from oral explanation of a text read aloud were permeable indeed. Rather than imagining the typical commentary as the product of an author—an exegete—confronting a text, alone and in silence, and producing in response a new text of his own, we must picture the commentary as a crystallization of a particular social interaction, most typically among a teacher and students. Like the traditional milieu of the school, the commentary was a conservative form, tending to dissolve away individual authorship in favor of a chorus of "authorities," whose voices became assimilated to a common, conversational tone.

Like the Greek and Latin grammatical commentaries, little of Christian biblical exegesis survives in its original form. On the Greek side, we have commentaries from the early third century attributed to a certain Hippolytus, perhaps a bishop of Rome, and a number of works by his younger contemporary, the famous Origen. After Origen, the next commentator to leave a substantial literary legacy was his follower Eusebius, who wrote on Isaiah and the Psalms in the early fourth century. The commentaries of Didymus the Blind that survive are preserved in a collection of early Byzantine papyrus codices dug up in 1946 at Toura, near Cairo. Other surviving Greek commentaries are of Jerome's own time, or later. Latin exegesis before Jerome was less developed than Greek, and is even less well preserved. In both languages, what has been lost vastly exceeds what has been preserved. Much of what we know about the exegesis of early Christian scholars comes from the *catenae,* or interpretative "chains," exegetical florilegia which, like the scholia to classical texts, present individual interpretations by a range of authorities dissociated from their original literary context.

The poor preservation of earlier Christian commentaries makes it difficult to describe the background against which Jerome worked. In many respects, early Christian commentaries probably resembled grammatical commentaries. Christian biblical exegesis grew out of the grammatical tradition. Biblical commentaries contained paraphrases of the text under exegesis, explanations of difficult words and obscure references, and other technical material. Christian commentators clearly took an interest, too, in elucidating the historical context of biblical narratives. These features were common to Greek and Latin exegesis. The place of allegorical interpretation in Christian commentary, however, was unusual, if not completely unprecedented. Allegory was a very ancient practice, but its wholesale incorporation into works in the commentary genre was probably rare outside Christian—and some Jewish—circles. This distinctive feature of biblical commentary may reflect the influence of philosophical exegesis. Although the concept of allegory found applications within the grammarian's tool kit, its most elaborate developments were among the philosophers. Origen's fascination with biblical allegory may well reflect the influence of his philosophical training at Alexandria.

The structure of Christian biblical commentaries seems to have varied widely. Thus Origen's commentaries (like Servius's commentary on Virgil) often deal with very brief units of text and do not necessarily contain a complete version of the work under exegesis. The commentary of Didymus on Zechariah, on the other hand—the only commentary that Jerome used as a source to survive intact—presents lengthy passages, of a few sentences or even a brief paragraph, and contains a complete text of Zechariah. The length of the comment, too, could range from the brief notes, little more than scholia, that Jerome attributes to Apollinaris of Laodicea, to the interpretative essays that Origen attaches to each phrase of the Song of Songs. Christian biblical commentaries could include a range of material running the gamut from simplifying paraphrase to mystical allegory. In practice, many interpreters seem to have emphasized a particular method over the others, so that already by the late third century there had emerged divergent traditions of commentary in Alexandria, where allegory ruled, and Antioch, where literal and historical exegesis dominated. Neither tradition, however, wholly excluded the characteristic approach of the other.

Commentaries were produced and used in several contexts in the lives of early Christian intellectuals and leaders. In late antiquity, there was no specifically Christian educational system. Many early Christian bishops and priests, however, had received traditional educations, including grammatical and often rhetorical and even philosophical schooling. Schooling in the narrow sense, then, was not a relevant context for Christian commentary in antiquity. But commentaries do seem to have been used in various instructional contexts, just as they reflect the influence of their authors' non-Christian education. The Christian study circles that grew up especially in Eastern cities were modeled loosely on the philosophical schools. Philosophical commentary, therefore, had an important influence on the development of Christian exegesis. Commentaries both reflected and aided the study of biblical texts by groups of Christian seekers who gathered around well-known teachers. Such teachers included Origen and Didymus, among many others.

Christian commentaries also had close links to the homily, a sermon preached on a specific, usually brief, passage of scripture. Homilies were intended to clarify for the congregation the meaning of a text used in the liturgy. Many preserved commentaries are collections of homilies. Conversely, we may imagine that a bishop or priest charged with preaching on a set text might turn to a commentary in search of material for his sermon. This direct link between the commentary and the public speech—both forms widely diffused in Greco-Roman culture, and connected to each other through their ties to the world of grammatical and rhetorical education—was unique to the Christian church and its use of scripture, and scriptural exposition, in worship.

Against this background, Jerome's commentaries are exceptional in several respects. They are massively preserved in hundreds of manuscripts, some dating as early as the fifth century.[27] In a number of respects, Jerome's commentaries are clearly modeled on Latin grammatical commentaries. Their exposition of difficult expressions, their discussion of textual variants, and their copious historical and contextual content all seem influenced by the grammatical tradition. The commentaries resemble even more closely the work of earlier Christian exegetes, particularly those who served as Jerome's principal sources. But their form and content seem to assert a new status as freestanding works, as independent of a liturgical or instructional setting as they are of the institutional authority of the bishop or the catechist. In spite of Jerome's protestations of humility, his exegetical oeuvre displays its author's intellectual ambitions on every page. As we shall see, it was Jerome's most characteristic achievement to imbue a literary form that was ostensibly humble and subordinate with tremendous authority.

THE *OPUS PROPHETALE*

Jerome's work on the Prophets addressed the central texts of the Old Testament as his contemporaries understood it. For early Christians, the Prophets and Psalms were the core of the Old Testament. Christian interpreters

---

27. The manuscripts of Jerome's works are catalogued in seven volumes in Lambert, *Bibliotheca hieronymiana*. Tome 2 deals with Jerome's commentaries, among other works.

regarded prophecy as the fundamental mode of discourse of the Hebrew scriptures. Whether directly or through allegory and typology, every page of the scriptures spoke of Jesus. The Prophets, and other works containing prophetic elements, were the basis of Christianity's claims to legitimacy against both Jews and pagans. Jesus, Christian apologists argued, was no new god. Rather, his career had been predicted in detail by Jewish prophets five or more centuries before his birth, and his relationship as Son and Logos to the time-honored God of Judaism was laid out in the Psalms as well as the Prophets.

In 392, when Jerome began his first commentaries on the prophetic books, it seems that he already planned to comment on all the Prophets. Certainly, he planned the commentaries on the Minor Prophets as a complete series, as remarks in the prefaces to several of the commentaries show. Much later, in a passage of his commentary on Ezekiel, he refers to the larger body of work of which that commentary formed a part as his *opus prophetale*. The phrase seems to reflect a unified conception of the undertaking.[28] It was an ambitious project, unequaled by any other patristic writer, whether in Greek or in Latin.[29]

In all of his commentaries on the Prophets, Jerome drew on a rich legacy of earlier exegesis. He used Origen's commentaries for his exegesis of all the Minor Prophets. For some of those texts he also used the work of Didymus of Alexandria, Hippolytus of Rome, and Apollinaris of Laodicea.[30] In his commentary on Daniel, he cites all of these writers except Didymus, along with Eusebius of Caesarea, Julius Africanus, Clement of Alexandria, and Tertullian. The great commentaries on Isaiah and Ezekiel continue to draw on Greek exegesis. The commentary on Isaiah, in particular, makes extensive use of the work of Eusebius.[31] The last work he wrote, the commentary on Jeremiah, takes a harsher attitude toward the Greek exegetical tradition, yet shows the influence of Origen and his successors nonetheless. Alongside the Greek sources Jerome collected in his library, he had access to Jewish interpretation through his teachers at Bethlehem. The extent of what he learned from his Jewish informants is difficult to specify but seems to have

---

28. *Comm. in Hiezech.* 6, pref. 11.

29. Other patristic treatments of the prophets were far less exhaustive that Jerome's. Even Origen's exegesis on the Prophets omitted the last third of Hosea and the last two-thirds of Zechariah; on Jeremiah, he left only homilies.

30. Didymus: Hosea and Zechariah; Hippolytus: Zechariah; Apollinaris: Hosea and Malachi.

31. Jay, *Exégèse*, 57–58.

been considerable.[32] He supplemented this material with historical information from Josephus and other Greek sources, both Jewish and Christian, and with the biblical philology that his Greek predecessors had developed, in part thanks to their own colloquies with learned Jews.[33]

Jerome worked on the commentaries on the Prophets, alongside numerous other projects, for almost thirty years.[34] He began work in 393, with commentaries on Nahum, Micah, Zephaniah, Haggai, and Habbakuk. He continued his work in the late spring of 397, commenting on Jonah and Obadiah. The series on the twelve Minor Prophets was completed only in 406. Over the course of several months, interrupted by recurrent illness, he wrote on Zechariah, Malachi, Hosea, Joel, and Amos, in that order.[35] In the following year, 407, he wrote the commentary on Daniel, which he had promised to Paulinus of Nola some years previously.[36] Finally, in 408, Jerome turned to the great task of commenting on the three Major Prophets. In that year, he began his commentary on Isaiah, finished in 410.[37] The commentary on Ezekiel, started on the heels of the completion of the work on Isaiah, was not finished until 414, its writing interrupted by the shock of the sack of Rome, by illness, and by barbarian attacks in Palestine.[38] In the last years of his life, Jerome turned to the prophet Jeremiah. His commentary on this book, begun perhaps as early as 414, was left unfinished when he died in 419 or 420, aged over seventy.[39] He had fallen just short of completing a full exegetical treatment of the entire prophetic canon.

The methodology and organization of Jerome's commentaries on the

---

32. See chapter 4 below; Kamesar, *Jerome;* Kedar, "Jewish Traditions" and "Vulgate"; Newman, "Jerome and the Jews."

33. On the combination of the *recentiores* and rabbinic materials, see Kamesar, *Jerome,* 81–82 et passim.

34. Jerome died in either 419 or 420: Cavallera, *Saint Jérôme,* 2 : 63; Kelly, *Jerome,* 331–32.

35. The primary data supporting this chronology appear in the prefaces to the commentaries on Jonah and Amos. See the discussion of Cavallera, *Saint Jérôme,* 29–30, 44, 51–52, for the identification of the evidence and its basic significance. His dates are about six to twelve months earlier than those given in the text. Nautin, "Études de chronologie IV," 257, 77, 79, placing the chronology in a new framework, dates the first four commentaries to the first three months of 393, and the commentaries on Jonah and Obadiah to shortly after Easter (April 5) 397, when Jerome was reconciled with Rufinus.

36. For dating, see Cavallera, *Saint Jérôme,* 2 : 52.

37. For dating, see Cavallera, *Saint Jérôme,* 2 : 52.

38. For dating, see Cavallera, *Saint Jérôme,* 2 : 52–53.

39. For dating, see Cavallera, *Saint Jérôme,* 2 : 55–56.

Prophets is largely consistent throughout, following a schema that will be described in detail below. There were variations within the great oeuvre, however, which deserve to be noted at the outset. The organization of the commentaries on the Minor Prophets, which Jerome wrote first, is the most complex. In the narrower compass of these commentaries, he was able to develop the full implications of his methodological principles. The same basic approach was to govern his later, far longer commentaries as well. But there, the volume of material under exegesis apparently led him to limit the length of his works by simplifying the way he presented his material. The structure of the commentaries on the Minor Prophets, therefore, gives the clearest view of the intellectual framework that shapes all but one of the commentaries.

The commentary on Daniel of 407 takes an approach different from that of all the other commentaries on the Prophets. Jerome states explicitly that he chose to limit the material he discussed because he feared that otherwise his commentary would be too long.[40] He cites and discusses only particularly difficult or noteworthy passages. Rather than quoting each passage in its entirety, he gives only enough of the text to make clear the topic of each comment, so that the commentary does not present a full text of the biblical book under exegesis. The new approach did not find favor with his readers. In the preface to book 11 of his work on Isaiah, written perhaps in 409, Jerome complains that the new format of his commentary on Daniel had evoked negative reactions.[41] He did not return to it.

The commentary on Isaiah, and the work on Ezekiel that succeeded it, were undertakings of an entirely new order by comparison with Jerome's earlier exegetical writings. The commentary on Isaiah alone is as long as all twelve of the commentaries on the Minor Prophets put together. In the prefaces to each book of these two great commentaries, Jerome displays a constant, explicit concern for the length, arrangement, and architecture of his work. He tries to keep related material together, and to divide the individual books of the commentaries at points that reflect the internal divisions of the text under exegesis. Still, as his frequent apologies for awkward divisions of the material between books reveal, the *volumen*, or book, was not merely a

---

40. Pref. to the *Comm. in Dan.* 81: *non iuxta consuetudinem nostram proponentes omnia et omnia disserentes ut in duodecim prophetis fecimus, sed breuiter et per interualla ea tantum quae obscura sunt explanantes, ne librorum innumerabilium magnitudo lectori fastidium faciat.*

41. *Difficile, immo impossibile est placere omnibus; nec tanta uultuum quanta sententiarum diuersitas est. In explanatione duodecim prophetarum longior quibusdam uisus sum quam oportuit, et ob hanc causam in commentariolis Danihelis breuitati studui praeter ultimam et penultimam uisionem, in quibus me necesse fuit pro obscuritatis magnitudinem sermonem tendere (Comm. in Esaiam 11, pref.)*

notional unit of composition. Instead, its dimensions seem to have imposed on him a real sense of constraint in the handling of his material.[42]

Jerome repeatedly mentions the disruptions that his exegetical labors suffered because of illness, political and military disturbances, and the influx of Latin refugees that Palestine and the holy places received after the sack of Rome in 410.[43] His complaints of the harassed existence he led as host to the illustrious displaced persons who filled the East in the decade after that disaster, and of the physical sufferings that were exacerbated by his ascetic regime, contain an element of self-promotion. Yet these passages convey not only the self-importance of a monk whose reputation spanned the Mediterranean world, but also a profound awareness of mortality. Shaken by the deaths of Paula in 404 and of Pammachius and Marcella at Rome six years later, Jerome must have felt a renewed pressure to complete his work without delay.[44] As a result, it seems, the complexity of the final, great commentaries was reduced.

Jerome's choice of the Minor Prophets as the focus of his first serious, extended exegetical work was a piece of calculated audacity. In this corpus, he confronted texts and problems of the first importance for contemporary Christianity within a restricted literary compass. The Minor Prophets include some of the most rebarbative materials in the biblical canon. They were written over a period of several centuries. Amos, Micah, and Hosea preached in the eighth century BCE, while portions of Zechariah may date to the Hellenistic period, as late as the second century BCE.[45] Many of the Minor Prophets were substantially revised and expanded over the centuries. The language, content, and concerns of the texts therefore vary widely, both among different prophets and within individual books. Almost all of the texts present serious interpretative problems. Hosea, to take a single example, is among the most corrupt texts in the Hebrew corpus.[46] Obscure and

---

42. See the prefaces to books 2, 3, 6, 8, 9, and 10. The preface to book 4 contains a particularly revealing passage: *Inaequales dictamus libros et pro diuersitate uisionum ac sensuum alius contrahitur, alius extenditur. Itaque finito tertio uolumine transimus ad quartum, qui tertia mensura uersuum priore minor est, praesertim cum quintus, quem huic libro subiecimus, historicae explanationis sit et paene duplicem numerum habeat.*

43. On the aftermath of the sack of Rome, see Cavallera, *Saint Jérôme*, 1:314–22; Kelly, *Jerome*, 296–308.

44. On the death of Paula, see Cavallera, *Saint Jérôme*, 1:292–94; Kelly, *Jerome*, 273–82. On the deaths of Pammachius and Marcella, see Cavallera, *Saint Jérôme*, 1:314–22; Kelly, *Jerome*, 296–308.

45. Blenkinsopp, *History of Prophecy*.

46. Andersen and Freedman, *Hosea*.

difficult as they are, these texts carried a disproportionate weight in early Christian messianic piety and anti-Jewish apologetics. The New Testament writers, especially Matthew and Paul, drew from them numerous proof-texts in support of their claims about Jesus. The critique of Israel and Judah advanced by prophets like Hosea, Amos, and Micah was a key element in early Christian anti-Jewish polemic.

Through these twelve texts—short but significant, and impressively obscure—Jerome made a direct assault on the core issues of fourth-century Christian appropriation of the Hebrew scriptures, while taking the opportunity for an impressive display of erudition. As he himself writes in his commentary on Hosea, composed in 406 as part of the final installment of the work on the Minor Prophets,

> When he says, "Who is wise, and will understand this? and understanding it, will know it?" he points to the obscurity of the book and how difficult it is to understand. But if he himself who wrote it confessed that it was difficult, if not impossible, to interpret, then what can we do, who with bleary eyes darkened by the filth of our sins, cannot look upon the most brilliant radiance of the sun, except to say with the scripture, "Oh, how deep are the riches of the wisdom and the knowledge of God! How inscrutable are his judgments, and unsearchable his ways!" (Rom. 11.33) [47]

These were Jerome's concluding words to this first stage of his work on the prophets, an undertaking that spanned the prime of his life, from the age of forty-six to almost sixty. Ostensibly a lament over the insufficiency of his own work, the passage can also be read in a more self-congratulatory light. In fact, Jerome had accomplished a great deal in providing his readers with new resources for understanding this difficult text, and the eleven that had preceded it. No doubt he realized as much.

The intellectual seriousness of Jerome's commentaries on the Prophets is reflected in their careful organization. In all of the commentaries, the comment is divided into two sections. First, Jerome discusses the literal and historical sense of the passage under exegesis, then its allegorical or spiritual meaning. He describes this procedure explicitly, for example in the commentary on Zephaniah of 393: "We must, therefore, in accordance with our

---

47. *Comm. in Osee* 3.14.10: *Quando dicit, "Quis sapiens et intelleget haec? intellegens et cognoscet ea?" obscuritatem uoluminis et difficultatem explanationis ostendet. Si autem ipse qui scripsit, uel difficile, uel impossibile confitetur; quid nos facere possumus, qui lippientibus oculis et peccatorum sordibus obscuratis, clarissimum iubar solis non possumus intueri, nisi dicere illud quod scriptum est: "O profundum diuitiarum sapientiae et scientiae Dei! Quam inscrutabile sunt iudicia eius et inuestigabiles uiae eius!"*

usual custom, first explain the historical sense, and only after that discuss higher things."[48] As this statement implies, the order of the two interpretations is an integral element in their presentation. The elucidation of the literal and historical sense provides the necessary preconditions for allegorical interpretation. The nature of the material under exegesis determines the balance between the two components. When the literal meaning of the passage seems obvious, Jerome limits his discussion to a brief paraphrase. Conversely, if an allegorical interpretation given in one of his sources fails to take account of the context, or interprets the passage in a sense totally at odds with its literal meaning, he may give it very short shrift indeed. But for many passages he applies the full panoply of exegetical strategies: first the elucidation of the literal and historical senses, then an allegorical interpretation.[49]

Unlike many of his Christian predecessors, Jerome devotes equal attention to the literal and allegorical senses of scripture. However, he associates them with separate exegetical traditions, whose status is markedly different. He brings together the literal and historical senses — *iuxta litteram* or *iuxta historiam* — under the common rubric of the interpretation *iuxta Hebraeos,* "according to the Hebrews," explicitly attributing the material adduced in the first part of his comment to Jewish sources. The allegorical sense — *iuxta allegoriam, iuxta tropologiam,* or simply *spiritaliter* — he credits to his Christian predecessors, whom he refers to as *nostri,* "ours."

The relation between the two primary senses of scripture was for Jerome a complex one. From one point of view, the spiritual sense was heavily privileged. Whereas the historical and literal meanings, associated with the Jews, had only a limited claim to truth, the allegorical or spiritual sense, associated with the Church, the true Israel, was the locus of salvation. Thus in expounding a verse of Hosea, Jerome can casually assert that "the salvation of Israel and their return to God, and their redemption from captivity, are not to be interpreted carnally, as the Jews think, but spiritually, as is most truly acknowledged."[50]

Jerome uses a variety of metaphors to refer to the historical sense, and to Jewish biblical interpretation in general, in their relation to Christian alle-

---

48. *Comm. in Sophoniam* 1:2–3, 84–86: *Debemus ergo, consuetudinem nostram sequentes, primum historiam texere, et postea de sublimioribus disputare.*

49. My own examination of the commentaries on the Minor Prophets confirms and further specifies the findings of Jay, *Exégèse.*

50. *Comm. in Osee* 3.14.5–9: *salutem Israelis et reuersionis ad Deum, et de captiuitate redemptionem, non carnaliter accipere, ut Iudaei putant, sed spiritaliter, ut uerissime comprobantur.*

gory. In a relatively neutral metaphor, he often describes the historical sense as a "staircase" leading up to the heights of spiritual interpretation: "You often begged me violently to interpret the historical sense for you, like steps of a kind, a sort of staircase leading upward," he writes to one of his dedicatees.[51] But the metaphor of the staircase is not without negative overtones. The Jews, while keepers of the historical sense, were also limited by it, so that they remained earthbound, unable to ascend the steps that they themselves provided.

Other metaphors, drawn from Paul's language in 2 Corinthians, make a sharper distinction. In 2 Corinthians 3:6, Paul contrasts letter and spirit in the sharpest possible terms: "the letter kills, but the Spirit gives life." Jerome repeatedly cites or echoes this scriptural tag.[52] A further text from the same passage of 2 Corinthians provided another key metaphor for the limitations of Jewish interpretation. In 2 Corinthians 3:12-15, Paul describes the "veil" that "lies over the minds" of those who hear the reading of the Old Covenant. For Jerome, as for most Christian interpreters of his day and since, this passage meant that the Jews were incapable of correctly interpreting their own scriptures, for they were blind to the spiritual truth of the Gospel hidden within them. Thus Jerome's vocabulary of abuse for Jewish exegetes centers on language of blindness, as well as on the accusation that the Jews are both spiritually dead, and themselves murderers, the killers of Christ and of spiritual truth. Christian readers, in accordance with the contrast Paul draws in 2 Corinthians, participate in spirit, in freedom, and in life, and regard the truth "with unveiled faces" (2 Cor 3.18).[53]

But the authority of the literal and historical senses, and of the exegetical approach that Jerome brought together under the rubric of the interpretation *iuxta Hebraeos,* was far greater than the abusive language he uses toward the Jews would lead one to believe. In some sense the spiritual interpretation remained for Jerome the ultimate goal of exegesis. Yet to acknowledge its superiority, to recognize it as "the spirit that gives life" over against "the letter that kills," is to appreciate only one side of the situation. For the historical sense retained great authority. Thus Jerome describes his exegetical

---

51. Prol. to *Comm. in Abacuc: Illud quoque disce—quia semel a me uiolenter exigis, ut quasi gradus quosdam, et scalas ad altiora nitenti, historiam tibi interpreter—prophetiam esse contra Babylonem.* See also *Comm. in Zach.* 1.4.54.

52. For example, there are nine references in the commentaries on the Minor Prophets.

53. What Paul himself meant by this passage is somewhat obscure, but it probably bore little resemblance to traditional Christian interpretations such as Jerome's: see Gaston, *Paul and the Torah,* 151–68. Georgi, *Opponents,* argues that Paul actually had his more charismatic rivals for leadership over the Corinthian congregation in mind, here as in other passages of 2 Corinthians.

method as in essence a combination of the two disparate traditions: "I have united the history of the Hebrews with the tropology of our own [interpreters], so that I might build upon rock and not upon sand, and thus lay a stable foundation."[54] Jerome here applies to the learning of the Hebrews the dominical parable, found in Matthew and Luke (Mt. 7:24-27 = Lk. 6:47-49), of the houses built on rock and on sand. The interpretation founded upon the *historia Hebraeorum* is like the house built on rock, which does not fall despite the storm. By implication, other exegetes, who "build on sand" because they do not have access to the *Hebraica veritas,* are condemned to futility.[55]

Not only did the historical sense precede allegorical interpretation; it also constrained it. Only when the literal meaning, literary context, and historical reference of a text had been clarified did it become available for higher exegesis. Moreover, when a proposed allegorical reading required a distortion of the literal or historical sense, that interpretation was to be rejected. For example, in the commentary on Hosea, Jerome rejects a sustained exegetical theme from one of his sources because it equates the historical figure of the king of Assyria with Christ, a connection that he finds inappropriate. Thus in his comment on Hosea 5:13, he gives the text of the relevant passage as follows in his translation *iuxta Hebraeos,* "and Ephraim went off to Ashur and sent to the king, the avenger"; and, in a Latin version of the Septuagint, "and Ephraim went off to the Assyrians, and sent emissaries to king Iarib." He then remarks, "I read in the commentaries of a certain writer that 'king Iarib' was to be interpreted as Christ." He paraphrases an allegorical interpretation based on this equation, then concludes, "So he said, but we interpret the king who is an avenger in a negative sense."[56]

The comment on Hosea 10:6a, which reads in Jerome's translation, "Even if he is carried down into Assyria, a gift for the king, the avenger,"[57] expands on the same problem:

> A certain writer, in his commentary on a preceding passage and on this one, claimed that the king Iarib, that is, the avenger, ought to be understood as

54. *Comm. in Zach.* prol. 37-39: *historiae Hebraeorum tropologiam nostrorum miscui, ut aedificarem super petram et non super arenam, ac stabile iacerem fundamentum.*

55. I am grateful to Peter Brown for pointing out Jerome's allusion to the New Testament here.

56. *Comm. in Osee* 2.5.13, ll.355ff.: (IH) *et abiit Ephraim ad Assur et misit ad regem ultorem . . .* LXX: *et abiit Ephraim ad Assyrios, et misit legatos ad regem Iarib . . . Legi in cuiusdam commentariis regem Iarib Christum interpretari* [he gives an allegorical reading that proceeds from this interpretation] *. . . Haec ille dixerit, nos in malam partem regem interpretemur ultorem.*

57. Hosea 10:6a (Vulg.): *Siquidem et ipse in Assur delatus est, munus regi ultori.*

Christ. We find this entirely unsatisfactory. For it is impious that what is interpreted according to the historical sense as a reference to the king of Assyria should be referred tropologically to Christ.[58]

The operative principle had already been articulated in the commentary on Habbakuk written in 393. There, Jerome had contrasted the liberty of allegorical reading with the strict attention to facts required by the historical sense:

> The historical sense is narrow, and it cannot leave its course. The tropological sense is free, and yet it is circumscribed by these laws, that it must be loyal to the meaning and to the context of the words, and that things strongly opposed to each other must not be improperly joined together.[59]

The interpretation of a phrase used by Hosea to denote the king of Assyria to refer to Christ provides a clear example of the third problem, "the improper joining together" of "things strongly opposed to each other." The historical reference of the text constrains its range of meaning on the spiritual level as well, restricting the liberty of the allegorical imagination. The *historia Hebraeorum*, therefore, plays a role of immense importance both in legitimating Jerome's exegesis, and in differentiating it from that of his competitors, past and present.

For Jerome's contemporaries, his emphasis on the version *iuxta Hebraeos* as the basis for his literal and historical interpretation had the potential to seem perverse. As he himself remarks in his commentary on Habbakuk, while interpreting a difficult passage where his two base texts differ significantly, "I know that the Hebrew diverges greatly from what has just been said; but what am I to do, who am assigned the task of interpreting at the same time both the Hebrew itself, and the scriptures as they are known throughout the world?"[60] The Septuagint text was authoritative; where the Hebrew diverged from it, Jerome had to defend his attention to it.

---

58. *Comm. in Osee* 3.10.5–6, ll. 211-15: *Quidam et supra et in praesenti loco in commentariis suis scriptum reliquit, regem Iarib, id est ultorem, Christum intellegendum. Quod nobis omnino displicet. Impium enim est quod iuxta historiam intellegetur de rege Assyrio, iuxta tropologiam ad Christum refert.*

59. *Comm. in Abacuc* 1.1.6–11, ll. 310-14: *Historia stricta est, et euagandi non habet facultatem. Tropologia libera, et his tantum legibus circumscripta, ut pietatem sequatur intellegentiae, sermonisque contextum nec in rebus multum inter se contrariis uiolenta sit copulandis.*

60. *Comm. in Abacuc* 2.3.14–16: *Scio multum Hebraicum ab his quae dicta sunt, discrepare; sed facere quid possum, cui semel propositum est et ipsum Hebraicum, et uulgatas in toto orbe scripturas interpretari?*

The division of the comment into historical and allegorical components, and their basic relation to each other, is a feature of all of Jerome's commentaries on the Prophets. Pierre Jay has studied this division in detail for the commentary on Isaiah.[61] The organization of the early commentaries on the Minor Prophets, however, presents a further level of complexity. The distinctive feature of that organization is the presentation of the lemma—the biblical text under discussion—in two complete versions. Jerome cites the text in his own translation *iuxta Hebraeos,* and again in a Latin version of Origen's recension of the Septuagint. Through this double lemma, each of his commentaries presents, at least in principle, two complete texts of each prophetic book.[62]

The complex organization of the commentaries on the Minor Prophets reveals the intellectual framework that underlies Jerome's exegetical approach as a whole. In these commentaries, Jerome deploys all of the many resources at his command, both textual and interpretative, according to a clear, two-

---

61. Jay, *Exégèse.*

62. In practice, Jerome often deviates from the ideal of the double lemma: when the Septuagint corresponds exactly to the Hebrew, he usually omits it, simply noting *LXX similiter.* In the commentaries on Nahum, Zephaniah, Habbakuk, and Micah (393), Jerome uses the double lemma fairly consistently, even when the two texts are almost identical. In the commentary on Haggai (393), he gives only a single text, after the MT, for most lemmata; he gives a double lemma for only about one-third of the prophet. The commentaries on Obadiah and Jonah (397) use the double lemma almost throughout (all lemmata for Obadiah, all but 6 for Jonah). The commentaries on Zechariah, Malachi, Hosea, Joel, and Amos (406) all give a double lemma consistently. The later commentaries use different approaches to the citation of the biblical text: in the commentary on Daniel, Jerome cites the text of Daniel only after his translation from the Semitic original. Furthermore, he cites only those passages that he thinks worthy of serious treatment, thus omitting most of the text of the prophet. In his last three commentaries, which deal with the lengthy books of Isaiah, Ezekiel, and Jeremiah, Jerome returned to a version of his practice in the commentaries on the Minor Prophets. All of these commentaries contain at least one complete text of the work under exegesis. Within the first two, there are significant sections, even entire books, that maintain the earlier format of the double lemma. Large parts of these works, however, and the entire commentary on Jeremiah, present only a single lemma. This lemma, like the lemma of the commentary on Daniel, is based on Jerome's own translations from the Hebrew. The commentary on Isaiah is particularly interesting. For most of the portion of the commentary composed in 408-10, Jerome gives a lemma based on the translation *iuxta Hebraeos* but with some significant variations (Jay, *Exégèse,* 89-126; at 111-13, Jay details his citation of a lemma after the Septuagint). For the commentary on the ten visions written for Amabilis in 398, contemporary with the commentaries on the Minor Prophets, Jerome gives *only* a lemma *iuxta Hebraeos* (Jay, *Exégèse,* 111). This latter observation is highly significant, for the exegesis of this earlier commentary was explicitly limited to the historical sense. The commentary on Ezekiel gives a single lemma for most passages, with the exception of book 5, which gives a double lemma throughout. The commentary on Jeremiah gives only a lemma *iuxta Hebraeos.*

fold division. He presents, at least in theory, a double commentary. Two versions of the text under exegesis, two methods of interpretation, and two exegetical traditions appear in parallel. In fact, many passages receive an abbreviated treatment. Yet the theoretical framework remains constant despite the flexibility with which it is applied.

In his deployment of his two texts and two interpretative methods, Jerome follows a regular pattern. He gives first the version *iuxta Hebraeos,* then the translation from the Septuagint. The comment then opens with a discussion of the literal and historical senses, which is based on the text *iuxta Hebraeos.* Only then does it move on to allegorical interpretation, which is almost always based on the Septuagint. Signposts mark the transitions: Jerome signals his reader, as in the passage from the commentary on Hosea quoted above, that he has completed his discussion of the sense *iuxta Hebraeos,* and will proceed to discuss the spiritual sense.

Jerome rarely offers an explicit rationale for this arrangement. On a few occasions he entertains, only to reject, the possibility of two complete parallel commentaries, which would present a double interpretation for each of his two lemmata. In the commentary on Hosea, for example, he writes: "The Hebrew and the Septuagint translation disagree greatly with each other. We will attempt therefore to give a historical interpretation of the Hebrew, and an anagogical interpretation of the Septuagint." Then, after a fairly lengthy historical interpretation of the passage, he continues:

> Let us pass on to the spiritual sense, at least according to the Septuagint translation, since if we were to undertake to interpret the two versions both according to the historical sense and according to the *anagogē,* we would extend the size of the book.[63]

And again, in the commentary on Amos:

> Having said this according to the Hebrew, let us pass on to the Septuagint translators, and what seems fitting to us in each instance according to the *anagogē* we will briefly set forth; for if we undertook to speak of each version according to each sense, the size of the books would suffer.[64]

---

63. *Comm. in Osee* 3.11.3–4: *Multum inter se Hebraicum et Septuaginta interpretum editio dissonant. Temptemus igitur iuxta Hebraeos historiam, iuxta LXX ἀναγωγὴν texere.* [He gives a historical interpretation of the passage at some length] *Transeamus ad intellegentiam spiritalem, iuxta Septuaginta dumtaxat interpretes; ne si utrumque et secundum historiam, et secundum ἀναγωγὴν uoluerimus exponere, tendamus libri magnitudinem.*

64. *Comm. in Amos* 2.4.4–6: *Haec iuxta Hebraicum diximus, transeamus ad LXX interpretes, et quid nobis iuxta anagogen uideatur in singulis, breuiter disseramus; neque enim si in utraque editione utrumque dicere uoluerimus, librorum patitur magnitudo.*

The sole reason Jerome gives in these passages for presenting only one interpretation for each text is that any other procedure would make his commentary too long. The notion of a complete double commentary is held forth as in some sense an ideal: if he had infinite space and time, presumably Jerome would have presented a full double commentary.

Although Jerome's concern for concision was real, as an explanation for the association of the two texts with their corresponding senses it is unsatisfactory. For Jerome uniformly connects the text *iuxta Hebraeos* with the historical sense, and the Septuagint with the allegorical sense. Something more than the desire for brevity must have determined this fixed association of text with interpretative tradition. On one level, the connection of each of the texts cited with a particular mode of interpretation simply reflected the sources Jerome used. His Jewish sources, which provided him with much of the material he used in his literal and historical interpretation, based their exegesis on the Hebrew text. Many of the Greek writers whose commentaries he mined for their allegorical interpretations commented exclusively on the Septuagint Greek. But other Greek exegetes, especially Origen and Eusebius, cited the *recentiores* regularly and gave elaborate allegorical interpretations of these versions, which were based on a Hebrew text similar to Jerome's. Indeed, we learn from Jerome himself that Origen's work on the Song of Songs provided a complete commentary not only on the Septuagint but also on the versions of Aquila and Symmachus.[65] Origen's commentary is not preserved in its original form, so we cannot be certain that Jerome's description is truthful. But the surviving commentary of Eusebius on Isaiah supports his claim: its numerous allegorical readings based on words and phrases from the *recentiores* may have paralleled Origen's own exegesis. Furthermore, Eusebius uses the additional versions primarily as a source of interesting variant readings that expand the possibilities for allegorical interpretation. His commentary, therefore, could have provided useful material for Jerome's own work on Isaiah, had Jerome wished to present allegorical interpretations of his translation from the Hebrew. Mere subservience to his sources cannot account for Jerome's rigid linking of the Hebrew text with the historical and literal senses, and of the Septuagint translation that was authoritative in the church with the spiritual sense. Nor can it account for

---

65. *Praef. in Origenis hom. II in Cant.* p. 26, l. 2: *Origenes, cum in ceteris libris omnes uicerit, in cantico canticorum ipse se uicit. nam decem uoluminibus explicitis, quae ad uiginti usque uersuum milia paene perueniunt, primum Septuaginta interpretes, deinde Aquilam, Symmachum, Theodotionem et ad extremum quintam editionem, quam in actio litore inuenisse se scribit, ita magnifice aperteque disseruit.*

the consistent language that he uses to represent base text and interpretation as intrinsically connected.

In a striking passage from the commentary on Nahum, Jerome breaks with his usual practice, providing a historical explanation of the text *iuxta Hebraeos*, and two quite different allegorical interpretations, one of the text *iuxta Hebraeos* and one of the Septuagint. The texts under exegesis differ sharply. Jerome's version of the Hebrew reads: "Celebrate, Judah, your festivals, and fufill your vows, since he did not also add to you that Belial should pass through you, so that the whole would perish." Having cited this text, he remarks, "I will put off the translation of the Seventy just a bit, since in this chapter also there is a disordered variety of interpretation in their version. Therefore when I have briefly expounded the historical sense, I will turn my speech to their edition." He gives a historical explanation that cites Chronicles for the interpretation of Belial as Sennacherib, whose death spared beseiged Jerusalem from destruction. But then he goes on to interpret the same text allegorically, "So much, then, for the literal sense. In other wise it is said, according to the *anagogē*, concerning the church . . . "

Finally, he cites the text after the Septuagint: "Celebrate, Judah, your festivals, fulfill your vows, since no longer do they oppose you any longer so that they pass into old age, it is completed, it is fulfilled; it arises blowing into your face, destroying with tribulation." He interprets this rather different version allegorically, but not historically: "As I recently said, according to the variety of the translation the chapter itself takes on an entirely different meaning, and it cannot be reconciled with the meaning of the chapter according to the translation of the Hebrew. Therefore what has now been said, is interpreted as follows: O ye of the church . . . "

Though both of the allegorical interpretations that Jerome proposes here read the "Judah" addressed in the passage as the church, they are strikingly different. The first interpretation reads the injunction to "celebrate and fulfill your vows" as regarding thanksgiving after persecution, with specific reference to the persecuting emperors Valerian, Diocletian, and Maximian. The second applies the entire prophecy to the end of time, when Christ would save his people from destruction.[66] This passage shows that Jerome

---

66. The crucial part of the Latin text (*Comm. in Nahum* 1.1.15) reads: (IH) *Ecce super montes pedes euangelizantes et annuntiantis pacem. Celebra, Iuda, festiuitates tuas, et redde uota tua, quia non adiciet ultra ut pertranseat in te Belial, uniuersus interiit. Paulisper LXX interpretes differam, quia et ipsa capitula apud eos interpretationis uarietate confusa sunt. Cumque historiam breuiter exposuero, editionem eorum meo eloquio temperabo.* . . . *Et hoc quidem iuxta litteram. Ceterum secundum anagwghn dicitur ad Ecclesiam* . . . *LXX: Celebra, Iuda festiuitates tuas, redde uota tua, quia nequaquam*

did not lack the resources to present an allegorical interpretation of his own translation *iuxta Hebraeos*—whether he found them in the works of other exegetes, who had perhaps based their own comments on the literal translation of Aquila, or created them himself. That he gave such an interpretation very rarely is striking evidence that his association of each mode of interpretation exclusively with one translation was intentional, not a mere by-product of the limitations of his sources.

By linking text and interpretation as he did in his early commentaries on the Minor Prophets, Jerome created for himself a unique position of exegetical authority—one that he never had to assert explicitly. The reader who accepted his translation *iuxta Hebraeos* as a more authentic version of the biblical text than the Septuagint was drawn into a paradoxical situation. For by rigidly and artificially dividing into two separate strands the traditions of Jewish and Christian biblical interpretation and criticism that he had inherited, Jerome inseparably linked the most authoritative biblical *text* with a tradition of interpretation that was essential, yet insufficient. At the same time, the authoritative interpretative tradition transmitted by Origen and his Greek successors was tied to a text that could not be regarded as reliable. This was more than a mere realization of scholarly reality: it was a carefully fashioned construct. It created for Jerome an implicit but unchallengeable authority as arbiter of biblical truth. The foundation of this entire edifice was the concept of the *Hebraica veritas*.

THE *HEBRAICA VERITAS* AND THE AUTHORITY OF THE CRITIC

The literal sense, though it was not the capstone of Jerome's biblical exegesis, played a central role in the construction of his authority as an interpreter. It was the primary locus of his claim to provide something that his Latin audiences could not obtain elsewhere. The most important element of the interpretation *iuxta litteram* was the establishment of an accurate text of the passage under exegesis. Jerome's text-critical method built on Origen's scholarship, but went beyond anything his Christian predecessors had at-

---

apponent ultra ut pertranseant in uetustatem, completum est, consummatum est; ascendit insufflans in faciem tuam, eruens de tribulatione. Semel dixi, iuxta interpretationis uarietatem capitula quoque ipsa aliter definiri, et non posse cum capitulis sensum Hebraicae interpretationis conuenire. Itaque quod nunc dicitur, huiuscemodi est: O Ecclesiastice (Jerome then gives a figural reading, which proceeds from a paraphrase of the passage).

tempted. It both depended upon and served to support his representation of the *Hebraica veritas* as the font of ultimate authority in biblical study. For Jerome, the Hebrew text held absolute primacy. Though he could not dismiss the Septuagint entirely, he never considered it an independent textual authority, much less allowed it to compete with the Hebrew.[67] He virtually never admits doubt as to the reliability of his Hebrew text. Instead, the role of textual criticism in the commentaries is to defend his translation from the Hebrew where it differs from the Septuagint. The textual difficulties he discusses in the commentaries on the Prophets are almost all cases of divergence between the Hebrew and the Septuagint versions. He treats the Hebrew text as the norm from which the Septuagint deviated, explaining variation between the Hebrew and the Septuagint in terms of misreadings or misinterpretations on the part of the Greek translators.

Numerous scholars, wishing to praise Jerome as an objective and scientific philologist, have written as though the value that he placed upon the Hebrew text simply reflected his appreciation of the facts. This is not strictly true. For the notion of error in translation, central to Jerome's biblical philology, plays little part in modern explanations of the differences between the Masoretic Hebrew text—essentially, the Hebrew text that Jerome knew at the turn of the fifth century—and that used in producing the Septuagint. Instead, as we saw in the previous chapter, modern scholarship posits that the Greek translators had before them a Hebrew text different from that transmitted by the Masoretes. Early diversity and later errors of transmission in the Hebrew textual tradition generated textual variety. The Masoretes, however, succeeded in imposing a single text and stamping out all others; these other texts are now represented only in the Hebrew scrolls from the Judean desert and in the ancient translations, which were transmitted by Christians. Jerome's assignment of primary authority to the Hebrew text, therefore, requires justification. It cannot simply be regarded as the result of scientific inference, an astute recognition of preexisting reality. Even in its application to the Hebrew text itself, Jerome's concept of the *Hebraica veritas* was carefully constructed to serve his larger purpose.

Closer examination of Jerome's handling of a complex textual problem reveals both the strengths and the limitations of his approach. Though Jerome confronted variance between the Septuagint and the Hebrew throughout his work on the Minor Prophets, Hosea presented extraordinary challenges. The commentary on that book is rich in discussions of textual difficulty. In

---

67. At *Comm. in Nahum* 1.14, Jerome speaks as though he would prefer not to exegete the Septuagint at all.

his comment on Hosea 9 : 11–13, Jerome deploys several of his standard text-critical tactics.[68] First, he cites the text as follows:

> [*Iuxta Hebraeos:*] Ephraim has flown away like a bird; their glory is from the birth and from the womb and from the conception. For even if they had nourished their sons, I would make them without progeny among men. But woe unto them, since I have withdrawn from them. Ephraim, as I saw, was Tyre founded in beauty; and Ephraim led out their sons to the one who slew them. LXX: Ephraim has flown away like a bird; their glory is in the birth and in the birth-givings and the conception; since even if they had nourished their sons, they would have been without sons among men, since also woe is unto them; my flesh out of them. Ephraim, as I saw, provided his sons unto captivity; and Ephraim, may he lead out his sons to slaughter. The versions differ greatly in this place.[69]

In addressing the problems these differences raise, he applies a variety of resources and tactics. His first recourse, here as in most cases, is to adduce the versions assembled by Origen in the Hexapla, those of Theodotion, Aquila, and Symmachus. For the first variant discussed here, he cites only Theodotion's version, which agrees with that of the Septuagint against the Hebrew. Jerome explains the divergence of the two Greek versions from the Hebrew as follows:

> For in that place, where we said, *woe unto them since I have withdrawn from them,* the Septuagint and Theodotion have translated, *woe to them, my flesh out of them,* seeking the reason why there should be such a difference, it seemed to me to arise from the following: *my flesh,* in the Hebrew language is said basari; but if instead we were to say, *my withdrawal,* or my turning aside, it would be said basori. The Septuagint therefore, and Theodotion, in place of that which means *my withdrawal* and *my turning aside,* translated *my flesh.*[70]

68. The textual difficulties presented by this passage are so great that the Anchor Bible commentators even have recourse to Jerome's evidence in their attempt to grapple with the text. Their comment is worth quoting to show exactly how little can be concluded with certainty here. "The most serious problem is v. 11aB, which is unintelligible or at least ungrammatical—literally, 'an adversary and around the land.' It requires more drastic emendation to read yesobeb. The LXX attests the preposition, but it levels to 'your land' and reads sr as 'Tyre,' which is often defective" (Andersen and Freedman, *Amos*, 408).

69. *Comm. in Osee* 2.9.11–13: *Ephraim quasi auis auolauit; gloria eorum a partu et ab utero et a conceptu. Quod et si enutrierint filios suos, absque liberis eos faciam in hominibus. Sed et uae eis cum recessero ab eis. Ephraim, ut uidi, Tyrus erat fundata in pulchritudine; et Ephraim educet ad interfectorem filios suos. LXX: Ephraim quasi auis auolauit; gloria eorum in partu et in parturitionibus et conceptu; quia etiam si enutrierunt filios suos, sine filiis erunt in hominibus, quia et uae eis est; caro mea ex eis. Ephraim, sicut uidi, in captionem praebuit filios suos; et Ephraim, ut educeret ad interfectionem filios suos. Multum in hoc loco inter se discordant interpretes.*

70. *Comm. in Osee* 2.9.11–13: *In eo enim loco, in quo nos diximus: uae eis cum recessero ab eis, Septuaginta et Theodotio transtulerunt: uae eis, caro mea ex eis, quaerensque causam cur sit tanta uarie-*

Jerome correctly identifies the word at stake in the Hebrew, and analyzes the source of the variant. The text he apparently had before him read *basori*. The alternative, which he gives as *basari*, he arrived at by retroversion of the Greek text of the Septuagint and Theodotion.

The form Jerome transliterates as *basori* is also the reading of the Masoretic text, the basis for modern Hebrew Bibles. In modern editions, it is printed with a *vav* to mark the second vowel, which is *holem*. A consonant used in this manner to mark the presence of certain vowels is termed a *mater lectionis*. These and other aids to reading were canonized by the Masoretes in the early Middle Ages. But in the fourth century, when Jerome was writing, the *matres lectionis* were not yet fixed.[71] The two readings he suggests may therefore have been graphically indistinguishable.

The passage contains another variant, for which Jerome gives a more complex explanation. Where he has translated a particular Hebrew word as *Tyrus*, that is, the Phoenician city of Tyre, the Septuagint gives *thēran*, that is, "hunting, or capture." Aquila, Symmachus, and Theodotion all translate "very hard rock, that is, flint." The versions of Jerome's translation *iuxta Hebraeos* and of the *recentiores* stem from a source of variation even more subtle than that discussed above. As Jerome states, "flint, which in the Hebrew language is called sur . . . if we were to say Sor, it would mean Tyre." Only a difference in vocalization separates two words with very different meanings. Since the use of written vowel signs was unknown in the fourth century, the alternatives would have been indistinguishable.[72]

The Septuagint version of this phrase, however, involves a more dramatic confusion, whose explication shows Jerome's Hebrew philology at once at its most assured and its most peculiar. Where the text Jerome regards as authoritative reads *sor*, the Septuagint translators seem to have read *sud*: "But the Seventy translators on account of the similarity of the letters resh and dalet, thinking that the letter was not resh, but dalet, read sud, that is, hunting, or capture, whence also Bethsaida is called 'house of hunters.'"[73] Je-

---

tas, hanc mihi uideor repperisse: caro mea, lingua Hebraea dicitur basari; rursum si dicamus: recessio mea, siue declinatio mea, dicitur basori. Septuaginta igitur et Theodotio pro eo, quod est recessio mea et declinatio mea, uerterunt: caro mea.

71. Tov, *Textual Criticism*.

72. *Comm. in Osee 2.9.11–13: Rursum ubi nos posuimus:* Ephraim, ut vidi, Tyrus erat, *Septuaginta interpretati sunt* θηραν, *id est uenationem, sive capturam; Aquila et Symmachus et Theodotio, petram durissimam, id est silicem, quae lingua Hebraica appellatur sur, quod si legamus Sor, Tyrus dicitur.*

73. *Comm. in Osee 2.9.11–13: Putantes autem septuaginta interpretes ob litterarum similitudinem res et daleth, non esse res, sed daleth, legerunt sud, id est uenationem, sive capturam, unde et Bethsaida domus dicitur uenatorum.*

rome recognizes here a confusion between two similar Hebrew consonants, resh and dalet. On the one hand, this is a tour de force of Hebrew knowledge. In order to explain the Septuagint version, Jerome again has to translate back from the Greek of that text to a Hebrew original. Not only does he offer this retroversion, but he explains it to his reader by offering a parallel in a familiar place name, Bethsaida, which he translates as "house of hunters." There are numerous examples of exactly this reasoning, and of similar arguments from the confusion of two letters that look alike, throughout the commentaries on the Prophets. On the other hand, Jerome's reasoning begins to seem eccentric when he goes on to explain the source of the problem. He has no doubt identified correctly the alternative reading that lies behind the version of the Septuagint. But his attribution of this variation to mistranslation, rather than to a different base text, is peculiar. He seems unable to imagine that the process of transmission had ever infected the Hebrew textual tradition with multiple readings.

This passage shows Jerome's philological work on the Prophets in its most developed form. Other texts receive a far more cursory treatment. Often, Jerome is content to defend his version where it differs from that of the Septuagint simply by adducing the similar translations of Aquila and Symmachus in support of his own. The Hebrew is a last resort, called upon only when a text is particularly challenging. Yet as the example of his treatment of Hosea 9:11–13 makes clear, its authority is complete. Jerome's textual criticism accords to the *Hebraica veritas* a weight far greater than modern text critics would assign to the Hebrew manuscripts that he used. Within the larger intellectual balance that shapes the commentaries on the Minor Prophets, this valorization of the Hebrew, and of the techniques of literal exegesis that support its authority, confers great importance upon the interpretation *iuxta Hebraeos*.

In a number of respects, Jerome set the value of the Hebrew text and its accompanying interpretative tradition far higher than did any of his predecessors. For Origen and Eusebius, the *recentiores* had often served not to support a decision as to the correct understanding of a difficult passage in the Hebrew original, but rather to broaden the range of meaning possible at a particular point in the text, increasing the opportunities for allegorical reading. Jerome's interpretation preserves the impress of their approach, particularly when he hesitates to reject an allegorical reading provided by a Christian source if it can in any way be reconciled with the Hebrew text. But in general his exegetical method aims to establish a single, authoritative text, which then becomes a criterion limiting further interpretation, rather than to expand the range of legitimate textual variation or to multiply meanings. In consequence, while Origen and Eusebius—who also admitted the notional priority of the Hebrew—could maintain the centrality of the Septuagint Bible of the church, Jerome eventually relegated the Septuagint to a thoroughly subordinate position.

At the same time, Jerome came increasingly to minimize his debt to his Greek predecessors' example and to present his interest in Hebrew and Jewish learning as a radical innovation. In some sense, it was: for while Origen had little if any direct access to Hebrew, so that it played a relatively minor role in his interpretation, Jerome continually presents sophisticated textual arguments based on that language. He may have drawn much of this information from Jewish informants rather than from his own study of the Hebrew text. But whatever its origins, Jerome's information about the Hebrew text did not come from his Greek sources, and represents a significant departure from their example. In another sense, though, the independence of Jerome's philological and interpretative system is more notional than real. Whenever he cites the *recentiores*—which he does on almost every page of his mature commentaries—he betrays his debt to Origen. Yet Jerome himself never explicitly acknowledges the connection, choosing instead to represent the later translations as "Jewish," and therefore part of an interpretative tradition independent of his Christian predecessors.

Thus over against his Greek Christian sources, exponents of the life-giving spirit, Jerome constantly sides with his Jewish teachers, and above all with the Hebrew text of which they were the custodians. The *Hebraica veritas* retains its ultimate authority. The Hebrew text itself is primary. Its sequence, its logic, and its relation to history—primarily to the history of the Jews—define the limits for all subsequent interpretation. Yet the meanings that Jerome and many of his readers considered most valuable were those extracted by the Alexandrian tradition of allegory. Only such imaginative transpositions of the biblical text to the situation of the church, or of the individual Christian soul, could give life to material that on its surface seemed obsessed with the events of a distant past. Jerome's image for the practice of allegorical reading is a telling one. Repeatedly he describes the move from the literal and historical to the spiritual sense as "spreading one's sails" and "taking to the high seas." Thus he writes in the commentary on Hosea, "Somehow or other we have escaped from the broken places; now stretching our sail upon the high seas, we pass on to the open ocean of allegory." [74]

---

74. *Comm. in Osee* 3.10.14–15: *Euasimus utcumque de confragosis locis; nunc in altum uela tendentes, allegoriae pelagus transeamus.*

The spiritual sense is a great ocean, on which the interpreter sails unconstrained, having escaped the rocky coastline of the literal sense with its many hidden reefs. One would imagine that the mariner, having experienced the freedom of the seas, would hesitate to put back in toward land, where the risk of a wreck was ever present.[75] Yet Jerome continually returns to the historical and literal senses.

This apparent contradiction in fact served to justify Jerome's authority as an exegete. For although he repeatedly invokes the inspiration of the spirit that moved the prophets to stimulate his own interpretative faculties, his credibility rested not on his superior insight but on his ability to marshal a dazzling array of sources.[76] Taking this approach, Jerome might have been dismissed as a feckless plagiarist. Indeed, some of his more hostile contemporaries saw him in such a light.[77] He preferred, of course, to be thought of as a man of immense learning who had mastered the work of a wide range of his predecessors and could subject their views to his own assured judgment. The arrangement of the materials used in the commentaries on the Minor Prophets effects just such a subordination of earlier exegesis to Jerome's authority. Yet it allows him to remain, ostensibly, humble before his teachers and predecessors.

Evidence from a surprising source supports the idea that, to his contemporaries, Jerome's self-representation as a commentator fit well with their understanding of the genre and its demands—whatever some of them chose to claim instead. In 402, Rufinus prepared a translation of Eusebius's *Ecclesiastical History* for his friend and patron, Bishop Chromatius of Aquileia. Rufinus's Latin *Ecclesiastical History* also includes substantial additions, which cover the period between the final redaction of Eusebius's work in the 320s and the composition of the new work eighty years later. There,

---

75. Deep-water archaeology has led to a wholesale reimagining in recent years of ancient sailing routes in the Mediterranean, replacing a model of cabotage, in which coast-hugging sailors risked the open sea only when absolutely necessary, with one of far more audacious blue-water navigation. See Rougé, *Ships and Fleets,* for an early version of the new view. Jerome's image makes sense only in a context where open-water sailing is viewed positively, while hugging the coast runs the risk of shipwreck.

76. For references to the inspiration of the Holy Spirit for Jerome as interpreter, see prologues to the commentaries on Jonah, Hosea, and Micah; in the latter, Jerome writes, *semper autem in exponendis scripturis sanctis illius [i.e., spiritu dei] indigemus aduentu.*

77. Julian of Eclanum, in the preface to his commentaries on Hosea, Joel, and Amos, writes: *Hieronymus porro, et ingenii capacis uir et studii pertinacis, in prophetarum quidem libros commenta digessit, sed quasi inter geminas traditiones ire contentus, de perquirenda consequentia nihil aut uoluit aut potuit sustinere curarum.*

Rufinus describes the first essays in Christian learning of the great Cappadocians, Gregory of Nazianzus and Basil of Caesarea:

> Gregory . . . removed Basil from the professor's chair which he was occupying and forced him to accompany him to a monastery, where for thirteen years, they say, *having put aside all the writings of the worldly pagans*, they gave their attention solely to the books of holy scripture, the understanding of which *they did not presume to derive from themselves* but from the writings and the authority of those of old, who were themselves known to have received the rule of understanding from apostolic tradition. They sought the treasures of wisdom and knowledge hidden in these vessels of clay by examing *their commentaries on the prophets* in particular.[78]

This passage resonates on several levels with aspects of Jerome's career. First, there is the renunciation of pagan literature in favor of the Bible and Christian exegesis, which Jerome had made a central part of his self-presentation in his Roman correspondence, and which had been one of the most important targets of Rufinus's attacks in his *Apology against Jerome* of the previous year. Then, there is the Cappadocians' deference toward their illustrious predecessors. Rufinus's understanding of the proper mode of Christian scholarship, based on the authority of tradition rather than on individual creativity, seems remarkably like that articulated by Jerome in his programmatic statements on the commentary.

Furthermore, Gregory and Basil concentrate their efforts on the Prophets. On first examination, this might seem an endorsement of Jerome's activity: Rufinus too sees these books as the proper starting point of Christian biblical investigation. At the same time, however, it promises to make Jerome's work redundant, if not useless. For had the Cappadocians—or their apostolic predecessors—produced commentaries on the prophetic literature, surely these would have far greater authority than Jerome's works if only they could be made available to the Latin-reading public. Read in this context, the passage reads like an advertisement for Rufinus's next translation project. But the threat, if it was one, was empty: there was no Cappadocian exegesis of the prophets for Rufinus to translate, nor did he undertake the massive effort of translating Origen's commentaries. What Rufinus says about Gregory and Basil bears little resemblance to what we know from other, more reliable sources. It has even been suggested that he

---

78. Rufinus, *Hist. Eccles.* 11.9, as translated in Rufinus and Eusebius, *Church History,* 71. Emphasis added.

deliberately fictionalized his entire account of their lives in order to make it more edifying for his readers.[79] If that were so, it would only show all the more clearly that to consider monastic humility as precluding the assertion of one's own exegetical opinions was a view that Jerome shared with his fellow monks and contemporaries.

To legitimate his definition of the commentator's task, Jerome asserted the precedent of the Latin grammatical commentaries he studied as a schoolboy. In fact, that definition responded to the specific demands of his social position as a learned monk. He claimed that the task of the commentator was to convey what others have said, not to advance his own interpretations. As we have just seen, he shared this understanding of the monastic approach to the study of the scriptures with his greatest rival. Doubtless others would have found such a description of how monks should read—and, by implication, write—readily comprehensible. When we turn to examine Jerome's commentaries on the Prophets, however, we find that their contents are arranged so as to construct a powerful, but tacit, position of authority for their compiler. By juxtaposing Jewish and Greek Christian interpretations as he does, Jerome places himself in the position of arbiter over both exegetical traditions. But because he does not explicitly assert his own authority, he can maintain a stance of humility appropriate for a monk. Here, Jerome may have been a more authentic representative of the tradition of Origen than was his rival, for all that he was willing to abjure Origen's theology.

79. Thelamon, *Païens*, 441–42; Rufinus and Eusebius, *Church History*, 94.

CHAPTER FOUR

— ✳ —

Jerome's Library

IN HIS account of Origen's life in the sixth book of the *Ecclesiastical History*, Eusebius tells a curious story about his subject's decision to abandon his first career as a teacher of Greek grammar. The anecdote condenses a number of important themes:

> Deeming the teaching of grammar discordant with training in divine learning, without hesitation he ceased to engage in grammatical studies, which he now held to be unprofitable and opposed to holy erudition. Then, having come to the conclusion that he ought not to depend upon the support of others, he gave away all the books of ancient literature that he possessed, though formerly he had fondly cherished them, and was content to receive four obols a day from the man who purchased them.[1]

Eusebius describes Origen's library as a sort of patrimony, which Origen renounced—in some sense, *had* to renounce—in order to support his new career as a Christian intellectual. At the beginning of his career in "sacred studies," Origen gave away his library, or rather sold it, presumably to a wealthy supporter. In return, he received a stipend sufficient for the meager needs of an ascetic.

This brief narrative suggests several problems that libraries could present for ancient Christian ascetics. Origen decided to sell his library presumably because it was made up of non-Christian writings, inappropriate for a reader devoted to "divine learning." Furthermore, his library was worth

---

1. Eusebius, *Hist. eccles.* 6.8–9.

money. Its sale was therefore an act of ascetic renunciation. Rather than give the proceeds to the poor, however, Origen converted his library into an ascetic endowment, to underwrite his own life of holy poverty. This implies that the value of Origen's library was considerable, its liquidation perhaps similar to the sale of a farm. Possession of such a library was an important signifier of membership in the classes whose property bought them leisure to read. Origen's library, instead, provided the income that made its former owner a man of leisure, if only a marginal one.

Could Eusebius's account of the fate of Origen's library have played a role — perhaps an unconscious one — in Jerome's concoction of the story of his dream? When he was accused of being a "Ciceronian" rather than a Christian, the primary offense in question was his unwillingness to abandon his library of Latin literature, "which I had formed for myself at Rome with great care and toil."[2] The contrast to Origen's contented renunciation of a similar library in Greek is sharp. Equally, the story could have been in Rufinus's mind when he attacked Jerome for having abandoned the pledge he had made in the dream, and in particular when he retailed the information that Jerome, at Bethlehem, had served as a teacher of literature to young boys. This was precisely the occupation that Origen had renounced, together with the library that supported it, at the very inception of his career as a Christian scholar and an ascetic.

Whatever the truth of these speculations, it is unsurprising that this description of one of the founding acts of Origen's career as an ascetic plays no overt part in Jerome's self-fashioning, otherwise so dependent on Eusebius's portrayal of Origen. For every page of Jerome's commentaries implies a library. The citations of multiple versions of the Bible, the historical information taken from Josephus's *Antiquities of the Jews,* the explanations of Hebrew names drawn from the Jewish and Christian onomastic literature, and especially the lengthy interpretations translated and paraphrased from a variety of Christian commentators — all of this material came from books that Jerome must have had on hand as he worked.[3] Many of Jerome's other works, too, can be shown to rely very closely on his sources, including both Christian and non-Christian writings.

In recent decades, the history of reading and of libraries has become central to a new approach to intellectual history. Scholars have realized that re-

2. Letter 22.30.

3. For a detailed discussion of Jerome's methods of using sources as he composed, see chapter 5 below.

constructing the ways in which books were used and collected in the past can reveal much about how intellectual life was conducted, and how it fit into society as a whole. Scholarship can no longer be regarded as an activity of disembodied minds. Scholars in the past, like those who study them today, went in search of books, collected them and pored over them. The works they produced, too, had to be embodied in material form in order to reach their audiences. These concrete aspects of scholarly activity were inseparable from more abstract processes of ratiocination. The form, content, and availability of books not only limited but structured what it was possible to think. The history of libraries, therefore, is not merely an antiquarian pursuit, but a central element of an intellectual history that recognizes that ideas are more than mere abstractions.

In Jerome's case, specific problems make it even more important—and more fruitful—to consider which books he had on hand and how he used them. As we saw in chapter 3, Jerome's method as a commentator was framed explicitly in terms of reliance on earlier authorities. This deference to the past was, among other things, an attempt to solve the difficulties that the claim to authority inherent in biblical exegesis presented for a monk devoted to humility. In solving one problem, however, Jerome seems to have created another. By making the citation and paraphrase of a range of earlier writers' works central to his scholarship, Jerome made possession of a considerable library essential. This would have involved great expense. Books in antiquity, as the passage from Eusebius just discussed implies, were very costly.[4] Their acquisition in the numbers that Jerome required would have demanded access to the kind of fortune that, in antiquity, was more often inherited than earned. Furthermore, the possession and use of books was in itself a marker of membership in the elite, from which the monk was supposed to have cut himself off.

Late antique libraries, and the books they contained, varied widely. People who worked with books, particularly in the provinces, generally had very different collections than did those whose books symbolized their freedom from paid labor. The distinction was expressed on every level, from the hands in which books were copied to the places where they were kept. At the same time, late antique book culture had a coherence that set it apart from the way books were made and used in both earlier and later periods, making it an expression of the times. In this context, a catalogue of Jerome's library will take on greater meaning. This chapter will consider the contents

---

4. For more on the cost of books in antiquity, see chapter 5 below.

of the library at Bethlehem in comparison to other ancient book collections. Our inventory will begin from Jerome's explicit references to books in his possession, take in the evidence of source-critical studies of his works, and consider also the books that Jerome probably had on hand but did not use as sources. Chapter 5 will flesh out the picture by collecting the evidence for the physical appearance of Jerome's books, their format, materials, and cost. Throughout, the primary concern will be to understand what it meant for Jerome, in the late fourth century, to reverse the trajectory that Origen had taken almost two hundred years earlier.

ANCIENT LIBRARIES

The library in antiquity reflected the way books were produced as well as the place of literary culture in the social world of the ancient Mediterranean. Unlike modern collections, ancient libraries were not primarily composed of books purchased on the market. Booksellers did play a role, especially in the orbit of the major cities. Great libraries, like other collections of precious objects, could also be assembled through plunder or corruption, as they were by some of the generals who fought in Rome's civil wars. But most of the books in most libraries were copied by or for their owners from originals borrowed from other participants in a network of literary exchange. Authors, too, disseminated new works by producing copies as gifts for their readers. Ancient libraries, therefore, grew by means of the exchange of books among like-minded members of a literate elite, each prepared to copy his own books (or more likely, to have a slave copy them) and pass them on to his friends. Jerome's own case, in his early days as an ascetic at Antioch in the 370s, exemplifies this model.[5]

So books were not only difficult to obtain but also, because they had to be hand-copied, very expensive. One would therefore expect book collections to be limited in size. Many ancient libraries, however, were very large. Some private libraries contained thousands of volumes; and some public libraries—at Alexandria, at Rome, even at Athens—tens or even hundreds of thousands. This may seem a paradox in a world where even basic literacy was limited to perhaps 10 percent of the population, and the kind of literacy required for the extensive use of books restricted to between 1 and 5 percent.

---

5. Interestingly, some of our strongest contemporary evidence for this mode of circulation of books comes from Antioch at the time that Jerome was there, in the work of Libanius: see Norman, "Book-Trade." For more on the circulation of books in antiquity, see chapter 7 below.

In fact, the steep pitch of the social pyramid, and the fact that the vast majority of resources were controlled by the top 2 or 3 percent of the population, meant that ancient elites could accumulate books—as they did other status-conferring objects of value—in almost incredible quantities.[6]

One of the factors that worked against the complete concentration of books in the hands of a narrow, hereditary class was the inherent instability of Mediterranean societies in the premodern world. For all their pretenses of ancient ancestry, few Mediterranean elite families succeeded in holding their status for more than a couple of generations.[7] Literary culture, mediated through books among other channels, provided both a major path of advancement for "new men," and a way of incorporating them seamlessly into existing elite circles, masking the precariousness characteristic of all Mediterranean populations in the premodern world. The acquisition of books, therefore, was a crucial element of upward mobility, meaning that books as well as learning circulated far more widely than one would expect in an equally stratified but more rigid society. It was perhaps in such contexts that the book markets and booksellers we know of from ancient literary references found their most important place.

Another factor that encouraged the growth of libraries was euergetism—the semi-institutionalized practice whereby citizens used their personal wealth to fund construction projects, pay for shows and games, and support other elements of the urban infrastructure. It was an element in the larger system of patronage that linked Mediterranean elites to the mass of the population, and sustained sub-elites who participated in the culture, if not the vast wealth, of the pinnacle of the social pyramid. The sense of obligation to one's city that expressed itself, in the Roman world of the late first through

6. The scattered literary, documentary and archaeological data on ancient libraries are presented most conveniently in Casson, *Libraries;* for the underlying data, see Staikos, *Great Libraries;* Cavallo, *Biblioteche;* Callmer, "Antike Bibliotheken"; for late Republican Rome, see Dix, "Libraries at Rome"; for the library discovered in the Villa dei Papiri at Herculaneum, perhaps the largest and best preserved library to survive from antiquity, see Gigante, *Philodemus.* See also Kenyon, *Books and Readers,* and Morgan, *Literate Education,* shedding light on the smaller libraries that might have belonged to, e.g., village grammarians. On Christian libraries, see Elderen, "Early Christian Libraries," and more generally, Gamble, *Books and Readers;* Carriker, *Library of Eusebius,* reconstructing the contents (but not the physical form) of Eusebius's library; and a similar treatment, marred by an overcritical approach, of Lactantius's library in Ogilvie, *Library of Lactantius.* For the number of books in some major ancient libraries, see Casson, *Libraries,* 36 (library of Alexandria), 50 (Pergamum), 88 (Forum of Trajan), 99 (early Latin libraries at Rome), 113 (library of Hadrian at Athens), 16 (library of Celsus at Ephesus), 39 (library of Caesarea). On the architecture of ancient libraries, see Johnson, "Hellenistic and Roman Library."

7. This pattern is at the center of the analysis of Horden and Purcell, *Corrupting Sea.*

the third century CE, through the donation of baths, temples, theaters, porticoes, and other monumental public amenities, also led to the construction of public libraries.[8] Similarly, the library of a powerful patron was open, together with the other amenities of his great urban house or sprawling rural villa, to a wide circle of acquaintances—both his peers and people of lower status, his protégés and clients.[9] Both euergetism, and patronage more broadly, served to make books and libraries available to those who did not have the funds to create or purchase them for themselves.

Evidence for the origins, size, content, and physical form of ancient libraries is sparse and frequently unreliable. From the scattered information that survives, however, we can patch together a modest history of the library in the Hellenistic and Roman worlds. The earliest documented libraries (as opposed to civic archives) are those of Alexandria and Pergamum. Both were founded by Hellenistic kings: the first by Ptolemy II in the third century BCE, the other by the Attalid ruler, Eumenes II, in the first half of the second. These collections served communities of scholars supported by the kings' largesse, and may have contained vast numbers of books: ancient figures for the library of Alexandria claim that it contained more than five hundred thousand book rolls at its peak. These libraries, it must be emphasized, were intended to enhance the prestige of Hellenistic rulers, very much in the manner of their collections of sculpture and precious objets d'art. What role they played in the larger culture of the cities that housed them is difficult to know.[10]

Late Republican grandees, and after them, Roman emperors, accumulated immense numbers of books in libraries both private and public. The first great libraries in the Roman world were built on the plunder of the conquered kingdoms of the Greek East. Later, Augustus and his successors donated numerous libraries to Rome, just as they did temples, bathhouses, and other public buildings. Indeed, libraries at Rome were generally associated with either temples or bathhouses. They were public amenities, at least in some sense, although there is much debate over who had access to their contents. These libraries were also, like triumphal arches and imperial forums, symbols of the emperor's standing as patron of all patrons. Lesser notables in cities throughout the empire endowed libraries as they did other places of

8. E.g., the library of Celsus at Ephesus, and probably the library excavated at Timgad in North Africa.

9. This emerges very clearly from Gigante, *Philodemus*.

10. Casson, *Libraries*, 31–60.

FIGURE 3. Ephesus, facade of the Library of Celsus. 110–35 CE.
Vanni / Art Resource, NY.

public recreation. Excavation has uncovered libraries in cities from Timgad, in modern Algeria, to Ephesus, on the Aegean coast of Asia Minor (fig. 3). Emperors, too, occasionally erected libraries in the provinces. Hadrian built a magnificent Greek library at Athens, whose remains have been thoroughly excavated (fig. 4).[11]

Roman villas, as we know from archaeological, inscriptional, and literary sources, also housed libraries. Some of these were extensive and specialized, like the libraries of Cicero and Atticus, for which Cicero's correspondence provides so much evidence.[12] Detailed confirmation for this conclusion emerges from the library excavated in the Villa of the Papyri at Herculaneum (fig. 5). Entombed by the eruption of Vesuvius in 69 CE, this library contained about two thousand papyrus rolls, stored in a room that connected to an expansive portico surrounding a garden.[13] The contents of the

11. Casson, *Libraries*, 61–79.

12. Casson, *Libraries*, 70–79.

13. For the number of rolls estimated to have been present in the original library, see Gigante, *Philodemus*.

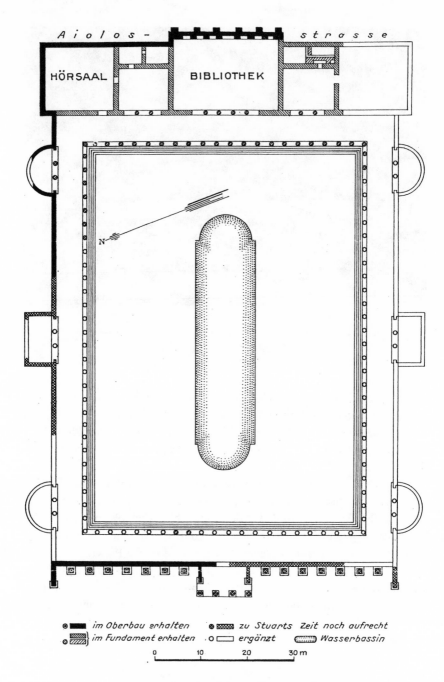

FIGURE 4. Plan of Hadrian's Library at Athens.
After Callmer, "Antike Bibliotheken," 173.

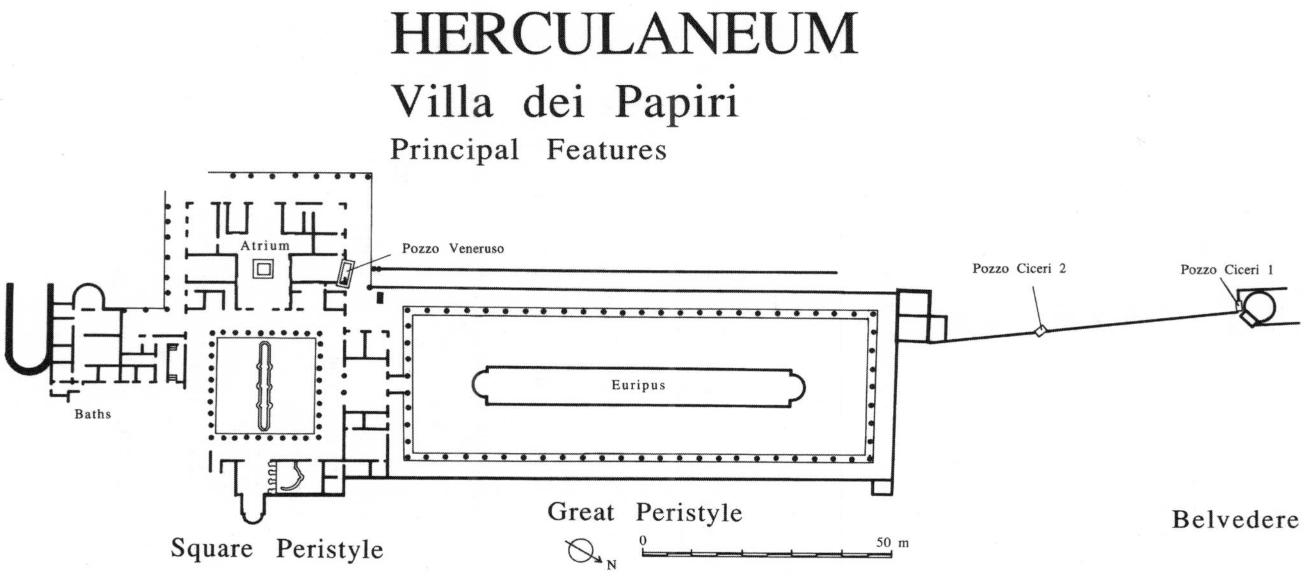

HERCULANEUM
Villa dei Papiri
Principal Features

Pozzo Ciceri 1

Pozzo Ciceri 2

Belvedere

Pozzo Veneruso

Euripus

Great Peristyle

Atrium

Square Peristyle

Baths

0   50 m

N

FIGURE 5. Plan of the Villa dei Papiri at Herculaneum. After Christopher Parslow, *Rediscovering Antiquity* (Cambridge: Cambridge University Press, 1995), 78. Courtesy of Christopher Parslow.

collection surprised its eighteenth-century discoverers, who were disappointed to find that the library specialized not in the literary works whose recovery they had breathlessly anticipated, but in Epicurean philosophy. In particular, it contained hundreds of copies of the writings of the obscure Philodemus, whose philosophical works were previously unknown.[14] Such highly specialized collections were probably not uncommon.

Physically, libraries public and private tended to combine relatively small areas for the storage of books with expansive "reading rooms" or open porticoes. The stoa, or portico, is more typical of the Greek library, while the reading room may have been a Roman invention. This allocation of space suggests that the library was as much a site for learned social intercourse as it was for the preservation and use of books. In Roman libraries, the books were stored in *armaria,* cabinets with doors and shelves, placed in niches around the room. Other niches typically enshrined statues, whether of the donor, of a patron deity, or of various authors.[15] The juxtaposition of niches containing books with those containing statues suggests a certain equivalence: like statues, books expressed their owners' wealth and aesthetic refinement; like books, statues advertised their owners' affiliation with a particular, well-defined cultural tradition. Interestingly, although the copying of books must have been a necessary concomitant of their collection and preservation, excavated libraries do not seem to have included facilities that can be recognized as scriptoria. The monumental rooms in which books were displayed and used served members of the elite and their privileged dependents. Repairing and copying books, on the other hand, were tasks for slaves. Presumably they did their work in the same quarters where other menial functions were carried out.

Many of the libraries, especially in Rome, created by the wealthy of the high empire as personal possessions or public amenities, survived into the fourth century and beyond. The survival of the libraries of Rome is well documented in the fourth and even the fifth centuries. In late antiquity, however, two new trends emerged: the rise of the codex and the formation of Christian libraries to rival older civic foundations, which were often associated with pagan temples. The roll had been the standard book of Mediterranean antiquity since its invention in Pharaonic Egypt. But by the late fourth or early fifth century, roll books became increasingly rare. In the

14. Gigante, *Philodemus.*

15. Casson, *Libraries.*

fourth century, libraries were sometimes recopied en masse.[16] Libraries written on rolls may have been converted to codex form. It is unlikely, however, that this was the general rule. The change in the form of the book must have had some impact on the library, but we lack evidence for these changes. The roll books in a classical library were housed in *capsae,* round buckets stored on shelves, or, more commonly in the West, laid flat on the shelves of *armaria.* Images of books in codex form show them stored in the same *armaria* that the Romans had used for rolls (fig. 6). Where the rolls had been stacked several layers deep, the codices lay flat on the shelves of the bookcases. The books had changed, but their containers had not. Probably, the transition was a gradual one, whose effect on the contents and physical arrangement of libraries was subtle and slow to be felt.

Christian churches possessed libraries from a very early time. We know this in part because the books were catalogued when they were confiscated by the authorities during the persecutions of the second half of the third century. The lists of books included in accounts of martyrdom tend to be pitifully short. But by the second half of the third century, Christian churches in major urban centers had begun to accumulate much larger and more varied collections. The trend only accelerated in the fourth century. In different senses, both elite private collections and the libraries of ancient temples served as points of origin for these new Christian libraries. Christian leaders in major cities were frequently men of wealth and learning, who might bequeath their books to the church. Moreover, Christian groups likely felt it necessary to keep books on hand for the purpose of religious instruction and research. Their needs would have gone beyond copies of the scriptures, which were used in the liturgy, to include works in exegesis, apologetics, and other Christian technical genres. Perhaps the best non-Christian analogy to this expanded form of the Christian library is the kind of library that sometimes accompanied a temple of Asclepius, enshrining large numbers of medical works and other texts useful for the healing work of the priests.

We even have some archaeological evidence for a Christian library at Rome: the fragmentary base of a statue, discovered in the Renaissance and heavily restored. The statue may have depicted Hippolytus, bishop of Rome at the end of the second century. Its base, in the form of a throne, is inscribed with a paschal table that agrees with the idiosyncratic opinions concerning the calculation of the date of Easter associated with this Hippolytus. The

---

16. See e.g. Jerome, *De vir. ill.,* on the activities of Euzoius, bishop of Caesarea in the mid-fourth century.

CODICIBVS SACRIS HOSTILI CLADE PERVSTIS
ESDRA DŌ FERVENS HOC REPARAVIT OPVS

FIGURE 6. Ezra (?) seated, writing, before an *armarium* holding nine codices. Codex Amiatinus, fol. 5r. Jarrow, early eighth century. Biblioteca Laurenziana, Florence. Scala / Art Resource, NY.

inscription also includes a lengthy catalogue of writings, which have traditionally been attributed to him as well. Recent scholarship has raised doubts about the identification, but whoever was originally memorialized by the statue was very likely a Christian writer, making this a Christian version of the statues of authors that adorned every ancient library of any pretensions. If so, it represents early evidence for the existence of a Christian library at Rome on the model of the more important non-Christian collections.[17]

By the later fourth century, the numerous Christian libraries of the imperial city harbored impressive collections, in Greek as well as Latin. In 393, Jerome wrote a long letter to his friend Pammachius at Rome to defend his recent work against Jovinian. In a further letter, he referred his correspondent to the commentaries of a variety of Greek writers on Paul's first letter to the Corinthians, which, he claimed, would reinforce his assertion that he had deprecated marriage no more than the apostle himself. Here, Jerome refers Pammachius to the libraries of the churches of Rome, where he will be able to find copies of all the texts Jerome cites.[18]

In Palestine, too, we know of great Christian libraries. We learn of one from a passing comment of Eusebius: Bishop Alexander of Jerusalem, he reports, established a library there in the first half of the third century, which survived for Eusebius to consult seventy or a hundred years later.[19] Far better known is the collection of the bishops of Caesarea Maritima. This library was established by the wealthy presbyter Pamphilus in the final decades of the third century; it was expanded by his disciple Eusebius, who became the city's bishop in 313, and was lovingly preserved by successive bishops in the fourth century.

Thanks to its connection with the prolific Eusebius, and to the testimony of later authors, particularly Jerome, we have more information for the library of Caesarea than for any other ancient Christian library. It is often reported that it was founded by Origen, but there is no evidence for this. In fact, what Eusebius tells us about the activities of Pamphilus, his revered mentor, indicates that Pamphilus was the library's founder. Eusebius states that Pamphilus sought out the works of Origen wherever he could find

17. For an exhaustive discussion of the statue and its possible relation to the second-century Christian writer Hippolytus, see Brent, *Hippolytus*, 3–367. For a different view of Hippolytus as an author, see Cerrato, *Hippolytus*. On the statue, see also Guarducci, *San Pietro*, 111–40.

18. Letter 49.3 mentioning Origen, Dionysius of Alexandria, Pierius, Eusebius of Caesarea, Didymus, and Apollinaris.

19. Eusebius *Hist. eccles.* 6.20.1.

them.[20] This must imply that Origen's own collection, which would have contained master copies of all his works, had been dispersed (though probably not destroyed) during the twenty or thirty years that separated his death from Pamphilus's arrival in Caesarea.

Pamphilus concentrated his collecting efforts on biblical manuscripts and Christian works, particularly those of Origen. The treasure of his library was undoubtedly the original copy of the Hexapla, prepared by Origen for his own use perhaps fifty years before Pamphilus acquired it.[21] Eusebius's works reveal that he himself must have added considerably to the library. Besides the Christian works he drew upon for his *Ecclesiastical History,* he used a wide range of non-Christian historical and chronographic works and an extensive library of Greek philosophy. Many of the books he depended on in his researches were lengthy, technical, and rare. To the vast collection he accumulated, he added a more modest one of his own works.[22] After Eusebius, we do not hear of other bishops of Caesarea as major authors, but Jerome tells us that the mid-fourth-century bishop Euzoius expended much labor and expense to copy the library from papyrus onto parchment, showing that it was the diocese's prized possession well after its founders' deaths.[23]

Most of the libraries just described were created by aristocrats, or even emperors, who used their own wealth to pay for books. Some were the property of wealthy institutions. The library of Caesarea, as we have seen, was founded by an individual, Pamphilus, who expended his personal fortune in forming its original nucleus. Eusebius, who seems to have inherited it from him, became bishop of the city in 314. Under him the library passed into the ownership of the see. In general, huge collections like Caesarea's would have been available only to those at the pinnacle of the social pyramid, or through their patronage. The exceptions are institutional libraries.

20. Eusebius, *Hist. eccles.* 6.32.3. Jerome, *De vir. ill. 75,* says that Pamphilus copied most of Origen's works in his own hand. On Pamphilus's library, see also Pamphilus et al., *Apologie,* 2:76 n. 8.

21. The most important evidence that Pamphilus did in fact obtain the original Hexapla, or a copy of it, comes from the subscriptions in ancient manuscripts of the Greek Old Testament that attest to Pamphilus's correction of the text against the Hexapla: e.g., Codex Sinaiticus, 2 Esdras and Esther. The implication is that Pamphilus had obtained Origen's Hexapla (or perhaps a copy of it) for his own use. On these subscriptions, see Mercati, "Nuove note"; Skeat, "Use of Dictation"; Swete et al., *Introduction;* and Petitmengin and Flusin, "Livre antique."

22. For a catalogue of the contents of Eusebius's library, see Carriker, *Library of Eusebius.*

23. *De vir. ill.* 113.51: *Euzoius apud Thespesium rhetorem cum Gregorio, Nazianzeno episcopo, adulescens Caesareae eruditus est, et eiusdem postea urbis episcopus, plurimo labore corruptam iam bibliothecam Origenis et Pamphili* in membranis *instaurare conatus, ad extremum sub Theodosio principe ecclesia pulsus est.* On this passage see Arns, *La technique,* 24.

Great libraries dominate the historical record, both literary and archaeological. For the personal book collections of lesser readers—Christian priests in small towns, village grammarians and scribes—we have less evidence. What we do know suggests that at least in provincial settings, such professional literates might have had access to ten or twenty books, rarely more.[24] Some who earned their living through books—men like Jerome's teacher Donatus, the greatest Latin grammarian of his age—would surely have owned much larger libraries. But they must have been exceptional. Most grammarians, for example, would have earned barely enough money to buy, or to have copied, the books they used for their own classes.[25] The possession of many books was a clear marker of elite status—or of dependence on the elite. In selling his library in return for a cash stipend, Origen had simply made this relationship explicit.

THE LIBRARY OF BETHLEHEM

The books that made up Jerome's library at Bethlehem fall into three broad categories. First, there were the biblical manuscripts that formed the essential basis of his scholarship. Then, there were the numerous—and often voluminous—works of Christian writers, exegetical and otherwise. Some of these Jerome used as sources, so that their presence in the library can be confirmed with relative certainty. In addition to the commentaries and technical works that Jerome consulted as he wrote, he also owned copies of many other Christian compositions. Hellenistic Jewish works, particularly those of Philo and Josephus, were also on hand, and served as important references. Finally, Jerome possessed a comprehensive, if sometimes idiosyncratic, collection of the works of Greek and Roman authors, from Plato and Cicero, Virgil and Horace, to Porphyry and Galen. For reasons that should be obvious, there is little explicit documentation for this component of his collection. What there is must be gleaned from the accusations of Rufinus. But source-critical analysis of Jerome's letters and polemical works reveals that he mined pagan works with the same assiduity as he did the commentaries of Origen and Didymus and the histories of Josephus.

It is surprisingly difficult to detail the biblical manuscripts that Jerome

---

24. Morgan, *Literate Education*, emphasizes the vast differences between the numbers and kinds of books available to sub-elite readers such as village grammarians and local Christian leaders and those available to members of metropolitan elites.

25. For a discussion of the grammarian's fees in comparison to the price of books, see chapter 5 below.

had on hand. Clearly, he was an avid collector of such books, assembling numerous copies in various languages, which he studied and sometimes cited. Jerome frequently refers to the "vulgate edition" of the Greek Old Testament. Often, this phrase simply means the Septuagint or Old Greek translation. Occasionally, though, he explicitly cites variants culled from different "vulgate" manuscripts. Perhaps these references indicate that Jerome had amassed a collection of Greek Bible manuscripts that he used in his textual researches.[26] He sometimes refers to copies associated with particular cities: in the commentary on Isaiah, for example, Jerome mentions "Alexandrian copies" of the Greek Old Testament.[27] His references to *Hebraica volumina,* "Hebrew scrolls," suggest that he may also have obtained Jewish biblical manuscripts in the original language, as he had attempted to do at Rome.[28] But his works provide little concrete evidence of the presence of such manuscripts in his library.

Jerome's commentarial method involves the regular citation of a consistent repertoire of biblical texts and translations. These include his own Latin

---

26. E.g., *Comm. in Esaiam* 16 preface, ll. 54–59: *in Hebraico non haberi, nec esse in septuaginta intepretibus, sed in editione uulgata, quae Graece* koine *dicitur et in toto orbe diuersa est;* but cf. *Comm. in Esaiam* 15.57–59: *Hoc iuxta Septuaginta interpretes diximus, quorum editio toto orbe uulgata est; Comm. in Hiezech.* 1.4.1332: *Satisque miror cur uulgata exemplaria "centum nonaginta annos" habeant et in quibusdam scriptum sit "centum quinquaginta," cum perspicue et Hebraei et Aquila, Symmachusque et Theodotio "trecentos nonaginta annos" teneant, et apud ipsos Septuaginta—et tamen non sunt scriptorum uitio deprauati—idem numerus reperiatur.*

27. *Comm. in Esaiam* 16.21.7–13: *Quod in alexandrinis exemplaribus in prooemio huius capituli additum est: " et adhuc in te erit laus mea semper" et in fine: "et ossa tua quasi herba orientur et pinguescent et hereditate possidebunt in generationes et generationes," in hebraico non habetur, sed ne in Septuaginta quidem emendatis et ueris exemplaribus; unde obelo praenotandum est.* Perhaps Jerome merely repeats information on such manuscripts given in Origen's lost *tomoi* or *excerpta,* or in annotations in Origen's recension of the Septuagint. Certainly, Origen did compare manuscripts of the Septuagint (see e.g. *Ad Africanum*). Equally, Jerome may be reporting on his own researches: none of the relevant parts of Origen's works survive. Particularly interesting is a passage from the commentary on Matthew, where Jerome writes, *In quibusdam latinis codicibus additum est: "neque filius," cum in graecis et maxime Adamantii et Pierii exemplaribus hoc non habetur adscriptum, sed quia in non nullis legitur disserendum uidetur (Comm. in Matt.* 4.591–94). In his *Contra Ruf.,* Jerome mentions various regional text-types within the Septuagint tradition: *Alexandria et Aegyptus in Septuaginta suis Hesychium laudat auctorem; Constantinopolis usque Antiochiam Luciani martyris exemplaria probat; mediae inter has prouiniciae Palaestinos codices legunt, quos ab Origene elaboratos Eusebius et Pamphilus uulgauerunt; totusque orbis hac inter se trifaria uarietate conpugnat (Contra Ruf.* 2.522).

28. For example, in his *Comm. in Matt.* 4.1525, Jerome writes: *Legi nuper in quodam hebraico uolumine quem Nazarenae sectae mihi Hebraeus obtulit Hieremiae apocryphum in quo haec ad uerbum scripta repperi.* The reference is, of course, not to a biblical text but to an apocryphon, but *a fortiori* it seems likely that Jerome also obtained Hebrew biblical scrolls.

translations of the Hebrew and of the Septuagint Greek, and several Greek and Hebrew versions. The primary texts under exegesis in the commentaries on the Minor Prophets are Jerome's Latin translation *iuxta Hebraeos*, and his Latin version of the Septuagint Greek, based on a text that Jerome considered to be Origen's critical recension. Beyond the texts of the lemma, a number of other versions are often adduced within the comment, including the so-called *recentiores*—the translations of Aquila, Symmachus, and Theodotion; a transliteration of the Hebrew into Greek, supplemented at times by the Hebrew itself spelled out with Hebrew letter names; and anonymous Greek translations designated by the numbers Quinta (appearing frequently), Sexta (rarely), and Septa (very rarely).

Behind this impressive catalogue of texts and translations, with its baroque terminology, looms the bulk of Origen's Hexapla. The Hexapla was the most sophisticated research tool for biblical criticism and interpretation available in Jerome's day, and for centuries afterward. It allowed the Christian scholar, whether or not he had a firm grasp of Hebrew, to have access to the original via the considerable repertoire of aids to comprehension that had developed among Greek-speaking Jews, from Hellenistic times through the third century CE. Jerome must have had his own copies of the Hexaplaric Bible.

Origen's great compilation consisted of six columns laid out over the two facing pages of a series of large and finely produced papyrus codices. The first column contained the Hebrew text in Hebrew characters; the second, a Greek transliteration of the Hebrew; the third and fourth, the Greek translations of Aquila and Symmachus; the fifth, the Septuagint text with Origen's critical signs; and the sixth, the translation of Theodotion. For certain books, up to three additional translations appeared in extra columns. Each line contained a single Hebrew word or, at most, two or three short words, with its corresponding material in the successive columns. Each page probably had about forty lines. Using a likely format for Greek Christian codices produced in the early third century, we can estimate that such a Bible would fill about twenty volumes of 400 leaves (800 pages) each.[29] This would have been a very large and expensive Bible, but not unimaginably so—by comparison, say, with the *Codex Grandior*, a Bible in nine volumes owned by the sixth-century Italian scholar Cassiodorus.[30]

---

29. The total number of words in the Hebrew Bible is 304,901, according to the Masoretic lists printed in modern rabbinic Bibles. For typical codex formats, see Turner, *Typology*.

30. For the details of this reconstruction, see Williams, "Jerome's Biblical Criticism," 151–60.

Jerome's access to Hexaplaric manuscripts has been challenged. Pierre Nautin argued that the Hexapla was never copied, and that by Jerome's day the original no longer existed in Caesarea. Jerome, therefore, could not have had known it.[31] Although many have accepted Nautin's views, other scholars have shown that they are ill-founded. The existence of two substantial fragments of biblical manuscripts containing the Hexaplaric columns proves that the work was in fact reproduced. Complete copies of the Hexaplaric Old Testament may have been rare, but individual books certainly did circulate. Since the two surviving fragments originated in widely separated places and times, it seems that Hexaplaric manuscripts were widely available. Furthermore, Nautin's contention that because Jerome's description of the Hexapla was inaccurate, he must not have seen it, has been refuted in detail.[32]

Nautin claims that Jerome's many references to the Hexapla were borrowed from Origen and Eusebius.[33] But comparison of Jerome's commentary on Isaiah with Eusebius's work on the same prophet, which Jerome explicitly cites as a source, has shown that Jerome did not obtain his references to the *recentiores* from Eusebius's work.[34] The possibility that Jerome

---

31. See Pierre Nautin, *Origène.* Scholars who have uncritically accepted Nautin's arguments include, e.g., Wright, "Scholar's Den," and Hollerich, *Eusebius.*

32. For refutations of Nautin's views, see Jay, *Exégèse,* 410–17; Kamesar, *Jerome,* 4–28; and Rebenich, "Vir Trilinguis," 57–62.

33. Nautin, *Origène,* 326–32.

34. On Jerome's use of Eusebius, see Jay, *Exégèse,* 56–60. As Jerome himself states, Eusebius's commentary on Isaiah served as a principal source for his own treatment of that prophet. Sufficient fragments of Eusebius's commentary survive in the *catenae* to reconstruct it with some confidence. In the reconstructed commentary on Isaiah, Eusebius makes frequent reference to the *recentiores,* as does Jerome in his own vast work. However, the two exegetes cite different material from the *recentiores* and use them for different purposes. For Eusebius, as for Origen before him, the purpose of assembling the more recent Greek versions was to correct the deterioration suffered by the Septuagint during the course of its lengthy transmission. Further, Eusebius uses the variety of translations to broaden the scope of his allegorical exegesis (Jay, *Exégèse,* 110; Barthélemy, "Eusèbe," 63–66; Kamesar, *Jerome,* 37; see also Hollerich, *Eusebius*). For Jerome, on the other hand, the *recentiores* helped to provide access to the Hebrew original, in particular by suggesting a range of solutions to interpretive problems presented by difficult Hebrew words and phrases (Jay, *Exégèse,* 102–10; Kamesar, *Jerome,* 80–81). Eusebius's commentary, therefore, could not have replaced texts of the *recentiores* themselves as the source of Jerome's citations in his work on Isaiah. Jay, comparing how Jerome and Eusebius use the *recentiores* in commenting on Isaiah, concludes: "De fait, on ne relève dans le détail que fort peu de recoupements entre les deux œuvres. Par exemple, sur les cinquante premières mentions d'Aquila chez Eusèbe, seule une dizaine se retrouve chez Jérôme. Quatre mentions sur cinq y restent donc sans écho. Pourtant, pour les mêmes chapitres, on relève chez lui soixante-trois références à Aquila. L'indépendance des deux auteurs est donc ici flagrante" (*Exégèse,* 110 n. 310).

drew upon Origen for such references cannot be tested by direct comparison, since Origen's commentaries on the Hebrew Bible are lost. However, we possess Jerome's exegesis of several prophetic books for which Origen had produced only partial treatments. The catalogue of Origen's works that appears in Jerome's letter 33 describes Origen's treatments of Hosea and Zechariah as incomplete. Jerome's commentaries on these two prophets, on the other hand, are among the most sustained and careful of his treatments of the Minor Prophets. Neither the frequency nor the manner of Jerome's citations of the *recentiores* changes between those sections where he drew on Origen's commentaries and those where Origen's exegesis was unavailable.[35] Thus, the attempt to explain Jerome's use of Hexaplaric material in terms of reliance on earlier exegetes fails to account for the evidence.[36]

Jerome's citational practices in the commentaries on the Prophets

---

35. "Expliquer d'autre part, comme le fait P. Nautin (p. 331), par la seule dépendance de Jérôme envers les commentaires d'Eusèbe et d'Origène les citations des différentes versions qui émaillent les siens n'est qu'une hypothèse que démentent les vérifications que nous pouvons faire. On l'a vu à propos du *Commentaire sur Isaïe* (ch. II, n. 301), la confrontation entre Jérôme et Eusèbe dans l'utilisation, pourtant fort abondante de part et de l'autre, des versions montre une large indépendance de Jérôme sur ce point. Et si c'était d'Origène qu'il était étroitement tributaire, il faudrait expliquer pourquoi l'on n'observe aucun changement dans la manière dont il continue de recourir à ces versions au-delà du chapitre 30 du prophète, auquel se limitait le Commentaire de l'Alexandrin. Ce qui est vrai du *Commentaire sur Isaïe* l'est encore plus du *Commentaire sur Osée*, pour lequel Jérôme ne trouvait, chez Origène, comme chez Eusèbe, que des sources très fragmentaires (*In Os.*, prol.: PL 25, 819 B). Or il y recourt aux versions tout autant que dans les commentaires contemporains, parmi lesquels le *Commentaire sur Zacharie* fournit l'occasion d'une dernière vérification. Sur ce prophète, en effet, il n'existait pas de commentaire d'Eusèbe. Et Origène en avait expliqué à peine le tiers. Didyme étant hors de cause (voir ch. II, p. 125 et la note 412), on devrait observer dans le recours aux versions une différence significative entre le livre I, qui correspond au Commentaire d'Origène, et les deux suivants. Or, si le livre II accuse une baisse sensible du nombre de références à nos trois versions: quatre au lieu du quatorze au livre I, le livre III en offre vingt-deux. C'est donc que leur présence dans le Commentaire, comme les variations de leur fréquence, ne sont pas fonction de la présence ou de l'absence d'une source origénienne" (Jay, *Exégèse*, 416).

36. Other solutions are also possible. For example, Dines, "Jerome," 421, proposes that Jerome used glossed manuscripts containing citations of the *recentiores* in the margins: "It is very probable that he possessed glossed Hexaplaric manuscripts of biblical texts, as these certainly existed in the fourth century." Dines provides no further information on these "glossed Hexaplaric manuscripts," however. Alternatively, Jerome could have used separate copies of the *recentiores*. He mentions that he had a manuscript of Aquila in letter 32.1: *iam pridem cum uoluminibus Hebraeorum editionem Aquilae confero, ne quid forsitan propter odium Christi Synagoga mutauerit.* (On the dating of this letter, see chapter 1 and the Appendix, section 5.) For the additional versions included by Origen for the biblical books written in verse, see *De vir. ill.* 54.32: Jerome claims that he obtained his copies from Origen's library at Caesarea, referring to *quintam et sextam et septimam editionem, quas etiam nos de eius bibliotheca habemus.* In *Contra Ruf.* 2.34, Jerome states that Rufinus had copies of the named *recentiores* and the Quinta and Sexta as well (cited by Jay, *Exégèse*, 417).

strongly support the inference that he had a manuscript containing the Hex-aplaric columns before him as he worked. Jerome's lemmata usually consist of at least one verse, sometimes several. But when he cites either the He-brew text (in the original or in transliteration) or the *recentiores,* he rarely gives more than a word, at most a short phrase. His philological arguments regarding the relation of the Septuagint to the Hebrew text also focus on in-dividual words, while ignoring larger syntactic or compositional units. Each line of the Hexapla presented a single Hebrew word, in parallel with its Greek translations. The Hebrew word is the basic logical unit within the compilation. Jerome's use of Hexaplaric materials in discussing the biblical text therefore seems to reflect the arrangement of the compilation itself.

Furthermore, when Jerome cites the *recentiores,* he very often refers to them as a group, suggesting that he saw them together on the page before him. At times he mentions only a single version, but usually he cites the three *recentiores* in series. At other points he refers to them as a group, stat-ing that they all present the same reading.[37] Jerome's manner of citing these translations thus reflects the arrangement of the texts as they were compiled in the Hexapla, which strengthens the inference that he worked with man-uscripts containing the Hexaplaric columns before him. These books would have been the most important biblical resource in Jerome's library, as well as the most unusual and most costly to obtain.

Given their importance, it is strange that Jerome rarely mentions that he possessed manuscripts containing the Hexaplaric columns, and never refers to the Hexapla at all in his commentaries on the Prophets. A passage from his early commentary on Titus refers to copies of the Hexapla that he cor-rected against the originals in the library of Caesarea.[38] In the prefaces to his

---

37. Jerome cites the *recentiores* in the commentaries on the Minor Prophets as follows: citation of three or more named versions or reference to *omnes:* 77 instances; citation of two versions: 27; citation of one version: 54; Aquila only: 24; Symmachus only: 23; Theodotion only: 4; Quinta only: 1. Clearly, the most frequent manner of citing the *recentiores* is to cite all three (or more); references to Aquila only or to Symmachus only are also frequent, but much less so. There are 59 instances of citation of the *recentiores* (counting citations of several versions together as one instance) in the commentaries written in 392–93 (Nahum: 9; Micah: 18; Zephaniah: 7; Haggai: 0; Habbakuk: 25). Of the two commentaries written in 396–97, the commentary on Jonah yields no references; that on Obadiah contains 3, each citing all three versions. There are 96 instances in the commentaries written in 406 (Joel: 7; Malachi: 5; Zechariah: 16; Amos: 32; Hosea: 36). Jerome's use of the *recentiores,* then, was very uneven, but seems to respond more to the difficulty of the text under exegesis, and perhaps to the care or lack thereof with which a given commen-tary was written, than to any obvious chronological development. There is no correlation be-tween the number of references to the *recentiores* and the identity of Jerome's dedicatee.

38. The Latin text of the passage reads: *in quibus et ipsa Hebraea propriis sunt characteribus uerba descripta: et Graecis litteris tramite expressa uicino. Aquila etiam et Symmachus, Septuaginta quoque*

translations of Job, Joshua, and Ezra from the Hebrew, made between the late 380s and about 404, Jerome again refers to manuscripts of the Hexapla in his possession.[39] But occurrences of the word "Hexapla," much less references to the work itself, are otherwise rare.

Two reasons for Jerome's relative neglect of the Hexapla suggest themselves. First, the Hexapla had the potential to blur the distinction between the Jewish and the Christian exegetical traditions that was so central to his mature exegetical program. Jerome acknowledged that Origen had preceded him in appropriating Jewish scriptural learning for Christian use. Indeed, Origen's example played an important role in legitimating Jerome's Hebrew studies. But if Jerome had made clear how much of his Jewish learning was filtered through Greek Christian sources, he would have undermined his own carefully constructed authority. The Hexapla, too, was phenomenally expensive. Indeed, when Jerome mentions it in the prefaces to his translations, he makes a point of how costly and difficult it was to obtain a copy of Origen's text-critical tool, and assures his audience that a copy of the translation *iuxta Hebraeos* could serve the same basic purpose at far less cost.[40]

---

et Theodotio suum ordinem tenent. Nonnulli uero libri et maxime hi qui apud Hebraeos uersu compositi sunt, tres alias editiones additas habent: quam quintam, et sextam, et septimam translationem uocant: auctoritatem sine nominibus interpretum consecutas. Translation: "in which also the very Hebrew words in their own letters are copied: and expressed in Greek letters in the neighboring column. Aquila also, and Symmachus, the Septuagint and Theodotion hold their places. But for not a few books, and especially those which among the Hebrews are composed in verse, three other editions have been added, which are called the fifth, sixth, and seventh translations: they are considered authoritative though the names of the translators are lost." *Comm. in Titum* 3.9 (PL 26 734D-735A). Jerome also describes the Hexapla in his *De vir. ill.*: there, however, he is clearly dependent on Eusebius's description in *Hist. eccles.* 6.16, discussed below. The description of the commentary on Titus is much shorter, yet gives considerably more detail regarding the arrangement of the work.

39. Prefaces to translations of Job, Joshua, and Ezra in Fischer and Weber, *Biblia sacra* (1975).

40. See especially the prefaces to Joshua: *pro Graecorum ἑξαπλοῖς, quae et sumptu et labore maximo indigent, editionem nostram habeant et, sicubi in antiquorum uoluminum lectione dubitarint, haec illis conferentes inueniant quod requirunt* ("In place of the Hexapla of the Greeks, which demands a great deal both in expense and in labor, they may have our edition and, wherever they have doubts about a reading in the ancient volumes, comparing this to them they may find what they need"); and to Ezra: *Graecorum studium et beniuolentiam, qui post Septuaginta translatores iam Christi Euangelio coruscante Iudaeos et Hebionitas legis ueteris interpretes, Aquilam uidelicet, Symmachum et Theodotionem, et curiose legunt et per Origenis laborem in ἑξαπλοῖς ecclesiis dedicarunt. . . . Primum enim magnorum sumptuum est et infinitae difficultatis exemplaria posse habere omnia, deinde etiam qui habuerint et hebraei sermonis ignari sunt, magis errabunt ignorantes quis e multis uerius dixerit.* ("The Greeks, who after the Seventy translators now while Christ's Gospel is shining forth both read with interest the Jewish and Ebionite translators of the old law, namely Aquila, Symmachus and Theodotion, and indeed through the labor of Origen in the Hexapla dedicate them in the churches. . . . For first of all to be able to have copies of all of them is a mat-

Perhaps, then, Jerome refrained from referring to the Hexapla in his mature exegesis so as to avoid reminding his readers, on virtually every page of his commentaries, how expensive scholarship was. By leaving unstated the source of his readings from the *recentiores* and the other materials compiled in the Hexapla, Jerome could draw a discreet veil over such matters.

Alongside his library of biblical manuscripts, Jerome must have had an even larger and more costly collection of Jewish and Christian works, filling hundreds, if not thousands, of codices. Three primary categories of material made up the collection. Easiest to catalogue are the Christian and Jewish works that Jerome cited, with or without explicit attribution, throughout his scholarly works. Second, there were many works that he may not have used as sources but whose influence on his writing, or physical presence in his library, can be documented with a reasonable degree of certainty. Finally, it is likely that Jerome's library became the repository for the writings of many of his contemporaries, from the Cappadocians to Augustine and John Chrysostom — all of them prolific authors.

Among the works that Jerome used as sources, the importance of the commentaries of the exegetical school of Alexandria — Origen, Didymus, Eusebius of Caesarea, and a few others — is clear. Not only did Jerome depend on these writers, but he frankly acknowledges the debt. In the prefaces to his commentaries on Galatians and Ephesians, in the prefaces to the final three commentaries on the Minor Prophets, in the prologue to his commentary on Isaiah, and in numerous other places, he states that he used Origen's exegesis, whenever it was available, as the primary source for his allegorical interpretations and that he also relied on Didymus and Eusebius extensively.

In terms of sheer volume, Origen's writings likely made up the bulk of Jerome's library. The entry on Origen in *On Famous Men* refers the reader to Jerome's letter to Paula, written in 385, for a catalogue of Origen's works. Listed in that letter are 285 books of commentaries on the Bible, 468 homilies, *excerpta* on seven biblical books, and other materials totaling 38 books, including the ten books of the *Miscellanies* (in Greek, *Stromateis*) and four of *On First Principles*, for a total of just under 800 items of widely varying length.[41] Jerome clearly possessed and used copies of many of these books.

Pierre Courcelle, in his study of Jerome's Greek reading, asserts that Je-

---

ter of great expense and infinite difficulty, then too those who have these are yet ignorant of the Hebrew language, and thus they have erred more greatly, not knowing which of the many [translators] has spoken more truthfully.")

41. Letter 33.4.

rome knew intimately all of Origen's works that survived at the end of the fourth century. For Courcelle, the catalogue of Origen's works in the letter to Paula represents accurately the contents of Jerome's own library.[42] This seems unlikely. If the letter was written, as it purports to have been, at Rome around 385, then he probably did not yet have copies of all the texts it lists. Only after he had access to the library of Caesarea could Jerome have completed his collection of Origen's works. At Bethlehem, Jerome's library must have come to contain dozens, if not hundreds, of volumes of Origen's exegesis. He also had other items listed in letter 33: *On First Principles, Against Celsus,* and the ten books of *Stromateis,* which he cites in his commentary on Daniel. Unfortunately, the contents of these many volumes are mostly lost, making a detailed reconstruction impossible.

Other exegetes of the Alexandrian school made up an important part of Jerome's library. Courcelle contends that Jerome must have had Eusebius of Caesarea's entire oeuvre on hand, including several works not mentioned in *On Famous Men.* This seems very plausible, given that Jerome had taken an interest in Eusebius from the very beginning of his career, and that the library at Caesarea certainly would have preserved the complete works of the city's former bishop. Jerome's library, then, would have included Eusebius's *Ecclesiastical History,* itself a major source for *On Famous Men;* the *Chronicle,* which Jerome had translated at Constantinople; *On the Locations and Names of Hebrew Places,* which became the basis for Jerome's own work of the same title; the *Demonstration of the Gospel,* cited in Jerome's commentary on Daniel; the commentaries on Isaiah and Psalms; *On the Disagreements between the Gospels;* the *Preparation for the Gospel; Against Porphyry;* the *Apology for Origen;* the *Life of Pamphilus;* the *Theophany;* and *On the Martyrs of Palestine.*[43] Again, Eusebius's works would have formed a substantial library on their own.

The works of Didymus of Alexandria no doubt formed another important component of the library. These would have included not only the commentaries on Zechariah and Hosea already mentioned but also commentaries on the Psalms, on Isaiah, on the gospels of Matthew and John, and on Job. Didymus also wrote important theological works, among them the treatise on the Holy Spirit translated by Jerome soon after his arrival in the East;

---

42. Courcelle, *Latin Writers,* 111.

43. Courcelle, *Latin Writers,* 116–17: "it is probable that Jerome possessed Eusebius's complete works, for he incidentally refers to certain of his commentaries whose titles do not appear in the *De viris.*"

two books against the Arians; and a treatise titled *On Teachings*.[44] The sixth-century monastic library unearthed at Toura in Egypt in 1941 included the commentaries of Didymus on Zechariah, Genesis, Psalms, and Job. The commentary on Zechariah is nearly complete. The codices of Didymus's exegesis of Genesis and Psalms, however, preserve only fragments of the treatments of these biblical books attributed to him by Jerome, and the volume on Job appears to contain about half of the original. Another codex from Toura contains a work on Ecclesiastes now attributed to Didymus; it is less a formal commentary than a collection of lecture notes.[45] The Toura finds, then, substantiate and extend the list of works attributed to Didymus in the *On Famous Men*. Jerome probably possessed all of these works, a number of which served as the basis for his own literary productions.

A few earlier writers from the Alexandrian school turn up among the authors of books Jerome used in his commentaries on the Prophets. He cites Clement of Alexandria's *Stromateis* at length in the commentary on Daniel. Pierre Courcelle is willing to allow that Jerome also knew other works of this forerunner of Origen.[46] Rather more exotic is the reference, in the preface to the commentary on Hosea, to the exegesis of Pierius, a late third-century Alexandrian exegete, homilist, and successor to Origen as a Christian teacher. Here again, Courcelle goes so far as to imagine that Jerome's library included not only the long homily on the opening chapters of Hosea, which he cites explicitly, but other works as well.[47] Jerome's collection of the exegesis of Origen, his predecessors, and his institutional and intellectual heirs was therefore both broad and deep.

Jerome also knew the work of a number of exegetes of the Antiochene school. Their works, though less important as sources for his own commentaries, must have been represented in his library. Their presence is difficult to assess, since none of the Antiochene commentaries to which Jerome refers survives. Where his claims can be tested, it seems likely that he did have access to a number of these works. Among the school of Antioch, Apol-

---

44. Jerome, *De vir. ill.* 109: *Hic plurima nobiliaque conscripsit; commentarios in Psalmos omnes, commentarios in euangelium Matthaei et Iohannis, et De dogmatibus, et Contra Arianos libros duos, et De spiritu sancto librum unum quem ego in Latinum uerti, in Esaiam tomos decem et octo, in Osee ad me scribens commentariorum libros tres, et in Zachariam, meo rogatu, libros quinque, et commentarios in Iob et infinita alia, quae digerere proprii indicis est.* See also the prefaces to *In Osee* and *In Zachariam*.

45. Doutreleau, "Que savons-nous?" 164-69; Doutreleau, "Nouvel inventaire," 551-62.

46. Courcelle, *Latin Writers*, 99: Jerome uses only the *Stromateis* extensively, but probably knew other works of Clement's. He cites the *Stromateis* in *Comm. in Dan.* 3.9.24a.

47. Courcelle, *Latin Writers*, 113.

linaris of Laodicea exerted the most important influence. Jerome claimed to have been his student, attending lectures that Apollinaris gave on biblical exegesis in the early 370s. Whatever the truth of these claims, the fact that the two men spent several years in the same city suggests that Jerome had ready access to Apollinaris's works.[48] *On Famous Men* attributes to Apollinaris "innumerable volumes on the Holy Scriptures," many of which Jerome probably owned.[49] He specifically cites Apollinaris's treatments of Paul's letters and of the Prophets, as well as his treatise in thirty books against Porphyry.[50]

Jerome also mentions, and seems to have read, the third-century author Theophilus of Antioch and the fourth-century writers Eustathius of Antioch, Eusebius of Emesa (who spent his career at Antioch), Theodorus of Heraclea, Diodore of Tarsus, and John Chrysostom.[51] *On Famous Men* attributes commentaries on Paul's epistles to Diodore and to Eusebius of Emesa.[52] The latter is also credited with works against the Jews, Gentiles, and Novatians and a number of homilies on the Gospels.[53] Jerome's own commentary on Galatians, as well as his *Hebrew Questions on Genesis,* also refer to a number of works by these writers on Paul's letters and on Genesis, some of which he may have owned.[54] He even procured a Greek translation of a work by the Syriac writer Ephrem.[55]

Along with the Greek exegetes, the Jewish historian Josephus held an important place in Jerome's working library. Citations of and references to Josephus pepper Jerome's entire oeuvre. Courcelle states that Jerome possessed Josephus's complete works, and picturesquely describes the first-century writer as Jerome's "bedside book." Jerome relied heavily on the lengthy *Jewish Antiquities* and also knew the *Jewish War* intimately.[56] Like those of Eusebius, Josephus's works constitute a small library on their own.

---

48. On Jerome's early years at Antioch, see chapter 1 above. For his use of Apollinaris's exegesis in his commentaries, see the prefaces to Galatians, Hosea, Malachi, Matthew, and Daniel. For further discussion, see Courcelle, *Latin Writers,* 117-19.

49. *De vir. ill.* 104.

50. *De vir. ill.* 104, and the prologue to the *Comm. in Dan.* on Apollinaris's *Against Porphyry.*

51. Prologue to *Comm. in Gal.;* Courcelle, *Latin Writers,* 119-20.

52. *De vir. ill.* 119.

53. *De vir. ill.* 91.

54. Prologue to *Comm. in Gal.;* Courcelle, *Latin Writers,* 119-20; for these writers in the *Quaest. Heb. in Gen.,* see Kamesar, *Jerome,* 126-75.

55. *De vir. ill.* 115.

56. Courcelle, *Latin Writers,* 83-84.

Another Jewish author who wrote in Greek was Philo of Alexandria, the first-century exegete and advocate of a fusion of Judaism with Greek philosophy. Jerome certainly knew some of the works of this prolific author, but we cannot specify which he actually owned.[57]

In addition to the Christian and Jewish writers in Greek whose works formed the bulk of his research collection, Jerome cites a number of other Christian writers in his prefaces and in the commentary on Daniel. These include the third-century Greek authors Hippolytus of Rome and Julius Africanus, and the Latins Tertullian and Marius Victorinus.[58] Jerome might have known Hippolytus and Julius Africanus through the mediation of Origen's works or perhaps of Eusebius's chronological writings. But that he had his own copies of their works is implied by the extensive verbatim citations in his commentary on Daniel. The citations of Latin authors in the same commentary testify to the continued presence in Jerome's library of volumes reflecting the earliest, exclusively Latin phase of his Christian literary culture, documented by the letters he wrote from Antioch and the Syrian desert in the 370s.

In *On Famous Men* Jerome catalogues the works of numerous other Christian writers. This text has long been discounted as a source of information on Jerome's reading, much less on the books actually present in his library. It is true that where Eusebius of Caesarea, in his *Ecclesiastical History* or his *Chronicle,* had already discussed a writer, Jerome simply paraphrased, summarized, or translated Eusebius's account, even omitting information he provided elsewhere if it was not in Eusebius. Eusebius, however, covered the period only to 330 or so, and he neglected Latin authors entirely. Therefore, however untrustworthy Jerome's methods were in general, at least some of the notices in this work are best explained in terms of his personal reading. It would be dangerous to assume that simply because he followed Eusebius in describing a writer's career, Jerome had no firsthand knowledge of that author's work.[59]

With the glaring exception of Origen, fourth-century writers seem to have made up the majority of Jerome's library. We have already seen this

---

57. Courcelle, *Latin Writers,* 81–82.

58. For Hippolytus, see prologues to *Comm. in Zach., Comm. in Dan.;* all of these writers are cited at some length at *Comm. in Dan.,* 3.9.24a.

59. Courcelle, *Latin Writers,* 90–91, describes the minimalist views of earlier scholars but concludes, "Such [a low] estimate is certainly unjust, unless we are careful to limit its implication. . . . The fact that Jerome plagiarizes from Eusebius for a particular account does not consequently force us to think that he personally knows nothing of the author in question."

phenomenon in listing the Greek exegetes Jerome used in his commentaries. Didymus of Alexandria, Apollinaris of Laodicea, and the other Antiochenes were all Jerome's older contemporaries. Even Eusebius wrote most of his works during the fourth century. Jerome's library, therefore, contained a substantial collection of the works of recent writers. It is unlikely that Jerome's friends, acquaintances, teachers, and rivals went unrepresented in the library — Gregory of Nazianzus and the other Cappadocians; Epiphanius of Salamis; Bishop Theophilus of Alexandria, whose letters Jerome translated; even the young presbyter of Antioch, John Chrysostom.[60] Surely, too, Jerome's library contained samplings of the writings of the great men of the midcentury, especially Athanasius of Alexandria, whose oeuvre Jerome had perused in the episcopal archives of Rome in 382.[61] We cannot verify the presence of these authors' writings in Jerome's library — the notices in the On Famous Men are often sketchy in the extreme, and in any case take us only to 393 — but we ought to assume that many of their voluminous works found their way into Jerome's hands over the years. Their penumbral presence there, outside the solid core of Greek exegetical works that supported Jerome's labors as a commentator, must be noted even if it cannot be quantified.

Among the authors whose presence in Jerome's library has so far been catalogued, only two Latin writers have found a place: Tertullian, whom Jerome regarded with immense respect, and Marius Victorinus, whom he disdained as a rhetor out of his depth as an exegete. We know that Jerome possessed an ample library of Tertullian's books, including works that are now lost.[62] Furthermore, he certainly knew and treasured the writings of at least two other early Latin writers, Cyprian and Lactantius.

But again, Jerome's library of Latin Christian literature was weighted toward the fourth century. He knew Ambrose's works well — and made them a target for vicious, though veiled criticism.[63] He read the earlier Latin exegetes of the fourth century: not only Marius Victorinus but Hilary of Poitiers, Reticius of Autun, and the early fourth-century writers Arnobius of Sicca and Victorinus of Poetovio.[64] We know that Jerome possessed the

60. *De vir. ill.* 129: Jerome says that he has only read John Chrysostom's *Peri hierosynes.*

61. See chapter 1 above; *De vir. ill.* 87.

62. E.g., the *De ieiunio*, used in his *Aduersus Iouinianum* (Hagendahl, *Latin fathers*, 147–48).

63. On Jerome's criticism of Ambrose, see chapter 2 above.

64. On Hilary, see *De vir. ill.* 100, prologues to *Comm. in epist. ad Ephesios*, translation of Origen's homilies on Luke, *Comm. in Michaeam* (his commentary on the Psalms used Origen heavily), letters 5.2 (copied Hilary's *De synodiis* at Trier), 20.1 (cites Hilary's commentary on Matthew). On

works of Reticius, in particular his commentary on the Song of Songs, only because letters mentioning these works happen to be preserved. It seems improbable that Jerome did not have those of the other authors as well, however little he regarded them. These Latin writers of the earlier fourth century, too, form part of the penumbra of the library's contents. Further, Jerome may well have acquired numerous Latin Christian works written after his own *On Famous Men*. We know that he had some of these—Rufinus's *Apology*, and the writings of Vigilantius, Jovinian, and Pelagius—because he composed detailed, point-by-point refutations of them. Doubtless the works of other Latin contemporaries—his immediate peers, and especially his prolific juniors, such as Augustine and Sulpicius Severus—came into the hands of the monk of Bethlehem as well.

That Jerome's library—with the massive exception of Origen—was largely composed of the works of fourth century writers should come as no surprise. The early critics of *On Famous Men*, when they discovered its immense debt to Eusebius, drastically reduced their estimates of Jerome's learning. A famous dictum compares Jerome's use of Eusebius's *Ecclesiastical History* to Eusebius's use of the entire library at Caesarea.[65] But this disparagement of Jerome's reading places too much emphasis on early writers, whereas fourth-century authors were not only more numerous but far more prolific and, for Jerome, more up-to-date. As an act of self-fashioning, *On Famous Men* situates Jerome firmly in a Eusebian tradition of Christian literary history that, like literary and philosophical historiography in the non-Christian world, prized the ancient and the hard to obtain. But Jerome's scholarly practice was very different from what this representation implies.

Jerome's Christian literary world was a new and rapidly changing one, whatever value it may have accorded to a few ancient landmarks—an Origen, a Tertullian—who served to give distinction to the landscape. The Christian literary culture of the turn of the fourth century was largely the product of the previous eighty or one hundred years. Furthermore, the productivity of Jerome's own contemporaries or near-contemporaries redoubled the pace of change and growth. In this context, Jerome hardly had time to delve into the musty volumes of a Justin the Apologist or a Melito of Sardis.

Reticius, see *De vir. ill.* 82; letter 5.2, in which he requests a copy of his commentary on the Song of Songs; letter 37.1, in which he criticizes the same commentary for its ineptitude. On Arnobius, see *De vir. ill.* 79, and letters 58.10 and 70.5 on his seven books *Aduersus nationes*. On Victorinus of Poetovio, see *Comm. in Hiezech.* 11.36.640; *Adv. Helv.* 17.211.16.

65. Harnack, *Altchristliche Literatur,* vol. 1, p. L, n. 1, cited in Courcelle, *Latin Writers,* 90.

Jerome's literary world had as much in common with that of a modern experimental scientist, for whom an article ten years old is woefully out of date, as with that of a modern classical scholar, who may find it worth her while to dig up a few references going back more than a century to adorn a learned bibliography. Of course, Jerome and his contemporaries still assigned immense authority to tradition, and used the names of earlier writers to authenticate their own views. But in practice, it may often have been more important for them to keep up with the new than to cultivate the old.

In addition to Christian and Jewish works, Jerome's library contained abundant materials of a very different kind. Despite his disavowals in the letter to Eustochium written at Rome in 385 and in the preface to his commentary on Galatians of the following year, it is beyond question that Jerome owned a large and diverse collection of writings by pagan authors,[66] both literary and philosophical. Although he did not advertise his possession of the writings of Cicero, Seneca, Virgil, and Horace—much less the pagan philosopher and advocate of persecution Porphyry, or the violently anti-Christian fourth-century historian Aurelius Victor—he had many such works on hand in Bethlehem. Several passages from his polemical works clearly rely on pagan writers whose texts he had before him as he wrote. Rufinus, too, provides detailed evidence for the presence of manuscripts of pagan writers in the library at Bethlehem.

The pagan books in Jerome's library fall into three main categories: historical works, philosophy, and literature. We do not know if he still had the books he used when he was composing the revised and extended Latin version of Eusebius's *Chronicle* at Constantinople. But it seems likely that at Bethlehem, Jerome had on hand a collection of historical works, many of which dealt with recent events. After he settled in Bethlehem, Jerome seems to have created a collection of pagan philosophical writings. He drew heavily on these in composing his polemical and antiheretical works. Finally, he seems to have held on to, or gathered anew, a collection of Latin literary works, including a good deal of Latin poetry. Perhaps he also had copies of commentaries on the classical texts that were studied in the grammatical schools.

---

66. Although I am uncomfortable with the term "pagan," I use it here in lieu of awkward circumlocutions such as "non-Christian, non-Jewish writers" and with the justification that my focus here is on these authors as Jerome and his Christian contemporaries would have seen them, not on their own views or those of Greek and Roman religious traditionalists who sought to appropriate the prestige of the canonical authors in defense of their own views.

The *Chronicle* depends on a number of Latin sources for the information that Jerome added to Eusebius's original column on Roman history and for its material on the fourth century. Jerome used Eutropius's *Brief History from the Foundation of Rome*, Festus's *Brief History of the Roman People*, and probably also the *Epitome de Caesaribus* of Aurelius Victor.[67] For the earlier references to Latin literary figures he relied on Suetonius's original *On Famous Men*.[68] Shortly after his arrival at Bethlehem, Jerome had projected the composition of a history of the church going down to his own times. His collection of historical works would have been a useful resource for such a project, suggesting that perhaps the books had traveled with him from Constantinople to Rome and then back to the East.[69]

Jerome's collection of philosophical works, from what little we can know of it, seems even more surprising. Rufinus reports that Jerome paid the monks in Rufinus's monastery on the Mount of Olives to make copies of "almost all" of Cicero's dialogues.[70] A number of allusions to the dialogues in his writings from the years at Bethlehem make clear that Jerome had these works and used them. Jerome mines Cicero's *Cato Maior*, his lost *Consolatio*, the *Tusculans*, and the *De fato* in specific works where these sources are apposite. He also cites or alludes to a number of other philosophical works of Cicero's, including *De Officiis*, *De re publica*, *Laelius*, *De finibus*, *Academica*, *De natura deorum*, and *De diuinatione*, and the lost *De gloria* and *De uirtutibus*.[71] Jerome used Seneca's lost *De matrimonio* heavily. He probably possessed a number of Seneca's other writings as well, perhaps including his tragedies as well as his philosophical works.[72]

Perhaps most startling is the evidence for Jerome's Greek philosophical library. Rufinus informs us that Jerome possessed at least one dialogue of Plato's. He may also have had direct access to the works of Theophrastus. He had studied the commentaries of Alexander of Aphrodisias on Aristotle at Antioch in the 370s, and may still have had them in Bethlehem.[73] Beyond

67. Jerome, *Jerome's Chronicon*, 19-33; Jerome had requested a copy of the work of Aurelius Victor from Paul of Concordia in his letter 5, though of course we cannot be certain that he got it.

68. Hagendahl, *Latin Fathers*, 107, citing Mommsen, "Quellen."

69. For the project of a history of the church in his own times, see the preface to the *Vita Malchi*, discussed in chapter 2 above.

70. Rufinus, *Apol.* 2.11.

71. Hagendahl, *Latin Fathers*, 192-94, 202-3, 64, 84-92.

72. Hagendahl, *Latin Fathers*, 266, 97; he cites Bickel, *Senecae fragmenta*, on the lost *De matrimonio*.

73. Rufinus, *Apol.* 2.11; Courcelle, *Latin Writers*, 71.

these authors, Jerome's holdings of the philosophical works of the classical and Hellenistic periods were probably few.[74] But he seems to have avidly collected the works of philosophers of the late empire. Unquestionably, he had an extensive collection of the works of the Neoplatonist Porphyry—despite that writer's vehement opposition to Christianity. It is unsurprising that Jerome should have obtained a copy of Porphyry's work *Against the Christians,* since he had to refute his charges in his commentary on Daniel. But it is peculiar, to say the least, to find in Jerome's possession copies of Porphyry's biography of Pythagoras, his treatise *De abstinentia,* his *Isagoge* or introduction to Aristotelian dialectic, and perhaps other works as well.[75] Jerome also used a work of Iamblichus, Porphyry's younger contemporary and rival. Alongside the anti-Christian treatise of Porphyry, Jerome also had the emperor Julian's *Aduersos Galilaeos.* He read at Bethlehem the *Life of Apollonius* of Philostratus, a work that fourth-century pagans had used to support the contention that Jesus was an inferior version of Apollonius. Jerome also seems to have had a number of works of Plutarch's, in particular the *Gamika paraggelmata,* which served him as a source for arguments in favor of virginity. Courcelle argues that he possessed a library of Galen's principal works, though he did not know any other Greek medical writers.[76]

It was his collection of Latin literary authors, however, that Jerome in the account of his famous dream explicitly claims to have renounced. We have already seen that during his years at Bethlehem he procured and studied Cicero's philosophical writings. Indeed, it may be that his acquaintance with these works began, or at least deepened significantly, during this period.[77] He certainly seems to have exerted himself to acquire new copies of them after 385.[78] Rufinus provides further evidence that Jerome also possessed the principal works of the Latin writers used in the grammatical curriculum. He accuses Jerome of serving as a *grammaticus,* teaching young

---

74. Courcelle, *Latin Writers,* 66–67.

75. Courcelle, *Latin Writers,* 72–78, discusses the works of Porphyry used by Jerome, detecting signs that he possessed all the works listed, but denying that he had a copy of the *Contra Christianos,* since it had been ordered destroyed under Constantine. However, given that Jerome knew personally Apollinaris of Laodicea, author of a refutation in thirty books of Porphyry's anti-Christian treatise, it is difficult to admit Courcelle's suggestion that all copies of Porphyry's work had perished: how then could Apollinaris have written his refutation? We may suppose, therefore, that Jerome takes his numerous and detailed references to the *Contra Christianos* from a copy of the original.

76. Courcelle, *Latin Writers,* 72, 76–77, 62, 87.

77. Hagendahl, *Latin Fathers,* 291–92.

78. Rufinus, *Apol.* 2.11.

boys to read Virgil, Horace, Terence, and probably Sallust as well.[79] While Rufinus's charge need not be believed in every detail, Jerome never goes so far as to deny it. We ought, therefore, to entertain at least the possibility that in his monastery at Bethlehem Jerome taught Latin literature to young boys. Once that is granted, the list of writers Rufinus puts forward appears to be stereotypical—and therefore all the more likely to be accurate.

Harald Hagendahl, in his study of Jerome's use of classical Latin authors, argues vehemently for the idea that Jerome continued to read the Latin poets and prose writers in his old age at Bethlehem. Hagendahl finds it impossible to believe that Jerome could remember, decades after the conclusion of his own grammatical studies, the many verses and *sententiae* he continues to cite from various writers.[80] Although Hagendahl certainly underestimates the role of memorization in classical literary culture, particularly in the use of *sententiae* and gnomic materials, his views support the conclusion that Rufinus's accusation was based on reality rather than on polemical fiction. In such a case, Jerome would certainly have had on hand the complete works of the three poets already mentioned, and perhaps others. Given his predilection for Sallustian *sententiae*, the historian's works were probably also present in the monastery at Bethlehem.[81] Finally, Jerome may have used Quintilian's *Institutions* directly in his letter 107, written between 400 and 402. His possession of that work might be connected with his work as a teacher of Latin literature. But it is also possible that he drew the material that parallels Quintilian from memory, since the similarities are fairly vague.[82]

---

79. *in monasterio positus in Bethleem, ante non multum adhuc temporis partes grammaticas executus sit, et Maronem suum comicosque ac lyricos et historicos auctores traditis sibi ad discendum Dei timorem puerulis exponebat, scilicet ut et praeceptor fieret auctorum gentilium, quos si legisset tantummodo, Christum se iurauerat negaturum.* (Rufinus, *Apol.* 2.11) "[When] he was settled in his monastery in Bethlehem, not a long time ago, he played the part of a *grammaticus,* and expounded to young boys who had been handed over to him in order that they might learn the fear of God his own Virgil and the comic, lyric, and historical writers. Note, then, that he acted as a teacher of those Gentile authors, whom he had sworn that if he even read them, he would be denying Christ."

80. Hagendahl, *Latin Fathers,* 321–22 et passim.

81. Hagendahl, *Latin Fathers,* 292–94.

82. Hagendahl, *Latin Fathers,* 196–201: letter 107.4 is a paraphrase of Quintilian *Institutio oratoria,* 1.1; however, there are few really close verbal parallels between Jerome and Quintilian. It seems possible, therefore, that Jerome was either remembering his reading of the *Institutio* at an earlier time or simply articulating commonplaces of the ancient educational system, traceable to Quintilian but not necessarily derived directly from him. The main support for the idea that Jerome was using Quintilian comes from the historical examples Jerome cites (Aristotle as the tutor of Alexander, the Gracchi, and Hortensius learned to pronounce Latin properly from their

One further possibility, speculative as it may be, is worth mentioning. In refuting Rufinus's charges of plagiarism against his commentary on Ephesians, Jerome argues that he merely proceeded after the model of grammarians when they commented on literary works. In support of this claim, he parades a catalogue of commentators, referring to "the commentaries of Asper on Virgil and Sallust, of Vulcatius on Cicero's orations, of Victorinus on his dialogues, and of my teacher Donatus on the comedies of Terence, similarly on Virgil, and of others on other writers, Plautus for example, Lucretius, Horace, Persius and Lucan."[83] Could Jerome have had copies of these same commentaries at Bethlehem? Certainly he might have drawn upon them in his work as a teacher. If the curriculum he provided to the boys at Bethlehem was similar to the one he himself had imbibed at Rome in the school of Donatus, then some of the grammarians' works might well have been on hand. Donatus's technical works on grammar and syntax, surely, must have been available. We cannot know if this speculation deserves credence, but it is tempting to imagine that alongside the many commentators on the Bible whose works he collected, Jerome also kept a cache of commentaries on Latin literature.

The library at Bethlehem, then, contained a very wide range of books. The biblical manuscripts discussed in the first section of this chapter may have included some of the library's rarest and most costly volumes. Its collection of Christian literature was vast and varied. Greek Christian exegetes unsurprisingly play the most important role: their works would have formed the bulk of the library. We can safely say that Jerome possessed several hundred codices containing such works. Other kinds of Christian works were surely present in significant numbers as well. Their precise representation is difficult to define, since Jerome did not rely on them so consistently as sources for his commentaries. Nevertheless, he clearly owned numerous codices of Tertullian, Cyprian, and other Latin writers from the second through the early fourth century, and of Latin exegetes like Reticius and Marius Victorinus. The library likely included an even larger number of codices containing the writings of Jerome's rough contemporaries, particularly such prolific writers as the Cappadocians, Ambrose, Hilary, Augus-

---

parents; Leonidas, Alexander's pedagogue), which are paralleled in Quintilian and do suggest dependence.

83. Jerome, *Contra Ruf.* 1.16: *puto quod puer legeris Aspri in Vergilium ac Sallustium commentarios, Vulcatii in orationes Ciceronis, Victorini in dialogos eius, et in Terentii comoedias praeceptoris mei Donati, aeque in Vergilium, et aliorum in alios, Plautum uidelicet, Lucretium, Flaccum, Persium atque Lucanum.*

tine, John Chrysostom, Athanasius, and Rufinus, as well as various others. Its collection of pagan books was more limited in numbers, but even this component of the library would still have run to dozens of codices, perhaps even a few hundred. As Rufinus's accusations document, Jerome spared no effort or expense to acquire books.

This was, unquestionably, a library after the aristocratic model. It was not the kind of collection that a grammarian—even a very successful one—would have assembled for professional use. It was probably considerably larger than the library discovered in the Villa of the Papyri at Herculaneum, for example. Indeed, the library at Bethlehem may well have rivaled the episcopal library of Caesarea as the foremost Christian library in Palestine. But that collection, by the late fourth century, was the property of a wealthy see, not of a single monk. Jerome's library was the personal possession of a man who had renounced wealth—and as we shall see, its contents were literally worth a fortune. Even if Jerome managed to address the challenge that his scholarship presented to the monastic value of humility, he would find it difficult to rationalize his violation of the norm of poverty.

CHAPTER FIVE

———— ✳ ————

Toward a Monastic Order of Books

IN THE preface to his translation of Job from the Septuagint, written in 390 or 391, Jerome compares his scholarly labors explicitly to the manual work that for the desert monks served as a form of self-mortification as well as a foundation of their independence from worldly ties. He develops in characteristically vivid language the comparison of his translation of Job to the rush baskets and palm-leaf mats woven by the fathers:

> If I were to weave a basket from rushes or to plait palm leaves, so that I might eat my bread in the sweat of my brow and work to fill my belly with a troubled mind, no-one would criticize me, no-one would reproach me. But now, since according to the word of the Savior I wish to store up the food that does not perish, and to purge the ancient track of the divine volumes from brambles and brushwood, I who have made authenticity my cause, I, a corrector of vice, am called a forger, and it is said that I do not remove errors, but sow them. . . . So, therefore, Paula and Eustochium . . . in place of the straw mat and the little rush baskets, the small presents of the monks, receive these spiritual and enduring gifts.[1]

Manual labor, Jerome complains, was an accepted occupation for a monk. Biblical translation raised eyebrows. We might not take his claims seriously

---

1. *si aut fiscellam iunco texerem aut palmarum folia conplicarem, ut in sudore uultus mei comederem panem et uentris opus sollicita mente tractarem, nullus morderet, nemo reprehenderet. nunc autem quia iuxta sententiam Saluatoris uolo operari cibum qui non perit, et antiquam diuinorum uoluminum uiam sentibus uirgultisque purgare, mihi genuinus infigitur, corrector uitiorum, falsarius uocor, et errores non auferre, sed serere. . . . quapropter, o Paula et Eustochium . . . pro flauello, calathis sportellisque, munusculo monachorum, spiritualia haec et mansura dona suscipite.*

if we did not know how unusual it was for a cenobite, in Jerome's time, to be an author without being accused of some heresy or other.

Furthermore, the goals of the monastic life, and its underlying world-view, were deeply at odds with the literary culture that was Jerome's real qualification as a writer. The central values of monasticism were humility, poverty, and obedience, whether to a spiritual father or to the head of a cenobitic monastery. Monastic *askesis* aimed at subduing, even at eradicating, self-seeking impulses, so as to transform the individual from a battleground of demonic passions into a pure vessel for the Holy Spirit. Humble, even degrading manual labor played a central role in the monastic program of radical self-transformation. Traditional education and the practices by which adult elite males sought to maintain what they had achieved through education, even while employing ascetic practices to channel the passions and to limit the grosser expressions of self-interest, had quite different goals. Greco-Roman literary culture sought to produce dispositions that allowed the elite male to control others as he controlled himself, and thus ultimately to develop its participants' personal authority. To equate literary production with the characteristic labor of the monk was implicitly to represent it as a way of destroying, rather than maintaining, those carefully cultivated dispositions. That took some daring.

Jerome's depiction of his scholarly activity as a form of labor appropriate to a desert monk, therefore, invites an investigation of his material practice as a scholar that goes beyond cataloguing the contents of his library. It matters how he worked because his labors as an exegete were the essence of *his* monastic vocation, just as the labors of the Egyptian fathers, weaving palm-leaf mats in their desert cells, were essential to *their* way of life. It was precisely the form of Jerome's labor—biblical scholarship, rather than menial toil—that set apart his form of monasticism as a novelty, and challenged reigning conceptions of the monk. We must ask, therefore, exactly how Jerome used the books that he had collected. His vast and costly collection was a library after the aristocratic model rather than that of a lowly provincial *grammaticus*, a small-town Christian presbyter, or an Egyptian monastery. In demonstrating the physical role it played in his activity as a scholar, we expose one of the sharpest edges of the cultural tension that cut across, and threatened to undermine, his self-fashioning.

At the same time, a reconstruction of the physical form of the books that Jerome used situates his literary activities more firmly in a specific place and time. A concrete idea of what Jerome's books looked like can serve as a useful safeguard against the tendency to picture him in the more familiar guises of a classical or a medieval scholar. No more can we imagine Jerome at work by thinking of a medieval author-portrait, the frontispiece of a Gospel for example, than we can by calling to mind an Attic funerary stele or a fresco from Pompeii advertising the culture of its wealthy subject. Jerome's literary monasticism was a thoroughly late antique phenomenon. This is as true for the physical media through which he used and produced texts as it is for the model of the monastic life with which he was presented, one that left open no obvious place for a literary career.

THE FOURTH-CENTURY BOOK
AND THE MONK AS READER

By the late fourth century, the book culture of the Roman Mediterranean had undergone a transformation that set it apart from that of the classical world. It had not, however, taken on the familiar features of the medieval European, or indeed Byzantine, culture of the book. Instead, late antiquity developed its own unique and highly sophisticated mode of producing and using books. The two principal distinguishing features of this book culture were, on the one hand, the wholesale adoption of the codex as the usual form of the book, and, on the other hand, the continued dominance of papyrus as the preferred material on which to write books.[2] These two features of the late antique order of books symbolize, respectively, the vitality of the late Roman culture of the book—its capacity for self-transformation and productive innovation—and its continuity with classical precedents.

It is well known that the codex had come to dominate the production of books of all kinds by the last decades of the fourth century. Juvenal testifies to its use for classical literature at the end of the first century. By the early second century, it had become the preferred form for Christian books in Egypt (fig. 7).[3] But the codex form remains rare among the papyri until the

---

2. I use the term "book" to refer to an object of whatever form and material that contains a substantial text or collection of texts, as distinct from, for example, a letter, pamphlet, or notebook. "Codex" refers to the form of the book familiar to modern readers, i.e., a book made up of pages bound between two covers, as opposed to the roll book. "Papyrus" can refer either to the writing material, made from the stalks of the papyrus plant, or to a text or book preserved on papyrus and discovered archaeologically in Egypt. Some Egyptian papyrus manuscripts were in roll form, others in codex form.

3. On the early adoption of the codex by Christians: Roberts and Skeat, *Birth of the Codex;* Gamble, *Books and Readers,* 42–82.

FIGURE 7. An opening from a papyrus codex of Numbers, copied in the second or early third century, now in the Chester Beatty Library, Dublin. P. Chester Beatty VI, fol. 11v–12. Reproduced with permission of the Chester Beatty Library.

third century, when it seems to increase in popularity. At the same time, the physical construction and layout of the codex became more sophisticated and more standardized. By the mid-fourth century, Christian codices could be produced to a very high standard, as the examples of the fourth-century pandect Bibles, Vaticanus and Sinaiticus (fig. 8), demonstrate. By Jerome's day, the codex had become the preferred form for classical literature as well. Two luxurious Virgil codices that probably date to the end of the fourth or the early fifth century, both richly illustrated with paintings that convey a strongly pagan interpretation of the text, show that the codex, if it had ever had specifically Christian associations, had them no more.[4]

Correspondingly, scholars long assumed that the fourth century saw the replacement of papyrus by parchment as the preferred writing material for literary codices.[5] Yet this view has been reevaluated, as estimates of the durability and convenience of papyrus have risen and as new discoveries have added to the lists of extant papyrus codices. Far from being the fragile, temperamental stuff that scholars once imagined, papyrus was a long-lasting, high-quality medium. Papyrus codices continued to be produced in Egypt, where the material remained plentiful, until well into the Islamic period. Outside Egypt, their use persisted at least into the sixth century.[6]

Fourth-century bookhands show both innovation and continuity with the past. Over a span of several centuries, the Greek hands found in papyri vary, but show little directional development. In particular, paleographers have failed to define precise criteria for dating late antique documentary

---

4. These manuscripts are the so-called Vergilius Romanus, Vat. lat. 3867, and Vergilius Vaticanus, Vat. lat. 3225.

5. For example, Arns, *Technique*, 23 n. 3: "Le *codex* est d'ordinaire en parchemin" (referring to a passage from the Pachomian rule, written in Egypt!). On the basis of this assumption, which would now be considered ill-founded, Arns interprets every reference to a codex in Jerome's work as implying a volume written on *parchment*, and gives credit to Jerome for the "victory" of parchment in the "battle" for dominance as the writing material of the fourth- and fifth-century monastic world.

6. For an earlier view, already cognizant of some of the important mid-twentieth-century discoveries but still emphasizing the superiority of parchment, see Kenyon, *Books and Readers*, 86–119. Arguing in favor of the longevity of the papyrus codex even outside Egypt, Turner, *Typology*, 40–41, writes: "there can be no automatic presumption that the codex of papyrus is restricted to Egypt. . . . there is good evidence that papyrus continued to hold its own against parchment in the early medieval world. We know that important and still surviving papyrus codices of the sixth century (e.g., the Paris Avitus, . . . the Vienna St. Hilary) were written in southern France, with which Egypt still maintained a flourishing commerce of papyrus. . . . Letters from [Antioch, Athens, Rome and Constantinople] of the third to the sixth centuries show that papyrus continued to be readily available in them."

FIGURE 8. An opening of the Codex Sinaiticus, fourth century, showing two pages of the Gospel of Luke. British Library Add. MS 43725, foll. 244v.–245r. Reproduced with permission of the British Library.

hands.[7] The hands used in books of lower quality also show considerable continuity. Development is much clearer in luxury books, where the fourth century saw the emergence of an entirely new hand. Because it is best known from the great fourth-century Bibles, this hand has been called "biblical uncial"—a term that has its limitations, since the same hand is found in other texts. Earlier Greek bookhands, and many late antique hands of lesser pretensions, combined minuscule and majuscule letter forms. The so-called "biblical uncial," however, was a fully developed majuscule hand, which allowed for great clarity and readability while sacrificing economy of materials. It was large, clear, and often very beautiful, its letter forms extraordinarily regular and homogeneous. To write such a hand would have required a high level of training and considerable effort.[8]

The new hand, while it seems to have developed first in Greek, quickly came to influence Latin scribal practice as well. An extraordinary witness to this transmission of Greek scribal practices to the West—at a time when knowledge of Greek in the Latin-speaking parts of the Mediterranean was already declining—comes from a few late antique bilingual papyri, in which the same scribe wrote, often in parallel columns, Latin literary texts in the original and in a Greek translation. Their provenance and purpose make clear that these papyri were the work of Greek scribes who produced books for Greek readers interested in learning Latin. Interest in Latin among Greek speakers peaked in the fourth and fifth centuries, with the rise of legal training, centered on Berytus and conducted in Latin, as a path to advancement in the imperial administration. The hand that these Greek scribes used to write their Latin texts is uncannily similar to that which begins, in the fifth century if not before, to replace older hands that imitated epigraphic lettering as the Latin luxury hand par excellence.[9]

In both East and West, the dominance of majuscule bookhands, espe-

---

7. For Greek bookhands in this period, see Cavallo and Maehler, *Greek Bookhands;* a convenient series of images is presented in Turner, *Greek Manuscripts;* for documentary hands from the same period, see Turner, *Greek Papyri.*

8. In the Greek world, uncial script was the most expensive hand, as being the most slowly written and the largest. Smaller, more cursive majuscule hands were used for less luxurious books. There was no Greek equivalent to the Latin *capitalis,* a hand based on inscriptional letter forms and reserved in Latin bookmaking for the most expensive volumes of pagan literary authors. "Biblical uncial" is described authoritatively in Cavallo, *Ricerche.* On Latin Christian hands in late antiquity, see Bischoff, *Latin paleography,* 53–81.

9. On the influence of Greek bookhands on Latin uncial in late antiquity, see Cavallo, *Ricerche,* 124ff.

cially for the writing of luxury books and copies of the Bible and the classics, was to continue as long as the culture that we call late antique survived. It was replaced in the East, in the wake of the Arab conquests and the consolidation of the Byzantine empire, by a new Greek minuscule hand; in the West, by Caroline minuscule and a range of regional developments. "Biblical uncial," therefore, can be taken as a material correlative of the last great pan-Mediterranean cultural synthesis, which emerged under the resurgent, and Christianizing, Roman empire of the fourth century.

Books in Jerome's day were stunningly expensive, as they had been for centuries. Our only real data for the cost of books in the late antique Mediterranean come from a single source, the Price Edict posted by Diocletian throughout his empire in 303. The edict was intended to regulate prices at a period of high inflation, and may therefore be out of step with normal prices. Furthermore, it was a rather hopeful piece of legislation, expressive at best of the emperor's intentions, not of economic reality. The prices listed become almost meaningless for Jerome's day, roughly a century later. Nonetheless, the Price Edict is useful insofar as it allows us to estimate and compare various prices. For example, a high-quality manuscript of Virgil's *Aeneid* would have cost 3400 denarii, while a second-quality manuscript of the same work, written in uncial letters rather than in *capitalis,* would have cost 2600.[10]

As far as we know, the only work Jerome ever did for which he might have been paid was teaching Latin grammar at Bethlehem. A grammarian's fee thus provides a useful basis for interpreting this data for the cost of books. The Price Edict sets fees at 200 denarii per student per month. The monthly fee of a medium-sized class, then, would be sufficient to cover the purchase of two books similar to the second-quality Virgil manuscript just mentioned.[11] Clearly, Jerome did not build up his library by paying for the copying of books with the money that he made as a teacher.

---

10. For these figures see Marichal, "Écriture latine," 214–16 and 14 n. 5; the data are as follows, from the edition of Lauffer, *Preisedikt,* 120: "[38] membranario in [qua]t<erni>one pedali pergamen[i uel] croca[ti] D XL; [39] scriptori in sc<ri>ptura optima versus n. centum D XXV; [40] sequ[enti]s scripturae bersuum no. centum D XX; [41] tabellanioni in scriptura libelli bel tabularum [in ver]sibus no. centum[D] X."

11. For grammarians' incomes, see Kaster, *Guardians,* 118–23, who cites *Edict. de pret.* 7.70–71 for the fee as set by Diocletian, and also addresses what little evidence we have for the size of classes, which comes mostly from Libanius. Clearly, there was wide variation, but a good-sized class might usually have had about thirty students. Such a class would generate a monthly fee, in the terms of the Price Edict, of 6000 denarii (72,000 denarii per year).

The scale of expenditure involved in the creation of Jerome's library can be readily appreciated when we consider a single example of a book that he must have possessed: the Hexapla. The writing alone would have cost approximately 75,000 denarii. Unfortunately, the passage of the Price Edict regulating the price of papyrus has not survived, but the parchment needed for a copy written on that relatively luxurious material would have cost an additional 75,000 denarii. Even in Palestine, copying the Hebrew column would presumably have required hiring an additional scribe, or else a more skilled one, capable of writing a good bookhand in both languages. Either would add to the expense. Furthermore, the Hexapla's complex layout would surely have increased the price of a copy. The minimum cost of a complete copy of the Hexapla, therefore, would have been about 155,000 denarii, sixty times the price of the kind of manuscript typical of a scholar's working library and equivalent to at least two years' earnings for a successful grammarian.[12]

On every level, late antique book culture allowed for a differentiation between elite and sub-elite registers. As the codex was gradually perfected, longer texts could be more easily contained within smaller books, reducing the cost of materials. Technology thus had the potential to make books less expensive. But the codex also provided new opportunities for the production of luxury books, through the development of elaborate bindings and the explosion of ornamentation, whether in the form of illustrations or of precious inks and purple-dyed parchment. Papyrus remained an accessible and relatively inexpensive material, but the superiority of parchment for the production of codices was becoming clear, creating what may have been a two-tiered hierarchy of writing materials: one for routine use, the other for books conceived of as precious objects. The new majuscule hands lent new distinction to fine copies of the scriptures and the classics, while largely erasing the cost advantage of the codex by increasing the space needed to write the text. But earlier, more modest bookhands persisted, allowing less

---

12. The total number of words in the Hebrew Bible is 304,901, according to the Masoretic lists printed in modern rabbinic Bibles. The fragments of the Hexapla suggest that the original may have had forty lines per page, arranged so as to display one Hebrew word per line. Taken together with the evidence of Turner, *Typology*, for plausible formats for codices written in the early third century, this information allows one tentatively to reconstruct a Bible that filled about twenty volumes of 400 leaves (800 pages) each. Although this is only a hypothetical estimate, it suffices to generate a relative order of magnitude for the cost of a copy to be compared with the figures in the Price Edict for the grammarian's fee. For the reconstruction, see Williams, "Jerome's Biblical Criticism," 151ff.

costly manuscripts to cram far more into a codex—whose pages were now written on both sides—than onto a single roll.

The new means of expression for the distinction between elite and sub-elite book cultures provided by the physical transformation of the book no doubt reinforced the existing differentiation between elite and sub-elite libraries. Roll books varied widely in quality, and the corresponding differences in price were presumably significant. But in the first centuries of the Roman empire, elite libraries were primarily distinguished from humbler ones by the number of books they contained, and the elaboration of the means for storing them. There could be no sharper contrast between the magnificent library constructed by Trajan as the centerpiece of his vast new forum at Rome, and the humble cupboards that sheltered the scriptures of persecuted Christians. The one was not only a place for storing books but also a monument to its creator and a locus for elite urban sociability; the other was a wooden box. In late antiquity, the distinction between the book culture of the elite and that of the merely literate was extended to cover every aspect of book production. The self-contained portability of the codex, we may imagine, had a symbolic as well as a practical dimension. Not only could a codex enclose an impressive range of texts, a library between two covers, but in and of itself it could indicate a precise social level, independent of the setting in which it might be found.

Monastic literature is ambivalent toward the book. Some texts require that monks read, while others suggest that books should be totally excluded from the ideal monastic life. The *Sayings of the Desert Fathers* is a sixth-century compilation that purports to record the words and deeds of desert monks whose lives spanned the previous three centuries. A story in the collection places books among those possessions which a monk would do better to renounce, even if they are sources of spiritual profit:

> Abba Theodore of Pherme had acquired three good books. He came to Abba Macarius and said to him, "I have three excellent books from which I derive profit; the brethren also make use of them and derive profit from them. Tell me what I ought to do: keep them for my use and that of the brethren, or sell them and give the money to the poor?" The old man answered him in this way, "Your actions are good; but it is best of all to possess nothing." Hearing that, he went and sold his books and gave the money for them to the poor.[13]

13. While the collections of the *Sayings of the Desert Fathers* in which this saying appears are all late, Macarius was a mid-fourth-century father, active already by 330. Regardless of its historicity, the episode may plausibly be taken to describe an ideal shared by many, if by no means all, fourth-century desert ascetics.

The fourth-century Pachomian rule, on the other hand, made reading an important element in the cenobitic routine. The monks were required to be literate enough to read the Gospels and the Psalms, and it was expected that they would have access to books. A Pachomian regulation further dictates, "If they seek a book to read, let them have it; and at the end of the week they shall put it back in its place for those who succeed them in the service."[14] Lest we imagine that the rule envisioned extensive collections for the monks' use, another provision refers to the place where books were stored: a niche that was also home to the monastery's tweezers![15]

In monastic circles, therefore, there was debate over whether reading had any spiritual value at all. Furthermore, these prescriptive and idealizing texts imply that where monks did read, their book culture belonged to that of the sub-elite rather than that of the elite and the institutions it endowed. These sources give little reason to imagine that monasteries collected vast libraries such as those found in major cities or in the homes of the aristocracy. Where monastic texts do refer to reading, the forms they prescribe are intensive rather than extensive, meditative rather than scholarly. Monastic reading began with the scriptures. Often—in particular, in its most idealized, meditative form—it also ended there. Monastic texts depict the reading of the desert fathers as focused on a limited number of texts, which they learned by heart. The monastic ideal was to internalize the scriptures as part of a program of refashioning the self.[16] Nor was the *lectio divina* coupled to literary production. We are informed that monks read, but not that they wrote.

Chance finds reveal what kinds of books some Egyptian monasteries in late antiquity actually owned. The famous Gnostic library discovered at Nag Hammadi in upper Egypt was probably hidden by monks from a nearby Pachomian monastery, presumably because the texts contained in the codices were prohibited and their possession had become dangerous. The Nag Hammadi codices are extremely simple, even crude, in their materials, construction and writing (fig. 9).[17] In this sense, they fit firmly within the kind of book culture that literary depictions of monastic life lead us to expect. Yet their unusual contents suggest that these books must have formed part

14. For books in the Pachomian rule, see Veilleux, *Pachomian koinonia*, 2:149 (25: monks may have a book to read); 2:160 (82: tweezers kept with books); 2:62 (101-2: handling of books); 2:66 (139-40: literacy required for all monks).

15. Veilleux, *Pachomian koinonia*, 2:160.

16. Burton-Christie, *Word*.

17. Robinson, "Codicology."

FIGURE 9. The fourth-century Egyptian monastic codices from Nag Hammadi in their original bindings. Reproduced with permission of the Institute for Antiquity and Christianity, Claremont, California.

of a fairly extensive library. Surely a monastery whose inmates kept such abstruse texts on hand would also have owned a variety of more popular works.

Another papyrus find, discovered at Toura a few kilometers from Cairo, is associated with the ruins of the monastery of Saint Arsenios. There too, the monks seem to have been driven to conceal works that had been banned. The Toura cache produced, among other texts, the only surviving copies of several works of Origen and of his follower Didymus the Blind. The form and the hands of the Toura codices vary, but in general their quality, though higher than that of the Nag Hammadi codices, is far from luxurious.[18] Nevertheless, the number—and the specialized nature—of the books hidden at Toura suggests that they too were culled from a library that was by no means restricted to copies of the scriptures.

These book caches, while they support certain aspects of the portrayal of the monastic use of books in the Pachomian rules and the *Sayings of the Desert Fathers,* also suggest that monastic literacy did not entirely conform to the models those texts set forth. The physical form of the books implies that, as we would expect, monks did not indulge in luxurious volumes. Indeed, these books may well have been the products of the monks' own labor as copyists. The hands used to copy them resemble those used for ordinary letters and documents in late antique Egypt—whether by local scribes or by literate individuals writing for themselves—far more closely than they do the developed, highly professional uncial bookhand. At the same time, the specialized nature of the works they contain suggests that these monasteries and their monks may have owned rather larger libraries than the literary evidence would lead us to imagine.

The evidence for monastic literary production parallels that for monastic libraries. Far from restricting their use of the book to the *lectio divina,* Egyptian monks could be prolific authors. Specialized works written by and for monks—Evagrius of Pontus is a famous example—circulated widely. Notably, Evagrius was a central figure in the rise of Origenism among the Egyptian monks, an intellectual movement that was to be sharply curtailed by the Alexandrian archbishop Theophilus, Jerome's contemporary and a central player in the Origenist controversy. The divergent ways of using and producing books reflected in literary and archaeological evidence may mirror a larger tension within the monastic world. The Origenist controversy

18. Didymus, *Sur Zacharie,* 139–46; Doutreleau, "Que savons-nous?"; Doutreleau and Koenen, "Nouvel inventaire"; Koenen, "Arsenioskloster."

itself can be understood, on one level, as a struggle between monks and clergy over the right of the monks to appropriate Origen's model, through which they sought to legitimate scholarly activity as part of the monastic ideal. Similarly, the evidence of finds like those from Nag Hammadi and Toura implies that monks physically resisted the attempts of outsiders to restrict their communities' reading practices. Rather than destroy their banned books, the monks carefully hid them, presumably with the intention of recovering them when the storm had passed. Both the contents of these caches, then, and the contexts in which they were preserved, provide concrete, material evidence that monks read far more, and more widely, than their ecclesiastical overseers would have preferred.

The monasticism of the Egyptian desert provided important models for Jerome. In 404, for example, he translated a collection of Pachomian writings, expressing the intention that he and Eustochium might follow Egyptian patterns in regulating their own monasteries.[19] In some respects the Pachomian ideal of cenobitic monasticism was more moderate than the path of desert hermits like Macarius and Theodore. Yet the Pachomian rules placed a heavy emphasis on the poverty of the monk, who ought to possess nothing beyond the clothing necessary to cover his body. The accumulation of a fortune in books did not square easily with such a way of life. Nor, indeed, did the Pachomian model at any point envision writing books as a form of monastic labor.

Yet as we have seen, the reality of monastic reading did not always match its idealized representations. Nor were monastic authors unheard of. So when we examine how Jerome produced his writings, and how he represented that activity, we should not view his case as entirely exceptional. Instead, Jerome represents an extreme — and very well-documented — example of a phenomenon that was part of the cultural potential of cenobitic monasticism itself. Despite the apparent conflict between monastic ideals and the reality of Jerome's literary practice, there were other ways in which the monastery made a natural home for bibliophilia and for literary labor. That Jerome was exceptional in his own day in the degree to which he realized that possibility shows only that the forces resistant to such developments were also powerful.

---

19. *Praefatio in Pachomiana Latina:* . . . *uenerabilis quoque uirgo christi, filia eius, Eustochium haberet quod sororibus agendum tribueret, nostrique fratres Aegyptiorum, hoc est, Tabennensium monachorum exempla sequerentur.*

JEROME AND HIS BOOKS

In his famous letter 22 to Eustochium, written at Rome in 385, Jerome arraigns the city's aristocracy for numerous ostentatious practices, including the production of costly books: "Parchment is dyed purple, gold is melted to make letters, the *codices* are clothed in gems, and the naked Christ dies outside their doors." [20] The context makes clear that the volumes to which Jerome refers are Christian books, perhaps biblical codices (fig. 10). Jerome has no patience with the notion that their luxury shows reverence for the scriptures. Instead, he condemns such precious volumes as mere opportunities for display, popular among aristocrats who only pretend to be Christians. [21]

Another passage, from the preface to his translation of Job *iuxta Hebraeos*, written in 391, uses similar language, but goes farther to contrast luxury books with those Jerome deems appropriate for his own use:

> Let those who want them have antique volumes, or books written on purple parchment in gold and silver ink, or in what the vulgar call "inch-high" [*uncialibus*] letters, so that they are burdens rather than books, so long as they let me and mine have our wretched pamphlets and our copies not so much beautified, as corrected. [22]

Jerome's scorn for those who prefer luxury Bibles allows him to represent his own mode of literary culture, characterized by books "not so much beautified as corrected," as properly ascetic. His attacks on costly books and their owners seem designed to carve out a space for bibliophilia within the

---

20. Letter 22.32.

21. The text cited comes in the midst of a diatribe against the hypocritical ostentation of certain Christian women at Rome: *Quae religiosior fuerit, unum exterit uestimentum et plenis arcis pannos trahit* . . . [The passage quoted in translation in the text appears here.] *Cum manum porrexerint, bucinant; cum ad agapen uocauerint, praeco conducitur. Vidi nuper* . . . *nobilissimam mulierum Romanarum in basilica beati Petri semiuiris antecedentibus propria manu, quo religiosior putaretur, singulos nummos dispertire pauperibus. Interea* . . . *anus quaedam annis pannisque obsita praecurrit, ut alterum nummum acciperet; ad quam cum ordine peruenisset, pugnus porrigitur pro denario et tanti criminis reus sanguis effunditur.* The reference to richly decorated codices appears, then, in a series of examples of ostentatious displays of piety meant to garner public admiration, practiced by wealthy women who are in their hearts no Christians. Not only does Jerome exhort his reader to charity and the radical renunciation of wealth, but he condemns the production of richly ornamented Christian books as itself a form of hypocrisy.

22. *Prologus in Iob de Hebraeo interpretato:* . . . *habeant qui uolunt ueteres libros uel in membranis purpureis auro argentoque descriptos, uel uncialibus, ut uulgo aiunt, litteris onera magis exarata quam codices, dum mihi meisque permittant pauperes habere scidulas et non tam pulchros codices quam emendatos.*

FIGURE 10. A codex written in "biblical uncial" with silver ink on purple dyed parchment. Codex Rossanensis, fol. 45r. Aleppo(?), sixth century. The Gospel of Matthew. Biblioteca Arcivescovile, Rossano, Italy. Erich Lessing / Art Resource, NY.

monastic life, distinct from the lavish expenditures that he rejects as un-Christian and, a fortiori, improper for a monk.

But Jerome's representation of his bibliographic practices did not, in fact, set him at odds with the cultural values of the elite. Two passages from the literature of the earlier empire, from Seneca's *De tranquillitate animi* and Petronius's *Satyricon*, neatly exemplify those values. Seneca, writing prescriptively, describes proper and improper ways of collecting and using books:

> Even for studies, where expenditure is most honorable, it is justifiable only so long as it is kept within bounds. What is the use of having countless books and libraries, whose mere titles their owners can scarcely read through in a whole lifetime? The mass of them does not instruct, but rather burdens the student, and it is much better to surrender yourself to a few authors than to wander through many. Forty thousand books were burned at Alexandria; let someone else praise this library as the most noble monument to the wealth of kings, as did Titus Livius, who says that it was the most distinguished achievement of the good taste and solicitude of kings. There was no "good taste" or "solicitude" about it, but only learned luxury—nay, not even learned, since they had collected the books, not for the sake of learning, but to make a show, just as many who lack even a child's knowledge of letters use books, not as the tools of learning, but as decorations for the dining-room.[23]

Petronius, conversely, satirizes the gauche ostentation of a rich freedman, a parvenu who attempts to ape the manners of the cultured upper classes: "though I don't plead cases myself, I studied literature for home use, and lest you should think I don't care about learning, let me inform you that I have three libraries, one Greek and the others Latin."[24] Taken together, these texts capture the expression, in bibliographic form, of an elite value of austere utility, seen in contrast to the ostentatious excess of the nouveaux riches.

Jerome may not have read Petronius, but he surely knew this passage

---

23. *De tranquillitate animi*, 9.4–7, trans. John W. Basore (slightly modified), Loeb Classical Library: *Studiorum quoque quae liberalissima impensa est tamdiu rationem habet, quam diu modum. Quo innumerabiles libros et bybliothecas, quarum dominus uix tota uita indices perlegit? Onerat discentem turba, non instruit, multoque satius est paucis te auctoribus tradere, quam errare per multis. Quadraginta milia librorum Alexandriae arserunt; pulcherrimum regiae opulentiae monimentum alius laudaverit, sicut T. Livius, qui elegantiae regum curaeque egregium id opus ait fuisse. Non fuit elegantia illud aut cura, sed studiosa luxuria, immo ne studiosa quidem, quoniam non in studium sed in spectaculum comparauerant, sicut plerisque ignaris etiam puerilium litterarum libri non studiorum instrumenta sed cenationum ornamenta sunt.*

24. Petronius, *Satyricon* 7: *Ego autem si causas non ago, in domusionem tamen litteras didici. Et ne me putes studia fastiditum, tres bybliothecas habeo, unam Graecam, alteram Latinam.* The translation is that ascribed to Oscar Wilde, Petronius and Wilde, *Satyricon*, 101–2.

from Seneca, whom he continued to read throughout his career. The two authors' descriptions of tasteful and excessive libraries, in any case, are part of a common elite aesthetic. In describing his own books, Jerome has cleverly transposed this aesthetic to a monastic setting. The reverse snobbery of the cultivated aristocratic confronted with the vulgarity of a nouveau riche has become the ascetic purity of the monk who stands aside from a church corrupted by worldly display. The ascetic, in appropriating elite values, becomes an aristocrat of the soul—a conception central to Jerome's understanding of the hierarchy of the saved within the church.

While Jerome's revulsion toward richly decorated books takes up themes present in Roman culture since a much earlier period, the physical form of his own books was part of his own late antique culture. Jerome's books would have been codices, not rolls. The only possible exception would be Jewish biblical manuscripts, which Jerome often refers to as *volumina* (scrolls).[25] Tellingly, Rufinus describes the copies of Cicero's dialogues that his monks made for Jerome as codices. He says that he personally checked over the *quaterniones*, a term that could only apply to codices.[26] If these manuscripts of a classical Latin author were in codex form, it is hard to imagine that Jerome's library included many roll-books.

Jerome's codices, furthermore, would have been written primarily on papyrus, not on parchment. In his entry on the martyr Pamphilus in *On Famous Men*, Jerome refers specifically to codices of Origen's commentaries on the Minor Prophets in his possession. He prized these books greatly, for they were written in the hand of the martyr himself. Jerome tells us that he obtained them from the library at Caesarea.[27] Pamphilus, copying Origen's works at the turn of the fourth century, would have used papyrus as his writing material. We know this because of another notice in *On Famous Men*, on the mid-fourth-century bishop of Caesarea Euzoius, whose most important literary contribution was to cause his see's entire library to be copied over from worn papyrus copies onto parchment.[28] Alongside

25. The phrase *Hebraea uolumina* appears more than forty times in Jerome's works, in comparison to five appearances of *Hebraeos codices*.

26. Rufinus, *Apol.*, 2.11.

27. *De vir. ill.* 75: *Pamphilus presbyter, Eusebii Caesariensis episcopi necessarius, tanto bibliothecae diuinae amore flagrauit ut maximam partem Origenis uoluminum sua manu descripserit, quae usque hodie in Caesariensi bibliotheca habetur. sed et in duodecim prophetas uiginti quinque ἐξηγήσεων Origenis uolumina manu eius exarata repperi, quae tanto amplector et seruo gaudio, ut Croesi opes habere me credam.*

28. *De vir. ill.* 113.51: *Euzoius apud Thespesium rhetorem cum Gregorio, Nazianzeno episcopo, adulescens Caesareae eruditus est, et eiusdem postea urbis episcopus, plurimo labore corruptam iam biblio-*

Origen's works among the books that Jerome had constantly before him as he wrote were the biblical commentaries and theological treatises of Didymus the Blind, the great scholar of late fourth-century Alexandria. Jerome tells us repeatedly that he obtained at least some of these books in Egypt, from Didymus himself.[29] These would almost certainly have been papyrus codices. Jerome's own works—written in Latin, intended for audiences in the West—were also copied on papyrus. Writing to a Spanish layman who sent six scribes to Bethlehem to make copies of Jerome's complete works, Jerome states expressly that the books they will take back with them are written in *chartaceis codicibus,* "in papyrus codices."[30] This suggests that many, if not most, of the books Jerome wrote were also copied on papyrus.

Modern scholars have occasionally seized upon the reference in *On Famous Men* to Euzoius's renovation of the library of Caesarea to argue that late antiquity was the period of the victory of parchment over papyrus, and the emergence of the medieval book.[31] Certainly, the text implies that parchment was seen as superior to papyrus in some sense, presumably because of its greater durability. But sweeping claims for the dominance of parchment at the turn of the fifth century find little corroboration in Jerome's works. Instead, he generally connects manuscripts written on parchment with Jews and, more specifically, with the Jewish practice of wearing phylacteries. Needless to say, these were not positive associations for Jerome or for his Christian audience.[32] Papyrus, meanwhile, appears to have remained the standard material for his own books.

Among the closest extant parallels to the kinds of books that would have been found in Jerome's library are those from the Toura cache, concealed by the monks of Saint Arsenios during a period of anti-Origenist fervor. Although the Toura codices date to the end of the fifth or the early sixth century, fashions in bookmaking did not change drastically, so these books can

---

thecam Origenis et Pamphili in membranis instaurare conatus, ad extremum sub Theodosio principe ecclesia pulsus est. On this passage see Arns, *Technique,* 24.

29. *De vir. ill.* 69, prologues to *Comm. in Osee* and *Comm. in Zach.*

30. Letter 71.5: *opuscula mea, quae non sui merito, sed bonitate tua desiderare te dicis, ad describendum hominibus tuis dedi et descripta uidi in chartaceis codicibus ac frequenter admonui, ut conferrent diligentius et emendarent.*

31. E.g. Arns, *Technique,* 24.

32. Out of a total of nineteen occurrences of *membrana* and related terms in Jerome's writings, six appear either in polemical contrasts between the Jews, who have the physical scriptures but do not understand them, and the Christians, who have the spirit, or in (negative) references to the Jewish custom of wearing phylacteries.

help us to imagine how Jerome's might have looked.[33] One well-preserved manuscript contains the complete text of the commentary of Didymus on Zechariah, a source for Jerome's lengthy treatment of the same prophet. Since that text played such an important role in Jerome's working library, the book that contained it deserves further discussion. The codex gives an impression of quality combined with restraint. Like most of the codices of Didymus found at Toura, it is nearly square, about 22.5 by 27 centimeters. This was a typical format for papyrus codices of the sixth century. The measurements of the individual pages vary by as much as a centimeter from the norm in either dimension. Again, this was not unusual in codices of the period.[34] The volume is made up of *quaterniones,* individual quires of four sheets laid one on top of the other, sewn, and folded down the middle to make sixteen pages. The codex as a whole originally contained 418 pages. The text on each page is enclosed within a ruled rectangle, but there are no lines ruled on the pages. The number of lines per page ranges from 22 to 30.[35] On each page, the text is laid out in a single, homogeneous block, without spaces between words. Only at the end of each book of the commentary has the scribe left a blank space to demarcate the sections. No decorations relieve the manuscript's austere simplicity.[36]

The hand of this codex is of particular interest. It is far from being an example of the so-called "biblical uncial," whose Latin equivalents Jerome criticizes as a sign of excess.[37] Instead, the hand broadly resembles those

33. Turner, *Typology,* 88–101, attempts to distinguish between the form of the earliest codices, of the second and third centuries, and what came after. His results, however, show how difficult it is to differentiate codices of different periods on the basis of their physical form.

34. The dimensions of the codices found at Toura are as follows (in centimeters): *In Eccles.* 23.5/24 × 27.5/27; *In Psalmos* 24.5 × 27/26.5; *In Genesim,* 23 × 27; *In Zach.,* 22.5 × 27; another codex (p. Tourah VIII), 22 × 28.5; *In Hiob,* 15.5/14.5 × 33; Origen, *Dialogue,* 14.5 × 32 (all 6th century); Tourah Codex II, Origen, Contra Celsum et al., 18 × 27.5 (6th or 7th century) These data come from Turner, *Typology,* 14–22; see 12–25 on the format of papyrus codices from late antiquity in general.

35. It was a single codex of 418 pages, arranged in quaterniones, with 4 blank pages and 414 pages of text. One *quaternio* in fact consists of four and one-half rather than four sheets, for a total of 18 pages; the half-sheet is badly damaged (Didymus, *Sur Zacharie,* 139–46).

36. Didymus, *Sur Zacharie,* 143–44.

37. *Prologus in Iob de Hebraeo interpretato: . . . uncialibus, ut uulgo aiunt, litteris onera magis exarata quam codices.* It is uncertain whether the hand Jerome had in mind was what Latin paleographers would call an uncial, a hand heavily influenced by the Greek hand referred to as "biblical uncial" or "biblical majuscule," or instead the *capitalis,* a hand based on inscriptional letter forms and reserved in Latin bookmaking for the most expensive volumes of pagan literary authors. The former is more likely, however, since Jerome is explicitly referring here to Christian books, indeed

used for several centuries in Egypt to copy carefully written but not luxurious books. A mixed hand using many majuscule letter forms, very roughly bilinear, with numerous ligatures and *nomina sacra*, it is written slowly, with care and regularity, but is far from ostentatious: a hand suitable, as the commentary's modern editor remarks, for copying such a lengthy work.[38] This volume, and the others found with it, were austere but impressive products of a sophisticated culture of the book.

Jerome's library, as we have just seen, contained hundreds of codices like this copy of Didymus's commentary on Zechariah—not to mention volumes of Virgil and other Latin poets. Even if the individual books were not especially lavish, the formation of the collection required a substantial investment, either of money or of labor.[39] The catalogue given in chapter 4 above implies that the library must have contained at least a thousand codices of the same length as a copy of the *Aeneid*. In the Price Edict's scale, these would have cost more than two and a half million denarii—a senatorial fortune.

In many ways, then, Jerome's books reflected the reality of monastic reading and writing far better than did the prescriptions of writers who aimed to shape monastic ideals. In other ways, they burst the bounds of the monastic model. Although the physical form of Jerome's books was probably similar to that discovered in the Egyptian monastic cashes, the sheer number of books he owned, and the ways in which he used them, had their models in the culture of the literate elite. As we have seen, Jerome transposed the asceticizing ideals of classical literary culture into a new, monastic context. In so doing, he created ways of talking about his use of books that could

---

to biblical manuscripts: and while there are several fourth- and fifth-century examples of very costly Latin Bibles written in hands influenced by the Greek hands found in fourth-century luxury Bibles like Sinaiticus and Vaticanus, very few biblical manuscripts and no manuscripts of other Christian works exist in *capitalis* (Bischoff, *Latin Paleography*, 58–59).

38. For discussion of the manuscript and the hand, see Didymus, *Sur Zacharie*, 139–46. The hand is described by Doutreleau as "ni une onciale, ni une cursive, mais une minuscule (rien de commun avec la 'minuscule' des manuscrits), commode pour les ouvrages de longue haleine. Les lettres sont soigneusement formées et gardent chacune leur individualité, sans être noyées dans les ligatures, quoiqu'elles soient souvent reliées les unes aux autres. Bonne écriture d'atelier, qui reflète les normes graphiques de la fin du VIe et du début du VIIe siècle." See also note 1 to p. 145: "L. Koenen, *ein theol. Pap. der Kölner Sammlung . . .* , p. 62–63, analyse aussi l'écriture de notre Papyrus (voir la liste des pièces comparées, p. 63, note 1) et conclut, avec la même approximation, à une date tardive dans les Ve–VIe siècles." In fact, the hand resembles in its regularity, and even in some of its letter forms, that of a papyrus letter dated on the basis of its contents to 325 and used by Turner (Turner, *Greek Manuscripts*, 23) to exemplify the second category of writing specified in the Price Edict of Diocletian, on which see below.

39. Rufinus, *Apol.*, 2.11.

compete with the models of renunciation of literacy, or of immersion in the *lectio divina*, presented by contemporary texts aiming to prescribe monastic ideals. What had been a form of reverse snobbery distinguishing the true aristocrat from the arriviste was pressed into the service of a far more radical social inversion, differentiating the ascetic Christian reader from the pseudo-Christian collector of luxury books.

The book culture that Jerome participated in and helped to shape was not simply a debasement of the practices of classical antiquity; nor was it an imperfect anticipation of the new world of the Western Middle Ages. Instead, it was characteristic of a specifically late-Roman order of books. The developed form of the papyrus codex, typical of Jerome's own books, can stand for an entire complex of material practices and cultural assumptions surrounding books, reading, and writing. Only in hindsight does the papyrus codex come to seem a transitional form, marking a boundary between eras rather than occupying a cultural space of its own. Similarly, while Jerome's fusion of cenobitic monasticism with a form of *askesis* based on textual scholarship may seem to us to point forward to medieval and even later phenomena, it was itself a peculiarly late antique development, not an anticipation of a future that was as yet several centuries distant. Monastic reading in late antiquity aimed at internalizing the sacred text rather than at producing interpretations for an outside readership.

The one real exception to this pattern was in Syria, where there arose the only ongoing tradition of ascetic Christian biblical scholarship before the Middle Ages. The Syrian church was in far closer contact with rabbinic Judaism than were its Western siblings. Late antique Judaism was the culture of study as piety par excellence. The importance of education and especially of biblical study in Syrian monasticism probably shows the influence of rabbinic models from Mesopotamia. Syrian influence, in turn, helps to account for the literary aspects of the monastic program of Jerome's sole successor in the late antique West, the senator and former imperial official Cassiodorus.[40] He had absorbed Syrian models while serving at the court in Constantinople, where the monastic school of Nisibis had taken refuge from Persian persecution. As a result, Cassiodorus's monastery at Vivarium had more in common with its cousins in distant Mesopotamia than with the ideals of his younger contemporary, Benedict of Nursia.[41]

---

40. On Cassiodorus's isolation within sixth-century Western Christianity, and the failure of his experiment at Vivarium to leave a long-term legacy, see Riché, *Education*, 160–269.

41. Riché, *Education*, 160–269.

THE LIBRARY IN USE

How, then, did Jerome actually use the many books he had accumulated with so much effort and expense? Two complementary sources of information allow us to answer this question: Jerome's own explicit statements, often made in reply to criticisms by his contemporaries, and the comparison of his works with those few of his sources that survive. Jerome's self-descriptions present problems. It is clear that he represented his use of sources in ways that subtly distorted reality. Furthermore, his self-presentation shifted over time, in response to controversy with his contemporaries, particularly over the propriety of his reliance on Origen. Nevertheless, a relatively consistent picture emerges.

Jerome described his method of commentary in terms of compilation. Reality seems, this once, solidly to support his self-portrayal. Even those who have tried to argue for his originality have limited their case to the claim that he reshaped the materials he borrowed.[42] He idealized his audience through the figure of the *prudens lector,* who could distinguish between false coin and true, making it unnecessary for Jerome to do so for him. Yet in practice, Jerome was far from shifting the burden of judgment onto his readers. Instead, he left his mark on everything he used. Even as he drew directly and without apparent hesitation on the many volumes in his library to fill the pages of his commentaries and other works, he rearranged and reworded his material, deploying it within a larger framework that was his own creation. In his polemical writings, where he did not wish it to be known that he drew on non-Christian sources like Seneca and Porphyry, he could skillfully conceal his debts. He did not lack the literary talents to do so in his commentaries as well, had that been his aim.

In texts written before the outbreak of the Origenist controversy in 393, Jerome advertised his use of Origen, claiming that access to the Greek exegete's works conferred on him an authority superior to that of his Latin predecessors. In the preface to his commentary on Galatians, discussed in chapter 2 above, Jerome refrains from boasting of his own expertise, and promises instead to base his exegesis entirely on Origen.[43] Having invoked

---

42. E.g., Jay, *Exégèse.*

43. *Non quod ignorem Caium Marium Victorinum, qui Romae, me puero, rhetoricam docuit, edidisse Commentarios in Apostolum; sed quod occupatus ille eruditione saecularium litterarum, Scripturas omnino sanctas ignorauerit: et nemo possit, quamuis eloquens, de eo bene disputare, quod nesciat. Quid igitur, ego stultus aut temerarius, qui id pollicear quod ille non potuit? Minime. Quin potius in eo, ut mihi uideor, cautior atque timidior, quod imbecillitatem uirium mearum sentiens, Origenis Commentarios sum secutus.*

Origen, however, Jerome goes on to obscure the degree to which he depends on him. First, he gives a long list of other commentators on Galatians. Unfortunately, the works catalogued are all lost, so that it is impossible to determine whether Jerome actually drew on such a broad array of sources, or simply wished to suggest that he did.[44]

Then he gives an explicit—yet probably misleading—description of how he worked: "Therefore I confess simply that I read all these things, and heaping them up together in my mind, I summoned my shorthand secretary and dictated either my own thoughts or another's, hardly remembering the order, the words, or the sense."[45] Ostensibly, Jerome is a passive channel, transmitting the opinions of his authorities. Though the phrase "either my own or another's" (*uel mea, uel aliena*) allows for the possibility that some of his own ideas might creep in, the emphasis is on his use of sources. Further, he portrays his methods as casual in the extreme, as if he had first ingested a mass of Greek exegesis, then vomited it forth to his *notarius,* without regard for its origins or the form in which it was expressed. On this level, the passage serves as a display of modesty, a simple confession that he is incapable of exegetical sophistication or literary polish. The authority of his work is only that of its sources. By denying that he has consciously selected the materials he deploys, Jerome avoids an explicit claim to power. At most, he admits that he followed the best teachers and labored hard at his studies.

Yet implicitly, Jerome's praise for Origen is an advertisement for himself. By asserting that he first read all the books he mentions, and only then began to compose, he interjects himself as a mediator between his sources and his readers. Having internalized the master, he can now speak in his place. He thereby appropriates the prestige of the Greek tradition for his own text, without overtly claiming for himself the authority to produce independent interpretations. If he had acknowledged that his reading of his sources was part of the process whereby his own texts were produced, not a separate phase preceding composition, Jerome's contribution would be reduced to translation or paraphrase. His own persona would no longer stand as a filter between the Greek interpretative tradition and his Latin readership.

---

44. *Praetermitto Didymum, uidentem meum, et Laodicenum Apollinarem de Ecclesia nuper egressum, et Alexandrum ueterum haereticum, Eusebius quoque Emesenum, et Theodorum Heracleoten, qui et ipsi nonnullos super hac re Commentariolos reliquerunt.*

45. *Itaque ut simpliciter fatear, legi haec omnia, et in mente mea plurima coaceruans, accito notario, uel mea, uel aliena dictaui, nec ordinis, nec uerborum interdum, nec sensuum memoriam retentans.* (Pref. to *Comm. in Gal.*)

In later works, Jerome was forced to retreat from such descriptions of his methods. In the face of his contemporaries' accusations, he had to admit that he worked not from memory but directly from his sources. Yet he continued to advertise his compilation of Greek exegesis as a virtue, while citing his sources anonymously and incorporating their opinions seamlessly into his own prose. In the prologue to the second book of his commentary on Micah, written in 392, Jerome complains to Paula and Eustochium that unnamed enemies have attacked his exegetical works: "They say that I have plagiarized the volumes of Origen, and have improperly corrupted old writings" (*dicunt, Origenis me uolumina compilare, et contaminari non decere ueterum scripta*). The accusations that he details concern plagiarism (*compilare, contaminari*); in his self-defense, he refers to translation (*transtulere, uertere*) and even to literary theft (*furta*). The language that Jerome uses in this passage indicates clearly how he used Origen's commentaries on the Minor Prophets, drawn from the precious codices written in Pamphilus's own hand. As he admits, his own commentary is a translation, or at best a paraphrase, of his source.

Instead of attempting to refute the accusations, Jerome confirms them. He contends, however, that his close adherence to Origen's work should be applauded rather than condemned. Not only has he modeled his own exegesis after the best of his illustrious predecessors, but he has followed in the footsteps of the great founding figures of Latin literary culture, drawing on the Greek tradition just as Ennius, Virgil, Cicero, and the comic playwrights had done. Other Latin exegetes too had blazed the trail that Jerome followed. The orthodox bishop Hilary of Poitiers, for example, had incorporated about forty thousand lines of Origen's work, loosely translated, in his treatment of the Psalms.[46] We may conclude that Jerome's procedure, here and elsewhere, was much the same.

A similar, though far more serious incident formed part of the mutual exchange of accusations between Jerome and his former friend Rufinus in the early 400s. As we saw in chapter 3, this phase of the Origenist controversy drove Jerome to articulate explicitly a theory of commentary, designed to

---

46. *quod illi maledictum uehemens esse existimant, eamdem laudem ego maximam duco, cum illum imitari uolo, quem cunctis prudentibus et uobis placere non dubito. Si enim crimen est Graecorum bene dicta transferre, accusentur Ennius et Maro, Plautus, Caecilius et Terentius, Tullius quoque et ceteri eloquentes uiri, qui non solum uersus, sed multa capita et longissimos libros ac fabulas integras transtulerunt. Sed et Hilarius noster furti reus sit, quod in psalmos quadraginta ferme millia uersuum supradicti Origenis ad sensum uerterit. Quorum omnium aemulari exopto neglegentiam, potius quam istorum obscuram diligentiam.* (*Comm. in Micaeam*, book 2, prol.)

defend himself against Rufinus's charge of Origenism. Rufinus's accusation was based on a close comparison of Jerome's commentary on Ephesians with Origen's own work on the same letter. In his *Apology against Rufinus,* Jerome not only claims with pride to have compiled the opinions of earlier authorities but asserts that this is the essential task of the commentator.

The role of the ideal reader, the *prudens lector,* as Jerome articulates it in his *Apology,* is also new. The *prudens lector* now takes over the ultimate responsibility for determining which interpretations are authoritative. In the preface to the commentary on Galatians, Jerome had reserved this role for himself, claiming that he first surveyed the Greek exegetical tradition, then produced a selective anthology. As we saw, his elaborate protestations of casualness served to minimize the claim to authority implied in this mode of composition, masking intellectual pretensions with a veneer of monkish self-effacement. In his reply to Rufinus, Jerome goes even farther in representing himself as a passive conduit. Not he but his reader will decide which interpretations are authoritative, which inaccurate or even heretical. This self-description was useful to Jerome when he had to defend himself against the charge of retailing Origen's worst heresies in his early works. Ironically, it also came closer to describing his actual procedure than did the earlier version.

Clearly, in all these passages Jerome drew upon common cultural tropes, which could be deployed not only by literary and philosophical commentators but by authors working in a range of other genres. Furthermore, the contrast between Jerome's open acknowledgment of his debts to earlier writers in his prefaces and other programmatic statements, and his citational practices, which tended to obscure the relation of his texts to their sources, was also typical of many literary genres.

But Jerome's citational practices were also deliberately chosen, as his commentary on Daniel reveals. In that work, written in 407,[47] Jerome experimented with a very different approach to his sources. This commentary does not provide a complete text of the prophet, as the works on the Minor Prophets had done. Jerome's sources had based their interpretations on the Septuagint. Rather than attempting to cope with that text, Jerome comments only on the translation *iuxta Hebraeos.* Furthermore, he does cover the entire book but omits sections he considers readily comprehensible. Rather than creating a smooth facade that masks the origins of his material, he cites his sources by name in the text of the commentary, and even quotes them verbatim.

---

47. For the date, see Cavallera, *Saint Jérôme,* 2:52.

Jerome departs most sharply from his usual approach in discussing the prophecy of the seventy weeks in Daniel 9 : 24. Here, he quotes lengthy passages from several sources, most of them verbatim extracts from the authors he cites. First, he translates about 140 lines from Julius Africanus, specifying that the passage appears "in the fifth volume of his Chronicles" (*in quinto Temporum uolumine*). He goes on to quote more than 120 lines from Eusebius of Caesarea, from the eighth book of the *Demonstration of the Gospel*, followed by material—often equally extensive—from Hippolytus of Rome, Apollinaris of Laodicea, Clement of Alexandria, Origen, and Tertullian and also from Jewish sources. He then invokes his *diligens lector* to adjudicate between these varied interpretations. Though he occasionally comments on the plausibility of the material he cites, Jerome explicitly refuses to take a stand on the meaning of the passage under exegesis.[48]

This unusual mode of proceeding ruptures the smooth surface created by Jerome's normal commentarial procedure. It demonstrates the seriousness of his engagement with this controversial prophecy, while exempting him from proposing an interpretation of his own. It also shows that Jerome deliberately chose to cite his sources as he did in his other works. His incorporation of the material he borrowed into a seamless, univocal text was not merely a conventional procedure. Rather, it was a crucial element of his self-presentation, and one of the key constituents of his authority as a biblical scholar. The elaborate parade of humility that characterizes his explicit descriptions of his commentarial method would lead one to expect all his commentaries to resemble the treatment of Daniel 9 : 24. By contrast, the voice of the other works on the prophets is self-assured, even arrogant, in its domination of the sources it appropriates.

In a passage from his commentary on Isaiah, written in 408–10,[49] a few years after the commentary on Daniel, Jerome describes the reaction to the experimental form of the previous exegetical work. He states that he had hoped to address criticisms of the excessive length of his commentaries on the Minor Prophets by adopting a more concise form for his treatment of Daniel, with the exception of Daniel 9 : 24, whose obscurity demanded fuller treatment. There, he had inserted lengthy passages from a number of Greek writers, from Tertullian, and from his Jewish informants. Having presented

---

48. *Comm. in Dan.* 3.9.138: *scio de hac quaestione ab eruditissimis uiris uarie disputatum et unumquemque pro captu ingenii sui dixisse quod senserat; quia igitur periculosum est de magistrorum ecclesiae iudicare sententiis et alterum praeferri alteri, dicam quid unusquisque senserit, lectoris arbitrio derelinquens cuius expositionem sequi debeat.*

49. For the date, see Cavallera, *Saint Jérôme*, 2 : 52.

excerpts from his authorities in translation, he left it up to his readers to adjudicate between them.[50] But the tactic met with criticism. He complains,

> Therefore what we saw fit to do for the sake of modesty, and for the honor of our expected readers, strongly displeased some, who desired not the opinions of the ancients, but our own views. It is easy to respond to them that I refuse thus to accept one view, since I see others condemn it. And certainly if so many and such learned men displeased fastidious readers, what would they make of me, who because of the poverty of my feeble intellect, suffer the attacks of my enemies?[51]

The passage makes very clear that the method of the commentary on Daniel—and of the other commentaries—was a deliberate choice. Furthermore, it explicitly links compilation, especially the citation of sources by name, with Jerome's desire to humble himself before his readers. Jerome was very much aware of the role played by his use of sources in his self-presentation as an exegete.

When we move from the evidence of Jerome's explicit descriptions of his methods to what we can extract from a comparison of his works with their surviving sources, the picture grows more complicated. Unfortunately, only a few of the Greek works Jerome used are extant in any form. These include extensive fragments of the commentaries of Origen on the letter to the Ephesians and of Eusebius of Caesarea on Isaiah, and Didymus the Blind's commentary on Zechariah. This work, preserved in a single papyrus codex (encountered already in chapter 4), is the only source Jerome used that survives intact. Where comparison is possible, the results support the idea that Jerome generally compiled or even paraphrased his sources. Paradoxically, however, his own works do not bear out his claim to humility and simplemindedness. Instead, Jerome dominated his sources, evaluated them in terms

---

50. *Comm. in Esaiam*, 11, prol.: *Difficile, immo impossibile est placere omnibus; nec tanta uultuum, quanta sententiarum diuersitas est. In explanatione duodecim prophetarum longior quibusdam uisus sum, quam oportuit; et ob hanc causam in commentariolis Danielis breuitati studui, praeter ultimam et penultimam uisionem, in quibus me necesse fuit ob obscuritatis magnitudinem sermonem tendere; praecipueque in expositionem septem et sexaginta duarum et unius hebdomadarum, in quibus disserendis quid Africanus temporum scriptor, quid Origenes, et Caesariensis Eusebius, Clemens quoque Alexandrinae ecclesiae presbyter, et Apollinaris Laodicenus Hippolytusque, et Hebraei, et Tertullianus senserint, breuiter comprehendi, lectoris arbitrio derelinquens quid de pluribus eligeret.*

51. *Itaque quod nos uerecundia fecimus iudicandi, et eorum honore qui lecturi erant, quibusdam forte non placeat, qui non antiquorum opiniones, sed nostram sententiam scire desiderant. Quibus facilis responsio est, noluisse me sic unum recipere, ut uiderer alios condemnare. Et certe si tanti et tam eruditi uiri fastidiosis lectoribus displicent, quid de me facturi erant, qui pro tenuitate ingenioli inuidorum morsibus pateo? (Comm. in Esaiam, 11, prol.)*

of his own critical standards, and incorporated them into new texts that were more than the sum of their parts.

Most previous scholarship on Jerome's use of sources has been harshly critical of his lack of originality and his failure to cite his sources by name. One scholar has characterized Jerome's use of Origen in his commentary on Ephesians as "shameless plagiarism."[52] In some respects, the description is probably not far from the truth. Comparing Jerome's commentary on Zechariah to Didymus's, Louis Doutreleau describes Jerome's work as a "faithful copy" of its Greek source. Revealingly, Doutreleau finds that Jerome replicated errors and inconsistencies perpetrated by Didymus. For example, Jerome copied Didymus's references to the Psalms slavishly. If Didymus gives the number of the psalm he quotes, so does Jerome; if Didymus omits it, Jerome does so also; and if Didymus's reference is inaccurate, so is Jerome's.[53] In a similar vein, where Didymus attributes an opinion to another commentator, Jerome translates his words almost exactly, giving the impression that it was he—rather than the author of the text that served as his source—who had read the book in question. He does the same in his commentary on Ephesians, where his source is Origen rather than Didymus.[54] We have in both these practices striking evidence that Jerome did not merely read his sources, digest them, and regurgitate their ideas to his *notarius*. Rather, he compiled passages directly from the books in his library to fill the pages of his own works.

But to condemn Jerome as a mere plagiarist fails, in several respects, to fully describe his methods. His commentaries—especially the later works on the Prophets—contain more than just the material he took from his main Greek sources. In his commentary on Isaiah, he clearly drew a number of interpretations from Eusebius, and follows him closely when he uses him. But the commentary as a whole contains a great deal of material not found in Eusebius.[55] It surely drew on other commentaries, such as Origen's, which are now lost. Whatever its sources, the final product is not a mere paraphrase of any one of them, or even an alternating version of them all, but a new work with its own integrity.

Much of the commentary on Zechariah is a Latin paraphrase of Didy-

---

52. "ein unverschämtes Plagiat" (Bammel, "Pauluskommentare," 207).

53. Didymus, *Sur Zacharie*, 130.

54. On *Comm. in Ephes.* see Layton, "Origen's Pauline Exegesis," 375–76 with 76, n. 11, 404–11. On *Comm. in Zach.*, see Didymus, *Sur Zacharie*, 131.

55. Jay, *Exégèse*, 56–58.

mus's work. But Jerome's version is much more than a mere copy of his source.[56] Jerome used at least three earlier works in writing on Zechariah. The prologue lists Origen's commentary, which covered only the first third of Zechariah; a commentary by another third-century writer, Hippolytus of Rome; and the work of Didymus, composed at Jerome's own request.[57] It does not cite Apollinaris of Laodicea, but Jerome elsewhere credits him with exegesis of all the Prophets. Perhaps his work also served as a source.[58] Detailed comparison of Jerome's treatment of Zechariah with that of Didymus reveals that Jerome took many passages directly, sometimes almost verbatim, from Didymus. But he reworked Didymus's exegesis extensively, incorporating it into a new literary fabric entirely of his own making. He combined the material drawn from all his sources into an almost inextricable mixture, unified by his own inimitable Latin prose.[59]

Jerome privileged some of his sources over others, and was critical of many of their individual readings. In the first book of the commentary on Zechariah, which covers Zechariah 1:1–6:8, he draws a few interpretations from Didymus. But the bulk of his material finds no parallel in that author. He must have relied primarily on another source for his allegorical exegesis of this portion of the prophet, probably the treatment of the first third of Zechariah by Origen mentioned in the preface. Only when Origen's exegesis was no longer available did Jerome's reliance on Didymus increase. When Jerome does adduce material from Didymus, he often does so only to reject it, especially in book 1, where Origen's commentary takes precedence. His most frequent criticism of Didymus's *allegoresis* is that it is not supported

---

56. For criticism of Doutreleau's evaluation, see Jay, *Exégèse*, 37 n. 95, as follows: "Comparant les deux oeuvres, L. Doutreleau parle dans son introduction de la 'copie conforme' de Jérôme (t. I, p. 129). L'expression est à la fois exacte et dangereuse, car elle peut donner à penser que le commentaire hiéronymien se réduit à une imitation servile de son modèle. Or la réalité n'est pas si simple. 'Exégèse spirituelle et citations scripturaires sont les deux seuls domaines où Jérôme pille Didyme; c'est ce qui constitue toute l'exégèse de Didyme et ce à quoi celle de Jérôme ne se limite pas' (C. Briffard, *L'exégèse de Jérôme dans le premier livre du Commentaire sur Zacharie*, Mémoire de maîtrise, Rouen, 1969, ex. dactyl., p. 55)."

57. *Comm. in Zach.* prol., ll. 28ff.: *scripsit in hunc prophetam Origenes duo uolumina, usque ad tertiam partem libri a principio. Hippolytus quoque edidit commentarios, et Didymus quinque explanationum libros, me rogante, dictauit, quos cum aliis tribus in Osee et mihi προσεψωνησεν; sed tota eorum εξηγησις, allegorica fuit, et historiae uix pauca tetigerunt.*

58. *Comm. in Osee prol.* 112ff.: *Apollinarem Laodicenum, qui cum in adolescentia sua breues et in hunc et in alios prophetas commentariolos reliquisset, tangens magis sensus quam explicans . . . ; De vir. ill.* 104: *Apollinaris, Laodicenus Syriae episcopus patre presbytero, magis grammaticis in adulescentia operam dedit et postea, in sanctas scripturas innumerabilia scribens uolumina.*

59. Didymus, *Sur Zacharie*, 128–29.

by the literal or historical sense of the text. For example, Jerome discusses in some detail the significance of the date of Zechariah's second revelation (Zech. 1:7). The Hebrew original, and all of the Greek translations, specify that the vision occurred in the eleventh month of the Hebrew calendar. Didymus, however, based his exegesis—a series of elaborate numerological speculations—on a text containing a unique variant, which placed the vision in the twelfth month of the second year of Darius. Jerome mentions Didymus's interpretation but rejects it as based on an inaccurate text, and goes on to cite a different rendering of the verse, based on the characteristics of the time of the year and month—in the depth of winter and at the dark of the moon—when Zechariah received the ominous vision about to be described.[60]

This passage is characteristic of the commentary as a whole. When Jerome criticizes allegorical interpretations drawn from his Greek sources, it is usually because they are based on an inaccurate text, less often because they violate the context of the passage under interpretation or run counter to its historical sense. But even when he gives good reasons to reject the material he has gathered from his sources, he catalogues their views anyway. He cannot be said to leave the decision up to the reader, yet he neither breaks wholly with the principle of compilation nor descends to parroting his sources, even when he follows them most closely. He was—at least in his mature exegesis—an active, critical user of earlier writers' work , so that the material he borrowed became part of a new text that was very much his own. The comparison of Didymus's commentary on Zechariah with Jerome's, then, produces a paradoxical result. While it reveals beyond doubt that Jerome mined his Greek sources for material, which he incorporated into his works virtually unaltered, it also shows that he chose carefully what he used, and regularly rejected the opinions of the writers whose authority he lauded so highly. His attitude toward those writers was by no means as humble as his programmatic statements imply. The readers who wanted Jerome to write commentaries that expressed his own views knew what they were asking for.

In the concluding passage of the *Contra Vigilantium*, a polemical treatise

---

60. *Comm. in Zach.*, 1.1.7.155–84. On Didymus's interpretation, Jerome writes, *Quidam pro undecimo mense ponunt duodecimum et uicesimum quartum diem eiusdem mensis arithmeticis rationibus interpretantes, quadrangulum firmum et stabilem numerum suspicantur, uolentes certa esse et stabilia quae scribuntur. Nos autem dicamus quod in eodem anno Darii regis secundo, tertio mense post primam uisionem, id est undecimo post octauum, qui apud Hebraeos appellatur Sabat, rursum ad Zachariam factus sit sermo Domini.*

he wrote in 406, Jerome describes the conflict between his office as a monk and the demands of Christian learning in stark terms. In context, the passage is ironic almost to the point of comedy. Having discharged himself of an unrestrained polemical screed, Jerome remarks that the monk ought to be conscious of his own weakness and therefore fear to offend. He goes on to assert that if he himself has retreated to the solitude of the desert, in defiance of Vigilantius's arguments against radical asceticism, it is because he prefers to avoid engaging his opponent in a combat of words.[61] He concludes,

> But a monk's office is not to teach, but to mourn, whether he laments for himself, or for the world, and in terror stands ready for the coming of the Lord: knowing his own weakness . . . he fears to offend.[62]

The passage, while hard to take seriously, is revealing nevertheless. It expresses what Jerome's world thought were the duties of a monk: "not to teach, but to mourn"—a view with which Jerome surely agreed, at least on some level. It was against this version of the monk's calling that Jerome had to justify the coupling of monasticism with scholarship. His self-presentation as a mere compiler played an important role in that effort.

A passage from Jerome's letter 112 to Augustine reveals the same view of the monastic role at work in a somewhat less facetious vein, while clarifying the problem presented by the monk as scholar. Here, Jerome not only describes the function of the monk as ultimately excluding scholarship, but associates Christian learning with the office of the bishop, for whom study, instruction, and even polemic are appropriate activities. Jerome wrote the letter in 404, finally replying to a series of letters from Augustine that had challenged Jerome's interpretation of Galatians 2:1-14 and questioned the propriety of his translating the scriptures from the Hebrew. In defending himself against his correspondent's criticisms of the commentary on Galatians, Jerome lists a bewildering number of Greek authorities who support his position, then turns to the attack and accuses his correspondent of advocating the rankest Judaizing. He caps off his rebuttal of the African bishop's first point with an elaborate obeisance to his addressee's status:

61. Apostrophizing Vigilantius, he writes: *cur, inquies, pergis ad eremum? uidelicet ut te non audiam, non uideam; ut tuo furore non mouear; ut tua bella non patiar (Contra Vigilantium 16).* The larger context deals with the monk's need to avoid women and thereby to avoid testing his resolve in their company, but these words, which follow closely on the passage cited in the text, seem to refer not to the threat of temptation but to the possibility of being drawn into debate.

62. *monachus autem non doctoris habet, sed plangentis officium: qui uel se, uel mundum lugeat, et Domini pauidus praestoletur aduentum: qui sciens imbecillitatem suam . . . timet offendere (Contra Vigilantium 15.3).*

If therefore you find something in our explanation worthy of criticism, it will be up to Your Erudition to discover whether what we have written is present in the Greek authorities, so that if they have not said it, then you may condemn my own personal opinion: especially since I freely confessed in the Preface [to my commentary on Galatians] that I had followed the commentaries of Origen, and had dictated both my own opinions and those of others. . . . You, as a bishop famous throughout the world, must put forward your view, and bring all your fellow bishops into agreement. I, in my poor little hut with the monks, that is, with my fellow sinners, dare not to take up a position on great matters, except insofar as I may honestly admit that I have read the writings of the ancients, and following in my commentaries the custom of all such works, have set forth various explanations, in order that out of many such each may follow what he wishes. I believe that you have read and commended such writings both in secular letters, and in works on the Holy Scriptures.[63]

Jerome claims that both his authority as an exegete and his invulnerability to accusations of theological error rest on his use of Greek sources. If Augustine wishes to challenge him, then let him take advantage of his position as a bishop, charged with teaching not only his congregation but his brother bishops, to drive home his views. Jerome, as a mere monk, would not dare to pass judgment on his betters—were it not that his adherence to the rules of the genre of commentary, which dictate the procedure of compiling earlier authorities, allows him to confess sincerely that his words are not his own. His entry into the lists of Christian literature as an exegete, therefore, entails no contradiction of the monastic rule of humility.

In letter 112, a number of threads come together. Jerome explicitly asserts that commentary is the proper genre for the monk *because* its nature as compilation allows him to preserve his humility rather than asserting his authority. A modern reader may be skeptical of Jerome's protestations. But his approach succeeded with many of his contemporaries. Augustine, for example, was won over. He became a firm advocate of Jerome's translations (if not of the views of Origen on Galatians 2:11–14 that Jerome had retailed in his commentary). Even more tellingly, Jerome managed to convince his

---

63. *Si quid igitur reprehensione dignum putaueras in explanatione nostra, eruditiones tuae fuerat quaerere, utrum ea quae scripsimus, haberentur in Graecis, ut si illi non dixissent, tunc meam proprie sententiam condemnares: praesertim cum libere in Praefatione confessus sim, Origenis Commentarios me esse secutum, et uel mea, uel aliena dictasse. . . . tu ut Episcopus in toto orbe notissimus, debes hanc promulgare sententiam; et in assensum tuum omnes coepiscopos trahere. Ego in paruo tuguriolo cum monachis, id est, cum compeccatoribus meis, de magnis statuere non audeo, nisi hoc ingenue confiteri, me maiorum scripta legere, et in commentariis secundum omnium consuetudinem, uarias ponere explanationes, ut e multis sequatur unusquisque quod uelit. Quod quidem te puto et in saeculari litteratura, et in diuinis libris legisse et probasse.*

Latin audience, despite all Rufinus's efforts to the contrary, that however slavishly he had copied Origen's works, he reviled his opinions. The fact that Jerome was exonerated of the charge of Origenism is strong testimony to his powers of persuasion.

But as this chapter's opening sections have shown, while Jerome's representation of his exegesis as humble compilation may have exculpated him from accusations of arrogance, it highlighted his dependence on access to great wealth. If he composed with a multitude of sources before him, then his scholarship was a costly activity indeed. Furthermore, as we have seen in the case of the commentaries on Daniel and Isaiah, Jerome deliberately considered the reactions of his audience in choosing his mode of composition. Perhaps he also chose to refer to sources, and to the books in his possession, in ways that did not call his readers' attention the riches of his library. Jerome's caginess about his use of Origen's Hexapla would then be just one example of his avoidance of anything that advertised how expensive his scholarship was. When he protests that he and his fellow monks reject luxuriously but uselessly adorned books, he is fashioning, out of the reverse snobbery of the literary elite, a kind of bibliophilia that could take its place in a monastic milieu suspicious of any books at all. By drawing attention to how plain the individual books are, he distracts his readers from the vast riches represented by his collection as a whole. He thereby obscures the integral part played by inherited wealth—whether his own or that of his patrons—in making his scholarship possible. In the final chapter of this book, we will see in more detail what problems this situation presented.

CHAPTER SIX

———— ✳ ————

The Book and the Voice

JUST AS the physical form of the ancient book was radically different from what we are familiar with today, so too was the social matrix within which literacy was exercised. Both elites and illiterates—users of literacy at either end of the social spectrum—made extensive use of literate assistants to access and to produce texts. The identity and status of these assistants varied widely. Rich men of letters might own educated slaves who served as their librarians and secretaries, as well as troops of stenographers, copyists, bookbinders, and other more menial processors of texts. The poor, even if entirely illiterate, were rarely excluded from access to letters. Paid scribes were present even in remote villages to handle simple transactions such as reading and writing personal correspondence and composing basic legal documents. Furthermore, illiteracy, or limited literacy, carried little social stigma, while the wealthy might consider it beneath their standing either to read or to write for themselves. Dictation was a dominant mode of composition. Listening to someone read aloud was perhaps the most common way to access texts.

Throughout his works, Jerome makes constant reference to his reliance on stenographers to take dictation as he composes. In a few texts he reports that his assistants also read to him. These modes of literacy have complex associations within Jerome's own texts. In the context of his broader social milieu, they mark his mode of literary production as elite, even aristocratic. His command of skilled assistants implied that he had the resources to pay them, or at least to support them. His emphasis on their presence drew attention to the similarities between the way he wrote and the habits that elite authors had developed over centuries. His readers may well have assumed that his assistants were his slaves or servants, purchased or paid out of his own funds. Perhaps some of them were.

Jerome deployed the notion of composition by dictation both to disclaim literary excellence for his writings and to stress that he worked in haste and under pressure, toiling day and night to meet the demands of his patrons. But these motifs were by no means restricted to Christian discourse. Thus we read in the *Historia Augusta,* composed in the mid-390s, perhaps at Rome, by a pagan author nostalgic for the old ways:

> Now bestow on anyone you like this little book, written not with elegance but with fidelity to truth. Nor, in fact, do I seem to myself to have made any promise of literary style, but only of facts. For these little works which I have composed on the lives of the emperors I do not write down but only dictate, and I dictate them, indeed, with that speed, which, whether I promise anything of my own accord or you request it, you urge with such insistence that I have not even the opportunity of drawing breath.[1]

The connotations of composition by dictation in this passage, as we shall see, are much the same as those which Jerome develops in his descriptions of his own literary work. The author of the *Historia Augusta* creates a picture of traditional literary *askesis.* He strives to meet his patron's demands, promising not elegance but simple fact—a striking claim coming from the author of a largely fictitious "history." Jerome, as we have seen, sought to represent his work as the monastic labor of the Christian scholar bent over his books in self-mortification—a conception that his references to dictation had the potential to undermine. If anything set Jerome's literary monasticism apart from the more traditional model of authorship, it was the status of those who served him as his amanuenses. To the extent that Jerome could rely on his monks to work as his assistants, he could claim a degree of independence from the classical economy of literary practice.

But scribes and copyists were not the only literary specialists upon whom Jerome relied. He also claims to have hired Jewish teachers to instruct him in biblical interpretation, and he probably did so. It is tantalizing to imagine these Jewish informants actually present in Jerome's workroom. But what is perhaps even more interesting is how he uses them to represent his exeget-

---

1. *Historia Augusta,* Trig. Tyrr. 33.8, LCL, tr. Magie: *da nunc cuivis libellum, non tam diserte quam fideliter scriptum. neque ego eloquentiam mihi videor pollicitius esse, sed rem, qui hos libellos, quos de vita principum edidi, non scribo sed dicto, et dicto cum ea festinatione, quam, si quid vel ipse promisero vel tu petieris, sic perurges ut respirandi non habeam facultatem.*

ical work as self-mortifying. Jerome depicts his Jewish teachers in terms that reinforce and further develop his rhetoric of Hebrew study as a specialized form of asceticism suited for a cultivated monk.

Jerome's representations of the participation of others in the making of his works, then, reflect the complexity of the relations of his scholarly undertaking to the elite literary tradition and to the ideals of cenobitic monasticism. At the same time, the skilled assistants who collaborated in making Jerome's literary oeuvre were real people, whose presence marks Jerome's scholarship as a labor-intensive as well as a capital-intensive undertaking. To be a prolific author in the conditions of late antiquity, was almost by definition to command a skilled staff.

THE *NOTARIUS* AND JEROME'S MODE OF COMPOSITION

A passage from the preface to book 7 of the commentary on Ezekiel, Jerome's penultimate exegetical work, paints a fascinating picture of the aged scholar at work, his labors supported by his monks:

> a twilight, nay rather a secret labor carried out by night—nights which as winter draws near begin to be longer—this we are compelled to dictate by the light of a little candle, and to digest the burning of our soul by means of the tediousness of exegesis. Nor do we boast, as some perhaps suspect, of the assistance of the brothers, but simply confess the causes of our delay . . . Composing has become so difficult, that with the clouded eyes of extreme old age, suffering to some extent what the blessed Isaac did, we can no longer read the Hebrew scrolls by the light of night. Indeed even in the blaze of the daytime sun, we are blinded by the smallness of the letters. Still more, the commentaries of the Greeks we know only through the voices of the brothers; and let there be no doubt, that food which has been chewed by someone else's teeth, causes nausea to the one who eats it. . . . We write by means of the stylus of a shorthand secretary and . . . hardly have time to correct [what he writes].[2]

2. *ut lucratiuis immo furtiuis noctium operis, quae hieme propinquante longiores esse coeperunt, haec ad lucernulam qualiacumque sunt dictare conamur et aestuantis animi taedium interpretatione digerere. Nec iactamus, ut quidam forsitan suspicantur, fratrum susceptionem, sed morarum causas simpliciter confitemur . . . Accedit ad haec dictandi difficultatem, quod caligantibus oculis senectute et aliquid sustinentibus beati Isaac, ad nocturnum lumen nequaquam ualemus Hebraeorum uolumina relegere, quae etiam ad solis dieique fulgorem, litterarum nobis paruitate caecantur. Sed et Graecorum commentarios fratrum tantum uoce cognoscimus; nullique dubium, quod alienis dentibus commoliti cibi, uescentibus nauseam faciant. Vnde obsecro te, filia Eustochium, ut ista quae notariorum stilo cudimus et ad quae emendanda spatium uix habemus . . .*

This passage links two aspects of Jerome's mode of literary production: compilation and dictation. The two played similar roles in his self-description. Jerome draws attention to both practices in order to present his works as unpolished, and therefore to describe his authorship in terms of the monastic norm of humility. But like his costly books, Jerome's *notarii* and other skilled assistants could have provided an opportunity for his opponents to charge him with violating the norm of poverty. As we shall see, Jerome himself lampooned at least one opponent in just such terms.

The monks who play such a crucial role in this vivid scene from the commentary on Ezekiel were familiar presences for Jerome's faithful readers. He seems to have composed by dictation for much of his career, and he advertised this practice in the prefaces to even his most technical works. From 380 to his death in 419, he continually referred to his reliance on a *notarius*[3] and to composition by dictation.[4] Some of these references are very brief. Especially in later works, Jerome seemed to take it for granted that composition involved dictation. He usually used the verb *dictare* in the technical sense of "to dictate." At times, however, the word seems to revert to its ancient meaning "to compose," which had preceded the invention of shorthand.[5] The *notarius*, unlike other members of the support staff whom we glimpsed in the passage just cited, played a central role in Jerome's self-presentation as a writer. While he emphasized his use of *notarii*, he referred only rarely and in passing to his reliance on skilled writers for other kinds of tasks, like copying books.

Jerome often ascribes his need to dictate to ill health or to eye problems.[6]

---

3. Explicit references to *notarii* who take Jerome's dictation occur in *praef. in Eus. Chronicon; praef. in Orig. hom. in Hiezech.; Comm. in Gal.* pref. to bk. 3; *Comm. in Abdiam* l. 776ff.; *Comm. in Hiezech.* pref. to bk. 7; *Comm. in Esaiam* prefs. to bks. 5, 10; *Comm. in Hier.* pref. to bk. 1; *Praef. in Pachomiana latina;* letters 34.6, 36.1, 57, 60, 65, 74.6, 117.12, 118.7, 130.1.

4. The references to composition by dictation are too numerous to list here: a number of citations appear in the following footnotes. The references appear in the prefaces to many of Jerome's commentaries on the Prophets, in his letters from the 380s until his death, and in prefaces to other works written throughout his career, from the *Chronicon* translated in 380 through the *Pachomiana latina* of 404. Indeed, exceptions to the rule are fewer than examples: these include the *Quaest. Heb. in Gen.* and several other works written at Bethlehem before 392, the *De vir. ill.,* the Commentary on Daniel, and Jerome's polemical works, including *Adv. Iov.* and *Contra Ruf.*

5. 130.1: *omnes materias, quas ab adulescentia usque ad hanc aetatem uel mea uel notariorum scripsi manu;* 75.4: refers to his mode of composing *all* his works as dictation. On the semantic evolution of *dictare,* see OLD, s.v.

6. For his ill health and eye problems, see the *praef. in Eus. Chronicon; praef. in Orig. hom. in Hiezech.;* letters 18A.16 and 21.42; *Comm. in Gal.* 3.427; *Comm. in Matt.,* pref.; *praef. in libris Solomonis de Hebr. interpr.; Comm. in Hiezech.* 7, pref. Cavallera, *Saint Jérôme,* 289–90, n. 2, cites

Equally, he attributes his methods to haste and the pressure of other obligations, and claims that he has been compelled to dictate late into the night.[7] He laments his reliance on a *notarius* as an expedient that prevents him from editing carefully, drawing a sharp stylistic contrast between the work that has been polished by its author's own hand and the *tumultuarium opus* produced by dictation. He associates a carefully elaborated literary style with declamation, a genre that he opposes to commentary. Declamation, and rhetoric in general, are associated with pagan literature, while commentary is the genre appropriate to a Christian.[8] The *notarius,* therefore, stands for a mode of composition that is utilitarian rather than literary; Christian rather than worldly; and ascetic rather than leisured—for the presence of an amanuensis, as Jerome assures his readers, simply allows him to work when he is ill, or to achieve a higher level of productivity through constant industry.

The preface to the third book of Jerome's commentary on Galatians already brings together all of these elements and makes clear their wider implications. It also contains one of Jerome's most vivid and concrete depictions of the role of the *notarius* in his working process. The preface opens with a description of the church of Jerome's day as corrupted by a fashion for rhetorical display. He claims that he is unqualified to enter the rhetorical competition that Christian discourse has become, for his literary asceticism has marred his language. He reminds his addressees, Paula and Eustochium, that in his case,

---

letters 71 and 73. Letter 74.6 states, *Nos enim et haec ipsa, lectulo decumbentes longaque aegrotatione confecti, uix notario celeriter scribenda dictauimus.* See also Cavallera, *Saint Jérôme,* 309–10, 12–13, 19, 34–35, for more references to Jerome's maladies, which usually interfered with his literary efforts.

7. On haste and late-night work, see *praef. in Eus. Chron. (uelocissime dictaverim); Contra Vigilantium* 3 and 17; *Comm. in Abdiam* 776 *(haec ad duas lucubratiunculas . . . dictaui); Comm. in Zach.,* prol. 19 *(uelim nolim, salte lucratiuis per noctem horis atque furtiuis dictare compellor),* and book 2, prol. 133 *(tanta celeritate dictauimus, ut paene non sit emendandi spatium); Comm. in Esaiam* 2, pref. *(ut potui, non ut uolui, celeri sermone dictaui),* 5, pref. (the commentary written for Amabilis in 398), 13, pref. *(hanc praefatiunculam tumultuario sermone dictaui); Comm. in Hieremiam,* 2.74.4 *(celeri sermone dictamus); Comm. in Hiezech.* 7, pref. *(haec ad lucernulam qualiacumque sunt dictare conamur);* letters 29.1 *(rem grandem celerius dicto, quam debeo),* 34.6, 36.1, 64.22, 108.32, 117.12, 119.1, 127.14, 129.8.

8. On declamation opposed to commentary, see letters 36.14; 52.4; 57.11; *Comm. in Hiezech.* 12.40.306 *(scientia scripturarum et non uanis oratorum declamationibus); Comm. in Osee,* 1.2.428; *Comm. in Sophoniam,* 3.549 *(non me controuersias et declamationes scribere . . . sed commentarios).* On association with pagan literature, see *Comm. in epist. ad Gal.* 3.427 *(si quis eloquentiam quaerit, uel declamationibus delectatur, habet in utraque lingua Demosthenem et Tullium, Polemonem et Quintillianum);* on declamation as childish, see *Dialogi contra Pelagianos,* 3.5.12 *(puerilibus declamatiunculis ludendum est).*

every elegance of speech, and beauty of Latin expression, the hissing sound of reading Hebrew has sullied. For you know yourselves that it has been more than fifteen years since I have held in my hands the works of Tully, of Maro, or of any author of secular works at all: and if perchance I even spoke of them in that time, I was stricken with fear, as if the vision of my dream rose again to haunt me.[9]

Jerome is no longer able to express himself in the manner inculcated in the rhetorical schools. His Latin has deteriorated under the influence of his Hebrew studies. He goes on to write, "What I have produced through my untiring study of that language [Hebrew], I leave to the judgment of others; I myself know what I have lost in my own [Latin]."[10] The study of Hebrew has ruined his pronunciation, while the complete avoidance of secular literature has robbed his diction of any former classical polish.

Jerome's assertions about his own literary style in this passage are highly problematic. Unless "elegance of speech, and beauty of Latin expression," *sermonis elegantiam et Latini eloqui uenustatem,* refer *only* to pronunciation, without any implications for literary style, Jerome's self-deprecating claims are falsified by the very text that advances them. Indeed, Jerome sets forth the contrast between "apostolic simplicity and purity of language," *apostolicorum simplicita[s] et purita[s] uerborum,* and "speech corrupted by the lie of the rhetorical art," *oratio rhetoricae artis fucata mendacio,* in a pair of balanced, Ciceronian phrases.[11] The lengthy preface moves from one vivid tableau to another, summoning before the reader's inner eye a parade of images of startling clarity. The use of rhetorical questions, which Jerome poses only to answer them, is another element of the preface's stylized diction. Altogether, the language of this discussion of the corruption wrought by rhetoric is as rhetorical as anything Jerome ever wrote.

Jerome goes on to specify that not only have the study of Hebrew and the neglect of Latin literature deprived him of his former eloquence, but his dependence on a *notarius* has made it impossible for him to carefully edit

---

9. PL 26.485–488: *omnem sermonis elegantiam, et Latini eloquii uenustatem, stridor lectionis Hebraicae sordidauit. Nostis enim et ipsae, quod plus quam quindecim anni sunt, ex quo in manus meas nunquam Tullius, nunquam Maro, nunquam gentilium litterarum quilibet auctor ascendit: et si quid forte inde dum loquimur, obrepit, quasi inaitui per nebulam somnii recordamur.* The chronological problems presented by the Pauline commentaries are discussed above in chapter 2, n. 4, and in the Appendix, section 6. As mentioned there, I have tentatively accepted the date of summer 386 suggested by Nautin, "Date des commentaires."

10. *Quod autem profecerim ex linguae illius infatigabili studio, aliorum iudicio derelinquo: ego quid in mea amiserim, scio* (PL 26.486).

11. PL 26.486.

his work. Instead, he composes orally, indeed extemporaneously. Here Jerome paints a striking picture of himself at work, his *notarius* poised to record his words:

> Add to this that because of the infirmity of my eyes and my entire body, I do not write with my own hand, nor can I muster sufficient effort and care to compensate for the slowness of my speech. Concerning Virgil, tradition recounts that he edited his books with the care of a she-bear guarding her cubs. I, on the other hand, simply summon my secretary, and either I immediately dictate whatever comes into my mouth or, if I pause for a moment to think, hoping to produce something a bit better, then he silently reproaches me, fidgeting with his hand, wrinkling his brow, and by the whole bearing of his body making plain that he thinks I am wasting his time.[12]

This lively scene shows Jerome racked by physical debility, unable to exercise any editorial control over his own literary productions. The portrayal of the *notarius*'s impatience may be intended to suggest that Jerome has deteriorated to the point that his servants are taking liberties with him. This pitiful self-portrait, however, masks an audacious assertion. Jerome claims that the polished Latin of this preface, with its striking images and elegant turns of phrase, is simply what rises to his lips unpremeditated (*quodcunque in buccam uenerit*). While Jerome avoids the floweriness of many a late antique writer, the vigor and clarity of his style by no means preclude rhetorical display. The contrast between Jerome's statements and the language in which he expresses them, therefore, constitutes a claim to power, an effort of self-promotion all the more effective because it is elaborately veiled.

Having violently disclaimed the normal means of attaining and perfecting a cultivated mode of expression, Jerome goes even farther in the next section of the preface. He opposes his own chosen literary genre, the commentary, to the rhetorical genre of declamation in sharp and explicit terms. Lamenting his inability to polish his language by editing his work with his own hand, he asks rhetorically what excuse he can make for himself, and replies,

> Why, surely, my answer to you, and to others (who might perhaps wish to read my work), would be that I am writing not a panegyric or a *controversia*, but a

---

12. *Accedit ad hoc, quia propter oculorum et totius corpusculi infirmitatem, manu mea ipse non scribo: nec labore et diligentia compensare queo eloquii tarditate: quod de Virgilio quoque tradunt, quia libros suos in modum ursorum fetum lambendo figurauerit: uerum accito notario, aut statim dicto quodcunque in buccam uenerit: aut si paululum uoluero cogitare, melius aliquid prolaturus, tunc me tacitus ille reprehendit, manum contrahit, frontem rugat, et se frustra adesse, toto gestu corporis contestatur* (PL 26.488).

commentary, that is, a work that has the following purpose: not that my words should be praised, but that what was well said by someone else, might be understood in the manner in which it was expressed. My task is to explicate the obscure, to make short work of the obvious, and to linger over doubtful passages. For this reason, too, many have termed their own commentaries "explanations." If someone seeks eloquence, or takes pleasure in declamations, these exist in either tongue, the work of Demosthenes and Tully, of Polemon and Quintilian.[13]

This passage develops a contrast that became a standard feature of Jerome's self-presentation: between the genre of commentary and its literary qualities (or lack thereof), and the genre of declamation. The two are set against each other as poles defining the field of learned language. Commentary, it is implied, is the proper discourse of the church, whereas declamation belongs to a godless secular realm, if not to paganism itself.

This distinction sharply opposes literary genres that in reality were not so far apart. Ancient grammatical commentaries, as observed already, retain a strong oral flavor, reflecting their genesis in the social setting of the schools and in the teacher's oral instruction to his pupils.[14] The formality and literary quality of Jerome's own exegesis is an innovation in this regard. The culture of declamation developed in the rhetorical schools had much in common with the literary exposition practiced by the grammarian. This continuity was as apparent within the literature of the church as it was in the social world of the schools. We have only to think of Origen's exegetical homilies, or of the biblical commentaries of Ambrose or Augustine and their origins in the two bishops' preaching, to see that Jerome's distinction between the commentary and the declamation was highly artificial.[15] The same degree of artificiality governs his deployment here of the figure of the *notarius*.

Within his lengthy discussion of his mode of composition and its place within the discourse of the church, Jerome's *notarius* appears briefly, yet plays a crucial role. The presence of the *notarius* is essential to Jerome's portrayal of his literary style as crude and unpolished. The need to dictate pre-

---

13. *uidelicet ut et uobis, et caeteris (qui forte legere uoluerint) sit responsum, me non panegyricum, aut controversiam scribere, sed commentarium, id est, hoc habere propositum, non ut mea uerba laudentur, sed ut quae ab alio bene dicta sunt, ita intelligantur ut dicta sunt. Officii mei est obscura disserere, manifesta perstringere, in dubiis immorari. Vnde et a plerisque Commentariorum opus, explanatio nominatur. Si quis eloquentiam quaerit, uel declamationis delectatur, habet in utraque lingua Demosthenem et Tullium, Polemonem et Quintillianum* (PL 26.400C).

14. Kaster, *Guardians*, especially chapter 4 on Pompeius.

15. See McLynn, *Ambrose*, 237–51; Pontet, *Exégèse de s. Augustin*.

vents him from editing his work with the care of a Virgil, as he points out. Yet the act of dictation, transforming literary composition from a written to an oral activity, makes of this preface a piece of declamatory rhetoric of precisely the sort that Jerome here condemns. The figure of the *notarius,* then, underwrites both Jerome's self-effacement and the self-aggrandizement it conceals. Through his description of how he composed, Jerome can parade his ascetic humility without relinquishing the class privilege conferred by rhetorical proficiency.

On another level, Jerome's advertising his use of a *notarius* raises the question of class privilege even more concretely. Reliance on highly skilled assistants was an expensive luxury, one that likely required the financial support of wealthy patrons. The ambiguous presence of the *notarius* in this and other prominent locations in Jerome's descriptions of his exegetical work is thus of a similar order to that of the Hexapla behind the pages of the commentaries on the Prophets. Jerome made a point of his command of a staff of educated younger men, some of whom could presumably have pursued careers in administration or the church. At the same time, he rarely disclosed any information about their identities or what kept them within his orbit.

We cannot prove that Jerome composed by dictating to *notarii.* However, certain references to *notarii* and other skilled writers in more specific, concrete contexts suggest that Jerome's representation of his mode of composition is not a mere fiction. It seems that Jerome did have a staff of skilled writers in his monastery at Bethlehem, though it may have been small. A few of Jerome's monks may have served him for decades as shorthand secretaries. In general, however, his assistants were recruited on an ad hoc basis. For example, both Western bishops and wealthy laymen sent men to obtain copies of his writings for the libraries of their masters or patrons.

Passages from two prefaces that Jerome wrote at Constantinople in the early 380s, long before he established himself at Bethlehem, help to bridge the gap between the role of the *notarius* in Jerome's self-representation and the concrete circumstances in which his works were composed and copied. The preface to the translation and revision of Eusebius's *Chronicle,* produced about 380, strikes a similar note to the preface to book 3 of the commentary on Galatians. Jerome composes in haste, dependent on a *notarius,* his work hampered not only by lack of time but by illness. He asks his dedicatees, Vincentius and Gallienus, to excuse any inaccuracies introduced as a result of this careless and unsystematic mode of proceeding:

> Therefore, my dearest Vincentius, and you, Gallienus, the other half of my soul,
> I beseech you, that although this is a disorderly work produced in haste, you

> nevertheless peruse it with the spirit of friends, not of judges, especially since, as you know, I dictated it most rapidly to a *notarius*.[16]

This description is extremely misleading. Two fifth-century manuscripts of Jerome's version of the *Chronicon* survive, giving a good idea of the appearance of the original (fig. 11). The manuscripts make plain that this was the very opposite of a *tumultuarium opus*.[17] The work consists largely of chronological tables, laid out in columns across the page. The columns are defined not only by the arrangement of the writing on the page but also by the ruling pattern that guides the writing. This pattern is complex and would have required careful planning. Notes expanding on the framework of dates that fills most of the page appear in the central space between the columns. In the earlier of the two manuscripts, these notes are neatly laid out in geometrical forms—diamonds, triangles, and so on.[18] Eusebius's invention of the chronological table had been a milestone in the history of the Greek book at the beginning of the fourth century. Jerome's translation would have been similarly innovative for the Latin tradition.

The production of the revised *Chronicle* would have required a considerable amount of skilled labor. The *notarius* took dictation in shorthand on wax tablets and transcribed the *notae* into a plain copy. Specialized work was also involved in ruling the leaves of the final presentation copy, transferring the text from the *schedulae* written by the *notarius* onto these leaves, and binding them into a codex. Prior to the preparation of the final copy, it may have been necessary to make at least one experimental version in order to be certain that the arrangement of the columns would accommodate the Latin translation of the annotations, as well as the substitution of Roman numerals for Greek. Unfortunately, the *Chronicle* has not survived in Greek, so we cannot have a precise idea of the differences in layout between Jerome's version and the Eusebian original. Two factors, however, suggest that Jerome's adaptation involved more than merely copying the format of the Greek *Chronicle*. First, Jerome inserted many additions into Eusebius's existing chronicle of Roman history. Second, he extended Eusebius's work forward by fifty-two years, to bring it up to the end of the most recent reign.[19]

---

16. *Itaque, mi Vincenti carissime et tu Galliene, pars animae meae, obsecro, ut, quidquid hoc tumultuarii operis est, amicorum, non iudicum animo relegatis, praesertim cum et notario, ut scitis, uelocissime dictauerim.*

17. For facsimiles, see Eusebius, *Bodleian Manuscript*; Jerome, *Chronicon*.

18. Jerome, *Chronicon*.

19. *Praef. in Eus. Chron.: a Troia usque ad uicesimum Constantini annum nunc addita, nunc admixta sunt plurima, quae de Tranquillo et ceteris illustribus historicis curiosissime excerpsi. a Constantini*

Both of these modifications would have required the preparation of new page arrangements. They would therefore have necessitated an intermediate step between the composition of the text and the copying of the final version. The making of the Latin version of Eusebius's *Chronicle* was a complex process, which could have required a small workshop of specialists. Jerome probably acted more as supervisor than as author in the usual sense of that word. Even though his version of the *Chronicle* was not much more than a translation, it was an extraordinarily ambitious undertaking in terms of planning, materials, and manpower.

In Jerome's preface, his characteristic emphasis on style diverts the reader's attention from the logistical complexity of making the book. Instead, the focus is on Jerome himself in his role as mediator of the Greek literary tradition. Implicitly, that role is defined not in terms of the technical production of complex books but of the cultured assimilation and reproduction of another writer's style. The figure of the *notarius*—here as in so many of Jerome's later works—both stands in for and serves to mask the complex cooperative process that the production of scholarly books involved in late antiquity. Whatever the deficiencies of Jerome's *Chronicle* as a historical account, the pose of casualness he strikes when he asks his friends to be lenient in judging a work produced in haste is artificial in the extreme.[20] On a purely bibliographic level, the *Chronicle* was complex, its production requiring careful coordination. The lesson of the *Chronicle* can be extended to other works Jerome claims to have dictated in haste and carelessly. These protestations should not be taken at face value, as too many scholars have done in the past. They need to be understood first in terms of the role they played in Jerome's representation of his literary activities as the humble efforts of a weak and diffident monk. Only after this context has been taken into account can their evidence shed light on how he actually worked.

A more modest work of the same period, the translation of Origen's homilies on Ezekiel, is also addressed to Vincentius, one of the two dedicatees of the *Chronicle*. In his preface, Jerome first describes his mode of composition—"these fourteen [homilies] on Ezekiel I dictated as I had the opportu-

---

autem supra dicto anno usque ad consulatum Augustorum Valentis sexies et Valentiniani iterum totum meum est.

20. Jerome's competence as a historian has been harshly criticized. Even Kelly, usually an apologist for Jerome, writes that his presentation of the materials he adds to the Chronicon "is seriously defective by the standards not only of present-day but even of contemporary historiography" (*Jerome*, 75).

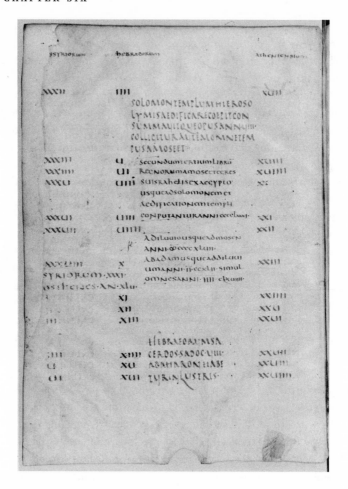

FIGURE 11. An opening of Jerome's translation of the *Chronicon*. Bibliothèque Nationale, Paris, BN latin 6400 B, fol. 287v. and 288r. Reproduced with permission of the Bibliothèque nationale de France.

nity.[21] Then he complains that although he depends on *notarii*, his poverty has made them difficult to afford. He addresses his dedicatee, Vincentius, as follows:

> You ask of me a great thing, my friend, that I should render Origen into Latin
> . . . but as you know, I am tortured by pain in my eyes, which I brought upon

21. *has quattuordecim [homilias] in Ezechielem per interualla dictaui* (*Praef. in Orig. hom. in Hiezech.*, PL 25.585A).

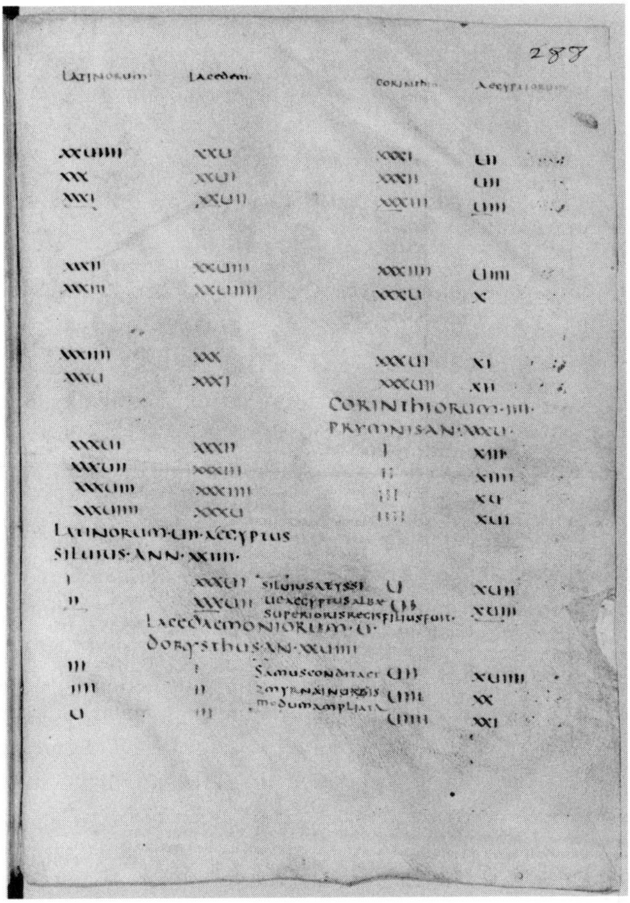

FIGURE 11. Continued

myself in my impatience by too much reading; and because of my lack of stenographers, since poverty has removed this support, I am unable to fulfill what
you rightly desire, however ardently you wish it. . . . this much, however, I
promise, that if by your prayers Jesus restores my health, I will translate Origen's works—I cannot say *all* of them, but a great deal at any rate—by means
of that principle, which I have often set before you, that I provide the voice, and
you the secretary.[22]

22. *Magnum est quidem, amice, quod postulas, ut Origenem faciam latinum . . . sed oculorum, ut ipse
nosti, dolore cruciatus, quem nimia impatiens lectione contraxi, et notariorum penuria, quia tenuitas
hoc quoque subsidium abstulit, quod recte cupis, tam ardenter ut cupis, implere non ualeo . . . hoc*

Vincentius, Jerome claims, has pressed him to undertake the immense labor of translating all of Origen's works. The demand, however unrealistic, is not incredible. Years later, Augustine wrote to Jerome in similar terms, urging him to return to translating all of Origen's exegesis.[23] Here, Jerome begs off, claiming ill health. He promises, however, that he will at least undertake to begin the task if he recovers and if Vincentius can remedy his lack of a shorthand secretary.

Two interpretations of the preface's final words—*ut ego vocem praebeam, tu notarium*—are possible. Either Jerome is asking Vincentius to *pay* for his *notarii,* or he is asking Vincentius himself to *serve* as his *notarius.* The first possibility is supported by the manner of Jerome's reference to dictation in the preface to the *Chronicle,* dedicated to Vincentius and Gallienus. When he there refers to his use of a stenographer with the words "As you know, I dictated it most rapidly to a *notarius,*" it is clear that this person is not identical with either of Jerome's addressees. The interpretation of the closing words of the preface to the homilies depends in part on the order in which the two translations were made. If the *Chronicon* came after the homilies, the preface to the homilies may have represented a bid for financial support, followed by the acknowledgment of its provision in the form of another dedication. If the *Chronicon* came first, this ambitious project may have exhausted Jerome's resources, leaving him unable to afford a *notarius.* Completing his translation of Origen's homilies despite these straitened circumstances, he proposes to his friend Vincentius that he himself could fill the gap, allowing Jerome to go on to even more ambitious translation projects. Unfortunately, there is no consensus on the dating to provide even tentative support for one option or the other.[24]

These contrasting narratives represent different economies of literary practice. If "that I provide the voice, and you the secretary" means that Jerome hopes his friend will defray the costs of hiring *notarii,* we are firmly in the traditional aristocratic economy, where writers might call upon their wealthy patrons for various forms of financial support, and *notarii* and copyists were typically slaves or freedmen. If Jerome is asking Vincentius himself to serve as his amanuensis, we are entering a new world: an economy

---

tamen spondeo quia, si orante te Iesus reddiderit sanitatem, non dicam cuncta . . . sed permulta sim translaturus, ea lege, qua tibi saepe constitui, ut ego uocem praebeam, tu notarium (Praef. in Orig. hom. in Hiezech., PL 25.583B–586A).

23. Letter 40, written in 394 or 395.

24. See Cavallera, *Saint Jérôme,* 2:20–22; Kelly, *Jerome,* 72–79.

of literary practice where the labor of monks replaces that of slaves, even (perhaps especially) in menial tasks like stenography. The very difficulty of determining which of these possibilities best corresponds to reality is revealing. Jerome stood on the cusp of a transition, a shift in modes of literary production that was just beginning in his lifetime and would not be complete for centuries to come. A mixture of the aristocratic and the monastic was to characterize Jerome's way of proceeding for the rest of his career. During his years at Bethlehem, Jerome was head of a flourishing monastic community. Even then, his literary staff included paid workers and slaves as well as his own monks, who may have worked for free. The dilemma of Vincentius's role is emblematic of this mixture.

Two further considerations place the question of how Jerome produced these early works in a broader context. First, Vincentius accompanied Jerome on his departure from Constantinople. Following his friend to Rome, and then to Bethlehem, he spent thirteen years as a monk in Jerome's monastery. Whether his contribution to Jerome's literary work consisted of cash or labor, Vincentius himself became incorporated into Jerome's monastic economy.

Second, a young man proficient in Latin stenography who found himself in Constantinople in 380 might well have traveled there seeking an administrative post. The 380s saw the culmination of a series of developments that transformed the social position of the shorthand writer from humble amanuensis to high imperial official.[25] If we are to believe the complaints of Libanius, by the 380s stenography had come close to replacing rhetoric as the skill that promised the easiest entrée into the imperial *officia*.[26] Vincentius, like Jerome, was a priest who seems never to have served as a pastor. It was probably the hope of an administrative—not an ecclesiastical—career that had brought him to the Eastern capital at the time of Theodosius's accession.[27] If this was the case, Vincentius's story would have been very similar to that of Jerome and his friend Bonosus during their brief stay at Trier in the late 360s. The figure of Vincentius as a young careerist turned ascetic would fit neatly with the suggestion that Jerome's concluding words in his preface to Origen's homilies were a bid for his friend's services rather than for financial support.

---

25. On stenographers in the imperial service in the 380s and before, see Teitler, *Notarii*, 54–72.

26. See Teitler, *Notarii*, 33–34, 65–67; Libanius, *Or.* 42.25.

27. For Vincentius's career, see Rebenich, *Hieronymus*, 84, 91–92, 132ff., 48, 93, 240–41.

We will probably never know exactly what Jerome meant by those words. Indeed, the very suggestion that Vincentius himself may have served as Jerome's *notarius* could be dismissed as quixotic. But the evidence for the status of the members of Jerome's staff at Bethlehem suggests that a similar inextricable mixture obtained even after Jerome had established himself there. He continued to combine modes of literary production that could be termed in turn aristocratic, monastic, and even episcopal or ecclesiastic.

Two sources from Jerome's correspondence provide precious concrete information on the identity of those who took his dictation and produced copies of his works for dissemination at the monastery in Bethlehem. The first is a letter from Jerome to Aurelius, newly elected bishop of Carthage, discovered in the 1990s among a collection of previously unknown letters of Augustine. Jerome is replying to a communication from Aurelius regarding Jerome's own works. Like Augustine's own letters in the new collection, Jerome's is more detailed and circumstantial on a number of matters than is any previously known source. He informs his correspondent that he enjoys the assistance of two monks in his monastery who serve as shorthand secretaries. These monks, however, have time only for taking dictation as he composes, and cannot be spared to copy his earlier works.[28] For the latter purpose, Jerome urges Aurelius to send a man from his own retinue to spend a year at Bethlehem, as other bishops from Italy and Gaul have before him. There, Jerome would provide his works to be copied for Aurelius's library.[29] In the meantime, Jerome sends Aurelius a sample of his recent exegetical work: the *Hebrew Questions on Genesis* and a brief commentary on Psalm 10. The date of the letter is in the early to mid-390s, when Jerome was well established at Bethlehem, but perhaps before the outbreak of the Origenist controversy.[30]

28. Letter 15/27*.3 *librariorum latinorum hierosolimae [non] est penuria; nam ego duos sanctos fratres quos habeo notarios, uix queunt his quae dictamus occurrere.* Three parallel passages where Jerome complains of a lack of Latin writers in Palestine support Divjak's emendation; see letter 134.2 to Augustine: *Grandem latini sermonis in ista prouincia notariorum patimur penuriam; Comm. in Isaiam,* pref. to book 10: *notariorumque penuria;* letter 75.4: *quia in hac prouincia latini sermonis scriptorumque penuria est.* The similarity of these formulas is characteristic of Jerome, and suggests that the *non* in letter 155/27* is all the more likely to be an interpolation.

29. Letter 155/27*.3: *ceterum quia orante te non parua de scripturis sanctis composuimus, si tibi placet et commodum uidetur, fac quod alii de Gallia et alii de Italia fratres tui, sancti episcopi, fecerunt, id est mitte aliquem fidum tibi qui unum annum hic faciat me exemplaria tribuente et deferat ad te cuncta quae scripsimus.*

30. The two works that Jerome sent to Aurelius were written in 391 (*Quaest. Heb. in Gen.*) and 392 (seven tractates on Psalms 10–16, mentioned in *De vir. ill.* 135; see Nautin, "Activité littéraire"); thus the letter must be dated to 392 at the very earliest. On the other hand, in 398 Je-

Jerome's claim that bishops from Italy and Gaul had sent scribes to Bethlehem in order to obtain copies of his works might seem far-fetched. But his correspondence with another reader, a certain Lucinus of Baetica, in northern Spain, preserves the story of a wealthy layman who had done just that. Lucinus, it appears, had sent six copyists, his slaves, to Bethlehem, where they were directed to make copies of all of Jerome's works. In the spring of 398, when Jerome had just recovered from a long and debilitating illness, he wrote to Lucinus, praising his generosity and discussing the slaves' work. The letter appears to have been written to accompany the volumes of Jerome's works to the West.

In this letter, and in another he wrote shortly afterward to Theodora, Lucinus's widow, upon receiving the distressing news of his patron's death, Jerome gives several interesting details regarding the books and their copying.[31] Lucinus seems to have had an exaggerated impression of Jerome's productivity. Jerome finds himself informing his Spanish correspondent that he has not, in fact, translated the work of Josephus, nor the writings of the saints Polycarp and Papias. Nevertheless it was a substantial task for Lucinus's servants to produce versions of all of Jerome's works. Jerome warns his addressee that because of the scope of the undertaking and his own illness, he has not had time to check the copies personally. He had to be content merely to supervise the process. A passing phrase reveals that the books have been copied *in chartaceis codicibus*, in papyrus codices—the late antique book par excellence, as familiar in the West as it was in Palestine.[32] Jerome tells Lucinus, too, that he frequently admonished the scribes to take care. But he assumes that like most copyists, they will have written "not what they

---

rome actually did write a commentary on Matthew, which he denied having done in the letter to Aurelius: *praeterea quod addis habere te et commentariolos meos in Mattheum, hoc ego opus edidisse me penitus ignoro, nisi forte caritate qua me diligis quidquid praeclarum uideris meum putas* ("you add that you also possess a brief commentary on Matthew of mine: for my part I am completely unaware of having produced such a work, unless perhaps because of the affection you cherish for me you attribute to me whatever seems to you worthy of repute"). This commentary, moreover, was dedicated to Jerome's friend Eusebius of Cremona, mentioned in the letter under discussion as already present in his monastery, before Eusebius's departure for the West in the spring of that year. The year 397, however, seems too late for the new letter, since Jerome wrote it to congratulate Aurelius on his election to the bishopric of Carthage, which must have taken place by October 393 when Aurelius presided at the Council of Hippo. A date as late as 395 is not unimaginable, but 392 or 393 seems most plausible. (See Yves-Marie Duval, "Notes complémentaires," 561, for this dating.)

31. For the dates and context of letters 71 and 75, and a discussion of Jerome's Spanish contacts, see Rebenich, *Hieronymus*, 293–98.

32. E.g., the sixth-century Latin papyrus codices of Avitus and Hilary cited at Turner, *Typology*, 40, made in southern France.

found but what they understood" and, worse still, "when they attempted to correct the errors of others, they merely made plain their own."[33]

Three categories of expert writers appear in these three letters: Jerome's monks, two of whom were trained as *notarii;* slave copyists sent by a wealthy layman from Spain; and, more hypothetically, ecclesiastical *notarii* dispatched from the courts of various Western bishops. Evidence from a different kind of source supports Jerome's claim that he lacked the staff to copy books in large numbers. In a passage of his *Apology against Jerome* (already discussed in chapter 4), Rufinus states that Jerome hired his monks on the Mount of Olives to copy books for him. The presumably routine transaction receives mention because the books were pagan works, the dialogues of Cicero. In order to emphasize his charge that Jerome took a lively interest in Cicero despite the oath he had taken in his dream, Rufinus stresses that Jerome paid extra to have the books copied with special care. Indeed, he claims not only that his monks served as copyists on Jerome's behalf, but that he himself "often held in his own hands" the *quaterniones* of the books in progress as he checked them for accuracy.[34] This final example of skilled writers at work in Jerome's service incorporates elements of the monastic and the aristocratic modes of literary production in an inseparable mixture.

In Jerome's letters from the 390s, several occurrences of the term *notarius* clearly refer to writers who functioned as copyists rather than as stenographers. In the letter to Aurelius, Jerome juxtaposes the word *notarius,* used in its specialized sense of a stenographer, with the contrasting term *librarius,* scribe or copyist, in a manner that suggests that both tasks were often carried out by the same individual. Complaining of the lack of Latin *librarii* in Palestine, Jerome explains that the two monks who serve as his *notarii* are barely sufficient for the task of taking dictation—implying that they could just as well have served as copyists, if it were not for the general scarcity of such personnel.[35] The references to Lucinus's servants present an

33. Letter 71 to Lucinus: *non quod inueniunt sed quod intellegunt . . . dum alienos errores emendare nituntur, ostendunt suos.* For the identification of Lucinus's *notarii* as slaves, see letter 71.5, *pueris tuis et notariis;* see also letter 75 on the death of Lucinus, where Jerome connects Lucinus's sending of the *notarii* with the lack of Latin copyists in Palestine: *. . . ut missis sex notariis, quia in hac prouincia latini sermonis scriptorumque penuria est, describi sibi fecerit, quaecumque ab adulescentia usque in praesens tempus dictauimus.*

34. *Alioquin, si inficias eas, etiam testes quamplurimos fratrum habere possum, qui in meis cellulis manentes, in Monte Oliueti, quamplurimos ei Ciceronis dialogos descripserunt, quorum ego et quaterniones, cum scriberent, frequenter in manibus tenui et relegi, et quod mercedes multo largiores, quam pro aliis scripturis solent, ab isto eis darentur agnoui* (Rufinus, *Apol.* 2.11).

35. Letter 155.3: *librariorum Latinorum Hierosolimae [non] est penuria; nam ego duos sanctos fratres quos habeo notarios, uix queunt his quae dictamus occurrere.*

opposite confusion of terminology. The men sent to Bethlehem are usually referred to as *notarii*, the term *librarius* appearing only in the phrase *tuis et imperitiae notariorum librariorumque incuriae* ("the inexperience and carelessness of your secretaries and copyists"). But their task clearly involved preparing fair copies of books rather than taking dictation.[36]

These confusions imply that the fluid status of those who might help to realize Jerome's works as finished books was matched by the interchangeability of the individuals involved. There seems to have been no rigid distinction between the kinds of labor assigned to individual skilled writers in Jerome's establishment, any more than there was between the work done by slaves, monks, and priests, or junior clerics. As he composed, Jerome likely relied on *notarii* skilled at the complex Roman shorthand system, but he did not draw a clear line between these men and others able to write a fair bookhand.

In chapter 4 we mentioned Rufinus's testimony that Jerome served as a Latin *grammaticus* at some point during his years at Bethlehem. We know so little about the boys Jerome taught that they invite speculation. If Jerome did in fact serve as a teacher for young boys, were they trained to serve him as scribes? The suggestion is both logical and far-fetched. Despite its improbability, the idea is worth exploring for what it can reveal about the precise conditions under which Jerome recruited his secretaries and copyists.

A modern reader, accustomed to the idea that the monasteries of the medieval West accepted child oblates and played an important part in education, might take Jerome's teaching for granted. This would be a serious anachronism. Late antique monasteries had little if any educational function.[37] Eastern monastic rules make no provision for the formal acceptance of child oblates, in the fourth century or later. Nor did Eastern monasticism develop a close association with secular or Christian learning before the seventh or eighth century.[38] For the fourth and fifth centuries, there is evidence that small children lived in Pachomian monasteries, and that attention was paid to their education.[39] However, the education these monasteries offered,

---

36. Letters 71.5, 75.55. On the definition of *notarius*, see Teitler, *Notarii*, 29–31: "it is quite possible that some of the *notarii* . . . mentioned in the sources were not stenographers, but only clerks."

37. On the institution of child oblation: Boswell, *Kindness*, 228–55; De Jong, *Samuel's Image*.

38. Wilson, *Scholars*, 28–60, discusses a number of grammarians and philosophers from the fifth and sixth centuries: while many are Christians, and a few are bishops, none are monks. By contrast, the ninth-century scholars discussed in Wilson, *Scholars*, 68–78, all seem to have been monks for at least part of their careers.

39. Boswell, *Kindness*.

both to children and to illiterate adults, was directed not at training them in classical literature, but at giving them the basic skills needed to read the New Testament and Psalms.[40] In the Latin West of Jerome's day, the development of monasteries as centers of literary culture lay far in the future,[41] as did the institution of child oblation.

Nevertheless, it is tempting to imagine that Jerome's role as a *grammaticus* foreshadowed the eventual institutionalization of the monastic economy of literary practice. For what could be more likely to set scholarship on an independent footing than for the social roles that perpetuated it to become self-replicating? If Jerome's young boys, trained in the Latin classics and presumably in biblical study as well from an early age, had gone on to become ascetics themselves, then his monastery could have become a self-sufficient center of Christian learning. It would no longer be enmeshed in relations of patronage and exchange with the aristocrats and aristocratic bishops whose servants we have seen visiting Jerome to make copies of his works for their masters.

As it was, Jerome's dependence on patronage to support his staff is undeniable. Either his monks' labor was not sufficient, or they had to be paid for their work. Jerome's translation of Proverbs, Ecclesiastes, and the Song of Songs from the Hebrew was completed in 398 and dedicated to Chromatius and Heliodorus.[42] In the preface, Jerome acknowledges the two bishops' support in unusually frank terms: "You sent us the consolation of money, you have supported our secretaries and our scribes, so that by your assistance our ability might toil the more."[43] Both dedicatees came from wealthy aristocratic backgrounds in northern Italy. They were also prominent and powerful ecclesiastics, particularly Chromatius, bishop of the great see of Aquileia. It is not surprising that they were able to contribute funds to Jerome's undertakings. Jerome's direct juxtaposition here of his reliance on a specialist staff with his need for money is reminiscent of the preface to his

---

40. Veilleux, *Pachomian koinonia*, 2:166, on teaching illiterates to read: "even if he does not want to, he shall be compelled to read. There shall be no one whatever in the monastery who does not learn to read and does not memorize something of the Scriptures . . . at least the New Testament and the Psalter."

41. Riché, *Education*, 100–122, describes the earliest Western monastic schools in the fifth and sixth centuries: these were wholly preoccupied with the scriptures and did not go much beyond basic literacy training.

42. Cavallera, *Saint Jérôme*, 2:46.

43. *mittitis solacia sumptuum, notarios nostros et librarios sustentatis, ut uobis potissimum nostrum sudet ingenium.*

translation of Origen's homilies written at Constantinople. Both passages imply that dictation was an expensive mode of composition. We might have hoped that after Jerome had established himself in his monastery in Bethlehem, he would no longer have to beg for cash in order to support his staff. This dedication implies that that was not the case.

Not only was dictation expensive, but the expense itself meant that Jerome's emphasis on his reliance on a staff might have laid him open to attack. Such at any rate is the implication of Jerome's own invective in a letter that he wrote in 396 against a recent guest in his monastery, the Gallic priest Vigilantius.[44] In the passage from the commentary on Ezekiel describing his reliance on his monks to read to him, Jerome hinted that he feared his enemies might accuse him of ostentation. In his lampoon of Vigilantius's literary culture, Jerome turns just such an accusation against his target: "At least spare your cash, you who hire secretaries and copyists to serve you both as your writers and as your fans—for they had better praise you, who pay them to write for you."[45] With typically Hieronymian concision, Vigilantius is portrayed as a spendthrift, an arrogant lout—a character from Petronius, rather than an ascetic like his attacker. But the sycophantic entourage of assistants conjured up for him here looks distressingly similar to the one on which Jerome himself placed so much emphasis. If confirmation were needed that the figure of the *notarius* was an ambivalent one, this passage provides it.

JEROME'S JEWISH TEACHERS

Notarii were not the only expensive specialists involved in Jerome's biblical scholarship, nor were they the most problematic. From his days at Constantinople on, Jerome made frequent mention of his consultations with learned Jews. Not only did he cite interpretations that he attributed to Jewish sources, but he explicitly claimed that he had received these traditions orally, from Jews who instructed him in the study of scripture. In the commentary on Ecclesiastes of 388, Jerome prefaces a discussion of a Hebrew term with the words, "As the Hebrew used to say to me, under whose instruction I thoroughly studied the holy Scriptures . . . "[46] With studied

---

44. Cavallera, *Saint Jérôme*, 2:45.

45. *parce saltem nummis tuis, quibus notarios librariosque conducens eisdem et scriptoribus uteris et fautoribus, qui te ideo forsitan laudant, ut lucrum scribendo faciant* (letter 61.4).

46. *Comm. in Eccles.* 1.14.337: *Dicebat mihi Hebraeus, quo scripturas sanctas instituente perlegi.*

casualness, he asserts that he has studied the scriptures with a Jew, presumably in Hebrew. This figure's appearance near the beginning of a commentary that contains twenty explicit references to Jewish material implies that Jerome consulted his Jewish teacher as he composed.[47] A Jew, Jerome seems determined to convey, was a regular presence in his workroom at Bethlehem, on hand to be consulted whenever his expertise was needed. Later works maintain this impression. Jerome frequently mentions his Jewish scriptural learning and his Jewish teachers in his commentaries on the Minor Prophets and on Daniel, and he continues to refer to them, though less often, in the longer works on Isaiah, Ezekiel, and Jeremiah written during the final decade of his life. The learned Jewish informant, then, played a prominent role in Jerome's self-presentation as an exegete throughout his career. Consistently, Jerome portrayed his access to Jewish exegesis as obtained from living Jewish teachers, never from books. When he refers to Jewish books, they are biblical scrolls, in a few instances Jewish or Jewish-Christian apocrypha, but not exegetical works.

Furthermore, Jerome accords immense authority to his Jewish teachers. It is on the basis of their information that he adjudicates between, and frequently rejects, the tropological readings drawn from his Greek sources. Using a variety of metaphors, he describes the historical and literal sense, which he attributes to his Jewish informants, as the standard by which allegorical interpretations are to be evaluated. One metaphor Jerome used frequently compares Jewish biblical learning to a staircase by which the interpreter may ascend to the summit of the spiritual sense, which is the exclusive possession of the church.[48] The staircase may be humble—but it is necessary. Going farther, in a passage of the commentary on Zechariah (already mentioned in chapter 3), he describes Jewish historical exegesis as the "foundation" upon which the edifice of Christian allegory must be erected, if it is to be built on rock and not on sand.[49] As his contemporaries complained, Jerome grounded his entire exegetical edifice on the disturbing figure of the learned Jew.

47. Cited at *Comm. in Eccles.* 1.7.193; 1.12.289; 3.2.15; 3.9.158; 4.13.179; 5.6.70; 7.9.97; 7.16.245; 7.17.272; 8.14.220; 9.5.86; 9.13.327; 10.4.73; 10.5.106; 11.2.35; 12.1.12; 12.1.63; 12.5.243; 12.13.384.

48. *Dicamus igitur singula percurrentes, primum quid uideatur Hebraeis, a quibus in ueteri testamento eruditi sumus; deinde per hos quasi gradus ad Ecclesiae culmina conscendamus.* (*Comm. in Zach.* 1.4.2–7, 54ff.)

49. *Comm. in Zach.*, prol. 28ff. See chapter 3, at note 53, for the text.

But Jerome was far from being an enthusiastic philosemite. Certainly, he was unusual, if not unique, in his fusion of the spiritual interpretation of Origen and his successors with a tenacious adherence to text-critical, contextual, and historical criteria. In this he differed sharply from the Alexandrian school, and showed the influence of his contacts with Antiochene exegetes, perhaps including Apollinaris of Laodicea.[50] Jerome considered all scriptural truth to proceed from and depend upon an accurate literal and historical understanding of the text, an understanding he sought to derive from Jewish sources. But he also regarded these senses as "carnal," limited to the things of the flesh and of this world, and blind to the higher truths revealed by the spiritual sense. Despite his regard for Jewish knowledge of the scriptures, he cites numerous Jewish traditions only to mock or to revile them, and assigns the same negative characteristics to Jews in general that he does to their biblical learning. In virulent language, he repeatedly describes the Jews as blind, fleshly, earthbound creatures, rejected by God for their murder of Christ and consequently enslaved by their gross physical appetites. Jewish interpretation, therefore, is necessary for a true understanding of scripture—yet it is insufficient on its own. Its role is essential, yet humble and functional.

The individuals from whom Jerome drew his knowledge of Jewish interpretive tradition are portrayed in a similarly paradoxical light. Jerome emphasizes their importance, placing them on the same level as his Greek teachers Apollinaris and Didymus, for whom he professed an immense regard despite their heretical tendencies. He recounts his studies with Jewish teachers after his relocation to Palestine as the culmination of the specialized education that legitimated him as an exegete.[51] He describes the tremen-

---

50. Jerome's example suggests that perhaps Jewish exegesis had a greater influence on the Antiochene tradition than is sometimes assumed. Certainly this is not impossible, given the extent of Jewish influence on Syriac exegesis, and the contacts between Greek-speaking Antioch and the Syriac world to the east. Furthermore, if Jerome's exegesis was more a fusion of Alexandrian with Antiochene exegesis than (as he describes it) of Alexandrian with Jewish exegesis, is he making such a radical misrepresentation, or was Antiochene exegesis in an important sense a conduit for Jerome's awareness of and respect for Jewish exegesis? This topic merits further study.

51. Jerome describes his education as an exegete in an important passage of letter 84.3: *Dum essem iuuenis, miro discendi ferebar ardore nec iuxta quorundam praesumptionem ipse me docuit. Apollinarem Laodicenum audiui Antiochiae frequenter et colui et, cum me in sanctis scripturis erudiret, numquam illius contentiosum super sensu doma suscepi. iam canis spargebatur caput et magistrum potius quam discipulum decebat; perrexi tamen Alexandriam, audiui Didymum. in multis ei gratias ago. quod nesciui, didici; quod sciebam, illo diuerso docente non perdidi. putabant me homines finem*

dous effort he expended to master their recondite expertise, and advertises them as men held in the highest regard within the Jewish community.[52]

But Jerome's descriptions also exoticize his Jewish teachers. He continually emphasizes their links to specific geographical locations in Palestine and their place in a milieu of Jewish learning that could only have been foreign, indeed distasteful, to his orthodox Christian audience.[53] He dwells upon their origins in Jewish Palestine, driving home the point that he had access to resources unavailable to his readers in the West. One of his teachers came from Lydda, another from Tiberias, both famous centers of rabbinic learning. The first, and the only one to be named, Baranina, seems to have been a native of the region of Jerusalem. Jerome recounts that Baranina had to meet with him by night, for he feared the attacks of his fellow Jews. The implication is that he had a reputation in his own community that he was concerned to safeguard.

In other cases, Jerome advertises the authority of his Jewish teachers by explicitly describing them as well regarded among their own people, and designates them and their mode of interpretation with terms that had a specialized meaning within rabbinic circles. One Jew with whom he studied was a "teacher of the Law," another a "sage and *deuterōtēs*."[54] The Greek *deuterosis*, which Jerome regards as a translation of a Hebrew word, *esna*, and defines as "to repeat," is surely related to the stem *š-n-h*, the root of the Hebrew terms *mishna* and *tanna*. The less technical Latin term *fabula* (story, tale) may reflect the Aramaic *haggadah*.[55] Despite Jerome's reliance on Jew-

---

fecisse discendi: rursum Hierosolymae et Bethleem quo labore, quo pretio Baraninam nocturnum habui praeceptorem! timebat enim Iudaeos et mihi alterum exhibebat Nicodemum.

52. *denique cum a me nuper litteris flagitassetis, ut uobis Paralipomenon Latino sermone transferrem, de Tiberiade legis quondam auctorem, qui apud Hebreos admirationi habebatur, adsumpsi, et contuli cum eo a uertice, ut aiunt, usque ad extremum unguem, et sic confirmatus ausus sum facere quod iubebatis* (Praefatio in libro Paralipomenon de graeco emendato). Also: *memini me ob intellegentiam huius uoluminis Lyddeum quemdam praeceptorem qui apud Hebraeos primas habere putabatur, non paruis redemisse nummis, cuius doctrina an aliquid profecerim nescio, hoc unum scio non potuisse me interpretari nisi quod ante intellexeram* (Praef. in Hiob de hebr. interp.).

53. A particularly strong example of Jerome's exoticizing his Jewish teachers (note the Greek designation δευτερωτης) appears in *Comm. in Abacuc* 1.2.578: *audiui Liddae quemdam de Hebraeis, qui sapiens apud illos et* δευτερωτης *uocabatur, narrantem huiuscemodi fabulam.* Perhaps this is the same individual mentioned in the prologue to the translation of Job *iuxta Hebraeos: memini me ob intellegentiam huius uoluminis Lyddeum quemdam praeceptorem qui apud Hebraeos primas habere putabatur.*

54. The relevant passages have been cited in the notes above.

55. *Fabula* (44 occurences in this sense) is much more frequent than *deuterosis* (11 occurences of *deuterosis*, 4 of *deuterotes*); Jerome equates the two terms in the commentary on Ezekiel: *iudaicas fabulas, quas illi* δευτερώσεις *appellant* (Comm. in Hiezech. 11.36.640). On *deuterosis* and *mishna*:

ish sources and his avowedly high regard for the literal sense, the valence of these terms is not as positive as it initially appears. For example, he repeatedly describes the "stories" of the Jews as "superstitious,"[56] "ridiculous," and so on.[57] Their accounts are mere *deliramenta*,[58] to be rejected by good Christians.

Similarly, when the titles of respect that Jerome applies to his Jewish teachers are read against the background of his use of these terms in other contexts, his seemingly laudatory descriptions reveal an edge of scorn. Jerome's letter 121 is a lengthy reply to eleven exegetical questions posed by the Gallic lady Algasia. A passage from the letter makes painfully clear that Jerome could deploy the vocabulary rabbinic scholars used to designate their own social group and the specialized learning they cultivated as terms of denigration:

> How many are the traditions of the Pharisees, which today they call *deuteroseis*, and what silly tales they are, I refuse to go over. For this book would suffer from its length, and many of them are so foul that I would blush to repeat them. Yet I will mention one example for the sake of shaming a enemy nation: the heads of the synagogues are charged with the following disgusting task, that in order to determine whether the blood of a virgin or a menstruant is pure or impure, if they cannot make the distinction by eye, they test it by tasting.[59]

This detail of Jewish ritual observance is clearly intended to disgust the reader. Having given it in spite of himself, Jerome goes on to mock the reliance of the Jews on the opinions of rabbinic authorities. He lists the names *Barachibas et Symeon et Helles*, that is, Akiba, Shimon, and Hillel. This catalogue displays a striking knowledge of rabbinic technical terminology — de-

---

esna δευτέρωσις, *quam nos a secundo numero dicere possumus secundantem, uel ignis uel edissertio* (*Liber nominum*, ed. Lagarde, 27, 5); *secundare* as "to repeat" is a medieval form, see Blaise, *Lexicon Latinitatis medii aeui*, s.v. *secundare*. Jerome also uses a verbal form of the same Greek word, in a passage that is interesting in its own right: . . . *doctores eorum* σοφοί, *hoc est "sapientes," uocantur. et si quando certis diebus traditiones suas exponunt, discipulis suis solent dicere:* οἱ σοφοί δευτεροῦσιν, *id est "sapientes docent traditiones"* (letter 121.10.17).

56. *Comm. in Esaiam*, 2.5.43; 16.59.19; *Comm. in Hiezech.* 11.38.1501.

57. *Comm. in Hiezech.* 8.25.169.

58. *Comm. in Esaiam*, 15, 54, 65; *Comm. in Hiezech.* 5, 16, 803; 12, 40, 1133; *Comm. in Mich.* 2, 5, 411; letter 121.10.2.

59. *quantae traditiones Pharisaeorum sint, quas hodie* δευτερώσεις *uocant, et quam aniles fabulae, reuoluere nequeo. neque enim libri patitur magnitudo et pleraque tam turpia sunt, ut erubescam dicere. dicam tamen unum in ignominiam gentis inimicae: praepositos habent synagogis sapientissimos quosque foedo operi delegatos, ut sanguinem uirginis siue menstruatae mundum uel inmundum, si oculis discernere non potuerint, gustatu probent* (letter 121.10.10).

ployed in the cause of hatred. In a timeworn tactic of Christian anti-Jewish polemic, Jerome claims that the Jews disregard the commandments of God only to rely on the traditions of men.[60] The only thing that differentiates Jerome's anti-Judaism from that of his Christian peers is that he actually had specific, up-to-date information about the beliefs and practices he attacked. His contemporaries, for the most part, relied exclusively on the portrayal of the Pharisees in the Gospel of Matthew for their knowledge of Judaism.

Jerome's representation of his Jewish teachers, then, is as contradictory as his use of the exegetical materials he attributes to Jews. His studies with Jews were the capstone of his development as a biblical scholar, yet he represented much of their learning as perverse, even repulsive. Similarly, he trumpets his Jewish teachers' prestige in their own community, while portraying that community and its values as repugnant to any right-thinking Christian.

One further detail of Jerome's portrayal of his Jewish teachers connects this conflicted representation with a larger social as well as intellectual context. Jerome repeatedly asserts that he paid his Jewish teachers, and paid them handsomely. Presumably, he did not remunerate the Antiochene bishop Apollinaris or the Alexandrian catechist Didymus for their instruction. Despite their heretical tendencies, these Christian biblical scholars, ascetics themselves, could be incorporated within a monastic literary economy. Jerome's Jewish informants played a different role in that economy, symbolized by his boasting about their steep fees. Fleshly and earthbound themselves, they nevertheless underwrote Jerome's own self-presentation as a monk for whom biblical study was a mode of *askesis*.

Before his Jewish teachers' function in this rhetorical context can be fully appreciated, however, it remains to be determined what reality lay behind it. From his own day forward, Jerome's use of Jewish biblical interpretation was praised by some and reviled by others. But the belief that he had studied with Jewish teachers, even before he settled in Palestine, went unquestioned until the twentieth century. One article in particular, published by Gustave Bardy in 1934, created a new, and profound, suspicion of Jerome's claim that

---

60. The passage continues: *praeterea, quia iussum est, ut diebus Sabbatorum sedeat unusquisque in domo sua et non egrediatur nec ambulet de loco, in quo habitat, si quando eos iuxta litteram coeperimus artare, ut non iaceant, non ambulent, non stent, sed tantum sedeant, si uelint praecepta seruare, solent respondere et dicere: "Barachibas et Symeon et Helles, magistri nostri, tradiderunt nobis, ut duo milia pedes ambulemus in Sabbato" et cetera istius modi, doctrinas hominum praeferentes doctrinae Dei. non quo dicamus sedendum esse semper in sabbato et de loco, in quo quis fuerit occupatus, penitus non recedendum, sed quo id, quod inpossibile legis est, in quo infirmatur per carnem, spiritali obseruatione conplendum sit.*

he consulted Jewish informants directly.[61] Although Bardy's arguments are, at best, sufficient to show that Jerome was capable of taking over a Jewish interpretation from a Greek Christian source without acknowledging the intermediary, his charges have had a considerable impact on modern estimates of Jerome's Jewish learning. This is unfortunate, since Bardy's admittedly preliminary treatment fails to do justice to the depth of Jerome's knowledge of Jewish matters.[62] Bardy analyzes a very limited number of instances of Jerome's use of Jewish interpretation.[63] Furthermore, his method often distorts the evidence. For whenever he can document a parallel in a Greek source for a tradition that Jerome describes as Jewish, or even for an interpretation apparently traceable to a Jewish source that Jerome adduces without attribution, he adds the instance to his list of Jerome's deliberate misrepresentations.

There are three main problems with this approach. First, in some of the cases Bardy discusses, Jerome identifies certain traditions as Jewish that his sources use without attribution. Second, Jerome sometimes adds important details to Jewish traditions that were also used by his sources. In either case, the likelihood is that Jerome had independent access to Jewish materials also

---

61. For unquestioning acceptance of Bardy's conclusions, see Nautin, "Hieronymus"; Opelt, "San Girolamo"; other literature cited by Newman in "Jerome and the Jews," 103–7; and Stemberger, "Exegetical Contacts."

62. For a similarly negative evaluation of Bardy's article and of the attempts of others to represent Jerome's use of Jewish exegesis as dependent on Greek sources, see Newman, "Jerome and the Jews," 103–22. Kamesar, *Jerome*, 180ff. proceeds on the assumption that Jerome had direct access to Jewish teachers.

63. A total of fourteen examples are given in Bardy, "Maîtres hébreux": reliance on Eusebius: *Comm. in Esaiam*, 5.22 = Eusebius, *Comm. in Esaiam* (PG 24.249 and 345); *Comm. in Esaiam*, 11.39 = Eusebius, *Comm. in Esaiam* (PG 24.361); reliance on Origen: letter 18A = Origen's homily 6 on Isaiah; *Comm. in Dan.* 13 (PL 25.580) cites Origen explicitly = Origen, *Stromateis* 10, frag. = *Comm. in Hierem.* 5 (PL 24.862): does not attribute the tradition to Origen, instead gives *Aiunt Hebraei . . .* ; *Comm. in Hiezech.* 2.5 (PL 25.54A) = Origen, *In Hiezechielem* 5.10 (PG 13.781D–784A); *Comm. in Hiezech.* 3.9 (PL 25.86D–87A) = Origen, *In Hiezechielem* 9.2 (PG 13.800C); *Comm. in Hiezech.* 3.14 (PL 25, 88–89) = Origen, *In Hiezechielem* 9.4 (PG 13.800D–801A); *Comm. in Hiezech.* 4.14 (PL 25.120C) = Origen, Homilies on Ezekiel, 4.8 (ed. Baehrens, 369); *Comm. in Hiezech.* 5.16 (PL 25.157CD) = Origen, Homilies on Ezekiel, 10.3 (ed. Baehrens, 420); *Comm. in Hiezech.* 7.24 (PL 25.230A) cites a tradition concerning the wearing of phylacteries that is also mentioned by Origen, *In Matt.* 2 (ed. Klostermann, 21–22); *In Matt.* 2, 14 (PL 26, 104) = Origen, *In Matt.* 11, 6 (PG 13, 917–920); *Comm. in Matt.* 4.23 (PL 26.173–74) = Origen, *In Matt. comment. ser.* 25 (ed. Klostermann, 42–43); *Comm. in Matt.* 4.27 (PL 26.205) = Origen, *In Matt. comment ser.* 117 (ed. Klostermann, 249). Bardy himself made no pretense that his investigations had been exhaustive: "Nous ne saurions prétendre avoir épuisé, dans les pages qui précèdent, le sujet que nous nous étions proposé d'aborder" (164).

transmitted by his Greek sources.[64] Third, when Jerome attributes to Jewish tradition interpretations that his Greek sources cited as Jewish, or simply cites such interpretations without any attribution, he cannot in fairness be convicted of falsehood as he can when he presents such materials as the fruits of his own inquiries with Jewish experts.[65] The final example advanced by Bardy in fact presents no parallel between any Greek text and the material Jerome cites as Jewish.[66]

Bardy does succeed in identifying two instances in which Jerome seems to have taken over from his Greek sources interpretations that those sources claimed to have obtained directly from Jewish informants. In these cases,

---

64. One case of identification as Jewish of traditions unattributed by his source appears in letter 18A. See also Kamesar, *Jerome*, 101–3, comparing Origen and Jerome on Gen. 41:43, the difficult word "avrech." Kamesar concludes, "It is therefore difficult to accept the view of B. de Montfaucon and others, who believe that Jerome is here dependent on Origen. In the first place, Origen [unlike Jerome: *Hebraei tradunt*] does not even say that the first interpretation which he cites is of Jewish origin, so from what source did Jerome obtain this information? In fact, we should probably see Jerome's comment as an indirect critique of the methods of his predecessor. For the Latin Father generally attempts to interpret the Hebrew text itself by critically employing the *recentiores* and Jewish teachers, not by simply sewing them together." In four of the cases Bardy cites, Jerome adds details to Jewish traditions also transmitted by Origen: *Comm. in Hiezech.* 3.9 (PL 25.86D–87A) (a Hebrew word); *Comm. in Matt.* 4.23 (PL 26, 173–74); *Comm. in Matt.* 4.27 (PL 26.205); *Comm. in Hiezech.* 7.24 (PL 25.230A). Bardy, "Maîtres hébreux," 160, acknowledges that Jerome probably knew this last tradition independently of Origen.

65. In six of Bardy's fourteen cases, Jerome does not attribute the material to his Jewish teachers: *Comm. in Esaiam* 11.39 (PL 25.86D–87A); *Comm. in Hieremiam* 5 (PL 24.862); *Comm. in Hiezech.* 2.5 (PL 25.54A); *Comm. in Hiezech.* 3.14 (PL 25.88–89); *Comm. in Hiezech.* 4.14 (PL 25.120C); *Comm. in Hiezech.* 5.16 (PL 25.157CD).

66. Comm. in Gal. 2 (PL 26.361–62) Jerome cites a Jew in explicating Deut. 21:22: *Memini me in altercatione Iasonis et Papisci, quae graeco sermone conscripta est, ita reperisse: λοιδορία θεοῦ ὁ κρεμάμενος, id est maledictio Dei qui appensus est. Dicebat mihi Hebraeus qui me in Scripturis aliqua ex parte instituit, quod possit et ita legi: quia contumeliose Deus suspensus est. Haec idcirco congessimus quia famosissima quaestio est et nobis soleat a Iudaeis pro infamia obici, quod Saluator noster et Dominus sub Dei fuerit maledictio.* Bardy ("Maîtres hébreux," ••) objects to this passage in an argument that can only be described as tendentious and unconvincing: "Faut-il croire que saint Jérôme a véritablement lu l'obscur dialogue de Jason et de Papiscus sur lequel nous renseignent si peu de témoignages anciens? Il est vrai que, dans les Questions hébraïques sur la Genèse, il a encore l'occasion de le citer [Bardy's footnote here cites *Quaest. Heb. in Gen.* 1.1 (PL 23.937)]; mais il doit ici à Origène le renseignement qu'il fournit. Il est très vraisemblable qu'il en va de même dans le commentaire de la Lettre aux Galates. Saint Jérôme se contente de copier son devancier, et il ne lui emprunte pas seulement la citation de l'Altercatio, mais encore l'explication proposée par le maître juif. Celui-ci paraît bien être un de ces judéo-chrétiens qui apparaissent fréquemment dans l'oeuvre d'Origène, mais que nous ne rencontrons guère dans l'entourage de saint Jérôme." While it is quite plausible that Jerome drew his knowledge of the dialogue of Jason and Papiscus from a lost Greek source, probably a work of Origen, that proves nothing about the origin of Jewish material cited in close proximity to a reference to that work. Bardy's argument depends on guilt by association, not on any real evidence.

Jerome presents himself as having conferred with learned Jews rather than having found his material in a Greek commentary.[67] Bardy shows, therefore, that Jerome was capable of a procedure repugnant to modern scholars, who have judged his exegetical methods by their own rigorous standards of citation and attribution. Bardy does not, however, present evidence that Jerome had no direct access to Jewish exegesis. To the contrary, he draws attention to several instances where Jerome knew independently, and in greater detail, Jewish materials also known to his Greek predecessors.

Recent scholarship by those well versed in the Jewish literature of late antique Palestine has not only confuted Bardy's claims but demonstrated the extent of Jerome's Jewish learning. Adam Kamesar's study of the *Hebrew Questions on Genesis* concluded that Jerome's very real knowledge of Jewish textual and historical scholarship formed the backbone of his biblical philology.[68] Hillel Newman, whose dissertation is the only comprehensive modern study of Jerome's relations to Jews and Judaism, evaluated his knowledge of Jewish exegesis in strongly positive terms. Newman concluded that Jerome obtained his knowledge of rabbinic tradition by oral transmission from Jewish teachers. In support of this view, he drew attention to a text already much discussed for the light it sheds on Jerome's use of sources: the commentary on Zechariah of Didymus the Blind, still unknown at the time of Bardy's researches. Didymus's commentary has providentially been preserved in a single papyrus copy. Newman pointed out that although this work served as Jerome's principal source for two-thirds of his own commentary on Zechariah, it contains none of the Jewish materials Jerome adduces.[69]

Further comparison of the commentary of Didymus on Zechariah with Jerome's work suggests that Jerome did not draw his citations of Jewish material from Origen. Jerome used two principal sources for his commentary on Zechariah: Origen's commentary, which covered only Zechariah 1:1–6:8, and Didymus's, which covered the entire book. While Jerome cites some interpretations from Didymus in the first section of his treatment of Zechariah, he draws most of his allegorical interpretations from another source, presumably Origen's commentary. In the second and third books, he relied heavily on Didymus.[70] The commentary on Zechariah contains one of the richest troves of interpretations attributed to Jewish sources of all

---

67. *Comm. in Esaiam*, 5.22 = Eusebius, *Comm. in Esaiam* (PG 24.249 and 345); *Comm. in Matt.* 2.14 (PL 26.104) = Origen, *In Matt.* 11.6 (PG 13, 917–20).

68. Kamesar, *Jerome*, 193–95.

69. Newman, *Jerome and the Jews* 107ff.; English abstract 6.

70. See the detailed discussion earlier in this chapter.

Jerome's exegetical works. As Newman observed, none of the Jewish interpretations that Jerome cites in his commentary on Zechariah are paralleled in Didymus's commentary. But the proportion of his lemmata for which Jerome cites Jewish interpretations does not vary between the first book, where he had Origen's commentary, and the second and third, where he relied primarily on Didymus. This strongly suggests that Origen was not a significant source of material cited as Jewish in the commentary on Zechariah.[71] For if he were, we would expect to find that Jerome cited more Jewish traditions in the section of his commentary where he used Origen's work than in the part where he did not.

If neither Origen nor Didymus provided Jerome with the bulk of the Jewish interpretations he adduces, where might he have found these materials? While lost Greek works may have supplied some of the interpretations Jerome cites, Jewish informants or Jewish texts seem the most plausible possibilities.[72] The material Jerome attributes to his Jewish teachers is extensively paralleled in Jewish sources. Jerome's commentaries also allude to material paralleled in rabbinic literature but not openly attributed to Jewish sources. A catalogue of his explicit citations of Jewish interpretation, therefore, may seriously underestimate his debt to his Jewish informants.[73] Furthermore, if Jerome's claim to rely on direct contact with Jews for so much of what was distinctive in his exegesis were simply an imposture, some of his many contemporary critics might have taken the opportunity to expose

71. The basic unit of the commentary on Zechariah, as of all the commentaries on the Minor Prophets, is the lemma, the segment of the base text under comment. Although the lemmata into which Jerome divides the text of Zechariah vary quite widely in length, each receives a similarly structured treatment, usually including literal/philological, historical, and allegorical interpretations, though these may also vary widely in length. Therefore, I have counted the number of lemmata that receive interpretations attributed to Jewish sources for the two sections of the commentary: book 1 (with Origen): 13 out of 26 (2 lemmata receive 2 separate Jewish interpretations, for a total of 15 Jewish interpretations) = 50% (57% counting each interpretation separately); books 2 and 3 (without Origen): 33 out of 65 = 51%. Jerome's use of Origen's commentary in book 1 exerted no significant effect on the frequency with which he cited Jewish materials.

72. Hippolytus of Rome (cited in *Comm. in Hiezech.*, pref.) and Apollinaris of Laodicea (not cited, but Jerome elsewhere says he wrote on all the Minor Prophets) are the most likely candidates, in particular for the millenarian material that Jerome attributes both to Jews and to Jewish-Christians (*nostri iudaizantes*). However, considerable further study will be required to pin down the precise origins of these materials. Wolfram Kinzig, in an unpublished paper of 2000, argued that Jerome's source was Apollinaris but did not present the evidence from the *catenae* that supports this conclusion. I am grateful to him for sharing the paper with me, and look forward to a published version.

73. Newman, "Jerome and the Jews," Rahmer, *Die hebräischen Traditionen.*

him. Finally, Jerome's numerous citations of Hebrew words in support of his preferred version of the biblical text force us to accept either that he had a thorough knowledge of that language or that he had access to informants who did. His occasional errors in presenting textual arguments based on the Hebrew suggest that the latter alternative is more likely, since it is easier to imagine that the errors crept in when Jerome misremembered information he had only imperfectly understood. There are strong arguments, then, for the idea that Jerome obtained the materials he cites that are paralleled in Jewish sources through direct consultation with Jewish teachers.

Clearly, it was of immense importance for Jerome to present himself as a student of Jewish teachers. He does so in the course of his exegesis, by incorporating material explicitly or implicitly attributed to Jewish informants at every turn. Similarly, the figure of the learned Jew as teacher plays a starring role in his most carefully constructed self-descriptions. Jerome wished his audience to believe that study with Jewish teachers was an integral element of his scholarly practice. Bardy showed that on occasion he even went so far as to lie in this cause. The more he did so, the more we must conclude that Jerome deliberately chose to present himself as a student of the Jews.

But why was this connection so desirable? Here again, it seems that Jerome represented himself in terms that allowed him to describe scholarship—a phenomenon strongly associated with the ethic of care of the self—in terms of monastic self-mortification. We saw in chapter 1 that from the very beginning Jerome's Hebrew studies played a central role in his attempts to portray biblical study in this light. Jerome's Jewish teachers themselves seem to serve a similar function. Their very coarseness, their carnality, could be made to support the representation of the form of scholarship made possible by their presence as mortifying to the cultivated sensibilities fostered by literary education. In a paradoxical turn, the very fact that the Jews were, for Jerome and presumably for many in his audience, the polar opposite of ascetic Christians, made intimate and sustained contact with them in itself a form of self-mortification. For Jerome to subject himself to study with Jewish teachers, even more than for him to master their language—which he describes with such evident distaste—was to attack at the root the dispositions his early literary education had instilled.

*

There were fundamental tensions both within and between the ways that Jerome represented the two main types of assistants who supported him. Jerome's *notarii,* if they were his monks, might have allowed him to work as an aristocratic author would do, without rendering him dependent on aristocratic patronage. The figure of the monk as amanuensis therefore holds out the hope, however chimerical in practice, of a mode of literary production in which the monastery becomes an independent center of scholarship. Monastic scholarship, furthermore, can appropriate both the ascetic qualities and the seriousness of engagement with a canon of authoritative works that characterized classical modes of learning. As a monastic practice, Christian biblical commentary could assert its independence from elite patronage and therefore wield greater intellectual authority. Yet the figure of the *notarius,* by allowing Jerome to represent his scholarship as lacking in literary pretensions, also allows a note of aristocratic negligence to creep into what are, after all, highly polished products of a refined tradition of Latin prose style. The Jewish assistant, on the other hand, for all that Jerome made of him an element in his own peculiar mode of self-mortification through voluntary immersion in Hebrew learning, came at a cost—a cost that could only be supplied by integration into elite networks of patronage.

———— ✳ ————

CHAPTER SEVEN

Readers and Patrons

PROFOUND contradictions ran through Jerome's scholarship and his self-presentation. Some of these contradictions served as productive tensions. For example, the opposition between ascetic Christian spiritual reading and "carnal" Jewish literalism in Jerome's commentaries was foundational to his authority as an exegete. Other contradictions threatened to undermine the entire enterprise. Most importantly, Jerome's representation of his mode of biblical commentary as a form of monastic *askesis* conflicted with the reality that he was dependent on elite patronage to fund the expensive infrastructure—the library and the staff of skilled assistants—demanded by that mode of commentary. Nowhere was this conflict more acute than in Jerome's efforts to construct rhetorically, and to reach in practice, an audience of appropriate readers for his works. His ideal reader embodied an uneasy mixture of Christian and non-Christian values. Similarly, his works circulated within the same elite networks on which he depended for patronage.

The question of Jerome's readership is inextricably linked to his relations with his patrons. In late antiquity, books circulated according to patterns quite alien to the modern author or reader, patterns that made the connection between readers and patrons a natural, indeed a necessary one. The book trade was hardly sufficient to supply copies of the classic literary texts used in education, much less of technical treatises newly produced by living authors. Books were circulated privately by those who had the time and the learning to read, and the means to make copies. Furthermore, books in antiquity functioned as elements within a heterogeneous economy of gift giving. This economy involved the circulation of a variety of favors, as well as material goods, within elite networks, which were characterized as much by the relative inequality of the participants as by their shared elite status. Essential to its functioning was the assumption that each initiative made by a member of the network on behalf of another was gratuitous, neither a re-payment of a debt nor an attempt to impose an obligation, but a recognition of the intrinsic merit of the recipient. Exceptions to this rule could and did occur. But the smooth operation of the system as a whole, as of any system of gift exchange, depended on a tacit agreement by all parties to disavow in principle the possibility of a *quid pro quo* in the exchanges that bound and constituted the network. Like any writer in his day, Jerome depended on his place in networks of the privileged for the circulation of his works. The Christian ascetic values dominant within his particular social world only in-tensified the imperative to ignore this dependence.

Numerous passages of Jerome's writings, especially his letters, show that texts circulated in his day, and among his peers and correspondents, in ways their authors did not anticipate and could not regulate. Jerome tells of a number of texts, his own and others', which escaped their authors' control, sometimes through deliberate theft, sometimes through negligence. These works embarrassed their authors by circulating without their titles or the names of their dedicatees, so that they seemed to be addressed to a broader public to which they had not originally been directed. The evidence Jerome provides for these "wild" modes of circulation reminds us of a larger truth about books in late antiquity, indeed in the ancient world in general. Where modern readers and writers assume a sharp distinction between published and unpublished or private texts — one which the potential for uncontrolled publication inherent in electronic media is only beginning to break down — ancient writers could not rely on any such clear boundary. On the one hand, to commit a text to writing was potentially to place its circulation beyond one's control, so that correspondents often entrusted sensitive information not to their written letters but to the trusted messengers who carried them. On the other hand, there was no means to guarantee that a text became avail-able to a public, much less that it would be taken up and read. There was thus a substantial gray area between private and public texts, one that could in principle include almost any written work.[1]

In his relations with readers and patrons — and in particular, with read-ers who were also patrons — Jerome had no choice but to cede control over

---

1. This ambiguity is closely connected to the problem of transmission and preservation: generally a text was transmitted to later generations only if it reached a public beyond the author's own circle, but many texts—whatever their literary ambitions—must never have broken that barrier.

his works. In some cases, this loss of control began even before he started work on a new project. Like some of his contemporaries—Augustine notable among them—Jerome seems to have attempted in various ways to resist the demands of his audience. Ultimately, however, he could not escape them. Not only did his readers control the physical circulation of his writings, but many of his works were written to order, their production stimulated less by his own, ambitious research program than by the requests of correspondents, friends, patrons and potential patrons. Most importantly, Jerome's writings could be inserted into theological debates in ways he could neither predict nor control. Even his involvement in certain controversies came not at his own instance but at that of his correspondents.

For the conflicts that shaped Jerome's life were not merely internal ones. During almost the whole of his productive career, Jerome's relations with readers and patrons played out in the midst of intense theological controversy. From 393, with the outbreak of the Origenist controversy in Palestine, until his death, Jerome never ceased to be involved in bitter debate. These disputes, furthermore, largely took place within the same close-knit network of elite, ascetic Christians in which Jerome's works had their primary currency, so that they intersected at crucial junctures with Jerome's efforts to draw upon that network to reach readers and to secure patronage. These intersections reveal the intensity of Jerome's aspiration to secure a new level of cultural independence for himself as a scholar and for the model of biblical scholarship as a form of monastic *askesis* that he promoted. At the same time, they illustrate the social and institutional constraints that eventually limited his success in doing so. Finally, the close literary and conceptual connections between Jerome's representation of his scholarship as monastic *askesis* and his polemics on behalf of radical renunciation, particularly for his wealthiest correspondents, compel us to take seriously one of the most prominent themes in these theological controversies: the nature and possibility of a Christian elite, and its proper relation to the secular elites of the late Roman world. For Jerome's proposals in that direction—his lifelong argument for a hierarchy of salvation based on a hierarchy of ascetic renunciation—were articulated in the context of intense argument, personified by figures such as Jovinian, Vigilantius, Rufinus, and Pelagius, but also by Paulinus of Nola, Sulpicius Severus, and, in Jerome's last years, Augustine.

THE READER IN THE TEXT

Jerome's texts, particularly his commentaries, subtly yet persistently invoke—indeed, construct—a notion of their own ideal reader. They do so, above all, through regular reference to the *prudens lector,* the "wise reader," who can sort through the various interpretations given for each passage of the biblical text and identify the truth. This construct serves Jerome's purposes on a number of levels. First of all, by representing the commentaries he compiles as incomplete without the judgment of readers, who will make the final distinction between true and false interpretations, Jerome can absolve himself from accusations of heresy for having transmitted the exegesis of Origen, Apollinaris, and others. More subtly, but perhaps more fundamentally, Jerome's use of the figure of the *prudens lector* shifts the responsibility for determining scriptural truth from himself to his reader, allowing him to maintain a pose of monastic humility as a mere transmitter of earlier traditions. Yet on closer examination the construct of the *prudens lector* also reveals the profound dependence of Jerome's Christian biblical scholarship on the Latin classical tradition. The qualifications of the *prudens lector* are those conferred by elite status and elite education, not those developed through ascetic practice in a cenobitic setting. Finally, Jerome himself emerges as the archetype of the *prudens lector.* By presenting himself—with his own classical education—as model for his reader rather than as channel for his sources, he defeats his own attempts to shift the burden of determining what is orthodox, and what heretical, in biblical interpretation. On this level, at least, he can only pretend to relinquish control.

Jerome uses the phrase *prudens lector* and, less often, its equivalents—*diligens lector, prudens et Christianus lector, benignus lector, studiosus lector*—repeatedly throughout his exegetical works. Through the repetition of these expressions, Jerome integrates his ideal reader into the complex structure of his commentary, drawing him or her into a conversation whose form that structure predetermines. The task of the reader in this conversation is to distinguish among varying interpretations of the same passage, retaining what is orthodox and rejecting what is heretical or simply false. Although Jerome begins to invoke the figure of the *prudens lector* early in his career as an exegete, he describes the reader's role most explicitly in the first book of his *Apology against Rufinus,* written in early 401. The passage is a *locus classicus* for Jerome's theory of commentary, and as such has already received considerable attention. In it, Jerome defends himself against the charge of endorsing Origen's heretical views by claiming that the function of a commentary is to present neutrally the conflicting views of diverse earlier authorities, allowing the *prudens lector* to decide which interpretations to accept, which to reject. In characterizing his ideal reader, Jerome turns to a simile drawn from an *agraphon,* a saying of Jesus transmitted outside the written canon. The saying instructs the hearer to be "like a good money-changer, knowing how to retain the true coin and reject the false." It resembles, and is often cited together with, 1 Thessalonians 5:21–22: "but test everything; hold fast what is good, abstain from every form of evil." Jerome's defense of his mode of commentary, with its reliance on a particular notion of the reader's role, thus draws upon powerful Christian associations as well as on the non-Christian context of Latin literary scholarship that is so heavily emphasized in this passage of his *Apology*.

The use of this *agraphon* and of the passage from 1 Thessalonians to characterize the orthodox Christian reader's attitude toward heretical texts had deep roots in the Greek Christian tradition, particularly in the works of the Alexandrians Clement and Origen, and of Origen's follower Eusebius of Caesarea. Eusebius cites the case of Dionysius, bishop of Alexandria during the persecutions of the mid-third century, quoting at length from Dionysius's own letter:

> But as for me, I read both the compositions and the traditions of the heretics, polluting my soul for a little while with their abominable thoughts, yet all the while deriving this advantage from them, that I could refute them for myself and loathed them far more. And indeed a certain brother, one of the presbyters, attempted to dissuade and frighten me from becoming involved in the mire of their wickedness, for he said that I should injure my own soul; and spoke truly, as I perceived. But a vision sent by God came and strengthened me, and a word of command was given me, saying expressly, "Read all things that may come to your hand. For you are able to sift and prove each matter, which was originally the cause of your faith." I accepted the vision, as agreeing with the apostolic saying addressed to the stronger: "Show yourselves trustworthy money-changers." [2]

Origen had already used the same *agraphon,* notably in passages preserved in the homilies on the prophets that Jerome translated in the early 380s in Constantinople for his friend Vincentius. There, Origen urges his audience, sure in the truth of their faith, to evaluate his own preaching "as approved money-changers." He claims that he applies this principle to the scriptures themselves in determining how they ought to be interpreted. [3] In doing so, he surely drew upon a tradition already prevalent at Alexandria, as represented by a passage of Clement's *Stromateis.* [4]

Wherever it appears, this dominical saying is used to underwrite the free-

---

2. *Hist. eccles.* 7.7.1–3.

3. Homily 2 on Ezekiel, Homily 9 on Jeremiah. See also Origen, *In Matt.* 17.31.

4. *Stromateis* 1.28.177.2.

dom, and also the obligation, of the individual Christian to evaluate whatever he reads, distinguishing for himself between orthodoxy and heresy. Such freedom and power of discernment were claimed by both sides in the Origenist controversy. Even before applying the *agraphon* to his intended readers in his *Apology* against Rufinus, Jerome had cited it in his commentary on Ephesians, written in 386, where he was perhaps paraphrasing Origen.[5] Rufinus, in turn, translated in 397 part of the *Apology for Origen* written by Pamphilus and Eusebius while the former was in prison for his faith. The text as Rufinus transmits it opens by invoking the saying to argue that those who say that Origen ought not even to be read are, in fact, unChristian. Both Jerome and his chief rival in the controversy of the turn of the fifth century, then, claimed the right and the ability to pick and choose among the statements of heretical writers, accepting the true and rejecting the false. Both men invoked the same scriptural and traditional justifications for this claim.

Jerome maintained this stance throughout his career. A letter written in late 406 to Minervius and Alexander, monks of Toulouse in southwestern Gaul, provides a fascinating example. Having addressed two exegetical questions posed by the monks, Jerome concludes:

> I have dictated all this with rapid speech, setting forth for Your Prudences what learned men have said about the two passages under discussion and by which arguments they have sought to support their opinions. For neither is my authority, little as I am—I who am nothing and yet suffer so much the attacks of enemies—such as theirs is, who have preceded us in the Lord; nor are we to accept their statements, in the manner of the disciples of Pythagoras, as the already established opinions of the learned, but rather to evaluate them in terms of the reasonableness of the doctrines [themselves]. But if one of the opposing faction murmurs against me, wanting to know why I read their exegesis, though I do not acquiesce in their teachings, let him know that I gladly hear the apostolic saying, "Test all things, keep what is good," and the words of the Savior, "Be you approved money-changers," in order that, if some coin is false and does not have the image of Caesar or the mark of the public mint, it will be rejected, but what clearly brings forth the face of Christ into the light will be hoarded in the purse of our hearts. For, if I were seeking to understand some dialectical proposition or teaching of the philosophers and—that I may return to our own learning—of the Scriptures, I certainly would not consult the simple men of the church (especially since in the great house of the Father there are said to be many vessels) but rather those who have learned the art from the

---

5. *Comm. in Eph.* 3.1.

Artificer and who meditate day and night on the Law. I too, both in my youth and in extreme old age, have profited from those most learned men, Origen and Eusebius of Caesarea, for all that they erred in respect of true teaching. How much more can we say for Theodore, Acacius, and Apollinaris! . . . My manner of proceeding is to read the ancients, to test individual interpretations, to retain those that are good, and not to depart from the faith of the catholic church.[6]

This lengthly exposition of the orthodox Christian's proper attitude toward earlier writers now deemed heretical is of interest not only for the basic attitude it proposes—"heretical" authors are to be read selectively, in accordance with 1 Thessalonians 5:21 and the *agraphon* already cited—but also for the slippage that occurs within it, between advice directed to the two monks of Toulouse as to how to read Jerome's letter, and a description of Jerome's own reading practices. This slippage is particularly important given that Jerome opens his justification for presenting the opinions of the earlier writers he cites by comparing their learning to his own inadequacy as an exegete, *meae pusillitatis auctoritas*. At this point Jerome represents himself as a mere conduit for the learning of the past, which it will be the task of his readers to evaluate and to accept or to reject. Quickly, though, he moves on to describe himself not as a channel for information but as a model for the proper mode for evaluating that information. Jerome thus reclaims—even as he has renounced it—authority over the tradition he transmits and, by implication, over the orthodox interpretation of scripture itself.

Jerome's explicitly stated attitude toward the Greek exegetical material he transmits parallels his handling of the same sources in his commentaries. There, as we have already seen, Jerome's authorial voice is far from neutral. Instead, he subsumes all his materials under a consistent, distinctive prose style, and intervenes to reject interpretations that violate his own exegetical principles. The application of these principles is regularly connected with the figure of the *prudens lector*. For example, in his commentary on Isaiah, interpreting Isaiah 11:15, Jerome connects the figure of the *prudens lector* with the rejection of "carnal" millenarianism:

> The wise Christian reader [*prudens et christianus lector*] will hold to this rule, that whenever the Jews and those of our own people—or rather, those who are not our own but are Judaizers—affirm that the prophesied redemption is to take place after the flesh, we deem that it is now being fulfilled after the spirit.[7]

6. Jerome, letter 119.11.1–5.

7. *Comm. in Esaiam* 4.11.15.43, on Isaiah 11:15: *Prudens et christianus lector hanc habeat repromissionum prophetalium regulam, ut quae Iudaei et nostri, immo non nostri Iudaizantes, carnaliter futura contendunt, nos spiritualiter iam transacta doceamus, ne per occasionem istiusmodi fabularum et*

Even more strikingly, the *prudens lector* is frequently collocated with the *Hebraica veritas*. In a passage from a lengthy exegetical letter written to the Roman divorcée Fabiola on the stations of Israel in the desert, Jerome gives a detailed discussion of the word "Dephca," the name of the ninth station. He acknowledges that he has given a different term, with a different interpretation, in his book of Hebrew names, and distinguishes the two in terms of a translation in the "vulgate" version based on the substitution of the letter *bet* for *phe*, producing the reading "Debca." After giving a Christian typological interpretation of "Dephca," he writes, "For the sake of the wise and assiduous reader [*prudentem studiosumque lectorem*] I wish to speak to the point, that he may know that I render the names according to the Hebrew truth; for the rest, in the Greek and Latin codices, except for a few instances, we find them all corrupt."[8] The implicit expectation is that Jerome's reader will naturally share both his concern for the *Hebraica veritas* and his rejection of the Greek and Latin codices in use in the churches as "corrupt"—an assumption that would have held true for few of Jerome's contemporaries. Not only does Jerome's *prudens lector* share many of his most idiosyncratic exegetical principles: he also shares Jerome's elite education and the biases that go with it. For example, in the preface to *On Hebrew Names* of about 390, Jerome writes that a previous writer "had dared to render the same book into the Latin language, though not in a Latin manner." The *prudens lector*, on comparing the two versions, will immediately be able to differentiate Jerome's from the other, whose translator Jerome describes as "one who had hardly learned his ABC" (*quidam vix primis imbutus litteris*).

The complexity of Jerome's representation of his implied reader is emblematic of Jerome's peculiarly late antique situation. At the turn of the fifth century, neither the monasteries nor even the Christian clergy had developed the institutional stability to support an independent, purely Christian intellectual life. Traditional education—still vibrant—remained the only education available. Thus Jerome's *prudens lector* retained the attitudes of the secular schools in which he and his peers had been formed. Despite Jerome's efforts to shape the reading of his works by constituting an ideal reader within them, he could do so only within the constraints of the elite literary culture shared by most of his actual readers.

---

inextricabilium iuxta Apostolum quaestionum, iudaizare cogamur. The reference to "the Apostle" is to 2 Timothy 2.

8. Letter 78.19: *Prudentem studiosumque lectorem rogatum velim, ut sciat me vertere nomina iuxta hebraicam ueritatem. Alioquin in graecis et latinis codicibus praeter pauca, omnia corrupta reperimus.*

THE READER IN THE WORLD

But how were these ideal readers—and more to the point, actual, flesh-and-blood ones—expected to obtain copies of Jerome's works? How did the means by which Jerome's works circulated shape their form, content, and reception? How did Jerome's writings function in the networks of exchange that also brought him the patronage he depended upon to produce them? References to the circulation of Jerome's works appear scattered through his correspondence, as if he had given no deliberate thought to the matter. Nevertheless, a pattern emerges. Jerome's self-consciousness about his own literary corpus prompted him to impose a greater degree of order on the circulation of his writings than was typical of his age. Thus he developed very early on a conception of his own "complete works," and found ways to make his entire oeuvre available to readers in the West. Again, Augustine provides an interesting parallel.[9] But Jerome also displays an instinctive mastery, from very early in his career, of the informal systems of exchange that served to disseminate literary works in his day. He dedicated his individual works to named persons, often patrons and supporters, perhaps in other cases those whom he hoped to recruit into those roles. Many of his writings were explicitly produced to satisfy the requests of individual readers, whether their interests lay in scholarship, spiritual guidance, or polemic. The skill with which he inserted these works into the economy of gift exchange among late Roman elites was rewarded both with an eager readership and with financial support for his literary activities. At the same time, it enmeshed him—perhaps more than he would have liked—in theological controversies, both local and empire-wide.

Jerome, as we have seen, was an extraordinarily self-conscious and self-reflective author. The coherence of the program of translation and commentary on the Hebrew scriptures that emerged from his experiments in the years 386 to 392 is evidence enough for this. We would expect, therefore, that he might seek ways to exert a degree of control over the circulation of his writings. Authors—and especially Christian authors—had long shown concern for the correct copying of their works.[10] Jerome seems to have gone

---

9. The early dissemination of Augustine's works is discussed in Vessey, "Conference and Confession," 180–91; p. 181 and the notes there deal with the letter of Jerome to Aurelius of Carthage that I discuss above in chapter 6 and later in the present chapter.

10. See, e.g., the adjuration to copyists at the end of Irenaeus's lost *On the Ogdoad* as cited in Eusebius, *Hist. eccles.* 5.20.1–3.

beyond this—as Augustine was to do late in life in his massive auto-bio-bibliography, the *Retractationes*—by attempting to create among his readers a conception of, and therefore a desire for, his complete works.

In the chapter 6, we considered in a different connection two instances in Jerome's correspondence, both from the 390s, that together with another, roughly contemporary letter raise the prospect of the dissemination of his works as a coherent corpus. The earliest text is a letter from Jerome to Aurelius of Carthage, written perhaps in 392 or 393. Aurelius seems to have written first, referring to certain works of Jerome's in his possession, and perhaps requesting copies of others. Such at any rate is the implication of Jerome's reply, in which he acknowledges having seen Aurelius at Rome during the council of 382; avers that he had, indeed, translated some of Origen's homilies on Jeremiah and on the Song of Songs; and denies having written a commentary on Matthew, as Aurelius seems to have believed. Jerome's elaborate protestations of modesty make it difficult to tell exactly what Aurelius had asked of him, but his response was to send his African correspondent copies of two of his recent works and to suggest that Aurelius—as his "holy brothers, bishops in Gaul and Italy," had already done—send a trusted subordinate to spend the year at Bethlehem, copying "everything that I have written." Whether Aurelius did so or not is unknown, but Jerome's works seem already to have been well disseminated in North Africa when Augustine first wrote to him a few years later.[11]

In the summer of 394, a year or two after the exchange with Aurelius in North Africa, Jerome wrote to a certain Desiderius at Rome, inviting him and his wife Serenilla to join him in Bethlehem. At the close of his brief letter, Jerome informs his correspondent that if he wishes to obtain any of his works that he lacked, he could borrow copies either from Marcella, in her palace on the Aventine, or from the Roman monk Domnio. Each of these close friends, Jerome claims, has copies of his complete works, as he had listed them only a year before in the closing passage of his *On Famous Men*. Jerome directs Desiderius to Marcella and Domnio not only for copies of his writings but for a copy of the list itself, which he does not see fit to append to his letter.[12] In a manuscript culture where private circulation was the dom-

---

11. Augustine's first letter to Jerome is Jerome, letter 56 = Augustine, letter 28. It was written perhaps in 394 or 395, but Jerome did not receive it until several years later. In the letter, Augustine refers to Jerome's translation of Job from the Septuagint with critical signs; to his translations from the Hebrew; and to his commentaries, of which Augustine knows at least the commentary on Galatians at first hand.

12. Jerome, letter 47.3. Kelly, *Jerome*, 283 n. 2, suggests that this Desiderius is the same as the Gallic Desiderius discussed later in this chapter.

inant mode for the dissemination of books, it would have been immensely useful for an ambitious author that a register of his works should be in circulation. It is ironic that Jerome produced such a catalogue in 393, so early in his own career that it rapidly became useless. But to have succeeded in including himself in such a useful work, alongside Christian authors from Paul onward, was still quite a coup.

Perhaps two years later—three years after *On Famous Men* was dedicated to the former imperial official Dexter, now retired in northern Spain—another Spaniard, Lucinus of Baetica, sent a troop of his own slaves to make and bring back copies of Jerome's entire oeuvre. Jerome wrote a cover letter to accompany the codices they carried with them when they departed in 397. Again there was some confusion about what Jerome had actually written: he had to insist that he had not, in fact, translated Josephus. But the conception of his complete works advocated already in his writings of the first half of the decade had apparently begun to take hold, even if the precise contents of the corpus remained difficult for would-be readers to pin down.[13]

Jerome's attempts to disseminate his writings as complete works can be read as an effort to exert control over their circulation, so as to circumvent the more chaotic patterns created by the insertion of literary works into existing elite systems of gift exchange. The suggestion to Aurelius of Carthage that the labor of copying could be undertaken—presumably for free—by a member of his clergy indicates the direction Jerome would have had to take to free himself from dependence on those elite networks and the rarely mentioned resources of inherited wealth and influence that allowed them to function. The fact that Lucinus, who imported Jerome's complete works into Spain, did so by means of the labor of six of his personal slaves—skilled copyists, and therefore valuable property—shows that that direction was not taken with any consistency. A mode of literary circulation that did not rely on the resources and hence fall into the patterns of elite networks of exchange was certainly beyond Jerome's attainment, if not beyond his imagining. Even if he did, at times, exert an unusual degree of personal control over the dissemination of his works, he did so by manipulating the system that already existed, not by substituting a new one. As he complained to Aurelius, in a passage quoted in chapter 5, the two monks who served as his personal secretaries were far from sufficient to make copies of his works for others. Monastic book production in late antiquity was dwarfed by long-standing patterns of personal copying and exchange of books among a literate, leisured, and usually slave-owning elite, whether lay or clerical.

13. Jerome, letter 71.

In a few cases, we can trace in detail the movement of letters, more formal literary works, and other kinds of gifts and favors between Jerome and his friends and patrons. The most vivid evidence pertains to Jerome's Roman friends, especially the senator Pammachius and the aristocratic female ascetic Marcella. Other members of the circle—Domnio, Oceanus, Fabiola, and a number of others who survive only as names, such as Rogatianus—were more peripheral, though they were the recipients of important letters and the dedicatees of major works. More scattered evidence provides glimpses of the channels through which Jerome's works reached other regions of the Latin world: Gaul, North Africa, Pannonia. One such case, where the evidence is particularly rich, will be discussed in detail below. Jerome's correspondents and dedicatees helped him to publicize and disseminate his works. They supplied financial support for his activities: in a few cases we have direct evidence for such patronage, and we ought to suspect it elsewhere. They also participated—sometimes in ways that Jerome might not have wished—in promoting his theological views, defending him against charges of heresy, and pressing the attack against his opponents. They sought his intervention from afar in local controversies. On every level, the initiative seems often to have rested not with the author but with his addressees, whether at the moment of a work's conception or in its later circulation.

The interventions of members of Jerome's circle at Rome in the Origenist controversy showcase the effects on his career of his correspondents' independent initiatives, and of unauthorized modes of literary circulation in general. In 399, Pammachius, Oceanus, and Marcella suppressed Jerome's conciliatory letter 81 to Rufinus. They substituted for it a private letter addressed to his Roman friends, letter 84, in which Jerome does not name Rufinus but attacks his literary activities in detail. This splenetic missive they circulated publicly, so that it appeared to be an open attack on Rufinus.[14] Their interference undid the achievements of spring 397, when Jerome and Rufinus were formally reconciled in the church of the Anastasis at Jerusalem, with the blessing of the city's bishop John, and set the two former schoolmates on the course of conflict that would last the rest of their lives. Even the most trusted of a writer's addressees, it appears from this incident, could not be prevented from exercising their own—perhaps dangerous—judgment.

During the same period, Eusebius of Cremona was involved in the unauthorized circulation not of a work of Jerome's, but of Rufinus's. Exactly what happened is probably beyond reconstruction, but Rufinus accused Eusebius not only of having stolen drafts of Rufinus's translation of Origen's

14. Cavallera, *Saint Jérôme*, 2:38; Kelly, *Jerome*, 236–40.

Peri Archon, which had been intended only for their addressee, a Roman named Macarius, but also of having adulterated his copies to make Origen's views appear more sharply heretical, where Rufinus's translation had omitted the work's most controversial passages. To what extent these charges correspond to reality cannot be determined. What is clear is that Eusebius pursued Rufinus across North Italy, from one episcopal court to another, adducing his pirated copy of Rufinus's Latin version of the *Peri Archon* as evidence that its translator endorsed Origenist heresy.[15]

Examples of this kind of behavior, on both sides of the Origenist controversy as well as in quite unrelated contexts, could readily be multiplied. Not only the delivery of a letter, but even the integrity of a work's content, might fall victim to the designs of a negligent, malicious, or overzealous intermediary. An author was not only dependent on his wealthy and well-connected friends for the dissemination of his works, but in fact lost control of those works when he turned copies over to them. Jerome's reliance on traditional modes of literary dissemination meant not only an inability to establish ascetic alternatives to elite culture, but powerlessness in the face of that culture's continued domination of the literary sphere, at least on this practical level.

The relations between Jerome, in Bethlehem, and a circle of monks, priests, and bishops in southwestern Gaul, carried on over a period of several decades and lasting until Jerome's death, exemplify the complex patterns by which letters, literary works, and financial patronage circulated between Jerome and his correspondents. We can identify perhaps ten men in the group, all linked to Jerome and known to at least one of the others. Vigilantius, a priest from southwest France, visited Bethlehem in 395 as the messenger of Paulinus of Nola, then returned to the West and carried Paulinus's letter 5 to the aristocratic monk Sulpicius Severus, at his monastery in Primuliacum, between Toulouse and Carcassonne, in 396. Jerome wrote to Vigilantius his vituperative letter 61 in the same year.[16] Desiderius, perhaps the addressee in 394 of Jerome's letter 47, discussed above, was a visitor to Beth-

---

15. Rufinus, *Apol.* 1.20, 2.44, with Jerome, *Contra Ruf.,* 3.20; for Eusebius's theft of Rufinus's draft translation, see Cavallera, *Saint Jérôme,* 1:234, and Kelly, *Jerome,* 234–35. For their confrontation before Simplician, bishop of Milan, and for Eusebius's general campaign against Rufinus in Italy, see Rufinus, *Apol.* 1.21, and Kelly, *Jerome,* 247.

16. There is considerable controversy over the dating of Vigilantius's travels and of Jerome's letter 61 refuting his charges of Origenism. The best treatment, refuting the earlier arguments of Rebenich, *Hieronymus,* 249–51, and giving 396 as the date of Vigilantius's return to Gaul, carrying Paulinus's letter 5 to Sulpicius, appears in Trout, *Paulinus,* 221 n. 136. For further discussion, see the Appendix, section 7.

lehem in 398, and eventually a priest of the diocese of Toulouse.[17] Amabilis, bishop of an unknown Gallic see, was the recipient of Jerome's literal commentary on the visions of Isaiah in 397.[18] Vitalis, a priest and an acquaintance of Amabilis's, was the recipient of Jerome's letter 72, carried by Desiderius on his return to Gaul.[19] Heraclius, a deacon, was the messenger of Amabilis in 397 and of Vitalis in 398.[20] Sisinnius, a deacon of Toulouse, visited Bethlehem in 402—bringing a copy of Augustine's first letter to Jerome, which he had found on an island off the Dalmatian coast[21]—and again in 406, when he brought an extensive dossier of letters and other writings from Gaul, as well as alms from his bishop. Riparius, another priest of the diocese of Toulouse,[22] reported on Vigilantius's recent activities to Jerome in 404, received in reply Jerome's letter 109, forwarded Vigilantius's writings to Jerome via Sisinnius in 406, and finally received *Against Vigilantius* that same year, addressed to him and to Desiderius. The same Riparius may also have been the addressee of Jerome's letters 138, 152, and 151, written in the 410s during the controversy over Pelagius.[23] Minervius and Alexander, monks of

17. On the identification of the Desiderius addressed in letter 47 with the Desiderius of the later correspondence, see Crouzel, "Amis toulousains," 145, and, more strongly in favor, Kelly, *Jerome*, 283 n. 2, where the dedication of Jerome's translation of the Pentateuch to a Desiderius is also in question. On Desiderius as a priest of Toulouse, see Crouzel, "Amis toulousains," 144.

18. Amabilis is typically identified as a Pannonian, because Heraclius in 397 also carried back a letter to Castricianus, a blind man whom Jerome identifies as a Pannonian in his letter 68 to him: for this identification see, e.g., Kelly, *Jerome*, 220. However, Heraclius was also the messenger, in 398, of Vitalis, as Jerome states in his letter 72.1 to Vitalis. That this is the same Heraclius is implied by the opening sentences of letter 72: *Zenon nauclerus, per quem mihi dicis tuae sanctitatis litteras esse transmissas, unam tantum et breuem epistulam beati papae Amabilis reddidit solita munuscula continentem. satisque miror, quid causae fuerit, ut, cum in benedictionibus et tuis et illius perferendis fidelis extiterit, in reddenda epistula neglegens adprobetur. Neque enim te falli arbitror, discipulum ueritatis, nisi forte Graeco homini Latinus sermo inter chartulas oberrauit. Itaque ad secundam rescribo epistualm, quam mihi sanctus filius meus Heraclius diaconus reddidit.* Zeno, who carried the letters of both Vitalis and Amabilis, delivered only that of Amabilis, to which no reply of Jerome's is preserved. Heraclius, on the other hand, acted in this case as the messenger of Vitalis, not Amabilis. Though this connection cannot be said to prove beyond any question that Amabilis was in Gaul when he wrote to Jerome in 397 and 398, it is much more solid evidence for his whereabouts than the description of Castricianus as a Pannonian; after all, a Pannonian by origin could be resident anywhere in the empire.

19. For Desiderius as Jerome's messenger to Vitalis, see Jerome, letter 72.5.

20. For Heraclius as Amabilis's messenger, see Jerome, *Comm. in Esaiam* 5.1.23-25, the preface to the original literal and historical commentary on Isaiah 13:1-23:18.

21. For Sisinnius's visit in 402 with the misdirected copy of Augustine's letter, see Jerome, letters 102 and 105.

22. Crouzel, "Amis toulousains," 144.

23. Crouzel, "Amis toulousains," 145.

Toulouse, were the addressees of Jerome's letter 119, carried to Gaul by Sisinnius in 406, and dedicatees in the same year of Jerome's commentary on Malachi. Exsuperius, bishop of Toulouse, was the dedicatee in 406 of Jerome's commentary on Zechariah.[24] Jerome may have made his first connection with the Christians of Toulouse at Constantinople in 380. There he must have met Dexter, the proconsul of Asia, to whom he would dedicate his *On Famous Men* in 393. Dexter was the son of Pacianus, a bishop of Toulouse and predecessor of Exsuperius.

The relations among these men reveal particularly well the power of elite networks in shaping Jerome's literary production. Jerome often had to defer a cherished project in order to meet the demands of a correspondent. Occasionally, texts that he had already written, in accordance with his own preestablished research programs, could be pressed into service as gifts offered to patrons in recognition of their support. The prestige of the series of commentaries and translations for which he became known could justify their insertion into relations of exchange. But these cases were the exception. In general, Jerome's readers knew what they wanted him to write, and it was not what he had planned for. This was true of Jerome's exegetical writings, but even more so of his polemics: as in the cases we shall examine, many of Jerome's controversial works were written on another's initiative, not his own. When financial support was forthcoming for Jerome's monastery and his literary labors, it was generally in the context of long-standing relationships—and often, paradoxically, against the background of conflict over the legitimacy of Jerome's mode of scholarship and of asceticism.

From 397 until his death, Jerome sent a large number of commentaries and exegetical letters to Gallic correspondents. Amabilis received a commentary on part of Isaiah in response to his specific request. Jerome later incorporated that work into his commentary on all of Isaiah, written between 408 and 410 and dedicated to Eustochium. Vitalis was the recipient of letter 72, which dealt with an exegetical question Vitalis had posed: How could both Solomon and Ahaz have become fathers at the age of eleven? In his reply, Jerome expressed impatience with this kind of pedantry, but nevertheless gave a full answer.

Letter 119, to Minervius and Alexander, is particularly revealing. In the

---

24. Exsuperius appears at other points in Jerome's works: perhaps in his letter 54 to Furia, written in 395, which mentions a *sanctus Exsuperius;* certainly in his letter 123 to Ageruchia of 409, where he is described as bishop of Toulouse; and again in letter 125 to Rusticus written in 412. The two certain references emphasize Exsuperius's charity and his gifts as a spiritual director: see Crouzel, "Amis toulousains," 131–33.

opening paragraph, Jerome writes that he had thought he had a good deal more time to compose his replies to the questions posed not only by the two monks from Toulouse but also by "many holy brothers and sisters from your province," whose letters had also been brought to him by Sisinnius. Instead, Sisinnius announced that he was leaving for Egypt much earlier than Jerome had expected, as he was anxious to bring alms there to relieve the suffering caused by the failure of the Nile's floods and a resultant famine. Jerome was therefore compelled first to write in haste to his other questioners — the letters are all lost — and then, having saved the most difficult problems for last, to send Minervius and Alexander not a full answer to their question but a dossier of selections from various authorities, on which they might base their own interpretations. Unlike many of Jerome's protestations of having composed in haste, this one seems too circumstantial to be merely a conventional formula.[25] It indicates how seriously Jerome took his task of satisfying the exegetical curiosity of correspondents in the West, who did not have access to the Greek commentaries that he translated and paraphrased, or to the many variant readings of the biblical text he could cite. In comparison to this burden of work imposed by his correspondents, the dedication of two of his commentaries on the Minor Prophets to readers at Toulouse seems almost inconsequential. No further volumes of Jerome's commentaries on the Prophets were dedicated to correspondents outside the circle of his intimates. But he continued to write lengthy exegetical letters in response to the technical and often challenging questions addressed to him by a variety of Western inquirers.[26]

Jerome's involvement in controversy with Vigilantius — once welcomed at Bethlehem but soon a bitter critic of his former host — is an even stronger example of this pattern. When he composed his letter 61 in 396, Jerome had heard that Vigilantius, upon returning to his homeland in Gaul, had begun to attack him personally, calling him an Origenist and a Manichee. Whatever Jerome's information was about Vigilantius's criticisms, he clearly had no hope of restoring their friendship but rather attempted to discredit him, counterattacking with great vituperation and sarcasm.

The precise circumstances of the rupture between Vigilantius and his former host are probably beyond recovery. A number of scholars have accepted the suggestion that Vigilantius, as the messenger of Paulinus of Nola, must

---

25. Jerome, letter 119.1.

26. E.g., letter 120 to Hedybia, on twelve exegetical problems; letter 121 to Algasia, on eleven exegetical problems; letter 140 to Cyprian, on Ps. 90.

have carried letters, and perhaps donations, for the monastery of Melania the Elder and Rufinus on the Mount of Olives as well as for Jerome in Bethlehem. If Vigilantius had visited them in 395, after the break between Jerome and Rufinus over Epiphanius's denunciations of Origen in 393 and 394, Rufinus's influence may have disposed him against Jerome. Furthermore, Vigilantius may have hesitated to align himself with a man who had been—as Jerome was in 395—excommunicated by his local bishop.[27] Jerome himself supplies support for this theory in the third book of his *Apology against Rufinus*, written in 402, where he implies that Rufinus lay behind Vigilantius's opposition to him.[28] But this explanation cannot fully account for the facts. If Vigilantius had aligned himself with Rufinus, why did he accuse Jerome of Origenism? In 395, Rufinus, together with John of Jerusalem, refused to anathematize Origen or his doctrines as heretical. A follower of theirs would have been unlikely to use the label "Origenist" as a term of opprobrium. While Vigilantius, as Paulinus's emissary, may well have visited Paulinus's relative Melania, the Gallic priest's attacks on Jerome cannot readily be explained by his connection to her or to her friend Rufinus.

Rather, Vigilantius's attacks on Jerome are probably best understood against the same background that shaped his later works, which no longer had Jerome directly in view. David Hunter has argued that Vigilantius wrote in the context of ongoing debates in Gaul over the cult of relics. When later he attacked asceticism and clerical celibacy, he likely did so with the support of a silent majority of the Gallic clergy.[29] Even in letter 61 Jerome makes clear that Vigilantius has already written extensively on a range of subjects, including the exegesis of Daniel. Jerome's interest, however, is limited to defusing the charges leveled against himself. Rather than engage with Vigilantius's doctrinal positions, Jerome portrays his accuser as beneath notice, an uneducated fellow from a lowly background whose pretensions to authorship are ridiculous rather than threatening. The result is that we learn very little about what Vigilantius had to say for himself. Presumably the controversies that drew so much interest in Gaul had little resonance in Palestine, long a center for the ascetic life.

There, it seems, Jerome would have been content to let the matter lie. But

27. For variations on this theme, see Nautin, "Études de chronologie (suite)," 231–33, followed by Kelly, *Jerome*, 286, Stancliffe, *St. Martin*, 303, and Clark, *Origenist Controversy*, 36. Stancliffe, *St. Martin*, 405–7, finds all the arguments inconclusive.

28. *Apol.* 3.19.

29. Hunter, "Vigilantius."

in 404 he received a letter from Riparius, demanding that he write against the dangerous views of Vigilantius, which had already won some sympathy from the latter's (unidentified) bishop. Jerome did so, but reluctantly. Responding to Riparius's descriptions of Vigilantius's arguments, which now included criticism of the cult of relics and the observance of vigils, Jerome waxes indignant at the mere possibility of such irreverence, but refuses to go into more detail until he has obtained copies of Vigilantius's own writings. No doubt Riparius had hoped that Jerome's international prestige might help him to oppose the teachings of a local rival. Jerome himself was less enthusiastic about the prospect.

In 406, however, Riparius and his fellow presbyter Desiderius followed up by forwarding to Jerome a dossier of Vigilantius's writings. Jerome responded with a full-dress polemic against Vigilantius, which he dedicated to the two presbyters. Jerome does his adversary the honor of quoting directly from his works, showing that he takes his views seriously enough to give some energy to refuting them. At the same time, he subjects his victim to an invective of unparalleled violence. Vigilantius had extended his polemics against the cult of relics and the observance of vigils at the martyrs' graves to include the very possibility of their intercession for the living or the dead. He had also renewed his attacks on clerical celibacy, while adding to them criticisms of both monastic vows of poverty and the sending of alms to monks in the Holy Land. While Jerome was an avid devotee of relics, it was these latter arguments that must have hit particularly close to home. Perhaps, then, Jerome responded more vigorously to this second request for a refutation of Vigilantius because his views now seemed more relevant to Jerome's own concerns; or perhaps it was simply his correspondents' persistence that elicited the work. In either case, *Against Vigilantius* was clearly written on their initiative, not Jerome's.

As David Hunter has argued, the practices that troubled Vigilantius were the focus of much controversy in early fifth-century Gaul. Indeed, on Hunter's interpretation, Vigilantius's views were those of the majority of the Gallic clergy at the time, while the ascetics and advocates of relics whose works survive to us represented a vocal but controversial minority. Hunter goes even farther to suggest that Exsuperius of Toulouse himself may have had a history of wavering, at least on certain late fourth-century developments in the cult of relics.[30] If this was the case, then we may hypothesize that Riparius, Desiderius, and their allies, had won over Exsuperius by 402 or

30. Hunter, "Vigilantius."

403 when he presided over the translation of the relics of Saint Saturninus, a martyr of Toulouse, to his newly completed basilica. Then, they sought to solidify their influence over their bishop and to counteract that of Vigilantius by involving the famous Jerome in what was actually a very local quarrel. Jerome, having had his fill of Vigilantius in the 390s, was hesitant to do so, but eventually came around. Perhaps his letter 109, despite its reluctance to engage the enemy directly, had some influence on Exsuperius, for when the full dossier of Vigilantius's writings was dispatched to Palestine in 406, it came accompanied by Exsuperius's generous donations. Both the composition of *Against Vigilantius* and the dedication of the commentary on Zechariah, under this interpretation, were intended to solidify a victory on behalf of relics and ascetics already partially consolidated in 404.

This scenario, of course, is highly speculative. But whatever the actual events that generated them, the history of Jerome's writings against Vigilantius exemplifies a broader pattern. Jerome's correspondents sought, often successfully, to involve him in controversies that were important to themselves, whether or not they were to Jerome. The *Against Jovinian*—despite the firestorm of criticism that it was to evoke—was written at the request of Jerome's friends at Rome when its author had already moved to Bethlehem. Jerome's letter 84, whose dissemination at Rome reopened the dispute with Rufinus, was written at the urging of his friends Pammachius and Oceanus, who feared that Jerome would be tarred as an Origenist if he did not defend himself—not a serious danger for him in Bethlehem, within the sphere of influence of John of Jerusalem. Later, as the quarrel degenerated, it was only in response to Rufinus's *Apology* that Jerome composed his own. As a polemicist, even more than as an exegete, Jerome was at the mercy of his readers. To be linked to the elite networks that supported his scholarship and disseminated his works meant also to satisfy the demands of their members.

SCHOLARSHIP AND POVERTY

In resisting the pressures that his audience exerted on him, and seeking to create for Christian scholarship a position of authority independent of wealth, social position, or clerical status, Jerome developed a rhetoric linking biblical scholarship, and Christian learning in general, to an extreme form of monastic poverty. That this linkage would inevitably prove unstable should already be clear. However, Jerome never retreated from the position that wealth and Christian learning were incompatible. Instead, he intensified his polemic against Christians who pretended asceticism while living in luxury, and raised the pitch of his call for renunciation coupled with a life of study. As early as 392, in the preface to his *Hebrew Questions on Genesis,* Jerome asserted unambiguously that it was impossible to possess scriptural erudition and worldly wealth at the same time:

> I therefore beg my reader . . . that in the books of Hebrew questions . . . he seek not eloquence, nor the pleasures of oratory. . . . we, humble and poor, neither have riches nor deign to accept them if offered—for as they too know, it is impossible to possess equally knowledge of the scriptures, which is the wealth of Christ, and the riches of the world.[31]

The passage is perhaps the most striking example in Jerome's work of the association of the eloquence that rhetorical education instilled with worldly wealth, and the opposition of both to the technical biblical scholarship of which the *Questions* provided a first taste. As we have seen in detail, that kind of scholarship required resources that could be had only by expending the world's riches. Its acceptance, even popularity, among Jerome's contemporaries was due in large part to his mastery of Latin eloquence. Yet the opposition of elite literary and rhetorical culture, and the wealth that underwrote it, to Christian biblical learning was a central feature of Jerome's cultural program. We need, finally, to ask how—and why—this paradox was sustained.

Jerome's vision of Christian learning as *necessarily* opposed to wealth did not end with himself. In a eulogy of his friend Heliodorus's nephew Nepotian, written for the grieving uncle after the young priest's untimely death, Jerome writes:

> In conversing at entertainments his habit was to propose some topic from scripture, to listen modestly, to answer diffidently, to support the right, to refute the wrong, but both without bitterness; to instruct his opponent rather than to vanquish him. Such was the ingenuous modesty that adorned his youth that he would frankly confess from what sources his various arguments came, and in this way, while disclaiming the glory attached to learning, he came to be held most learned. This, he would say, is the opinion of Tertullian, that of Cyprian; this of Lactantius, that of Hilary; thus speaks Minucius Felix, so Victorinus, and in this manner Arnobius. Myself too he would sometimes put forward, since he loved me because of my intimacy with his uncle. Indeed by assiduous reading and lengthy meditation he had made his breast a library of Christ. . . . Let oth-

---

31. Pref. to *Quaest. Hebr. in Gen.*: *unde lectorem obsecro . . . ut in libris Hebraicarum quaestionum . . . non quaerat eloquentiam, non oratorum leporem. . . . ut enim nos, humiles atque pauperculi, nec habemus diuitias nec oblatas dignamur accipere, ita et illi nouerint non posse se notitiam scripturarum, id est diuitias christi, cum mundi pariter habere diuitiis.*

ers add coin to coin, and, with their purses choking, complaisantly chase after the wealth of matrons; let them be richer as monks than they were as men of the world; let them have wealth as servants of a poor Christ that they never had as servants of a rich Devil; and let the church gasp at those rich men who in the world were beggars. Our Nepotian, treading gold into the ground, eagerly pursues mere leaves of paper.[32]

Jerome's description of Nepotian, like the portrait he had painted of Blesilla after her death in 385, is clearly intended not only to praise an individual but to articulate an ideal. Nepotian, now tragically dead, was the very model of a Christian scholar. Interestingly, Jerome omits any references to his subject's secular training, though as a former imperial official he must have had a traditional education.[33] The nascent canon of Latin Christian authors seems to have replaced the classics as the foundation of an intellectual life. In keeping with Jerome's ideals, Nepotian's reputation for learning depends on his knowledge of earlier authorities — a relation linked here, as elsewhere, to an appropriate humility, an authority that makes no claims for itself.

In a complex passage of his famous letter 57, "On the best method of translation" (*De optimo genere interpretandi*), addressed to Pammachius in July 396 in the heat of the first phase of the Origenist controversy, Jerome reveals a further dimension to his advocacy of Christian learning. The opening of the passage acknowledges the prestige of holy simplicity among the ascetically minded, making clear how powerful a challenge to Jerome's model of scholarly *askesis* this conception could be. But Jerome then turns first to attack an unnamed opponent — clearly Rufinus, whom Jerome regularly charged with luxury — and finally to assert the absurdity of claims to holiness based solely on simplicity:

> I reprove no Christian for inexperience in speaking — and would that we could hold to that Socratic maxim, "I know, that I know not," and the saying of another wise man: "Know yourself." My reverence has always been not for wordy

---

32. Letter 60.11: *Sermo eius et omne conuiuium de scripturis aliquid proponere, libenter audire, respondere uerecunde, recta suscipere, praua non acriter confutare, disputantem contra se magis docere quam uincere, et ingenuo pudore qui ornabat aetatem quid cuius esset simpliciter confiteri; atque in hunc modum eruditionis gloriam declinando eruditissimus habebatur. "Illud," aiebat, "Tertulliani, sic Cypriani, hoc Lactantii, illud Hilarii est. Sic Minucius Felix, ita Victorinus, in hunc modum est locutus Arnobius." Me quoque, quia pro sodalitate auunculi diligebat, interdum proferebat in medium. Lectione quoque adsidua et meditatione diuturna pectus sum bibliothecam fecerat Christi. . . . alii nummum addant nummo, et marsuppium suffocantes matronarum opes uenentur obsequiis, sint ditiores monachi quam fuerant saeculares, possideant opes sub Christo paupere quas sub locuplete diabolo non habuerant, et suspiret eos ecclesia diuites quos tenuit mundus ante mendicos; Nepotianus noster aurum calcans scedulas consectatur.*

33. For Nepotian's career in the imperial service, see letter 60.9.

boorishness, but for holy simplicity: he who claims to imitate the apostles in speech ought first to imitate their lives. The greatness of their holiness excused the simplicity of their speech, and a dead man resurrected confuted the syllogisms of Aristotle and the perverse cunning of Chrysippus. But it is ridiculous if one of us, while living among the wealth of Croesus and the luxuries of Sardanapalus, were to boast of his ignorance alone, as if all thieves and those accused of various crimes were in truth eloquent, and they concealed their bloody swords in the books of the philosophers and not in the trunks of trees.[34]

The tone of the passage makes plain that, for all his awareness of the powerful model of the untutored ascetic who refutes philosophers—a model grounded in the Gospels and the letters of Paul, and prominently set forth in Athanasius's immensely popular *Life of Anthony*—Jerome is willing to *excuse* simplicity when it is coupled with holiness, not to praise it as a virtue in itself. The final, startling image, by rendering absurd the claim of Jerome's critics that learning is morally inferior to simplicity, implies the opposite case. Jerome accepts the prestige of the ignorant holy man, but places him in the second rank.

Jerome stakes his most explicit claim for the learned Christian—an ascetic, of course—as holder of the first rank of holiness in commenting on Daniel 12:3, "And those who are wise shall shine like the brightness of the firmament; and those who turn many to righteousness, like the stars for ever and ever." He first discusses the passage in the preface to the third book of his commentary on Ephesians, dedicated to Paula and Eustochium in 386. There, reading the passage of Daniel very much as its author intended it, he argues that the reward reserved in the afterlife for the man who is both just and learned—which, he explains, means "possessing knowledge of the scriptures," *habens scientia Scripturarum*—will be as distant from that of the man who is just but ignorant as the light of heaven from the brightness of the stars.[35] As a higher place is reserved in heaven for virgins than for the

---

34. Letter 57.12: *Nec reprehendo in quolibet Christiano sermonis imperitiam—atque utinam Socraticum illud haberemus: 'scio, quod nescio,' et alterius sapientis: 'te ipsum intellege'—uenerationi mihi semper fuit non uerbosa rusticitas sed sancta simplicitas: qui in sermone imitari dicit apostolos, prius imitetur in uita. Illorum in loquendo simplicitatem excusabat sanctimoniae magnitudo, et syllogismos Aristotelis contortaque Chrysippi acumina resurgens mortuus confutabat. Ceterum ridiculum, si quis e nobis inter Croesi opes et Sardanapalli delicias de sola rusticitate se iactet, quasi omnes latrones et diuersorum criminum rei diserti sunt, et cruentos gladios philosophorum uoluminibus ac non arborum truncis occulant.*

35. *Comm. in Eph.* 3, preface to book 3, PL 26, 515A: *Fulgebunt, inquit, justi sicut stellae in aeternum: et intelligentes, id est, habentes scientiam Scripturarum, sicut splendor coeli. Non quo doctus vir justus quoque esse non debeat: sed quo qui justus est, nisi fuerit eruditus, tam procul sit a sapiente justo, quam est stellarum fulgor a lumine firmamenti.*

married or those who adopted a celibate life after the loss of their virginity, so too does the Christian scholar stand above the simple monk, given that their degree of virtue is the same.

The same scriptural citation, with the same significance, appears in a text that is crucial for a full appreciation of Jerome's linking of Christian scholarship and monastic poverty. Jerome's letter 53, his first to Paulinus of Nola, was written in the second half of 394. In it, Jerome makes no bones about the division between learned and untutored Christians:

> Daniel, at the end of his most holy vision, says that the just shine like stars, and the discerning, that is, the learned, like the firmament. You see, how great a difference there is between righteous ignorance and learned righteousness? The first are compared to the stars, the others to the heavens, although according to the Hebrew truth both comparisons can be applied to the latter; therefore in their texts we read, "Those who were learned will shine like the splendor of the firmament, and those who instructed many to justice like stars in endless eternity." [36]

The praise of "learned righteousness" is even more fulsome than it was in the passage from the commentary on Ephesians. In this letter, however, Jerome develops much more fully his conception of Christian learning. As he does so, dissonant elements begin to creep in.

Throughout his correspondence with Paulinus, Jerome represents Christian learning as a specialized exegetical discipline, open only to those who have been properly initiated. In letter 53, he opposes it explicitly to the learning of grammarians and rhetoricians, and criticizes those like himself who have studied secular literature before turning to the scriptures. Such exclusivity seems at first to strengthen his implied claim that the Christian scholar's authority is independent of other markers of status. But he concludes this paean to scriptural study by exhorting Paulinus,

> Let not the simplicity of the scripture or the poorness of its vocabulary offend you, for these are due either to the faults of the translators or to deliberate purpose: for in this way it is better fitted for the instruction of an unlettered congregation as the educated person can take one meaning and the uneducated another from one and the same sentence. [37]

36. Letter 53.3: *Danihel in fine sacratissimae uisionis iustos ait fulgere quasi stellas, et intellegentes, id est doctos, quasi firmamentum. Vides, quantum distent inter se iusta rusticitas et docta iustitia? alii stellis, alii caelo comparantur, quamquam iuxta Hebraicam ueritatem utrumque possit; ita enim apud eos legimus: "qui autem docti fuerint, fulgebunt quasi splendor firmamenti, et qui ad iustitiam erudiunt multos, quasi stellae in perpetuas aeternitates."*

37. Letter 53.10: *Oro te, frater carissime, inter haec uiuere, ista meditari, nihil aliud nosse, nihil quaerere, nonne tibi uideretur iam hic in terris regni caelestis habitaculum? nolo offendaris in scrip-*

Thus he betrays the baggage that his notion of scriptural study as a specialized discipline carries with it. The presupposition is that his addressee is among the educated, those possessed of cultivated literary sensibilities that could potentially be offended by the *vilitas* of the language of scripture. The senator Paulinus was, of course, one such reader.

Letter 58, written to Paulinus a year later, closes with a long passage praising the eloquence of Paulinus's panegyric on Theodosius, forwarded by its author with his letter (both are lost). Jerome lauds his correspondent's literary style to the skies, while denying any intention of flattery. Indeed, his praise is not without a sting, for he continually urges Paulinus to take up the study of the scriptures. By this, Jerome clearly means the kind of technical exegesis that he himself practiced. Where in letter 53 he had presented himself as Paulinus's equal, a fellow student, now he offers to instruct his addressee in what he has already learned himself. The notion of scriptural study as a specialized discipline seems even sharper here. Yet the relation of Christian learning to rhetorical proficiency is not so much one of opposition as of completion. Jerome's criticisms of earlier Latin writers—Marius Victorinus, Arnobius, and Hilary of Arles are all faulted for various stylistic flaws, while Cyprian and Lactantius possess eloquence but neglect exegesis—indicate that the ideal he holds out to Paulinus fuses stylistic perfection with biblical erudition. To achieve "the highest excellence" within the church, one must be educated in secular rhetoric as well as in the technical study of scripture.[38]

What must be teased out of Jerome's positive prescriptions for the life of Christian learning becomes painfully obvious when he lampoons his opponents. To choose but one example among many, in letter 61 to Vigilantius, Jerome defends himself against his addressee's charges of Origenism by claiming that he himself is qualified to select only the "flowers," that is, the orthodox interpretations, found in the works of heretical writers. In support of his position, he paraphrases 1 Thessalonians 5:21, "Read everything, keep what is good." Attacking Vigilantius's scriptural ineptitude, Jerome turns the closely related image of the "approved money-changer" on its head. He insinuates that his addressee, reared in a tavern, lacks the education to distinguish orthodox from heretical exegesis: "From early childhood you have learned other lessons, you are accustomed to other forms of train-

---

turis sanctis simplicitate et quasi uilitate uerborum, quae uel uitio interpretum uel de industria sic prolatae sunt, ut rusticam contionem facilius instruerent, et in una eademque sententia aliter doctus, aliter audiret indoctus.

38. Letter 58.8–11.

ing. For the same man cannot test both gold coins and the scriptures, taste wines and understand the prophets and apostles." Lest we wonder what kind of training Vigilantius lacks that would make him into an "approved money-changer" in respect to the scriptures, Jerome adjures him later in the same letter, "If you wish to exercise your mind, turn yourself over to the grammarians and rhetoricians . . . so that, when you have learned everything, you will perhaps begin to keep silent." Vigilantius, the innkeeper's son, is not only uneducated and therefore incapable of serious scriptural study but by virtue of his status is unsuited even to learn what he lacks. Schooling, at best, might teach him to hold his tongue. He will never be more than "an ass playing a lyre," as Jerome assures him with a deftly deployed Greek tag.[39] According to our only other ancient witness, Vigilantius was in fact a polished writer.[40] Regardless of his actual literary abilities, the premise of Jerome's polemic is clear: scriptural learning must be grounded on elite literary education, exhibited through rhetorical proficiency.

The tension between the two types of material discussed thus far is clear. On the one hand, Jerome presents worldly riches and Christian learning as intrinsically incompatible. On the other hand, he assumes that true scriptural erudition can be attained only by those imbued with a culture restricted to the elite. He goes so far as to assign to the learned Christian a higher place in the afterlife than that allotted to the simple holy man. Status within the church depends — if at one remove — on status in the world. The highest degree of renunciation is available only to him who has the most to renounce. In such a circumstance, the independence of Christian learning can be only partial, its authority always linked to that of traditional culture and thus to that of the traditional elites.

It is against this background that we must understand Jerome's demands for radical renunciation on the part of his wealthiest addressees, Paulinus among them. In order for a hierarchy of ascetic renunciation and Christian learning to replace secular hierarchy, or even to stand independent of it, ascetic renunciation must be total. What Jerome hoped for is expressed graphically in his words to Paulinus at the end of letter 53, where he urges him to come to Palestine to study alongside him:

> Make haste then, I beseech you, and cut instead of loosing the hawser which prevents your vessel from moving in the sea. The man who sells his goods because he despises them and means to renounce the world can have no desire to

39. Letter 61.1, 3–4.

40. Gennadius, *De viris illustribus* 36, on Vigilantius.

sell them dear. . . . . If your property is in your own power, sell it; if not, cast it from you. . . . You are all for delay, you wish to defer action: unless—so you argue—unless I sell my goods piecemeal and with caution, Christ will be at a loss to feed his poor.[41]

Let us pause for a moment to consider what Jerome is demanding of his interlocutor. Paulinus, as Jerome well knew, was the master of a great senatorial fortune. What Jerome urges is in effect the destruction of this patrimony. The sarcastic words that conclude the passage just quoted preclude any thought of bringing Paulinus's fortune intact into the church. Rather than preserving Paulinus's status in the face of Christian critiques of the world by transmuting his patrimony into the property of the church, Jerome wishes to see it dissolved willy-nilly. This was not, needless to say, the course that Paulinus eventually chose. Instead, he used his senatorial fortune to set up, on his estates at Nola in Campania, an ostentatious complex of monastery and church, built around the relics of the martyr Felix. He seems to have continued to use his wealth to support the poor as well as funding the activities of learned ascetics such as Jerome and his erstwhile friend, now rival, Rufinus.

If Paulinus proved a disappointment to Jerome, another aristocrat turned ascetic, the widow Marcella, exemplified his ideal. So she appears in the eulogy that Jerome wrote for her after her death, in the wake of the Gothic sack of Rome in 410; and in this case at least there is no reason to doubt his sincerity. As so often, a female ascetic provides Jerome with the opportunity to contemplate the possibility of a Christian culture purified from the taint of classical rhetoric. Marcella, like Nepotian, acquired much expertise in Christian theology, and also in biblical exegesis. Like him, she refused to flaunt her learning, instead deferring to the authority of her sources—including Jerome, who declared:

> I will praise her for nothing but the virtue which is her own and which is the more noble, because forsaking both wealth and rank she has sought the true nobility of poverty and lowliness. . . . For we judge people's virtue not by their sex but by their character, and hold those to be worthy of the highest glory who have renounced both rank and wealth. It was for this reason that Jesus loved the evangelist John more than the other disciples. For John was of noble birth and

---

41. *Festina, quaeso te, et haerentis in salo nauiculae funem magis praecide quam solue. Nemo renuntiaturus saeculo bene potest uendere quae contempsit et uenderet. . . . Si habes in potestate rem tuam, uende; si non habes, proice. . . . Scilicet, nisi tu semper recrastinans, et diem de die trahens caute et pedetemptim tuas possessiunculas uendideris, non habet Christus, unde alat pauperes suos.*

known to the high priest, yet was so little appalled by the plottings of the Jews that he introduced Peter into his court, and was the only one of the apostles bold enough to take his stand before the cross.[42]

When Jerome claims that Marcella's ascetic achievement directly corresponded to the wealth and privilege that she renounced, we can only take him seriously. Status among the new, ascetic Christian elite depends not only—perhaps not primarily—on the severity of the ascetic practices one undertakes, but rather on the distance between what one was and what one has become. Standing within the Christian ascetic elite, therefore, paradoxically both depends upon and rejects the values of the world.

Read against this background, Jerome's own renunciation of the pleasures of the literary text, and the status that came with mastery over it, takes on new meaning. The complex hierarchy of Christian renunciation defined by Jerome's scholarship and his ascetic and polemical writings sets up the possibility of a Christian elite both intimately connected to, and in some senses independent of, the secular elites of the late Roman empire. The goods that a Christian bent on heroism might renounce on adopting a monastic life were not restricted to wealth and social status. Through the transmuting power of Hebrew philology, classical literary culture could also become the locus for a privileged form of ascetic renunciation.

Jerome's scholarship and the dissemination of his works depended largely, as we have seen, on his position within the late Roman elite. The relation of that elite milieu, and its characteristic values, to the Christian church was a pressing issue in Jerome's day. A key theological problem for the late fourth and early fifth centuries was the definition of Christian perfection. What is the highest goal to which a Christian can aspire in this life? What sets an individual Christian apart from his fellows as an exemplar of spiritual achievement? From one point of view, all the controversies in which Jerome became involved, from the 380s until his death, revolved around these questions. Since Constantine, and especially since the accession of Theodosius I, the champion of Nicea, orthodox Christians had no longer been able to define themselves as a spiritual elite over against a corrupt and essentially alien society. Instead, it became increasingly important to distinguish among Christians, to mark out a hierarchy of the saved. Furthermore, the end of martyrdom meant that it was far more difficult to identify the pinnacle of Christian achievement. The harsh clarity of the arena

---

42. Letter 127.1, 5.

gave way to confusion, or at least to multiplicity. These theological concerns intersected with a new social reality. Over the course of the fourth century, as Christianity slowly gained the adherence of the mass of the population of the Roman empire, its internal dynamics became more and more integrated with those of the larger society. Those who wielded power outside the church—especially the urban elites—exerted increasing influence within the church as well. Although many must have thought this only right, the ascetic movement could not readily accept the assimilation of the values of the church to those of the world. The skills of those trained to rule the Roman empire were useful for governing the churches. But the values such dispositions implied were alien to them.

EPILOGUE

—— ✳ ——

THE tension between the classical literary culture of the imperial elite, and the ascetic Christian focus on the Bible that emerged in its shadow, shaped everything Jerome did, thought, and wrote. Others in his day articulated similar tensions in different terms. Some of them were more influential than Jerome. Nevertheless, Jerome's life and work, viewed as a cultural program, impresses upon the observer a sense of coherence, even monumentality. This study has traced some of the contours of that monumental legacy.

Jerome's scholarly innovations were linked at several points to the imperatives of his monastic vocation. The monastic ideal enjoined strict rules of chastity, poverty, and humility. Biblical exegesis itself threatened to violate the norm of humility on at least two levels. First, it implied an assertion of authority over the biblical text and therefore potentially over the Christian community for whom that text served as charter. More subtly, biblical interpreters—especially Jerome—relied on modes of reading that derived not from within the church itself but from the literary culture instilled by the traditional schools that shaped the Roman empire's ruling elite. Embedded within these modes of reading were values, and an elite aesthetic, very much at odds both with the style of the Christian scriptures and with the faith that anything of profound significance could be extracted from such unpromising texts.

Jerome softened these tensions by distancing himself from them, through the method of compilation that he enshrined at the heart of biblical commentary. The multiple earlier exegetes he cited became his authorities, displacing the claim to power inherent in the practice of interpretation. Abasing himself, at least rhetorically, before these illustrious predecessors, Jerome could reemphasize his own monastic humility. And through his juxtaposition of competing traditions of interpretation with texts of differing authority, Jerome could further confuse the issue, wielding his power as commentator covertly.

But compilation presented another problem, perhaps even more threatening: the books that Jerome needed for this kind of research were extremely expensive. Nor did he control a private fortune of his own, to be piously expended on sacred books. Jerome's ascetic ideals were inspired above all by the rigorous champions of the Egyptian desert. How uncomfortable was the fit between these ideals and his mode of scholarship is suggested by Jerome's failure overtly to deploy his considerable powers of persuasion and publicity to raise an endowment for his library. It seems that Paulinus of Nola, for example, did at one point send money to Jerome at Bethlehem. Clearly, Chromatius of Aquileia and Heliodorus of Altinum did so, as did bishop Exsuperius of Toulouse later on. Jerome accepted these bishops' money with restrained gratitude. But when he wrote to wealthy laymen and women, like Paulinus or the Anician heiress Demetrias, he used the full persuasive power of his rhetoric not to ask them for money but to advocate a program of renunciation so total that it would have entailed the destruction, rather than the redistribution, of their vast patrimonies. By adopting this uncompromising stance—and by attacking other learned monks who, he imputed, led lives of less than total austerity—Jerome could distract his audience's attention from the costliness of his own studies.

Jerome's devotion to what he came to call the *Hebraica veritas*, the "Hebrew truth," also defused the problems raised by the position of elite literary culture at the foundation of his intellectual program. Hebrew, in Jerome's portrayal of it, violated the aesthetic sensibilities inculcated by literary education. Hebrew study could therefore serve as a mode of ascetic discipline peculiarly suited to test and to refine the resolve of an educated monk like Jerome. A biblical philology founded on the Hebrew original could be clearly set apart from the traditional disciplines of literary learning, whose proper objects were the works of Homer and Demosthenes, of Cicero, Horace, and Virgil. The element of aesthetic self-mortification at the center of Jerome's program of Hebrew study comes across most vividly in his description, in a late letter, of his initial motivation for engaging with the language: to suppress his youthful lusts.[1]

1. Letter 125.12.

If these were the internal dynamics of Jerome's cultural program, how are we to evaluate its larger historical, or even intellectual, significance? It should be clear by now that the temptation to write a biography of Jerome is one that the sensible historian will firmly resist. Among his peers, Jerome is one of the more poorly served by contemporary, external documentation. For Augustine, we have the *Life* of Possidius, bishop of Calama in North Africa and Augustine's personal disciple.[2] For Jerome, we have only the late fantasies compiled in the *Golden Legend* of Jacobus de Voragine in the thirteenth century. Other documentation is similarly sparse, or derivative of Jerome's own writings.[3] Although those writings are copious, we know that the collection we have is incomplete and has been shaped by its author's deliberate editorial control.[4] Furthermore, the criticisms — often astute — of modern scholars have cast suspicion on much of what Jerome says about himself, particularly on those kinds of information that would be of most interest to a biographer.

To take but one, crucial example, for which the evidence has already been weighed above: it is impossible to be certain when, where, or why Jerome began to learn Hebrew. As we just saw, Jerome claimed, toward the end of his life, that he began to study Hebrew in the 370s as a means to suppress his carnal desires.[5] But this is an interpretation retrospectively imposed upon his younger self, which contradicts what he had written at that time. In the 380s, at Rome, he wrote of his ongoing work on Jewish texts of the Hebrew scriptures, as well as on the translation of Aquila.[6] But if he had indeed begun the study of Hebrew during the 370s, why do the letters he wrote in that period omit any allusion to this activity? As we have already seen in chapter 1,

2. See Erika Thorgerson, "The *Vita Augustini* of Possidius: The remaking of Augustine for a post-Augustinian world" (doctoral dissertation, Princeton University, 1999); Eva Elm, *Die Macht der Weisheit: Das Bild des Bischofs in der Vita Augustini des Possidius und anderen spätantiken und frühmittelalterlichen Bischofsviten* (Leiden: Brill, 2003).

3. On the external documentation for Jerome's life, see Cavallera, *Saint Jérôme*, 1: 27–44. Kelly, *Jerome*, exemplifies the lack of such documentation by basing his biography almost entirely on Jerome's own works. Vessey, "Jerome's Origen," details how Jerome's own efforts shaped the way his contemporaries and later generations perceived him; Vessey refers to Jerome as his own "autobiographer," who thus, unlike figures of similar prominence, "escaped the attentions of contemporary biographers" (136).

4. Vessey, "Jerome's Origen," passim, and especially 140–45 on Jerome's collection of his letters to Marcella written while he was at Rome.

5. Letter 125.12.

6. Particularly letters 32 (to Marcella) and 36 (to Damasus), which describe these projects in some detail.

the letters Jerome wrote from Syria give considerable detail about his intellectual and literary pursuits, so that if he had undertaken Hebrew study, we would probably know about it. This contradiction cannot be resolved.

The question of motivation, moreover—central to many a modern biographer's concerns—must remain wholly opaque. Typical of late antique writers trained in the rhetorical schools, and even more so than many, Jerome aimed not merely to provide his readers with information, but first and last to persuade. Above all, what is interesting about Jerome is not what conventional biography would set out to capture—even if that effort were likely to bear fruit. To an extent that challenges modernist assumptions about the unitary self, what compels attention to Jerome is not the person, but the persona. Questions of character, in the face of self-fashioning so nimbly executed and so often readjusted, become if not irrelevant, then uninteresting.

When we turn from Jerome's life to his legacy, we face equal, if rather different, frustrations. Jerome left little behind, other than his own massive body of writing. No buildings or institutions outlived him at Bethlehem, as far as we know. Though he may have wished to train a successor, there is no evidence that he did so or even seriously tried. His bid to recruit Paulinus of Nola as a disciple, with the potential to become a collaborator and equal, clearly failed.[7] Other young men who passed through Jerome's orbit either left no surviving writings or went their own ways—as did Sulpicius Severus and Orosius. And only with his female patronesses—Marcella at Rome, Paula and her daughters Blesilla and Eustochium—did Jerome claim to have shared his Hebrew studies. This central and most characteristic innovation of his biblical scholarship therefore left no legacy outside his own writings.

Nor did the marriage that Jerome arranged between the costly practice of textual research and the institution of the cenobitic monastery have offspring in the next generation. Later monastic founders—certainly Cassiodorus, perhaps Benedict as well—may have looked to Jerome as a model in this respect. Across further centuries, the linking of monastery and library would provide a framework for the first universities of Christian Europe. But the genealogy of the university, with its Islamic roots and its worldly impulses, is far too ramified to be traced directly to Jerome. It was his own works rather than his library, his teaching, or the social milieu he created at Bethlehem that were to carry Jerome's influence across the following millennium. Even his writings seem to have served less as example than as provocation. When Christian scholars in the West—whether among the Vic-

---

7. Vessey, "Conference," explores Augustine's role in this failure. See also Trout, *Paulinus*, 199–235.

torines of medieval Paris, or in Renaissance Germany—began again to place the Hebrew language at the center of their biblical scholarship, they did so almost more in rebellion against the overwhelming influence of Jerome's translations and commentaries than in continuation of his project. Tellingly, Eugene Rice's classic study *Saint Jerome in the Renaissance* deals much with his representation in the visual arts: it was as an icon, almost more than as a scholar, that Jerome's influence was felt.

Why was Jerome's impact on the cultural world of late antiquity so much less formative than, say, Augustine's? His personality as well as the shape of his intellectual project may well have played a part. Proud, irascible, eager for controversy despite his ascetic training, Jerome made a bad impression on many. But more important, it seems, was a fundamental failure of imagination. For all the violence with which he rejected classical literary culture, Jerome does not seem to have envisioned its end—at least at any point short of the final, eschatological consummation, whose early warning signs he may have read in the sack of Rome in 410, nine years before his own death.[8] What Jerome created, in the model of the Christian biblical scholar that he described and, uniquely, embodied, was not so much a program for a new Christian culture as for the Christianization, through a specialized ascetic discipline, of an intellect already formed by a solid classical education. He was, in other words, his own life's work, one for which the mold was to be broken in the century immediately following his death.

Must our interest in Jerome, then, end by being merely antiquarian? I believe not. For the place of aesthetic pleasure in a professional practice of reading and criticism is an issue still very much alive. In our own culture, the relations of elite education to the dispositions it inculcates, to the delimitation of the proper objects of criticism, and to the pleasures of the text are profoundly troubled. If we are Jerome's heirs in anything, it is in our institutional and personal commitment to specialized, technical disciplines of reading that claim authority over texts central to our culture—however little we may agree which texts those are. As in Jerome's day, any agreement that may once have existed as to what canon might delimit the proper objects of such readings has been severely disrupted. It has become painfully clear that the interests of a particular elite—one charged, from time to time, with the oversight of empire—strongly shape education, which in turn produces the sensibilities that make possible appropriate aesthetic responses to literary texts.

The pretense that it is merely natural, and therefore good, to respond

---

8. See for example the preface to the first book of the commentary on Ezekiel, written in 410.

with pleasure to certain books—a pretense essential to the representation of literary criticism as an essentially personal and charismatic activity—has been shattered for us as surely as it was for Jerome when he committed himself to valuing the crude utterances of Hebrew prophets over the polished periods of Cicero. Jerome's biblical scholarship replaced the aristocratic male reader, occupying his leisure by correcting a text of Virgil with the aid of a slave secretary, with a far stranger pair: the Jewish teacher with his pupil the monk. These intruders stand, in Jerome's cultural program, for the element of mental labor—as opposed to leisure—intrinsic to his biblical studies. Such brute labor, Jerome hoped and claimed, could deform the cultivated sensibilities that in the young man had responded with such intensity to the beauties of classical Latin style. Poured out upon the texts he studied, Jerome's labor added a perversely banausic element to his exegesis, in addition and in opposition to the training all educated men shared. Labor therefore underwrote an authority that could be opposed to the charisma of the aesthetic response and to the aristocratic privilege that that charisma embodied.

Ironically, to the extent that Jerome persuaded his readers to adopt, or at least to admire, his technical and laborious practice of reading, he did so by wielding without scruple the weapons of Latin rhetoric, so sharp on his pen. That is, Jerome promoted the renunciation of pleasure as the ground of interpretative authority by means of language whose force depended on its readers' enjoyment of what they read, indeed on their admiring acquiescence to his powers of seduction as a consummate product of elite education. Modern critics, in general, have refused this course. Adopting instead a rebarbative jargon, and a style of argumentation that demands that its audience be willing to labor indeed, critics suspicious of the configurations of power that long shaped their trade have placed pleasure even farther from the center of their enterprise. Are we to admire their ascetic rigor?

I can offer no answer to this question. Jerome, however much one may find to say about him, cannot be made an Archimedean point from which to shift the burdens that currently form, or deform, our literary culture, weighing upon authors and critics alike. At best, perhaps, he can serve as a warning, a reminder that, while pleasure in reading can be a dangerous allurement—drawing us all too readily to collude in aspirations to power over more than mere texts—its denial or suppression may lead us more seriously astray. Pleasure is shaped by power, and is power. And whatever the efforts of Jerome or of his epigones, it endures. The reader forgets this at his peril.

———— ✳ ————

Chronology of Jerome's Career

ALTHOUGH the general outlines of Jerome's life are better known than those of most of his contemporaries, a number of specific issues remain sharply contested. The last comprehensive effort to establish a chronology of Jerome's life and writings was that of Cavallera, published in 1922. Since then, the biography of J. N. D. Kelly in 1975, a long series of articles published by Pierre Nautin between 1972 and 1983, and the study of Jerome's circle by Stefan Rebenich in 1992 have all made new proposals for dating major periods and events in Jerome's life. Numerous other authors have addressed individual issues of chronology in various publications.

No effort of synthesis has been made, however, to integrate these new views and interpretations with Cavallera's work, much less to test new proposals against each other. This appendix will address the issues raised by almost a century of scholarship since Cavallera, while placing new datings within the still robust framework he created. Each period of Jerome's life is treated in terms of the most important or controversial chronological problems raised. Scholarly controversies are discussed and, where possible, resolved. Jerome's works are placed in the context of events at the time they were written. I introduce a few modest proposals of my own. However, this Appendix gives no continuous biographical narrative. The most technical discussions, together with citations to the scholarly works discussed in the text, appear in the notes.

The appendix is divided into ten sections, each covering a coherent period in Jerome's life. Each section ends with a chronological list of Jerome's works dating to that period, together with other significant events. The exception is the first two sections, covering the years to 373. Since no surviving works of Jerome's date to that period, no chronological lists are given. Dates given without citation in these lists are from Cavallera's *Regesta Hieronymiana.*

1. BIRTH, CHILDHOOD AND EDUCATION, CA. 347–CA. 368

Jerome was born into a Christian family in a small town in the western Balkans in the mid-fourth century.[1] The family was one of some wealth and local prominence, as comments in his later writings imply.[2] The impression is corroborated by his descriptions of his childhood friend Bonosus, a native of the same town.[3] So much is generally accepted.

The date and place of Jerome's birth have been the subject of much controversy. His hometown, Stridon, cannot be located with certainty. In his account of himself in *On Famous Men* (135), Jerome describes it as *oppido Stridonis, quod a Gothis eversum Dalmatiae quondam Pannoniaeque confinium fuit,* "the town of Stridon, now destroyed by the Goths, which once stood on the boundaries of Dalmatia and Pannonia,"[4] that is, in the western Balkans, probably to the north and thus within the sphere of North Italian influence.

On the far more significant issue of Jerome's birth date, two major proposals exist. The ancient evidence of Prosper of Aquitaine supports a date of 331. Prosper's dates, however, are notoriously unreliable.[5] Thus, Cavallera painstakingly reconstructed, on the basis of the internal evidence of Jerome's own writings, an alternative date of 347. His primary evidence was Jerome's statement that he was a student in the rhetorician's school in 363, at the time of Julian's edict barring Christians from teaching literature. But he also correlated this information with other passages scattered across Jerome's works.[6] Jerome's most recent biographer, J. N. D. Kelly, rejected Cavallera's hypothesis, adopting 331 instead, after the argument of P. Hamblenne.[7]

---

1. For his family's Christianity, see *Prol. in Iob de Hebr. interp.;* Rebenich, *Hieronymus,* 22 with n. 8; Kelly, *Jerome,* 7; Cavallera, *Saint Jérôme,* 1:4.

2. Letter 66.14, *Apol. adv. Ruf.* 1.30.

3. Bonosus, Jerome's childhood friend, in letter 3.4. For discussion of the status of Jerome's family, see Rebenich, *Hieronymus,* 22 with n. 7; Kelly, *Jerome,* 6–7; Cavallera, *Saint Jérôme,* 1:4.

4. A similar description is reiterated in Letter 66.14. See Rebenich, *Hieronymus,* 21 with n. 5 for the literature on this topic.

5. Prosper, *Chronicle,* cited in Cavallera, *Saint Jérôme,* 2:3.

6. *Comm. in Abacuc* 3.14, Cavallera, *Saint Jérôme,* 2:3–12.

7. Hamblenne, "La longévité de Jérôme: Prosper avait-il raison?" *Latomus* 28 (1969).

Since Kelly's *Jerome* (1975), a number of scholars have rejected his re-instatement of 331 for Jerome's birth date, including Pierre Jay and Stefan Rebenich; the latter summarizes the history of the debate.[8] The date of 331 seems particularly improbable, given that Kelly, who accepts this date and therefore places Jerome's education in the 340s, is then unable to account for his activities during the 350s: "a whole decade and more of his life is lost to us," he writes.[9] Surely a date of birth roughly fifteen years later better fits the evidence. Over-precision is probably dangerous, however: the mid-340s is perhaps our best guess.

Two of Jerome's contemporaries who would play important roles in his own career were also born in the mid-340s. Rufinus was born in 345 at Concordia, near Aquileia.[10] His patroness Melania the Elder's birth date is extremely difficult to determine, but was probably also in the 340s.[11]

---

8. Pierre Jay, "Sur la date de naissance de s. Jérôme," *Revue des études latines* 51 (1973); A. D. Booth, "The Date of Jerome's Birth," *Phoenix* 33 (1971); Booth, "The Chronology of Jerome's Early Years," *Phoenix* 35 (1981). For a summary of the debate, concluding for 347, see Rebenich, *Hieronymus*, 20 with n. 3.

9. Kelly, *Jerome*, 24.

10. For Rufinus's chronology, see in general Murphy, *Rufinus;* below, I cite Hammond, "Last Ten Years," who proposes a number of modifications to the dating of events in the last ten years of Rufinus's life.

11. Melania the Elder's chronology is very difficult to establish. The data are thin and contradictory. Palladius, *Historia Lausiaca,* is the basic source. He tells us that Melania was widowed at twenty-two; liquidated her fortune, placed her son under a guardian, and departed from Rome for the East during the reign of Valens (364–78); traveled to Alexandria; spent six months with the fathers in the Egyptian desert; followed Isidore of Alexandria into exile in Palestine; after the recall of Isidore and his companions (i.e., after the death of Valens) founded a monastery on the Mount of Olives, where she remained for twenty-seven years; returned to Italy at the age of sixty; and finally made her way back to Jerusalem, where she died, a refugee from Alaric's attack on Rome. The date of Melania's return to Italy is fixed by that of Paulinus of Nola, letter 29, which was probably written around 400 (see Trout, *Paulinus,* for the date of this letter). But if one takes that date as a starting point, then according to Palladius, Melania founded her monastery in 373, before the death of Valens, which does not agree with his narrative at all. On the other hand, if Melania was sixty when she returned, then she was born in 340, and (according to Palladius) widowed in 362. Again, this does not fit with Palladius's claim that her renunciation took place under Valens. Perhaps the reality behind the confused data given by Palladius was that Melania traveled to the East in 373, spending a *total* of twenty-seven years away from Italy. In fact, 373 was the date of Rufinus's move east, and Palladius seems unclear as to whether Melania preceded Rufinus there or not. Such an interpretation makes it possible to reconcile the other data Palladius provides. But the inconsistencies of his account render it a suspect basis from which to proceed further. On Melania's chronology, see Murphy, "Melania the Elder," and Moine, "Melaniana." Jerome refers to Melania in letter 3.3 (written after 374) and in his *Chronicon* (written in 381), under the year 374: he describes her as "a second Thecla." Perhaps this indicates that Jerome believed it was in this year that she renounced her former life: this would support the interpretation of Palladius's information just proposed.

Jerome's parents sent him away for his grammatical education, first to Aquileia and then to Rome. He probably left home aged about eleven to thirteen, that is, around 358–60. As we have seen, in 363 Jerome was still a teenage student at Rome,[12] where he continued his studies in the school of a rhetorician. Students normally graduated to rhetorical studies at about age sixteen or seventeen, completing their studies as late as their early twenties. Thus Jerome probably spent almost a decade at Rome as a boy, from about 358 or 360 to about 368, when he was roughly twenty-one.

There is very little evidence for Jerome's life as a Christian during his first stay at Rome. Christianity and the Christian politics of the city probably played some role in his development at this time. The affairs of the Roman Church in the late 360s had a considerable element of drama. Damasus, future bishop of Rome, had been a deacon under the ultra-Nicene bishop of Rome Liberius, who was exiled to Greece by Constantius II after the Council of Rimini in 355. Damasus accompanied his bishop into exile, but returned while Felix II, Constantius's nominee as Liberius's replacement, still held the see. In 366, on the deaths of both Felix II and his rival Liberius, Damasus was raised to the Roman see in a violently contested election.[13]

In letters Jerome wrote to Damasus from Syria in the 370s, he claimed the right to appeal to Damasus as one who had been baptized at Rome.[14] If he had been baptized by Damasus after his election, the rite would have taken place when Jerome was between nineteen and twenty-one, very early for any Christian in that period, particularly for an elite male. We know from later remarks of Jerome's that he was sexually active as a young man at Rome. If this activity took place before his baptism—a ritual that, in the fourth century, generally marked a conversion if not to asceticism then at least to a fairly serious form of Christian life—then we can speculate that Jerome's Christianity intensified in the wake of the drama of Damasus's election. In a sentimental passage written several decades later, Jerome describes visiting the catacombs of the martyrs on the outskirts of the city with his group of friends from school.[15] Damasus was a major promoter of the catacombs

12. See the reference to his days as a schoolboy at Rome at the time of Julian's death at *Comm. in Abacuc*, 3.14, dating this to ca. 363–64.

13. Damasus, letter 3: PL 13.356f. and PL 56.684–86. For the date of this letter see Kelly, *Jerome*, 57–58. On Damasus's career, see Rade, *Damasus*. See also Basil of Caesarea's letters 214, 216 to Damasus.

14. Jerome writes to Bishop Damasus of Rome from the Syrian desert in the late 370s, referring to his baptism in the Roman Church: letters 15.1, 16.2. On Jerome's Christianity during his years as a student at Rome, see Kelly, *Jerome*, 21–24.

15. *Comm. in Hiezech.* 40.5–13.

as sites of piety toward the martyrs: perhaps we can see his influence already in this episode.[16]

If these speculations have any truth, they may provide helpful background for the trajectory that Jerome's development followed in the next four years. Already a Christian when he arrived at Rome, in his late teens and early twenties Jerome was drawn to a more intense form of piety by the charismatic example of Damasus, and perhaps by involvement in his contested election. Choosing early baptism, Jerome became a devotee of the martyrs and abandoned at least some aspects of the unruly life typical of a young student living away from home in a major city. When he moved to Trier shortly after his baptism, his Christian aspirations intensified.

2. TRIER AND AQUILEIA, CA. 368–WINTER 372

When Jerome left Rome, he went to Trier in northern Gaul, accompanied by his childhood friend Bonosus from Stridon. It is generally believed that the two went there to seek administrative careers. Trier was the residence of the emperor Valentinian I from 365 to 375, when he died of a stroke while on campaign north of the Danube. Thus, Trier would have been an attractive destination for well-educated young men hoping to enter imperial service.[17]

We have little evidence for when Jerome moved to Trier or how long he stayed there. In a later work, Jerome mentions seeing the Attacotti, a British tribe, "during his youth in Gaul."[18] This seems most likely to have occurred when the *comes* Theodosius (father of the future emperor Theodosius) returned to Trier from a victorious campaign in Britain in 369. So Jerome was probably in Trier by this time.[19]

Abandoning Trier, perhaps because he had renounced his secular ambitions, Jerome moved to Aquileia. Both the chronology of Jerome's stay at Aquileia and the nature of his activities there are somewhat obscure. Jerome himself provides almost all our evidence about the ascetic circle — the "chorus of angels"—that he joined there, and about its eventual disruption by a "sudden storm" of undescribed nature.[20] It seems probable that he went

---

16. On Damasus and the catacombs, see most recently Trout, "Damasus."

17. Matthews, *Western Aristocracies,* 32–55.

18. *Adv. Iov.* 2.7.

19. Kelly, *Jerome,* 26–27.

20. Jerome, *Chron.* (ed. Helm, p. 247): the group was a "chorus of angels." *Subito turbine:* Jerome, letter 3.3. On Jerome's years at Aquileia: Rebenich, *Hieronymus,* 42–51; Kelly, *Jerome* 30–35; Cavallera, *Saint Jérôme,* 19–24.

to Aquileia to join friends from his years at Rome who had undergone similar conversions to asceticism. Rufinus was baptized at Aquileia in approximately 369–70, perhaps before Jerome's arrival. He was already a monk at the time of his baptism.[21]

At Aquileia, Jerome became friends with Chromatius, at that time a priest and later to become bishop of the city and an important patron of both Jerome and Rufinus. Around 370, Chromatius's family, including his mother and sisters, his brother Eusebius (a deacon at the time), and their friend the archdeacon Jovinus, seem to have renounced the world collectively and adopted a sort of monastic life. The entire group came under the patronage of Valerianus, bishop of Aquileia, of whose clergy Chromatius, Eusebius, and Jovinus were members.[22] The three younger men — all future bishops — participated together in Rufinus's baptism.[23]

The most important new contact that Jerome made at Aquileia was with an Easterner, Evagrius of Antioch. Evagrius, a priest and correspondent of many prominent churchmen in both East and West, had traveled to Illyricum in 363 with the returning ultra-Nicene bishop Eusebius of Vercelli, and there became involved with other western clerics, including Damasus of Rome. He returned to the East in about 371 on a mission from Damasus to Basil of Caesarea, then went home to Antioch.[24]

When the circle at Aquileia broke up, Jerome and several of his friends from Italy departed in search of new ascetic experiences. Some quickly returned to their Italian homes, but others remained away for decades. Rufinus, who may have left Aquileia before Jerome did, was at Alexandria in 373. He remained there through about 380, then moved to Palestine, where he settled in the monastery recently founded on the Mount of Olives by Melania the Elder, whom he had met in Egypt.[25]

In late 372, Jerome himself left for the East, traveling by sea down the Adriatic, then overland along the Via Egnatia via Athens, Constantinople, Pontus and Bithynia, Galatia and Ancyra. He traversed Cilicia in the sum-

---

21. In Jerome, *Apol.* 1.4, we read that Rufinus was baptized at Aquileia "about thirty years before" the composition of his *Apology* against Jerome (401).

22. Jerome, letter 7.6; *Prosopographie Chretienne* s.v. Chromatius 1. Chromatius's birth and death dates, and the date of his accession to the see of Aquileia, are unknown. He died after 407, so he may be imagined as a contemporary of Jerome and Rufinus, perhaps a few years older than they.

23. Rufinus, *Apol.* 1.4.

24. Rebenich, *Hieronymus*, 71–75; Basil, letter 138.2.

25. Melania the Elder probably founded her monastery on the Mount of Olives after Valens's fall in 378 (see Palladius, *Historia Lausiaca*, s.v.).

mer of 373, and toward the end of that year arrived at Antioch, where he was received by Evagrius.[26]

3. ANTIOCH AND THE DESERT, WINTER 373–80

At Antioch, Jerome seems to have become a sort of long-term houseguest of Evagrius. He was still in Antioch when he wrote his first surviving letters. Only in early 375 did Jerome leave Evagrius's household to take up the life of a hermit in the desert of Chalcis, a short distance outside the city. He stayed there for perhaps eighteen months, returning to Antioch probably in 376. From then on, he remained in Antioch—presumably as the guest of Evagrius—until he departed in 380 to attend the Council of Constantinople.[27]

Shortly after Jerome left Aquileia, his boyhood friend Bonosus became a hermit on an island in the Adriatic. After a letter of Jerome's praising his friend's heroism, we hear nothing more of Bonosus.[28] During Jerome's first year or so at Antioch, his friend Heliodorus of Altinum, a fellow student from Rome, visited him while touring the East. But when Jerome moved to the desert, Heliodorus refused to join him. Instead, Heliodorus returned to his hometown in northern Italy, where he was eventually ordained bishop.[29]

The central chronological problem for this period of Jerome's life is the length of his stay in the desert, and the date and cause of his return. The confusion in the scholarship over this issue is such that Rebenich, for one, is dubious of any attempt to determine a precise chronology for Jerome's movements in the years 375–77.[30] The key to the problem, however, has been overlooked: the letter of Damasus of Rome to Paulinus of Antioch from the summer of 376, which addresses Paulinus as sole orthodox bishop of Antioch.[31] The impact of Damasus's letter may be measured in the distress expressed by Basil of Caesarea in two letters written around this time.[32]

---

26. Kelly, *Jerome*, 36–38; the journey is described in Jerome, letter 3.3.

27. On the chronology of Jerome's letters and other writings from the 370s, see Rebenich, *Hieronymus*, 86; Kelly, *Jerome*, 46, 52–56; Cavallera, *Saint Jérôme*, 2:12–20.

28. Letter 3.4–5.

29. On Heliodorus's visit, see Jerome, letter 14.

30. Rebenich, *Hieronymus*, 98; for further discussion of the dates of Jerome's arrival at Antioch, his move to the desert, and his return to the city, see Rebenich, *Hieronymus*, 86; Kelly, *Jerome*, 46, 52–56; Cavallera, *Saint Jérôme*, 2:12–20.

31. Damasus, letter 3: PL 13.356A–357A.

32. Basil, letters 214.2 and 216. Kelly, p. 58 n. 1 cites E. Schwartz, "Zur Kirchengeschichte des vierten Jahrhunderts," *Zeitschrift für die neutestamentlichen Wissenschaft* 34 (1935): 185.

Initially, Jerome's stay in the desert was happy, despite the rigorous life-style he had adopted. This is reflected in a number of letters in which he explicitly states that he is living in the desert outside Antioch. Sometimes he complains of loneliness, or deprecates his own fitness for the eremitic life in rhetorical terms, but there is no sign of conflict with his fellow hermits.[33]

Three further letters, however, mention other monks who harassed Jerome, demanding that he subscribe to a trinitarian formula he deemed suspect. The first two letters, 15 and 16, were addressed to Damasus of Rome. Ostensibly, Jerome requested that Damasus adjudicate his theological dispute with the monks, but it is evident that he hoped to draw Damasus into the controversy over the see of Antioch on the side of Paulinus. In letter 15, Jerome describes the monks who are persecuting him as *campenses,* a derogatory term for the adherents of Bishop Meletius, who held services in a field outside the city when he and his congregation were denied a basilica.[34] In letter 16, Jerome refers to "Arians" as installed in Antioch with government support.[35] The third letter, 17, was written to the priest Marcus, begging leave to stay in the desert until spring.

Jerome's letters to Damasus make sense only if written before Damasus's own letter had reached Antioch. A letter from the bishop of Rome would probably have cut no ice with uneducated Meletian monks in the Syrian desert, but Jerome would not have written as he did if he had known of Damasus's recognition of Paulinus. Working backward from the likely arrival of Damasus's letter in Antioch in summer 376, we may thus conjecture that Jerome's situation in the desert had begun to sour relatively quickly, perhaps as much as a year earlier. Likely, letter 15 was sent to Rome in the summer

33. The chronology of the letters written from Syria is as follows: letters 1 and 2 were written before the death of Innocentius toward the end of 374; letters 3 and 4 were sent together to Jerusalem after his death. Letters 5, 6, 7, 11, 14, 15, 16, and 17 explicitly state that Jerome is writing from the desert. Letters 15 and 16 definitely precede Valens's revocation of his sentence of exile on the orthodox bishops in late 377, and probably precede Damasus's letter to Paulinus of Antioch of summer 376, on which see below. Among the other letters written during the years Jerome was in Syria, 8 and 12 carry no specific indications of date; 9 was written after Heliodorus's return to the West in 374; 13 was probably also written after 374, since Jerome says his quarrel with his aunt Castorina in Dalmatia has endured for several years; letter 10 too, sent as a cover letter to Paul of Concordia with the *Life of Paul the First Hermit,* should probably be dated after Jerome's move to the desert.

34. Letter 15.5.

35. Letter 16.2: *hinc enim praesidiis fulta mundi Arriana rabies fremit.* In late 377 Valens revoked his sentence of exile on the orthodox bishops. Kelly, *Jerome,* 52 with n. 28, citing Cavallera, *Saint Jérôme,* 2:16, argues that Jerome's words in letter 16 (just cited) date the letter to before Valens's action.

of 375. Jerome would not have expected an immediate response. Perhaps, then, his second letter to Damasus was written the following spring, before the arrival of Damasus's letter in Antioch.[36] The letter to Marcus, which reveals no knowledge of Damasus's letter, might have been written in late 375. So we may conclude that Jerome probably left the desert to return to Antioch in 376, before the arrival of Damasus's letter.

In 376, Epiphanius, a monk from Palestine who had become bishop of Salamis in Cyprus, came to Antioch, where he publicly declared his support for the episcopacy of Paulinus. As discussed in chapter 3 above, Jerome's friendship with Epiphanius, which presumably dated from this visit, was to play a central role in several later phases of his life.[37] Some time during his years at Antioch, Jerome was ordained a priest by Paulinus. It is logical to suppose that this took place after his return from the desert, when he had abandoned—at least for the moment—his earlier monastic ambitions.

Chronology

373–early 375

Letters 2 (to Theodosius and a group of monks);[38] 1 (to Innocentius);[39] 3 (to Rufinus in Jerusalem);[40] 4 (to Florentinus in Jerusalem)[41]

---

36. Given the difficulty of sending letters between the East and Rome in the winter season when sailing was all but suspended, it is hard to account for Jerome's two letters arriving at Rome before Damasus wrote to Paulinus. But perhaps Jerome wrote letter 15 in 375 or early 376, and it reached Damasus before he wrote his letter to Paulinus; Jerome's second letter could have been sent after Damasus replied in summer 376, but before his letter reached Antioch. For the importance of the shipping season for dating correspondence between East and West, see Pierre Nautin, "Études (393–397)," setting forth the principle, but cf. also the caveats of Jay, *Exégèse*, 407–9. On shipping in the Roman Mediterranean, see Rougé, *Ships and Fleets*.

37. Cavallera, *Schisme*, 195–96.

38. The letter was written before the death of Innocentius, a friend of Evagrius's, in 374 (Kelly, *Jerome*, 33 n. 43).

39. The addressee, Innocentius, died in 374.

40. The letter informs Rufinus of Innocentius's death: letter 3.3: *Syria uelut fidissimus naufrago portus occurrit. ubi ego quicquid morborum esse poterat expertus e duobus oculis unum perdidi; Innocentium enim, partem animae meae, repentinus febrium ardor abstraxit. nunc uno et toto mihi lumine Euagrio nostro fruor, cui ego semper infirmus quidam ad laborem cumulus accessi.* The letter also mentions the death of the slave of Melania the Elder, Hylas, who was also a convert to asceticism, suggesting that Rufinus's association with Melania was well known by this time. However, the fact that Jerome sent these letters to Rufinus in Jerusalem, when he was in fact in Egypt at the time, implies that Jerome's information was less than perfect.

41. This letter accompanied letter 3.

375

Jerome moves to the desert outside Antioch. Commentary on Obadiah (now lost)

375–76

Letters 5 (to Florentinus); 6 (to Julian); 7 (to Chromatius and friends); 11 (to the virgins at Emona); 14 (to Heliodorus, written shortly after Heliodorus's departure when Jerome had just moved to the desert); 15 (to Damasus, summer 375); 17 (to the priest Marcus, winter 375); 16 (to Damasus, spring 376)

373–80

Letters 8 (to Niceas of Aquileia); 12 (to Anthony, a monk at Emona)

Letters 9 (to Chrysocomas, a monk at Aquileia, after Heliodorus's return to the West in 374); 13 (to Castorina, Jerome's maternal aunt, probably also after 374) [42]

Life of Paul the First Hermit and letter 10 (cover letter dedicating it to Paul of Concordia), probably after Jerome's return to Antioch [43]

Altercatio Luciferiani et Orthodoxi, date unknown, perhaps after Jerome's return to Antioch in 376 [44]

4. CONSTANTINOPLE, 381–82

For the next period of Jerome's life, the main controversy has been over the timing and motivation of his departure for Constantinople. It is certain that Jerome went to Constantinople some time after the fall of Valens in the battle of Adrianople in 378 and that he left the city to attend the Council of Rome in 382. In November 380, within a few days of his official entry into the city, the new emperor Theodosius removed the Arian bishop of Constantinople and replaced him with the leader of the tiny Nicene congregation in the city, Gregory of Nazianzus.[45] At the same time, he sent out letters convening a council at Constantinople, in part to resolve the disputed episcopal succession of Antioch.[46]

Few scholars have given these events their proper role in the chronology

---

42. In the letter, Jerome says his quarrel with his addressee, his aunt Castorina in Dalmatia, has endured for several years.

43. Cavallera, *Saint Jérôme*, 2:16–17.

44. Cavallera, *Saint Jérôme*, 2:18–19; Kelly, *Jerome*, 62–64.

45. For this dating, see Matthews, *Western Aristocracies*, 123–25; Rebenich, *Hieronymus*.

46. Cavallera, *Schisme*, 211ff.

of Jerome's movements. Likely, Jerome's motivation for going to Constantinople was to attend this council. In a later work, Jerome specifically refers to his presence at the Council of Constantinople, together with his new friend, the priest Vincentius.[47] Furthermore, when Jerome left Constantinople for Rome, it was in the company of two protagonists of the controversy, Paulinus and Epiphanius, and in order to attend a further council convened to address the situation. Given this information, it is hard to avoid the conclusion that Jerome had initially gone to the Eastern capital in the same connection.[48]

Chronology

381–82

Translation and extension of Eusebius's *Chronicon* (dedicated to Vincentius and Gallienus)

Translations of Origen's homilies on Ezekiel (dedicated to Vincentius), and on Isaiah and Jeremiah (no dedications)

Letters 18A and 18B (to Damasus, on the exegesis of the Psalms)

5. ROME, 382–85

The primary chronological problem for this period of Jerome's career has been created by challenges to the authenticity of his Roman correspondence, and to the accuracy of his account of his relations with Damasus. The latter problem has been discussed above, in chapter 1. Here, I will restrict myself to the issue of the Roman correspondence.

Certain scholars have questioned the dating of many of the letters ascribed to Jerome's years in Rome in the 380s. These writers have argued that parts of the correspondence with Damasus (specifically letters 35 and 36), letter 33, the catalogue of Origen's works addressed to Paula, and the entire dossier of letters to Marcella in fact date to the period 386–92, after Jerome's departure for Bethlehem but before the publication of *On Famous Men*, where they are listed in the catalogue of Jerome's works. The evidence these scholars present may point to some editorial work on the letters before their official publication by Jerome in Palestine after 385, but it does not suffice to support a wholesale redating of the letters.

---

47. Jerome, *Contra Ioh. Hier.*, 41, cited by Clark, *Origenist Controversy*, 31 n.191.

48. See Kelly, *Jerome*, 66–67; Rebenich, *Hieronymus*, 115–17; Cavallera, *Saint Jérôme*, 2:20–22.

Pierre Nautin, in a late article, contended that the letters printed as 35 and 36 in Jerome's collection were not an actual exchange of letters between Damasus and Jerome but a fiction created by Jerome after Damasus's death and Jerome's flight to Palestine.[49] Nautin argues against the authenticity of these two letters on the following grounds: Damasus's letter contains typically Hieronymian phraseology; the content of the two letters is not in keeping with Damasus's dignity as a pope of Rome; and, finally, the questions Damasus poses to Jerome are suspiciously parallel to some of those addressed by the anonymous Roman writer known as Ambrosiaster in a contemporary exegetical work. None of these arguments is persuasive.[50] They are sufficient to suggest only that Jerome might have retouched an authentic letter of Damasus after the bishop's death and before he published a collected correspondence.

Ilona Opelt has challenged the authenticity of Jerome's letter 33, the catalogue of Origen's works addressed to Paula.[51] Opelt's argument turns on the following observations: letter 33 expresses a polemic against nameless enemies of Origen; the language of this polemic is similar to that of Jerome's attack on Jovinian in 393, and also to language Jerome uses against Rufinus in 401; similar formulae occur in Jerome's letter 50, a defense of *Against Jovinian*, which was also written in 393; and the enmity of the nameless attackers to whom Jerome alludes in letter 33 would not have been possible during Damasus's lifetime. Thus, letter 33 dates to the period just before the composition of *On Famous Men* in 392–93, which refers explicitly to the letter. Again, none of these arguments withstands closer examination.[52] But

---

49. Nautin, "Premier échange."

50. First, the similarity between the two sets of exegetical problems, if anything, argues that Jerome did write letter 36 at Rome before 385. The presence of the same problems in the work of Ambrosiaster establishes that these questions were current in that place and time. If Jerome did in fact concoct this list of problems in an attempt to rival the work of Ambrosiaster, all the more reason to think that he did so when Ambrosiaster was a live presence rather than a distant memory. Second, Nautin's criticism of the language and actions of Jerome and his patron as inappropriate for the relations of a young priest to a pope is simply anachronistic. Nautin appears to have a modern, or at least a Counter-Reformation, pope in mind. Finally, Nautin's description of the language of letter 35 as typically Hieronymian is not confirmed by a check of the CETEDOC Christian Latin Fathers database: none of the locutions cited is unique to Jerome; several occur frequently among Jerome's contemporaries.

51. Opelt, "Origene," cited in Vessey, "Jerome's Origen," 139 n. 14.

52. The notion that Jerome had no enemies during Damasus's lifetime seems improbable: if this were the case, whence did the opposition that drove him from Rome after his patron's death so suddenly emerge? Further, Opelt's claim that previous readers of the letter had failed to note its polemical quality ignores Vallarsi's interpretation (printed in the notes to the PL) of the references to Epicurus and Aristippus: *Romani Presbyteri his traducuntur nominibus qui Hieronymum statim*

there is evidence that letter 33 may have circulated in a variant form, without the dedication to Paula.[53]

Building on the challenges of Nautin and Opelt, Mark Vessey insinuates that the figure of Marcella as Jerome paints her in his letters from the period at Rome contains an element of fiction.[54] However, the concreteness of Jerome's mention of Marcella in letter 47, written in 393, where he refers a correspondent to her as a source of his works at Rome, makes Vessey's suggestion less than plausible.[55] Rufinus, too, refers to Marcella in his *Apologia contra Hieronymum*, in which he attacks her in veiled terms for her anti-Origenist activities at Rome in the late 390s.[56] Surely, if Jerome had forged letters to her, Rufinus would have pointed it out, in a polemic that makes so much of other distortions in Jerome's self-descriptions as a writer. We have no reason, therefore, to consider Jerome's relations with Marcella during his years at Rome a fiction created ten years later.

None of the writers who have criticized the dating of individual letters or groups of letters traditionally assigned to this period has considered the implications for Jerome's biography of reassigning the entire corpus to the period after 385. The works that Jerome produced shortly after his relocation to Bethlehem, such as the commentaries on Ecclesiastes and on the four Pauline epistles, already presuppose an understanding of the authority of the Hebrew text developed in the disputed letters. Furthermore, Jerome's letters from 393, notably letter 52, depict him as long silent, withdrawn from controversy since his departure for Bethlehem. This image is out of keeping

---

a Damasi obitu insectabantur. Initially, the connection of the reference to Aristippus and Epicurus with the *Adv. Iov.* and the *Contra Ruf.* seems more robust. Aristippus appears six times in Jerome's work: Opelt cites all of these except for a mention in the *Comm. in Eccles.*, which is nonpolemical; of 32 references to Epicurus, all of those that carry a polemical application to a specific person appear in either the *Adv. Iov.* and letter 50, or the *Contra Ruf.* However, this argument is inconclusive: the separation in time of the two datable appearances of this language, in 393 and 401, shows that Jerome was capable of developing a polemical motif, then reusing it many years later when his target seemed to warrant it. Finally, Jerome in the *De vir. ill.* could not refer his readers to letter 33 for a catalogue of Origen's works if that letter was not already widely available. Given the conditions under which literary works circulated in the late fourth century, it seems more plausible that, just as Jerome claimed, letter 33 had already been published some time before the *De vir. ill.* itself.

53. Vessey, "Jerome's Origen," 139 n. 14, adducing Rufinus, *Apol.* 2.12.

54. Vessey, "Jerome's Origen," 144. Rebenich, *Hieronymus*, 154–70, accepts the relationship and the outlines of Jerome's depiction of Marcella.

55. Letter 47.3

56. Rufinus, *Apol.* 1.19. He says little explicitly of Marcella, but it is clear that (like Jerome) he sees her as the prime mover behind anti-Origenist activity at Rome.

with the idea that Jerome was actively issuing forged letters throughout the intervening period. Finally, some of the arguments advanced contradict each other: for example, if the intimacy between Damasus and Jerome were sufficient to make it improbable that Jerome should feel the need to engage in polemic during his patron's lifetime, as Opelt claims, then the correspondence attacked by Nautin on the grounds of Jerome's irreverence stands every chance of being authentic. The traditional problem, of placing the Roman letters in relation to each other within the period 382–85, therefore remains, and Cavallera's proposed chronology should be reinstated as the best available solution.

Chronology

382
    Fall: Jerome arrives in Rome
383
    Letter 19 (to Damasus)
    Against Helvidius (no dedication)
383–4
    Translation of Origen's homilies on the Song of Songs (for Damasus)
384
    Spring: Letter 22 (to Eustochium)
    June: Letters 30 (to Paula); 31 (to Eustochium)
    July: Letter 32 (to Marcella)
    Fall: Letter 38 (to Marcella)
    October: Letters 23 (to Marcella, on the death of Leah); 24 (to Marcella, on Asella)
    Late fall: Death of Blesilla
    November: Letter 39 (to Paula, on the death of Blesilla)
    Before December: Letter 35 (Damasus to Jerome), 36 (Jerome to Damasus)
    December 11: Death of Damasus; election of Siricius as bishop of Rome
    Precise dates unknown: Revision of the Gospels against the Greek for Damasus; Letters 26, 27, 28, 29, 25, 24, 40 to Marcella; Revision of the Psalter against the Greek (the so-called *Psalterium Romanum*)
385
    Before August: Letters 37, 41, 42, 43, 44 (to Marcella), 33 (to Paula, on Origen)
    August: Letter 45 (to Marcella, in farewell as Jerome departs for the East)

6. EARLY YEARS IN PALESTINE, 386–92

The six years from 386 to 392 were ones of extraordinary literary productivity for Jerome. He arrived in Bethlehem in December 385,[57] then spent the spring traveling in Egypt and Palestine. By summer, it seems, he had begun the series of exegetical, hagiographic, and other works that were to fill his next years. No letters survive from this period except Jerome's letter 46, written in the personae of Paula and Eustochium to Marcella at Rome. On the other hand, *On Famous Men*, which lists almost all the works traditionally ascribed to this period, serves as an endpoint for it.

The key chronological problem here is to place the many works attributed to this period in relation to each other. The framework created by Cavallera now requires much revision. A new chronology must incorporate the proposals of Pierre Nautin, mostly based on his conceptions of how Jerome calculated dates and of how travelers were able to pass between Rome and Bethlehem. Other writers, particularly Pierre Jay and Adam Kamesar, have convincingly put forward new dates for specific works. The list given here follows the new dates of Nautin, Jay, and Kamesar, adhering to Cavallera's original dates only when none of these authors has advanced any suggestions. Where there are difficulties, the date given for each individual work is justified in the notes.

Chronology

386

Early in the year: *Life of Malchus* (no dedication), *Life of Hilarion* (no dedication)[58]

Early spring: Letter 46 (to Marcella at Rome, in the names of Paula and Eustochium)[59]

Summer: Commentaries on Titus, Ephesians, Galatians, and Philemon (Commentary on Galatians dedicated to Paula and Eustochium; remaining Pauline commentaries undedicated)[60]

---

57. Nautin, "Études (suite)," 216.

58. Nautin, "Activité littéraire,"248 n. 8.

59. For this date see Nautin, "Activité littéraire," 258.

60. The Pauline commentaries are traditionally dated to the end of the 380s; Cavallera, *Saint Jérôme*, 27, gives 389 or 390; Kelly, *Jerome*, 145, gives 387–88. They have been convincingly redated by Nautin, "Date des commentaires," to summer 386; but see the caveats of Jay, *Exégèse*,

387

Translation of Didymus, *On the Holy Spirit* (to Paulinian; originally requested by Damasus)[61]

Commentarioli in Psalmos (addressee unidentified in preface)[62]

Tractatus in Psalmos (no dedication)

388-89

Commentary on Ecclesiastes (to Paula and Eustochium)[63]

389-92

Translations *iuxta LXX* of the Solomonic Books (to Paula and Eustochium); of Chronicles (to Domnio and Rogatianus); of Psalms and Job (to Paula and Eustochium)

407-9, accepting Nautin's general line of argument but warning that he aims at excessive precision. There are at least four texts that provide evidence for the date of the commentaries, of which three were noted by Nautin. First, the commentaries are mentioned in the *De uir. ill.* and were therefore written before the beginning of 393. Second, in the preface to book 3 of *Comm. in ep. ad Gal.*, Jerome claims not to have read any secular literature for fifteen years. The allusion is to his famous dream, recounted in letter 22, which, if it occurred at all, would have taken place during his years in Antioch, 373-79. This evidence thus implies a date for the commentary of 388-94. Third, in the *Contra Ioh. Hier.* 17, Jerome says that the commentaries on Ecclesiastes and Ephesians were written "about ten years ago." Since the *Contra Iohannem* was written in 396, the date implied is about 386. This evidence was overlooked by Nautin. Finally, in his *Contra Ruf.* I.22, Jerome says that he wrote his *Comm. in Eph.* "about eighteen years ago." Since *Contra Ruf.* was written in 401, this implies a date of 383, which is clearly impossible. Nautin explains the reference as actually meaning 386, because Jerome counted the years inclusively based on a consular table. Nautin's reasoning is over-clever, but reinforced by the evidence of the *Contra Ioh.*, his arguments for a date of 386 become more convincing. Perhaps the best answer is to date the Pauline commentaries to the years 386-88, after Jerome settled in Bethlehem but before the composition of the *Comm. in Eccles.*

61. Dated positively to 387 by Nautin, "Activité littéraire," 257-58.

62. If this work must be dated before 393, despite its absence from the *De uir. ill.*, its Old Latin lemma of unknown origin should place it earlier than the Commentary on Ecclesiastes. Cavallera gives a range of 389-93: "Les *Commentarioli in Psalmos* sont antérieurs à la traduction du Psautier, comme il ressort de la controverse, sur le psaume II, avec Rufin (Jérôme, *Apol.* I, 19 ; PL XXIII, 413, A B)." He describes the Psalms text of the *Commentarioli* as "une version latin qui ne s'identifie avec aucune des versions hiéronymiennes et qui peut être une traduction directe sur le grec des Septante, faite par saint Jérôme à mesure qu'il dicte ses remarques" (*Saint Jérôme*, 2:30). Kelly, *Jerome*, 157, describes his text as "a fresh rendering from the Greek with careful attention to the Hebrew," citing A. Vaccari, *Scritti di erudizione e di filologia*, 1 (Rome: 1952): 213f.

63. The commentary is dated by Jerome's remark in the preface that Blesilla's death in 384 was "about fifteen years ago" (*ante hoc ferme quinquennium*). Nautin, "Activité littéraire," 251-52, unequivocally supports 388; his application of his own view on Jerome's method of calculating dates, i.e., using a consular table and counting inclusively, seems overprecise in this case.

Translation of Psalms *iuxta Hebraeos*[64] (first translation *iuxta Hebraeos*, dedicated to Sophronius)

Translations *iuxta Hebraeos* of the Prophets (to Paula and Eustochium); of Samuel and Kings (to Domnio and Rogatianus); and of Job (no dedication)

390

Book of Hebrew Names (to Lupulus and Valerianus)[65]

Liber nominum Hebraicorum locorum (no dedication)

392 – early 393

Hebrew Questions on Genesis (no dedication)[66]

Translation of Origen's *Homilies on Luke* (to Paula and Eustochium)[67]

Winter: Commentaries on Nahum (to Paula and Eustochium); on Micah (to Paula and Eustochium); on Zephaniah (to Paula and Eustochium); on Haggai (to Paula and Eustochium); on Habbakuk (to Chromatius of Aquileia)[68]

---

64. Kedar, "Vulgate," attempted to provide independent support for Jay's arguments in favor of re-dating the first translations from the changes in translation technique apparent between the different books. The translation of Job, which had already reached audiences in North Africa by ca. 395 (Cavallera, *Saint Jérôme,* 2:48), may be as early as 389 (Cavallera, 2:157, says 389-92); the preface to Joshua may be as late as 404 or 405 (Cavallera 2:290-91). Jerome cites the prefaces to Job and Ezra at length and verbatim in his *Contra Ruf.* 2.28-29. Thus they must be earlier than the *Apol.,* written in 401.

65. Nautin, "Activité littéraire," 253-56, dates this work to 390; he associates this work with the *De nom. Hebr. loc.* and *Quaest. Hebr. in Gen.;* the latter, however, seems a work of a different kind.

66. Jerome was working on the *Quaest. Hebr. in Gen.* when he made the translation of Origen's homilies on Luke. In the preface to that translation he complains that this project had interrupted the work on the *Quaestiones.* This suggests that this translation should be dated *before* the publication of the *Quaestiones.* See Nautin, "Activité littéraire," 253-56, dating this work to 390. However, Nautin's criteria for choosing a particular date between 390 and 392 are somewhat arbitrary and perhaps predicated on a cynical estimate of Jerome's contribution in these works, particularly the *Quaestiones,* to which he refers rather sneeringly. Kamesar, *Jerome,* 76, dates the *Quaestiones* to 392.

67. Kamesar, *Jerome,* 74; Nautin, "Activité littéraire," 252-53, dates the translation on the basis of its relation to the publication of Ambrose's commentary on Luke, which itself followed his own *Apology of David,* dated by its correlation with the massacre of Thessalonica in April or May 390.

68. The primary data supporting this chronology for the Minor Prophets commentaries appear in the prefaces to the commentaries on Jonah and Amos. See the discussion of Cavallera, *Saint Jérôme,* for the identification of the evidence and its basic significance. His dates are about six to twelve months earlier than those given in the text. Nautin, "Études (suite et fin)," 257, 77-79 places the chronology in a new framework. He dates the first five commentaries to the first three months of 393, and the commentaries on Jonah and Obadiah, to shortly after Easter (April 5) 397, when Jerome and Rufinus were reconciled.

7. THE BEGINNING OF THE ORIGENIST CONTROVERSY, 393-96

This period saw both the appearance of many of Jerome's most important early works, and the first phase of the Origenist controversy. Unlike the previous six years, for this period many of Jerome's letters survive. Thus the chronological problems are particularly complex, involving the correlation of events in the ongoing controversy in Palestine, Egypt, and elsewhere with Jerome's correspondence and with his literary production in other modes. A crucial issue that emerges here for the first time is the reconstruction of the dossiers of letters and other works that Jerome sent West every year during the navigation season, and the identification where possible of the messengers who carried them.

In 393 alone, Jerome completed the first five of his commentaries on the Minor Prophets; *On Famous Men; Against Jovinian* and, probably, letter 49 to Pammachius defending that treatise against its Roman critics; and a number of other letters.

At the same time, the Origenist controversy erupted in Palestine with a series of challenges from Jerome's old friend Epiphanius of Salamis. The monk Atarbius, sent by Epiphanius, approached both Jerome and Rufinus to demand that they sign an anti-Origenist formula. Jerome complied; Rufinus refused. In September 393, during the feast of the Encaenia, Epiphanius himself preached an anti-Origenist sermon in one of the principal churches of Jerusalem, implicitly accusing the city's bishop, John, of Origenist heresy. John replied the next day with a sermon defending his orthodoxy but evading the specific charges leveled by Epiphanius.

In 394, after Pentecost, Epiphanius returned from Cyprus to Palestine, where he ordained Paulinian, Jerome's younger brother, as a priest, and wrote a letter accusing John of Jerusalem of Origenist heresy, which he circulated among the monks of Palestine.[69] Ostensibly on the grounds of the irregular ordination of Paulinian by a foreign bishop on John's territory, John of Jerusalem excommunicated Jerome and his monks in the spring or summer of 394.[70] The breach was to last until Easter 397.

Probably also in 394, Jerome received several visitors from the West: the monk Oceanus and the converted divorcée Fabiola from Rome,[71] and the

---

69. Nautin, "Études (suite et fin)," 277, and Nautin, "Études (suite)," 76-78.

70. Nautin, "Excommunication"; they remain excommunicated until Easter 397 (at least according to Nautin's argumentation, which is somewhat tendentious).

71. Nautin, "Études (suite et fin)," 278, gives the date as 395, "après la reprise de la navigation."

priest Vigilantius, a protégé of Sulpicius Severus and the emissary of Sulpicius's friend Paulinus of Nola.[72] Toward the end of the year, Jerome translated Epiphanius's anti-Origenist letter for the use of one of his monastic
companions, the Latin Eusebius of Cremona.[73]

The year 395 saw further disruptions. In July, the Huns threatened to attack Palestine. Jerome's visitors—Oceanus, Fabiola, and probably Vigilantius as well—departed for the West. Jerome himself was threatened with exile: John of Jerusalem and his allies at court obtained a decree against him
from the praetorian prefect of Constantinople, Rufinus, which was rendered
ineffective only by that official's death on November 27, 395.[74]

By 396, Jerome's translation of Epiphanius's anti-Origenist letter had become public, leading to charges of mistranslation by Jerome's opponents. At
the same time, Vigilantius, who had returned to his homeland in Gaul, had
begun to attack his former host Jerome, accusing him among other things of
Origenist heresy. Jerome wrote his letter 61 to Vigilantius in an attempt to
defuse these charges, probably in summer 396.[75]

---

72. Vigilantius arrives at Bethelehem with a letter from Paulinus of Nola and a copy of his panegyric of Theodosius I. He departs with Jerome's letter 58 to Paulinus in 395. See Nautin, "Études
(suite)," 213–39, for the dating of Vigilantius's visit and of the first phase of the correspondence
between Jerome and Paulinus of Nola. Vigilantius was a protégé of Sulpicius Severus in Gaul,
who made the connection between Vigilantius and his close friend Paulinus of Nola.

73. See letter 57.2, where Jerome describes the circumstances of his making the translation at the
request of Eusebius of Cremona. The description there places the making of the translation
shortly after the composition and release of the letter, in the context of the interest it immediately
aroused among the monks of Palestine. However, the translation remained secreted in Eusebius's
desk (*scriniis eius*) for a year and six months (*anno et sex mensibus*), at which point it was stolen
by a nameless monk who rummaged through Eusebius's papers and stole Jerome's translation
(*conpilatis chartis eius et sumptibus Iudas factus est proditor deditque aduersariis latrandi contra me
occasionem*). The translation, therefore, was made in mid-394, but began to circulate only in late
396, eighteen months later.

74. Cavallera, *Saint Jérôme*, 2 : 46; Nautin, "Études (suite)," 78 and n. 35, citing Socrates, *Historia
ecclesiastica*, 6.1.

75. There has been some disagreement over the date of letter 61. Cavallera, *Saint Jérôme*, 2 : 45,
dates letter 61 to 396, stating that "La date de la lettre LXI, à Vigilance, dépend de celle de la lettre LVIII, puisque c'est à son retour de Palestine qui Vigilance se mit à déblatérer sur le compte
de Jérôme." This argument remains persuasive, despite later attempts to re-date the letter. Nautin, "Études (suite)," 232, dates the letter to 399, without argumentation. Rebenich, *Hieronymus*,
240 with n. 32, places the letter in "388 oder 399 [*sic*]." The later date allows Rebenich to connect Vigilantius's attacks on Jerome with the second phase of the Origenist controversy, after
the return of Rufinus to Italy, where Rebenich envisions Vigilantius as a member of Rufinus's
"circle"; see Rebenich, *Hieronymus*, 243. Pronberger, *Beiträge*, 50–51, on whose analysis Rebenich bases his own interpretation, argues that letter 61, which he sees as concerned with controversies over Origen at Rome, can therefore only be dated after 397. But Jerome's language in
letter 61 in fact suggests that Vigilantius has returned to Gaul, and that it is from there, not from

It may be possible to reconstruct a dossier of letters and other works that Jerome and Epiphanius of Salamis sent to Rome in summer 396 to respond to John of Jerusalem's appeal to Siricius of Rome. The dossier would have included Jerome's letter 57 *On the Best Method of Translation* (a defense of his translation of Epiphanius's letter against John, addressed to Pammachius); a copy of Epiphanius's original letter against John in Greek; a letter of Epiphanius to Siricius; and Jerome's letter 60 to Heliodorus on the death of Nepotian.[76]

Jerome's *Against John of Jerusalem*, another polemical work intended for a Western audience, was probably written in the winter of 396–97 and reached the West in the spring of 397.[77] This treatise finds close echoes in letter 82 to Theophilus of Alexandria, another work from the end of 396.[78] During the same months, Jerome found time to complete two further commentaries on the Minor Prophets: his treatments of Obadiah (dedicated to Pammachius) and Jonah (dedicated to Chromatius of Aquileia).[79]

Chronology

393

Easter 393: Epiphanius of Salamis visits Jerusalem
On Famous Men (to Dexter)

Italy, that word of his criticisms has reached Bethlehem: letter 61.3.1, *scilicet gloriari cupis, ut in patria tua iactites me non potuisse respondere eloquentiae tuae et acumen in te Chrysippe formidasse.* Letter 61.4 makes clear that Vigilantius himself has written extensively attacking Jerome, though the genre and precise subject matter are unclear; Jerome's discussion suggests that some of Vigilantius's writings contained exegetical material. Later, Jerome did connect Rufinus and Vigilantius: Jerome, *Contra Ruf.* 3.19, cited at Clark, *Origenist Controversy*, 36 n. 249. On balance, however, it seems more persuasive to think of Vigilantius's attacks on Jerome, which the latter attempted to refute in letter 61, as an earlier, separate controversy centered in Gaul, rather than a facet of the second-phase Origenist controversy in Italy. For a conclusive discussion, supporting the same date that I give, see Trout, *Paulinus*, 221 n. 136.

76. Nautin, "Études (suite et fin)," 279, places letter 57 in summer 396. However, in the *Contra Ioh. Hier.*, Jerome recounts that he translated Epiphanius's letter for Eusebius of Cremona six months after it was written (after Pentecost 394), but the translation was only released eighteen months later, i.e., in late spring 396. This does not allow much time for the translation of Epiphanius's letter of 394 to reach Italy and cause a controversy, word of which then got back to Jerome in Palestine. It might then be more reasonable to date letter 57 to winter 396 and its arrival in Rome to the following spring, in the same dossier as the *Contra Iohannem*.

77. Nautin, "Études (suite et fin)," 279.

78. Nautin, "Études (suite et fin)," 279.

79. Cavallera, *Saint Jérôme*, 2:159.

Against Jovinian (no dedication, sent to Pammachius)

Letters 50 (to Domnio), 48, 49 (to Pammachius), 47 (to Desiderius), 53 (to Paulinus of Nola), 59 (to Marcella)

Augustine, Letter 27*, Jerome to Aurelius of Carthage (perhaps written in 393)[80]

Letters 55 (to Amandus, written between 393 and 397) and 106 (to Sunnia and Fretela, written between 393 and 401)

394

Translation *iuxta Hebraeos* of Ezra and Nehemiah (to Domnio and Rogatianus)

Early in the year: Ordination of Paulinian by Epiphanius of Salamis; letters of Epiphanius to John of Jerusalem and to the monks of Palestine

Spring–summer 394: Excommunication of Jerome and his monks by John of Jerusalem[81]

Late in the year: Letter 51 (translation of a letter of Epiphanius of Salamis to John of Jerusalem)

Precise date unknown: Letter 52 (to Nepotian, nephew of Heliodorus of Altinum)

394–95

Letters 54 (to Furia); 56 (Augustine to Jerome, letter 28 among Augustine's letters)

395

Letter 58 (to Paulinus of Nola)

396

Translation *iuxta Hebraeos* of Chronicles (to Chromatius of Aquileia)

Summer: Letters 57 (to Pammachius); 60 (to Heliodorus of Altinum, a consolatory epistle on the death of Nepotian); 61 (to Vigilantius)

---

80. The two works that Jerome sent to Aurelius were written in 392 (the *Quaest. Hebr. in Gen.* and seven tractates on Pss. 10–16, mentioned in *De vir. ill.* 135; see Nautin, "Activité littéraire"); thus the letter cannot be earlier than 392. On the other hand, in the letter to Aurelius, Jerome denies having written a commentary on Matthew. In 398, however, he did write a commentary on Matthew, which he dedicated to Eusebius of Cremona. The letter under discussion also mentions Eusebius as a resident of Jerome's monastery. In spring 398, however, Eusebius departed for the West, taking the new commentary on Matthew with him. The letter must therefore be earlier than spring 398. Finally, Jerome wrote the letter to congratulate Aurelius on his election to the bishopric of Carthage, which must have taken place already by October 393 when Aurelius presided at the Council of Hippo. It is most likely, therefore, that Jerome wrote the letter relatively soon after Aurelius's election. A date as late as 395 is not unimaginable, but ca. 393 seems most plausible. (See Duval, "Notes complémentaires," 561 for this dating.)

81. Nautin, "Excommunication," 14–18.

Winter 396-97: *Against John of Jerusalem* (to Pammachius); letter 82 (to Theophilus of Alexandria); commentary on Jonah (to Chromatius); commentary on Obadiah (to Pammachius)

8. BROADENING OF THE ORIGENIST CONTROVERSY, 397-402

The years 397-402 began with the healing of the rupture between Jerome and his old friend Rufinus that Epiphanius's anti-Origenist interventions had occasioned, only to end with a final break between the two friends, symbolized by their mutual *Apologies,* written in 401-2.

Around the time of the celebration of Easter in 397, which fell on April 5 that year, John of Jerusalem lifted his excommunication of Jerome and his monks, and Jerome and Rufinus were publicly reconciled in the church of the Anastasis. Jerome's letter 64 to Fabiola was written immediately after the reconciliation. Shortly thereafter, probably before Pentecost, Jerome sent Vincentius to Rome bearing the commentaries on Obadiah and Jonah, *Against John,* letter 64 to Fabiola, and a copy of letter 82 to Theophilus.[82]

After Pentecost, Rufinus himself departed from Jerusalem for the West, never to return. That summer, at Rome, he translated the *Apology for Origen* of Pamphilus and Eusebius; in the preface, he defends himself against attacks made by Jerome in *Against John.*[83] He accompanied this translation with a treatise on the adulteration of the works of Origen.

Toward the end of 397, Jerome fell seriously ill.[84] He was unable to work until the spring of 398, recovering only shortly before Easter.[85] His recovery saw a renewed spate of literary productivity: he composed several letters, a commentary on Matthew written for Eusebius of Cremona immediately before he left for Italy,[86] and his translations of the Solomonic books

---

82. See Nautin, "Études (suite et fin)," 275, for the identification of Vincentius as the bearer of these items.

83. See Rufinus, *Apol.* 1.11, on Macarius's dream and his repeated requests to Rufinus for translations of Origen, immediately after Rufinus's arrival in Rome from Palestine; Rufinus first translates the Apology for Origen, and states that he tried to excuse himself from making the translation by saying that he had had no practice with this kind of work for nearly thirty years.

84. Letter 71.7, to Lucinus of Baetica: *longo tentus incommodo uix diebus quadragesimae* [i.e., Lent], *quibus ipsi proficiscebantur, respirare coepi.*

85. Cavallera, *Saint Jérôme,* 2:159.

86. For the dating, see Cavallera, *Saint Jérôme,* 2:159. The preface to the commentary on Matthew refers to Jerome's recent illness and to Eusebius's imminent departure for the West, where Jerome expects him to visit Rome, where he will be able to give a copy of the commentary to the

from the Hebrew, dedicated to Heliodorus of Altinum and Chromatius of Aquileia.[87]

After Easter 398, Jerome's brother Paulinian and Eusebius of Cremona both left for the West. Eusebius took with him the commentary on Matthew, letter 44 to Principia at Rome, letter 66 to Pammachius on the death of his wife Paulina, and probably also Jerome's new translations from the Hebrew, which were dedicated to Italians.[88]

During the same Lent, at Rome, Rufinus was translating books 1 and 2 of Origen's *On First Principles,* with a preface in which he invoked Jerome's authority for the project. After Easter, he translated books 3 and 4 of the same work, with a new preface.[89] This project, and the reaction it evoked among Jerome's friends in the West, were to lead to the final rupture between the two boyhood friends.

By autumn of 398, Eusebius of Cremona had obtained copies of Rufinus's versions of *On First Principles,* which he disseminated across Italy, accusing Rufinus of heresy. Sometime this year, Jerome's friends Pammachius and Oceanus wrote an urgent letter to Jerome, requesting a literal translation of *On First Principles* that could be compared with Rufinus's expurgated version.[90] Jerome probably began work on the translation immediately, since he sent it west in the spring of 399.

Jerome's emissary in 399, Rufinus the Syrian, who was the guest of Pammachius at Rome, carried Jerome's letters 84 and 81.[91] Letter 84 served as a cover and defense for Jerome's version of *On First Principles,* as well as a reply to Rufinus's imputations in the latter's preface to *his* translation. In letter 84, Jerome defended his orthodoxy while attacking the unnamed but easily recognizable Rufinus. Letter 81 was a friendly letter addresssed directly to Rufinus at Aquileia. Jerome's friends suppressed letter 81 and cir-

---

virgin Principia, the companion of Marcella, who had asked Jerome to compose a commentary on the Song of Songs. Principia was the addressee of Jerome's letter 65, also written at this time.

87. Mention in the preface of a "long illness" followed by the preparation of the translation in eight days points to a date in the spring, when Jerome also wrote the commentary on Matthew and letter 71 to Lucinus. Cavallera, *Saint Jérôme,* 2:160, dates this translation to summer 398, but this date contradicts the notice in letter 71 to Lucinus that at that time Jerome had completed the translation of the entire Bible from the Hebrew *excepto octateucho,* "except the Octateuch," i.e., the Pentateuch plus Joshua, Judges, and Ruth. It seems more plausible to place these translations a bit earlier in the year, in time for Eusebius of Cremona to carry them to Italy.

88. Cavallera, *Saint Jérôme,* 2:160, with the modifications proposed in note 87.

89. Cavallera, *Saint Jérôme,* 2:160.

90. The letter is preserved as Jerome, letter 83.

91. On the identity of Rufinus the Syrian, see Wermelinger, *Rom und Pelagius,* 13, against Marrou, "Attaches orientales."

culated letter 84 publicly.[92] Rufinus's friend and frequent dedicatee Aproni-
anus sent Rufinus a copy of letter 84, probably soon after it reached Italy.[93]
The letter alienated Rufinus and may have been the stimulus for his *Apology*
against Jerome.

Early in 400, Theophilus of Alexandria altered his position on Origenism, from neutrality to violent hostility. His actions were to shape the controversy's final phase, and to extend its reach to the bishop of Constantinople, John Chrysostom. One of Theophilus's first moves was to expel
Origenist monks from Nitria. These monks, led by the so-called Tall Brothers, went first to Palestine and then to Constantinople, where they appealed
to Chrysostom for protection. During the same months, Theophilus wrote
to Anastasius of Rome seeking a condemnation of Origenism; his emissary stopped off in Bethlehem to visit Jerome. Later in the year, Theophilus
wrote another anti-Origenist letter to the bishops of Palestine and Cyprus.[94]
A synod held at Jerusalem produced a reply. Jerome was in the thick of the
debate, acting as Theophilus's Latin translator, as he would do during the
rest of the controversy.

During the same year, Eusebius of Cremona appeared at Milan carrying
a letter from Anastasius to Simplician, bishop of Milan, in which he accused
Rufinus of having presented unorthodox views in his translation of *On First
Principles*. Simplician died in August; Anastasius sent another letter to his
successor Venerius, demanding that he reject Origenism. Venerius, together
with Chromatius of Aquileia, acceded to Anastasius's demand, producing a
letter condemning Origenism. Rufinus wrote to Anastasius to excuse himself from appearing at Rome.[95] John of Jerusalem, too, wrote to Anastasius
on Rufinus's behalf. Anastasius's response was a letter prohibiting the reading of Origen.

Sometime in 401, Rufinus finally released his *Apology* against Jerome.[96]

---

92. Letter 81 itself contains information on the chronology of this period: Jerome knows that Rufinus has moved to Aquileia, after a long stay in Rome; he also remarks that his brother Paulinian, who left Bethlehem in 398, was still abroad. Jerome therefore had already received word of
Rufinus's move to Aquileia, which probably took place during winter 398–99, by the time he
sent letter 81 west with Rufinus the Syrian. Thus Rufinus the Syrian probably did not leave immediately at the beginning of the season for navigation, but later in the summer.

93. Hammond, "Last Ten Years," 387.

94. For the date of this letter see Hammond, "Last Ten Years," 375, and Cavallera, *Saint Jérôme*,
2:161, specifying "before September 14."

95. Hammond, "Last Ten Years," 388.

96. For the dating of Rufinus's *Apology*, see Hammond, "Last Ten Years," 388. Jerome, in his
own *Apology* written in 401, says that Rufinus has been at work on his *Apology* for three years

Jerome's brother Paulinian, returning to Bethlehem from the west, brought a description of the work but not a copy of it. Jerome began to reply immediately, producing two books of his own *Apology* in 401, before he received Rufinus's.

At Easter 402, Theophilus's paschal letter was a further condemnation of Origen. Jerome translated this letter and sent it west, together with translations made already in 401. The complete dossier included translations of Theophilus's letter to the bishops of Palestine and Cyprus (Jerome, letter 92); the replies of John of Jerusalem and the Palestinian bishops (letters 93, 94); a letter of Theophilus to Epiphanius (letter 90); one from Epiphanius to Jerome (letter 91); Theophilus's Easter pastorals for the years 401 (letter 96) and 402 (letter 98); and Jerome's letter 97, a cover letter for the dossier. Around the same time, Jerome seems finally to have received a copy of Rufinus's attack of the previous year. It was not until after Easter 402, at any rate, that Jerome produced the third book of his *Apology.*

During the summer of 402, Theophilus was summoned to Constantinople to be tried by a synod, the result of his attack on the monks of Nitria two years earlier. The outcome of the synod, however, would be the deposition of John, who had summoned it, and the vindication of the wily Theophilus. With the events of these two years, the tide had turned decisively against the followers of Origen's theology, even to the point of sweeping others away as well.

Chronology

397

Easter 397: reconciliation of Jerome and Rufinus

After Pentecost 397: letter 64 (to Fabiola); Rufinus departs for Italy; Letter 65 (to Principia); literal commentary on the visions of Isaiah (to Amabilis); Letter 68 (to Castricianus)

Summer: Letter 70 (to Magnus, on the use of secular literature); lost letters of Augustine to Jerome and Jerome to Augustine; Rufinus, translation of the *Apology for Origen* of Eusebius and Pamphilus (to Macarius), treatise *De adulteratione librorum Origenis*

Fall: Letter 62 (to Tranquilinus, on reading Origen)

Winter: Jerome is ill for several months

(he refers to Rufinus's work as *libri tui quos limasti per triennium*). If Rufinus began the work in response to the letters of Jerome that reached Italy in summer 399, then 401 would be the earliest possible date, even if Jerome were counting the three years inclusively.

397-98

Letter 145 (to Exsuperantius of Toulouse)

397-99

Augustine, letter 40 (Jerome 67), his second letter to Jerome; Jerome, letter 103 to Augustine introducing Praesidius (these two letters may date to 398 or 399)[97]

Letters 69 (to Oceanus, written between 397 and 400) and 147 (to Sabinianus, date unknown, probably between 397 and 400)

398

January–March: Jerome is ill

Lent 398: Commentary on Matthew (to Eusebius of Cremona), letter 66 (to Pammachius, a consolatory letter on the death of his wife Paulina); Rufinus, translation of books 1 and 2 of *On First Principles* (to Macarius; preface is Jerome, letter 80)

After Easter: Paulinian and Eusebius of Cremona depart for the West

Summer: Letters 71 (to Lucinus), 72 (to Vitalis), 73 (to Evangelus, on Melchisedek), 74 (to Rufinus, a priest of Rome, on the judgment of Solomon); Rufinus, translation of books 3 and 4 of *On First Principles* (to Macarius)

Fall: Letter 83 (Pammachius and Oceanus to Jerome, requesting a literal translation of *On First Principles*)

Death of Lucinus

Rufinus moves to Aquileia[98]

Letter 146 (also to Evangelus, on the priesthood, at an unknown date, probably after 398)

399

Death of Evagrius Ponticus

Literal translation of *On First Principles* (for Pammachius and Oceanus, now lost)

Letters 75 (to Theodora, on the death of her husband Lucinus, addressee of letter 71); 76 (to Abigaus, a blind priest in Spain); 84 (to Pammachius, against Rufinus); 81 (to Rufinus); 63 (to Theophilus of Alexandria); 85 (to Paulinus of Nola)

---

97. An argument has also been made for dating Jerome's letter to 402: see Kelly, *Jerome*, 220, citing Donatien de Bruyne, *Zeitschrift für die neutestamentlichen Wissenschaft* 31 (1932): 233–48.

98. See Jerome letter 127.9, the eulogy of Marcella, addressed to Principia, and written in 413; Hammond, "Last Ten Years," 385–86, is ambiguous on whether the move took place late in 398 or in 399.

November 19: Death of Siricius, succession of Anastasius as bishop of Rome

400

Early in the year: Theophilus of Alexandria expels Origenist monks from Nitria

Letter 77 (to Oceanus on the death of Fabiola); 78 (to Fabiola, posthumously)

Spring: Theophilus of Alexandria writes to Anastasius of Rome against Origenism; Letter 89 (Theophilus of Alexandria to Jerome, brought by Theodore on his way to Rome)

Summer: Letters 86 (to Theophilus of Alexandria); 87 (Theophilus to Jerome); 88 (to Theophilus of Alexandria)

Before August 15: Anastasius of Rome writes to Simplician of Milan urging him to condemn Origenism (letter 95)

Altercation of Eusebius of Cremona and Rufinus at Milan

Rufinus, *Apology* to Anastasius of Rome

Melania the Elder returns to Italy from Jerusalem [99]

August 15: Death of Simplician of Milan, succeeded by Venerius

Before September 14: Theophilus of Alexandria writes to the bishops of Palestine and Cyprus against Origenism (letter 92) and to Epiphanius of Salamis (letter 90)

Epiphanius forwards the letter of Theophilus to Jerome for translation (letter 91)

September 400: Palestinian bishops respond to Theophilus of Alexandria (letter 93); Dionysius of Lydda writes to Theophilus (letter 94)

Anastasius of Rome writes to Venerius of Milan urging him to condemn Origenism

Letter 79 (to Salvina); translation of letters 90, 91, 92, 93, 94

400–402

Jerome's letter 107 (to Laeta, wife of Paula's son Toxotius, on the education of their newborn daughter, Paula the younger, who would eventually head the women's monastery at Bethlehem)

Translation of an anonymous treatise on the visions of Isaiah

401

January: Theophilus of Alexandria, paschal letter for 401 against Origenism, translated shortly afterward by Jerome (letter 96)

---

99. Hammond, "Last Ten Years," 374 n. 2, bases the date upon Paulinus of Nola, letter 29 to Sulpicius Severus, describing her arrival; cf. P. Fabre, *Essai sur la chronologie de l'oeuvre de saint Paulin de Nole* (Strasbourg, 1948), 35–39.

Rufinus, *Apology* against Jerome

Paulinian to Bethlehem with description of Rufinus's *Apology*

Jerome, *Apology* against Rufinus, books 1 and 2

402

Letters 98 (translation of Theophilus of Alexandria, paschal letter for 402); 97 (to Pammachius and Marcella, cover letter for letter 98)

After Easter: *Apology* against Rufinus, book 3 (after receiving the *Apology* of Rufinus)

Summer: Theophilus summoned to Constantinople for trial

Sisinnius to Bethlehem with letter 67 (Augustine to Jerome), found on an island in Dalmatia

Asterius to Bethlehem, bringing letter 101 (Augustine to Jerome); departs with letter 102 (to Augustine) and Jerome, *Apology*, book 3

December 19: Death of Anastasius of Rome, succession of Innocent I

9. CONTROVERSY AND COMMENTARY, 403-9

Between 404 and 409, the disputes that had begun with the Origenist controversy continued, focused on the person of John Chrysostom. At the same time, the material for a new controversy was being created through the teaching of Pelagius and others at Rome. Their ideas, however, would not provoke a reaction until after the sack of Rome in 410, when Pelagius and Caelestius took refuge in North Africa. These six years also saw Jerome complete his commentaries on the Minor Prophets and begin the great commentaries on Daniel and Isaiah that would occupy his final years. The massive work on Isaiah was completed in 410, before word of the sack of Rome had reached Palestine.[100]

The dispute over John Chrysostom's episcopacy, and the involvement of Theophilus of Alexandria, continued for several years. Chrysostom had made himself unpopular with important elements of the imperial court. In 403, when Theophilus presented himself for trial at Constantinople, he succeeded in turning the tables on his accuser and converting the synod convened for his trial into an attack on Chrysostom. The bishop of Con-

---

100. The prefaces to the eighteen books of the commentary on Isaiah track Jerome's progress through the work. In the preface to the first book, Jerome mentions Paula's death (in 404); Pammachius is mentioned as alive. There are no further indications of date until the prefaces to books 13 and 14, which allude to an illness of Jerome's, presumably that of 409. The commentary was complete before Jerome received word of the sack of Rome, as there is no mention in it of those events.

stantinople was outmaneuvered: at Easter 404, his clergy was attacked by imperial troops, and in June of that year he was sent into exile.[101]

Meanwhile, he had sent a delegation west to Italy, which evoked support from a number of prominent Italian bishops, including Chromatius of Aquileia. In early 405, the Italians met in a synod at Rome. They produced a petition for a church council to be convened at Thessalonica, which they sent to the Eastern court with a delegation that included bishops who were closely connected both with Rufinus and Melania and with Julian of Eclanum, who was to become a prominent advocate of Pelagianism in decades to follow. But the Roman delegation returned from Constantinople in humiliation, and Chrysostom was sent into even harsher exile on the eastern borders of the empire. He died in 407.[102]

Melania the Elder, Rufinus's patron during his decades in the East, had returned to Italy from Jerusalem in 400, receiving a warm welcome from Paulinus of Nola among others. Perhaps in 404 or 405, Rufinus left Aquileia to join Melania at Rome.[103] There, they joined a group that included Melania's granddaughter Melania the Younger, her mother Albina, and her husband Pinian: the three had adopted an ascetic lifestyle together. Also joining them in 405 was Palladius, author of the *Lausiac History* and a protégé of Melania's, who with other partisans of Origen had taken refuge in the West. During these same years, also at Rome, a circle around the British priest Pelagius began to produce a literary legacy, including the *Libellus fidei* of Rufinus—probably Rufinus the Syrian, Jerome's emissary in 399—and Pelagius's own commentary on Paul's epistles, written between 404 and 409.[104]

At Lent in the year 406, Jerome once again fell seriously ill. He had just

101. Hammond, "Last Ten Years," 375, citing C. Baur, *John Chrysostom and His Time*, trans. M. Gonzaga (London: Sands, 1960), 2:287ff., 293ff.

102. Hammond, "Last Ten Years," 376, citing Palladius, *Dialogue on the Life of Chrysostom*, chaps. 1–4, PG 47.7–16, and Sozomen, *Historia ecclesiastica* 8.26, who quotes letters from Innocent to Chrysostom and to the presbyters, deacons, clergy and people of Constantinople.

103. On Rufinus's move to Rome, see Hammond, "Last Ten Years," 378, who states, "If Rufinus did not already travel south in 403 or 404, encouraged by the change of pope, the return of Melania, and the rising interest in the affair of Chrysostom, one might conjecture that he took the opportunity to accompany Chromatius on his way to attend the Roman synod [in early 405]."

104. On the emergence of Pelagian ideas at Rome before 410, see Wermelinger, *Rom und Pelagius*, 13; more generally, see Bohlin, *Theologie des Pelagius*; Evans, *Pelagius*; Ferguson, *Pelagius*; Rees, *Pelagius*. For the relevant chronology, see Duval, "Pélage en son temps." For various aspects of the origins and development of Pelagianism and the controversy it inspired, see Bonner, "Rufinus of Syria"; Bostock, "Influence of Origen"; Clark, "Origenism to Pelagianism"; Duval, "Censeur inconnu."

prepared translations of some of Theophilus's writings against Chrysostom, but these were left unfinished for several months. After his recovery, Jerome completed the last five of his commentaries on the Minor Prophets. In autumn of 406, Sisinnius arrived from Gaul, bringing copies of the works of Vigilantius. Jerome composed his *Against Vigilantius* and a number of letters to correspondents in Gaul during the winter. He then sent all of these works, together with the commentaries composed in 406, to the West with Sisinnius, who returned via Egypt.

In 407, Jerome composed his commentary on Daniel, dedicated to Pammachius at Rome; in 408, he began work on the great commentary on Isaiah, which would take him about two years to finish. During these years, he kept up a correspondence with admirers in Gaul, some of whom traveled to Bethlehem to visit him. Since 403, too, his correspondence with Augustine in North Africa had become more regular. The two exchanged letters in 403 and in 404 or 405, establishing a more cooperative relationship that was to lay the foundation for their joint attack on Pelagius and his associates during the last decade of Jerome's life.

Chronology

403

> May 12: Death of Epiphanius of Salamis
> June: Theophilus of Antioch to Constantinople for trial; Synod of the Oak deposes Chrysostom; emperor Arcadius banishes him
> July: return of Chrysostom
> Letters 104 (Augustine to Jerome, carried by the deacon Cyprian); 105 (to Augustine, written before letter 104 was received)

404

> January 26: Death of Paula
> Early in the year: translation of the *Pachomiana* (for Eustochium)
> Spring: Letters 100 (translation of the paschal letter of Theophilus of Alexandria for 404) and 99 (cover letter for letter 100)
> Council convened at Constantinople to decide the case of Chrysostom
> Easter (April 17): Imperial troops attack Chrysostom's clergy [105]
> Delegation sent to Rome by Chrysostom with letters to Innocent of Rome, Venerius of Milan, and Chromatius of Aquileia
> Delegation sent to Rome by Theophilus of Alexandria

---

105. Hammond, "Last Ten Years," 375, citing Baur, *John Chrysostom and His Time*, 287ff.

June 9: banishment of John Chrysostom

Chromatius of Aquileia writes to John Chrysostom and to the emperor Honorius

Letters 108 (to Eustochium, eulogy of Paula); 109 (to Riparius against Vigilantius); 110 (Augustine to Jerome); 111 (to Praesidius); 112 (to Augustine, carried by the deacon Cyprian)

404–5

Translation *iuxta Hebraeos* of Esther (to Paula and Eustochium); translation of Tobit and Judith (to Chromatius of Aquileia and Heliodorus of Altinum)

Letters 115 (to Augustine, carried by Firmus, response to letter 110); 116 (Augustine to Jerome, response to letter 115); 117 (to an anonymous mother and daughter in Gaul)

Rufinus leaves Aquileia for Rome

405

Early 405: Synod of Italian bishops at Rome; deputation of Western bishops sent to Constantinople (including Gaudentius of Brescia, friend of Rufinus and dedicatee of his translation of the *Clementine Recognitions*, and Aemilius of Beneventum, friend of Paulinus of Nola and of Melania's family)[106]

Palladius and other Origenist refugees arrive in Rome from the East

Roman delegation returns after four months, rebuffed by the Eastern court[107]

406

Lent: Jerome is seriously ill

Translation of Theophilus's polemic against John Chrysostom (now lost); letters 113 (translation of a letter of Theophilus sent to Jerome as a cover for the polemic against Chrysostom) and 114 (apology to Theophilus for delay in translating the polemic)

---

106. Hammond, "Last Ten Years," 376 with n. 4. Beneventum was near Nola and had a Publicola, probably Melania's son, as its patronus (Palladius, *Dialogue*, 4, PG 47.15 and PLRE s.v. Publicola, cited by Hammond). Aemilius of Beneventum is mentioned by Paulinus of Nola, *Carmen*, 21.330 and *Carmen* 25, which describes Aemilius's role in officiating at the wedding of Julian of Eclanum to Aemilius's daughter; for this information see Clark, *Origenist Controversy*, 216, citing Palladius, *Dialogus* 4 [15] (Coleman-Norton ed., 22).

107. Four months later: delegation from Rome returns empty-handed, having been treated ignominiously and refused an audience with Arcadius: "the insult affected the Western court as well as the Pope"; reconciliation between Innocent and the East occurred only after Theophilus's death in 412 and was gradual even then (Hammond, "Last Ten Years," 377–78).

Commentaries on Zechariah (to Exsuperius of Toulouse), Malachi (to Minervius and Alexander, monks at Toulouse), Hosea, Joel, Amos (to Pammachius)

Autumn: Arrival of Sisinnius from Gaul with treatise of Vigilantius against relics, sending alms to Jerusalem, monastic poverty, and clerical celibacy

Against Vigilantius (to Riparius and Desiderius, priests of Toulouse)

Letter 119 (to Minervius and Alexander, monks at Toulouse)

Late in the year: departure of Sisinnius for Egypt

407

Visit of Apodemius from Bordeaux with letters from Hedybia and Algasia

Letters 118 (to Julian, carried by his brother Ausonius); 120 (to Hedybia); 121 (to Algasia); 122 (to Rusticus, on his wife Artemia, who is at Bethlehem, carried by Apodemius to Gaul)

Commentary on Daniel (to Pammachius and Marcella)

408

Beginning of work on the commentary on Isaiah

409

Letters 123 (to Ageruchia) and 124 (to Avitus)

Further work on the commentary on Isaiah (to Eustochium)

Jerome is ill

Commentary on Isaiah completed before Jerome receives word of the sack of Rome by Alaric in August 410

10. JEROME'S FINAL YEARS, 410–19

Jerome's final years were darkened by the increasingly dire state of affairs in Italy in the wake of the invasion of the Visigoths under Alaric, and their sack of the city of Rome in August 410. Jerome's old friend Pammachius died in the Gothic attack, while Marcella's death in 411 was the result of her sufferings at the hands of the barbarians. Rufinus fled Rome with the two Melanias, Albina, Pinian, and others. In 411, Rufinus died an exile in Sicily, having witnessed the Gothic sack of Regium in southern Italy from the other side of the Straits of Messina. The Melanias and their party went on to Hippo in North Africa, where they took refuge with Augustine. Pelagius, too, fled Rome and found his way to Hippo. Other prominent Roman Christians went to Carthage: these included Anicia Faltonia Proba, her daughter Juliana, and her granddaughter Demetrias, an immensely wealthy heiress who then took a vow of virginity. Caelestius, too, a companion of Pelagius, escaped to Carthage. Ironically, many of these refugees would end up in Palestine, in Jerome's immediate sphere of influence.

The Pelagian controversy, the primary theological concern of Jerome's last years, came about as a result of the flight of prominent members of the Roman clergy to North Africa. The doctrines of Pelagius and Caelestius had caused no concern, and attracted much interest, at Rome; in the rather different theological environment of North Africa, however, they evoked immediate and stern condemnation. In 411, a council at Carthage — originally convened to deal with the ongoing Donatist problem — condemned Caelestius. That same year, Pelagius departed for Palestine. There, he found a home for several years. But in 415, an emissary of Augustine, the Spanish priest Orosius, arrived there and accused Pelagius of heresy before a synod convened at Jerusalem. For the moment, Pelagius was acquitted, both at Jerusalem and by another gathering at Diospolis in December 415. In the spring of 416, however, Pelagian monks attacked Jerome's monastery. This act, in the end, brought down the ire of Innocent, the new bishop of Rome, and in the fall of 417, a council at Antioch expelled Pelagius from Palestine.[108]

In the midst of his grief and horror at the fate of Rome, and the ongoing struggle over Pelagius's theology, Jerome still managed to produce his two final commentaries on the Prophets. The treatment of Ezekiel was written over the course of four years from 410 to 414. The commentary on Jeremiah, begun in 414, was left incomplete at his death.

In 418, Melania the Elder, her grand-daughter, Melania the Younger, and the latter's mother Albina and husband Pinian, arrived at Jerusalem. Melania the Elder died soon after their arrival, but her namesake was to establish cordial relations with Jerome during his final year.

During these last years, Jerome wrote numerous letters to prominent Westerners, and kept up an active correspondence with Augustine. His letters grow very brief, however: one can sense that he has entered his final decline. On September 30, 419, Jerome died, aged perhaps seventy-two, having outlived most of his contemporaries and even many members of the next generation, such as his patroness Eustochium, who died at the end of 418.[109]

108. See note 104 for bibliography on the Pelagian controversy.

109. For the chronology of Jerome's final years I have followed Cavallera entirely, having found no reason to challenge his arrangement of the material. The narrative just given summarizes events recounted in detail by Jerome's biographers and elsewhere.

Chronology

410

Before August: Beginning of work on the commentary on Ezekiel (to Eustochium)

August: Rome taken and sacked by Alaric and his Goths; death of Pammachius

411

Death of Marcella

Death of Rufinus in Sicily

Further work on the commentary on Ezekiel, interrupted again by a barbarian attack

Letter 126 (reply to Marcellinus and Anapsychia, who write to Jerome from Africa)

412

Further work on the commentary on Ezekiel

Letter 125 (to Rusticus, a monk at Marseille)

Death of Theophilus of Alexandria, succeeded by Cyril

413

Letters 127 (to Principia, a eulogy of Marcella) and 128 (to Gaudentius, on the education of Pacatula)

414

Letters 129 (to Dardanus); 140 (to the priest Cyprian); 133 (to Ctesiphon, against Pelagianism); 130 (to Demetrias)

Completion of the commentary on Ezekiel

Beginning of the commentary on Jeremiah, left unfinished at Jerome's death (to Eusebius of Cremona)

415

Orosius arrives in Bethlehem from Hippo, bringing two treatises of Augustine (Jerome, letters 131 and 132)

July: Synod at Jerusalem, Orosius debates Pelagius

Dialogues against the Pelagians (no dedication)

December 20–26: Synod at Diospolis; Pelagius acquitted of heresy by a group of Palestinian bishops including John of Jerusalem

416

Spring: Orosius returns to Hippo with letter 134 (to Augustine)

Pelagian monks attack Jerome's monastery

Letter of Jerome to Aurelius of Carthage about the Pelagian attack (lost)

Letter of Eustochium to Innocent of Rome about the Pelagian attack (lost)

417

    January 10: Death of John of Jerusalem, succeeded by Praylus

    February: Letters 137 (Innocent of Rome to John of Jerusalem); 136 (Innocent of Rome to Jerome); 135 (Innocent of Rome to Aurelius of Carthage); all concern the Pelagian attack at Bethlehem

    Autumn: Council at Antioch condemns Pelagius and expels him from Palestine

    Letter 138 (to Riparius)

418

    Innocentius to Bethlehem

    Letters 141 (to Augustine); 142 (to Augustine); 152 (to Riparius)

    Albina, Pinian, and Melania the Younger to Jerusalem

    Death of Pelagius

    Late 418-early 419: death of Eustochium

419

    Letter 151 (to Riparius)

    Innocentius to Bethlehem, bringing letters from Apronius and from Boniface, the new bishop of Rome

    Letters 139 (to Apronius), 153 (to Boniface of Rome), 154 (to Donatus), 143 (to Augustine and Alypius)

    September 30: Death of Jerome

Bibliography

Primary Sources

Anthony. *See* Rubenson (*under Secondary Sources*).

Aphthonius. *Aphthonii Progymnasmata.* Edited by Hugo Rabe. Leipzig: B. G. Teubner, 1926.

Athanasius. *The Life of Anthony and the Letter to Marcellinus.* Translated by Robert C. Gregg. New York: Paulist Press, 1980.

Augustine. *Epistolae ex duobus codicibus nuper in lucem prolatae.* Edited by Johannes Divjak. Vienna: Hoelder-Pichler-Tempsky, 1981.

Basil. *The Letters, with an English Translation.* Edited by Roy J. Deferrari. LCL. London: Heinemann; New York: Putnam, 1926.

Biblia sacra. See Fischer and Weber.

Didymus. *Sur Zacharie.* 3 vols. Translated by Louis Doutreleau. Vol. 1, *Sources chrétiennes.* Paris: Éditions du Cerf, 1962.

Doran, Robert, trans. *The Lives of Simeon Stylites.* Kalamazoo, MI: Cistercian Publications, 1992.

Edictum Diocletiani de pretiis = Diokletians Preisedikt. Edited by Siegfried Lauffer. Berlin: De Gruyter, 1971.

Eusebius. *The Bodleian Manuscript of Jerome's Version of the Chronicle of Eusebius, Reproduced in Collotype.* Edited by John Knight Fotheringham. Oxford: Clarendon Press, 1905.

———. *Historia Ecclesiastica = Die Kirchengeschichte des Eusebius.* Edited by Eduard Schwartz. 2nd edition. Leipzig: J. C. Hinrichs, 1914.

Eusebius and Jerome. *Die Chronik des Hieronymus, Hieronymi Chronicon.* GCS, Eusebius Werke, Bd. 7. Edited by Rudolf Helm. Leipzig: J. C. Hinrichs, 1913–26.

Fischer, Bonifatius, and Robert Weber, eds. *Biblia sacra: Iuxta Vulgatam versionem.* Stuttgart: Württembergische Bibelanstalt, 1969; ed. altera emendata, 1975.

Gerontius. *The Life of Melania the Younger: Introduction, Translation, and Commentary.* Edited by Elizabeth A. Clark. New York: E. Mellen Press, 1984.

Hermogenes. *Opera.* Edited by Hugo Rabe. Editio stereotypa editionis anni 1913. Stuttgart: Teubner, 1969.

Jerome. *Adversus Helvidium.* PL 23. Edited by J. P. Migne. Paris, 1844–64.

———. *Adversus Iovinianum.* PL 23. Edited by J. P. Migne. Paris, 1844–64.

———. *Altercatio luciferiani et orthodoxi.* CCSL 79B. Edited by Aline Canellis. Turnhout: Brepols, 2000.

———. *Commentaires de Jérôme sur le prophète Isaie.* Edited by Roger Gryson and Paul-Augustin Deproost. 5 vols. Freiburg: Verlag Herder, 1993–99.

———. *Commentarii in Epistulam Pauli Apostoli ad Ephesios.* PL 26. J.P. Edited by J. P. Migne. Paris, 1844–64.

———. *Commentarii in Epistulas Pauli Apostoli ad Galatas.* PL 26. Edited by J. P. Migne. Paris, 1844–64.

———. *Commentarii in Epistulas Pauli Apostoli ad Titum et ad Philemonem.* CCSL 77C. Edited by Federica Bucchi. Turnhout: Brepols, 2003.

———. *Commentarii in Epistulas Pauli Apostoli ad Philemonem.* PL 26. Edited by J. P. Migne. Paris, 1844–64.

———. *Commentarii in prophetas minores.* CCSL 76–76A. Edited by Marcus Adriaen and Domenico Vallarsi. Turnhout: Brepols, 1969–70.

———. *Commentariorum in Danielem libri III (IV).* CCSL 75A. Edited by Franciscus Glorie. Turnhout: Brepols, 1964.

———. *Commentariorum in Hiezechielem libri XIV.* CCSL 75. Turnhout: Brepols, 1964.

———. *Commentariorum in Mattheum libri IV.* CCSL 77. Turnhout: Brepols, 1969.

———. *Contra Iohannem.* CCSL 79A. Edited by Jean-Louis Feiertag. Turnhout: Brepols, 1999.

———. *Contra Rufinum.* CCSL 79. Edited by Pierre Lardet. Turnhout: Brepols, 1982.

———. *Contra Vigilantium.* PL 23. Edited by J. P. Migne. Paris, 1844–64.

———. *Dialogus adversus Pelagianos.* CCSL 80. Edited by Claudio Moreschini. Turnhout: Brepols, 1990.

———. *Epistulae.* CSEL vols. 54–56. Edited by Isidore Hilberg. Vienna and Leipzig: F. Tempsky and G. Freytag, 1910–18.

———. *Hebraicae quaestiones in libro Geneseos; Liber interpretationes Hebraicorum nominum; Commentarioli in Psalmos; Commentarius in Ecclesiasten.* CCSL 72. Edited by Paul de Lagarde, Germain Morin, and Marcus Adriaen. Turnhout: Brepols, 1959.

———. *Hieronymi Chronicorum codicis floriacensis fragmenta leidensia, parisina, vaticana phototypice edita.* Edited by Ludwig Traube. Louvain: A. W. Sijthoff, 1902.

———. *Praefatio in Eusebii Chronicon.* PL 27. Edited by J. P. Migne. Paris, 1844–64.

———. *Praefatio in Origenis homiliae II in Canticum canticorum.* PL 23. Edited by J. P. Migne. Paris, 1844–64.

———. *Praefatio in Origenis homiliae in Hiezechielem.* PL 25. Edited by J. P. Migne. Paris, 1844–64.

———. *Praefatio in Origenis homiliae in Lucam.* PL 26. Edited by J. P. Migne. Paris, 1844–64.

———. *Praefatio in Pachomiana Latina.* PL 23. Edited by J. P. Migne. Paris, 1844–64.

———. *A Translation of Jerome's Chronicon with Historical Commentary.* Translated and edited by Malcolm Drew Donalson. Lewiston, NY: Mellen University Press, 1996.

———. *Vita Pauli primi eremitae.* PL 23. Edited by J. P. Migne. Paris, 1844–64.

———. *Vita Malchi monachi captivi.* PL 23. Edited by J. P. Migne. Paris, 1844–64.

Jerome and Gennadius. *Hieronymus liber De viris inlustribus; Gennadius liber De viris inlustribus.* Edited by Ernest Cushing Richardson and Oscar von Gebhardt. Leipzig: J. C. Hinrichs, 1896.

Kennedy, George A., and Leonhard von Spengel. *Progymnasmata: Greek Textbooks of Prose Composition Introductory to the Study of Rhetoric.* 2nd ed. Fort Collins, CO: Chez l'auteur, 2000.

Libanius. *Libanii Opera.* Edited by Richard Foerster et al. Leipzig: Teubner, 1903–27.

Origen. *Commentaire sur l'Évangile selon Matthieu.* Edited by Robert Girod. Paris: Éditions du Cerf, 1970.

Palladius. *Historia Lausiaca.* Edited and translated by Edward Cuthbert Butler. Cambridge: Cambridge University Press, 1898–1904.

Pamphilus, Eusebius, and Rufinus. *Apologie pour Origène.* Translated and edited by René Amacker and Eric Junod. *Sources chrétiennes,* vols. 464–65. Paris: Éditions du Cerf, 2002.

Petronius Arbiter. *The Satyricon of Petronius Arbiter in the Translation Attributed to Oscar Wilde.* New York: Covici Friede, 1934.

Rufinus. *Opera.* CCSL 20. Edited by Manlio Simonetti. Turnhout: Brepols, 1961.

Rufinus and Eusebius. *The Church History of Rufinus of Aquileia, Books 10 and 11*. Translated by Philip R. Amidon. New York: Oxford University Press, 1997.

Sayings of the Desert Fathers: The Alphabetical Collection. Translated by Benedicta Ward. Kalamazoo, MI: Cistercian Publications, 1975.

Seneca. *Moral Essays, with an English Translation*. Translated by John Basore. LCL. London, W. Heinemann; New York, G. P. Putnam's Sons, 1928-.

Theodoret of Cyrrhus. *A History of the Monks of Syria*. Translated by R. M. Price. Kalamazoo, MI: Cistercian Publications, 1985.

Veilleux, Armand. *Pachomian koinonia*. Vol. 1, *The Life of Saint Pachomius and His Disciples*. Vol. 2, *Pachomian Chronicles and Rules*. Vol. 3, *Instructions, Letters, and Other Writings of Saint Pachomius and His Disciples*. Kalamazoo, MI: Cistercian Publications, 1980-.

Secondary Sources

Adkin, Neil. "Gregory of Nazianzus and Jerome: Some Remarks." In *Georgica: Greek Studies in Honour of George Cawkwell*, edited by Michael A. Flower and Mark Toher. London: University of London, Institute of Classical Studies, 1991.

———. *Jerome on Virginity: A Commentary on the Libellus de virginitate servanda (Letter 22)*. Cambridge: Francis Cairns, 2003.

Andersen, Francis I., and David Noel Freedman. *Amos: A New Translation with Notes and Commentary*. New York: Doubleday, 1989.

———. *Hosea: A New Translation with Introduction and Commentary*. Garden City, NY: Doubleday, 1980.

Ando, Clifford. *Imperial Ideology and Provincial Loyalty in the Roman Empire*. Berkeley: University of California Press, 2000.

André, Jean-Marie. *L'Otium dans la vie morale et intellectuelle romaine, des origines à l'époque augustéenne*. Paris: Presses universitaires de France, 1966.

Antin, Paul. *Recueil sur saint Jérôme*. Bruxelles: Latomus, 1968.

Arns, Paulo Evaristo. *La technique du livre d'après saint Jérôme*. Paris: E. de Boccard, 1953.

Bammel, C. P. "Die Pauluskommentare des Hieronymus: Die ersten wissenschaftlichen lateinischen Bibelkommentare?" In *Cristianesimo Latino e cultura Greca sino al sec. IV, XXI Incontro di studiosi dell'antichità cristiana, Roma 7-9 maggio 1992, Studia Ephemeridis 'Augustinianum' 42*. Rome: Institutum Patristicum 'Augustinianum,' 1993. Reprinted in *Tradition and Exegesis in Early Christian Writers*. Aldershot (UK): Variorum, 1995.

Bardy, Gustave. "Jérôme et ses maîtres hébreux." *Revue bénédictine* 46 (1934): 145-64.

Barthélemy, Dominique. "Eusèbe, la Septante, et 'les autres.'" In *Études d'histoire du texte de l'ancien testament*, 179-93. Göttingen: Vandenhoeck & Ruprecht, 1978.

Beckwith, Roger T. *The Old Testament Canon of the New Testament Church and Its Background in Early Judaism*. Grand Rapids, MI: Eerdmans, 1985.

Bickel, Ernst. *Diatribe in Senecae Philosophi fragmenta. Volumen 1: Fragmenta de matrimonio*. Leipzig: Teubner, 1915.

Bischoff, Bernhard. *Latin Palaeography: Antiquity and the Middle Ages*. Translated by Dáibhí Ó Cróinin and David Ganz. Cambridge: Cambridge University Press, 1990.

Blaise, A. *Lexicon Latinitatis Medii Aevi: Praesertim ad res ecclesiasticas investigandas pertinens = Dictionnaire latin-français des auteurs du Moyen-Age*. Turnholt: Brepols, 1975.

Blenkinsopp, Joseph. *A History of Prophecy in Israel*. 2nd ed. Louisville, KY: Westminster John Knox Press, 1996.

Bohlin, Torgny. *Die Theologie des Pelagius und ihre Genesis*. Uppsala: Lundequistska bokhandeln, 1957.

Bonner, Gerald. "Rufinus of Syria and African Pelagianism." *Augustinian Studies* 1 (1970): 31-47.

Bonner, Stanley Frederick. *Education in Ancient Rome: From the Elder Cato to the Younger Pliny*. Berkeley: University of California Press, 1977.

Bostock, Gerald. "The Influence of Origen on Pelagius and Western Monasticism." In *Origeniana Septima*, 381–96. Louvain: Leuven University Press, 1999.

Boswell, John. *The Kindness of Strangers: The Abandonment of Children in Western Europe from Late Antiquity to the Renaissance*. New York: Pantheon Books, 1988.

Bourdieu, Pierre. *Outline of a Theory of Practice*. Translated by Richard Nice. New York: Cambridge University Press, 1977.

Bourdieu, Pierre, and Randal Johnson. *The Field of Cultural Production: Essays on Art and Literature, European Perspectives*. New York: Columbia University Press, 1993.

Brakke, David. *Athanasius and Asceticism*. Baltimore: Johns Hopkins University Press, 1998.

Brent, Allen. *Hippolytus and the Roman Church in the Third Century: Communities in Tension before the Emergence of a Monarch-Bishop*. Leiden: Brill, 1995.

Brown, Peter R. L. *The Body and Society: Men, Women, and Sexual Renunciation in Early Christianity*. Lectures on the History of Religions, n.s.13. New York: Columbia University Press, 1988.

———. *The Making of Late Antiquity*. Carl Newell Jackson Lectures. Cambridge, MA: Harvard University Press, 1978.

———. *Power and Persuasion in Late Antiquity: Towards a Christian Empire*. The Curti Lectures, 1988. Madison: University of Wisconsin Press, 1992.

Burton-Christie, Douglas. *The Word in the Desert: Scripture and the Quest for Holiness in Early Christian Monasticism*. New York: Oxford University Press, 1993.

Callmer, C. "Antike Bibliotheken." In *Opuscula archaeologica*, edited by the Svenska institutet i Rom. Lund: C. W. K. Gleerup, 1935.

Carriker, Andrew. *The Library of Eusebius of Caesarea*. Leiden: Brill, 2003.

Casson, Lionel. *Libraries in the Ancient World*. New Haven: Yale University Press, 2001.

Cavallera, Ferdinand. *Le schisme d'Antioche (iv–v siècle)*. Paris: A. Picard, 1905.

———. *Saint Jérôme, sa vie et son œuvre*. Louvain: "Spicilegium Sacrum Lovaniense" Bureaux, 1922.

Cavallo, Guglielmo. *Le Biblioteche nel mondo antico e medievale*. 2nd ed. Rome: Laterza, 1989.

———. *Ricerche sulla maiuscola biblica*. Florence: Le Monnier, 1967.

Cavallo, Guglielmo, and Herwig Maehler. *Greek Bookhands of the Early Byzantine Period, A.D. 300–800*. Bulletin Supplement 47. London: University of London Institute of Classical Studies, 1987.

Cerrato, J. A. *Hippolytus between East and West: The Commentaries and the Provenance of the Corpus*. Oxford: Oxford University Press, 2002.

Chartier, Roger. *Cultural History: Between Practices and Representations*. Cambridge: Polity Press, 1988.

———. *The Order of Books: Readers, Authors, and Libraries in Europe between the Fourteenth and Eighteenth Centuries*. Stanford: Stanford University Press, 1994.

Clark, Elizabeth A. "From Origenism to Pelagianism: Elusive Issues in an Ancient Debate." *Princeton Seminary Bulletin*, n.s. 12, no. 3 (1991): 283–303.

———. *The Origenist Controversy: The Cultural Construction of an Early Christian Debate*. Princeton: Princeton University Press, 1992.

Courcelle, Pierre. *Late Latin Writers and Their Greek Sources*. Translated by Harry E. Wedeck. Cambridge, MA: Harvard University Press, 1969.

Cribiore, Raffaella. *Gymnastics of the Mind: Greek Education in Hellenistic and Roman Egypt*. Princeton, NJ: Princeton University Press, 2001.

———. *Writing, Teachers, and Students in Graeco-Roman Egypt*. Atlanta: Scholars Press, 1996.

Cross, Frank Moore, and Shemaryahu Talmon. *Qumran and the History of the Biblical Text*. Cambridge, MA: Harvard University Press, 1975.

Crouzel, Henri. "Saint Jérôme et ses amis toulousains." *Bulletin de littérature ecclésiastique* 73 (1972): 124–46.

Curran, John R. *Pagan City and Christian Capital: Rome in the Fourth Century*. Oxford Classical Monographs. Oxford: Clarendon, 2000.

De Jong, Mayke. *In Samuel's Image: Child Oblation in the Early Medieval West*. Leiden: E. J. Brill, 1996.

De Labriolle, Pierre. "Le songe de s. Jérôme." In *Miscellanea Geronimiana*, edited by Vincenzo Vannutelli, 227–35. Rome: Tipografia Poliglotta Vaticana, 1920.

Dines, Jennifer. "Jerome and the Hexapla: The Witness of the Commentary on Amos." In *Origen's Hexapla and Fragments: Papers presented at the Rich Seminar on the Hexapla, Oxford Centre for Hebrew and Jewish Studies, 25ᵗʰ[July]-3rd August 1994*, edited by Alison Salvesen, 421–36. Tubingen: Mohr-Siebeck, 1998.

Dix, Thomas Keith. "Private and Public Libraries at Rome in the First Century B.C.: A Preliminary Study in the History of Roman Libraries." Dissertation, University of Michigan, 1987.

Doutreleau, Louis. "Que savons-nous aujourd'hui des papyrus de Toura?" *Recherches de science religieuse* 43 (1955): 161–76.

Doutreleau, Louis, and Ludwig Koenen. "Nouvel inventaire des papyrus de Toura." *Recherches de science religieuse* 55, no. 4 (1967): 547–64.

Duval, Yves-Marie. "Jérôme et les prophètes: Histoire, prophétie, actualité et actualisation dans les commentaires de Nahum, Michée, Abdias et Joël." In J. A. Emerton, ed., *Congress Volume, Salamanca 1983*. Leiden: Brill, 1985.

———. "Notes complémentaires [sur Ep. 27*]." In *Lettres 1*-29*: Nouvelle édition du texte critique et introduction par Johannes Divjak*, edited by Johannes Divjak, 562–63. Paris: Études Augustiniennes, 1987–99.

———. "Pélage en son temps: Données chronologiques nouvelles pour une présentation nouvelle." In *Studia patristica. XXXVIII, St Augustine and His Opponents, Other Latin Writers*, 95–118. Leuven: Peeters, 2001.

———. "Pélage est-il le censeur inconnu de l'Adversus Iovinianum à Rome en 393? ou Du 'portrait-robot' de l'hérétique chez S. Jérôme." *Revue d'histoire ecclésiastique* 75, nos. 3–4 (1980): 525–57.

Elderen, Bastiann Van. "Early Christian Libraries." In *The Bible as Book: The Manuscript Tradition*, edited by John Sharpe and Kimberly van Kampen, 45–59. London: British Library; New Castle, DE: Oak Knoll Press; in association with the Scriptorium: Center for Christian Antiquities, 1998.

Elm, Eva. *Die Macht der Weisheit: Das Bild des Bischofs in der Vita Augustini des Possidius und anderen spätantiken und frühmittelalterlichen Bischofsviten*. Leiden: Brill, 2003.

Elm, Susanna. *Virgins of God: The making of Asceticism in Late Antiquity*. Oxford: Oxford University Press, 1994.

Estin, Colette. *Les psautiers de Jérôme à la lumière des traductions juives antérieures*. Rome: San Girolamo, 1984.

———. "Les traductions du Psautier." In *Le monde latin antique et la Bible*, edited by Jacques Fontaine. Paris: Beauchesne, 1985.

Evans, Robert F. *Pelagius: Inquiries and Reappraisals*. New York: Seabury Press, 1968.

Ferguson, John. *Pelagius: A Historical and Theological Study*. New York: AMS Press, 1978.

Foucault, Michel. *The Care of the Self: Histoire de la sexualité*, vol. 3. New York: Vintage Books, 1988.

Francis, James A. *Subversive Virtue: Asceticism and Authority in the Second-Century Pagan World*. University Park: Pennsylvania State University Press, 1995.

Gall, August von. *Der hebräische Pentateuch der Samaritaner*. Giessen: Alfred Töpelmann, 1914–18.

Gallay, Paul. *La vie de Saint Grégoire de Nazianze*. Lyon: E. Vitte, 1943.

Gamble, Harry Y. *Books and Readers in the Early Church: A History of Early Christian Texts*. New Haven: Yale University Press, 1995.

Gaston, Lloyd. *Paul and the Torah*. Vancouver: University of British Columbia Press, 1987.

Geerlings, Wilhelm, and Christian Schulze, eds. *Der Kommentar in Antike und Mittelalter: Beiträge zu seiner Erforschung*. Leiden: Brill, 2002.

Georgi, Dieter. *The Opponents of Paul in Second Corinthians*. Philadelphia: Fortress Press, 1986.

Gibson, Roy K., and Christina Shuttleworth Kraus. *The Classical Commentary: Histories, Practices, Theory.* Leiden: Brill, 2002.

Gigante, Marcello. *Philodemus in Italy: The Books from Herculaneum.* Ann Arbor: University of Michigan Press, 1995.

Gleason, Maud W. *Making Men: Sophists and Self-Presentation in Ancient Rome.* Princeton, NJ: Princeton University Press, 1995.

Gordis, Robert. *The Biblical Text in the Making: A Study of the Kethib-Qere.* Augmented edition. New York: Ktav, 1971.

Grafton, Anthony, and Megan Williams. *Christianity and the Transformation of the Book: Origen, Eusebius, and the Library of Caesarea.* Cambridge, MA: Harvard University Press, 2006.

Guarducci, Margherita. *San Pietro e Sant' Ippolito: Storia di statue famose in Vaticano.* Rome: Istituto Poligrafico e Zecca dello Stato, Libreria dello Stato, 1991.

Hadot, Pierre, and Arnold Ira Davidson. *Philosophy as a Way of Life: Spiritual Exercises from Socrates to Foucault.* Oxford: Blackwell, 1995.

Hagendahl, Harald. *Latin Fathers and the Classics: A Study on the Apologists, Jerome, and Other Christian Writers.* Göteborg: Elanders, 1958.

Hammond, C. P. "The Last Ten Years of Rufinus' Life and the Date of his Move South from Aquileia." *Journal of Theological Studies* n.s. 28 (1977): 372–429.

Harries, Jill. *Sidonius Apollinaris and the fall of Rome, AD 407–485.* Oxford: Clarendon Press, 1994.

Holl, Karl. *Gesammelte Aufsätze zur Kirchengeschichte.* Tübingen: Verlag von J. C. B. Mohr (P. Siebeck), 1927.

Hollerich, Michael. *Eusebius of Caesarea's Commentary on Isaiah: Christian Exegesis in the Age of Constantine.* Oxford: Clarendon Press, 1999.

Holtz, Louis. "Les manuscrits latins à gloses et à commentaires, de l'antiquité à l'époque carolingienne." In *Il libro e il testo,* edited by Cesare Questo and Renato Rafaelli, 141–67. Urbino: Università degli Studi di Urbino, 1984.

Holum, Kenneth G. *Theodosian Empresses: Women and Imperial Dominion in Late Antiquity.* Edited by Peter Brown. Vol. 3, *Transformation of the Classical Heritage.* Berkeley: University of California Press, 1982.

Horden, Peregrine, and Nicholas Purcell. *The Corrupting Sea.* Oxford: Blackwell, 2000.

Hunter, David G. "Vigilantius of Calagurris and Victricius of Rouen: Ascetics, Relics, and Clerics in Late Roman Gaul." *Journal of Early Christian Studies* 7, no. 3 (1999): 401–30.

Janko, Richard. "The Physicist as Hierophant: Aristophanes, Socrates, and the Authorship of the Derveni Papyrus." *Zeitschrift für Papyrologie und Epigraphik* 118 (1997): 61–94.

Jay, Pierre. "La datation des premières traductions de l'Ancien Testament sur l'hébreu par saint Jérôme." *Revue des études augustiniennes* 28 (1982): 208–12.

———. *L'exégèse de saint Jérôme: D'après son "Commentaire sur Isaïe."* Paris: Études augustiniennes, 1985.

Jellicoe, Sidney. *The Septuagint and Modern Study.* Winona Lake, IN: Eisenbrauns, 1993.

Johnson, Lora Lee. "The Hellenistic and Roman Library: Studies Pertaining to Their Architectural Form." Dissertation, Brown University, 1984.

Kamesar, Adam. *Jerome, Greek Scholarship, and the Hebrew Bible: A Study of the Quaestiones hebraicae in Genesim.* Oxford: Clarendon Press, 1993.

Kaster, Robert A. *Guardians of Language: The Grammarian and Society in Late Antiquity.* Vol. 11, *The Transformation of the Classical Heritage.* Berkeley: University of California Press, 1988.

Kedar, Benjamin. "Jewish Traditions in the Writings of Jerome." In *The Aramaic Bible: Targums in Their Historical Context,* edited by D. R. G. Beattie and M. J. McNamara, 420–30. Sheffield: Sheffield Academic Press, 1994.

———. "The Latin translations." In *Mikra: Text, Translation, Reading, and Interpretation of the Hebrew Bible in Ancient Judaism and Early Christianity,* edited by M. J. Mulder and Harry Sysling. Assen: Van Gorcum; Minneapolis: Fortress Press, 1990.

———. "The Vulgate as a Translation: Some Semantic and Syntactical Aspects of Jerome's Version of the Hebrew Bible." Dissertation, Hebrew University, 1968.

Kelly, J. N. D. *Golden Mouth: The Story of John Chrysostom—Ascetic, Preacher, Bishop.* Ithaca, NY: Cornell University Press, 1995.

———. *Jerome: His Life, Writings, and Controversies.* London: Duckworth, 1975.

Kenyon, Frederic G. *Books and Readers in Ancient Greece and Rome.* 2nd ed. Oxford: Clarendon Press, 1951.

Kinzig, Wolfram. "Jewish and Jewish-Christian Eschatologies in Jerome." Unpublished paper.

Koenen, Ludwig. "Zu dem Papyri aus dem Arsenioskloster bei Tura." *Zeitschrift für Papyrologie und Epigraphik* 2 (1968): 41–63.

Kraft, Robert A. "Christian Transmission of Greek Jewish Scriptures." In *Paganisme, judaïsme, christianisme (Mélanges Marcel Simon),* 207–26. Paris: E. de Boccard, 1978.

Lambert, Bernard. *Bibliotheca hieronymiana manuscripta: La tradition manuscrite des œuvres de Saint Jérôme.* The Hague: Martinus Nijhoff, 1969.

Lauffer, Siegfried. *Diokletians Preisedikt.* Berlin: De Gruyter, 1971.

Layton, Richard A. "Recovering Origen's Pauline Exegesis: Exegesis and Eschatology in the *Commentary on Ephesians.*" *Journal of Early Christian Studies* 8, no. 3 (2000): 373–411.

Lim, Richard. *Public Disputation, Power, and Social Order in Late Antiquity.* Berkeley: University of California Press, 1995.

Loewe, Raphael. "The Medieval History of the Latin Vulgate." In *The Cambridge History of the Bible,* vol 2: *The West, from the Fathers to the Reformation,* edited by G. W. H. Lampe, 102–54. Cambridge: Cambridge University Press, 1969.

Madec, Goulven. *Saint Augustin et la philosophie: Notes critiques.* Paris: Institut d'études augustiniennes, 1996.

Marichal, Robert. "L'écriture latine et la civilisation occidentale du Ier au XVIe siècle." In *L'écriture et la psychologie des peuples: XXIIe semaine de synthèse,* edited by Marcel Cohen, 199–247. Paris: Librairie Armand Colin, 1963.

Marrou, Henri Irénée. *A History of Education in Antiquity.* Translated by George Lamb. New York: New American Library, 1964.

———. "Les attaches orientales du Pélagianisme." *Académie des Inscriptions et Belles Lettres: Comptes rendus des séances* (1969): 461–72.

Marrou, Henri-Irénée, et al., eds. *Prosopographie chrétienne du Bas-Empire.* Paris: Éditions du Centre national de la recherche scientifique, 1982–.

Matthews, John. *Western Aristocracies and the Imperial Court, A.D. 364–425.* Oxford: Oxford University Press, 1975.

McCarthy, Carmel. *The Tiqqune Sopherim and Other Theological Corrections in the Masoretic Text of the Old Testament.* Freiburg: Universitätsverlag; Göttingen: Vandenhoeck & Ruprecht, 1981.

McLynn, Neil B. *Ambrose of Milan: Church and Court in a Christian Capital.* Vol. 22, *The Transformation of the Classical Heritage.* Berkeley: University of California Press, 1994.

McNamee, Kathleen. "Marginalia and Commentaries in Greek Literary Papyri." Dissertation, Duke University, 1977.

———. *Sigla and Select Marginalia in Greek Literary Papyri.* Papyrologica Bruxellensia. Brussels: Fondation égyptologique Reine Elisabeth, 1992.

Meershoek, G. Q. A. *Le latin biblique d'après Saint Jérôme: Aspects linguistiques de la rencontre entre la Bible et le monde classique.* Nijmegen-Utrecht: Dekker & Van de Vegt, 1966.

Mercati, Giovanni. "Nuove note di letteratura biblica e cristiana antica." *Studi e Testi,* 95. Vatican City: Biblioteca Apostolica Vaticana, 1941.

Meredith, Anthony. *The Cappadocians.* London: Geoffrey Chapman, 1995.

Millar, Fergus. *The Emperor in the Roman World (31 BC–AD 337).* Ithaca, NY: Cornell University Press, 1992.

Moine, Nicole. "Melaniana." *Recherches augustiniennes* 15 (1980): 3–79.

Mommsen, Theodor. "Über die Quellen der Chronik des Hieronymus." In *Gesammelte Schriften,* 606-32. Berlin: Weidmannsche Buchhandlung, 1909.

Morgan, Teresa. *Literate Education in the Hellenistic and Roman Worlds.* Cambridge: Cambridge University Press, 1998.

Most, Glenn. *Editing Texts—Texte edieren.* Göttingen: Vandenhoeck & Ruprecht, 1998.

Mulder, M. J., and Harry Sysling. *Mikra: Text, Translation, Reading, and Interpretation of the Hebrew Bible in Ancient Judaism and Early Christianity.* Compendia rerum Iudaicarum ad Novum Testamentum. Assen: Van Gorcum; Minneapolis: Fortress Press, 1990.

Murphy, Francis Xavier. "Melania the Elder: A Biographical Note." *Traditio* 5 (1947): 59-77.

———. *Rufinus of Aquileia (345-411): His Life and Works.* Washington, DC: Catholic University of America Press, 1945.

Nautin, Pierre. "L'activité littéraire de Jérôme de 387 à 392." *Revue de théologie et de philosophie* 115 (1983): 247-59.

———. "La date des commentaires de Jérôme sur les épîtres pauliniennes." *Revue d'histoire ecclésiastique* 74 (1979): 5-12.

———. "Études de chronologie hiéronymienne (393-397)." *Revue des études augustiniennes* 18 (1972): 209-18.

———. "Études de chronologie hiéronymienne (393-397) (suite)." *Revue des études augustiniennes* 19 (1973): 69-96.

———. "Études de chronologie hiéronymienne (393-397) (suite)." *Revue des études augustiniennes* 19 (1973): 213-39.

———. "Études de chronologie hiéronymienne (393-397) (suite et fin)." *Revue des études augustiniennes* 20 (1974): 251-84.

———. "L'excommunication de saint Jérôme." *Annuaire de l'école pratique des hautes études Ve section—Sciences religieuses* 80-81 (1972-73): 7-37.

———. "Hieronymus." In *Theologische Realenzyclopädie,* edited by Gerhard Müller, 304-15. Berlin: Walter de Gruyter, 1986.

———. "Le premier échange épistolaire entre Jérôme et Damase: Lettres réelles ou fictives?" *Freiburger Zeitschrift für Philosophie und Theologie* 30 (1983): 331-44.

———. *Origène: Sa vie et son oeuvre.* Edited by Pierre Nautin. Christianisme antique. Paris: Beauchesne, 1977.

Newman, Hillel I. "Jerome and the Jews." Dissertation, Hebrew University, 1997.

Norman, A. F. "The Book-Trade in Fourth Century Antioch." *Journal of Hellenic Studies* 80 (1960): 122-26.

Ogilvie, R. M. *The Library of Lactantius.* Oxford: Clarendon Press, 1978.

Opelt, Ilona. "Origene visto da san Girolamo." *Augustinianum* 26 (1985): 217-22.

———. "San Girolamo e i suoi maestri ebraei." *Augustinianum* 28 (1988): 327-38.

Petitmengin, Pierre, and Bernard Flusin. "Le livre antique et la dictée: Nouvelles recherches." In *Mémorial André-Jean Festugière,* edited by E. Lucchesi and H. D. Saffrey, 247-62. Geneva: Cramer, 1984.

Pfeiffer, Rudolf. *History of Classical Scholarship from the Beginnings to the End of the Hellenistic Age.* Oxford: Clarendon Press, 1968.

Pontet, Maurice. *L'exégèse de s. Augustin, prédicateur.* Paris: Aubier, 1946.

Pronberger, Nicolaus. *Beiträge zur Chronologie der Briefe des hl. Hieronymus.* Amberg: Druck von H. Böes, 1913.

Propp, William H. "The Skin of Moses' Face—Transfigured or Disfigured?" *Catholic Biblical Quarterly* 49 (1987): 375-86.

Rade, Martin. *Damasus, Bischof von Rom: Ein Beitrag zur Geschichte der Anfänge des römischen Primats.* Freiburg: J. C. B. Mohr, 1882.

Rahmer, Moritz. *Die hebräischen Traditionen in den Werken des Hieronymus, durch eine Vergleichung mit den jüdischen Quellen.* Vol. 1. Breslau: Schletter, 1861.

Rapisarda, C. A. "Ciceronianus es, non Christianus: Dove e quando avvenne il sogno do S. Girolamo?" *Miscellanea di studi di letteratura cristiana antica* 4 (1954): 1–18.

Rebenich, Stefan. *Hieronymus und sein Kreis: Prosopographische und sozialgeschichtliche Untersuchungen.* Stuttgart: F. Steiner, 1992.

———. "Jerome: The 'Vir Trilinguis' and the 'Hebraica Veritas.'" *Vigiliae Christianae* 47 (1993): 50–77.

Rees, B. R. *Pelagius: A Reluctant Heretic.* Woodbridge (UK): Boydell Press, 1991.

Rice, Eugene F. *Saint Jerome in the Renaissance: The 13th Johns Hopkins Symposium in Comparative History.* Baltimore: Johns Hopkins University Press, 1985.

Riché, Pierre. *Education and Culture in the Barbarian West, Sixth through Eight Centuries.* Translated by John J. Contreni. Columbia: University of South Carolina Press, 1976.

Roberts, Colin H., and T. C. Skeat. *The Birth of the Codex.* London: Published for the British Academy by Oxford University Press, 1983.

Robinson, J. M. "On the Codicology of the Nag Hammadi Codices." In *Les textes de Nag Hammadi: Colloque du centre d'histoire des religions,* edited by M. Krause. Leiden: Brill, 1975.

Rougé, Jean. *Ships and Fleets of the Ancient Mediterranean.* Middletown, CT: Wesleyan University Press, 1981.

Rousseau, Philip. *Pachomius: The Making of a Community in Fourth-Century Egypt.* Berkeley: University of California Press, 1985.

Rubenson, Samuel. *The Letters of St. Antony: Monasticism and the Making of a Saint.* Studies in Antiquity and Christianity. Minneapolis: Fortress Press, 1995.

Saebo, Magne, ed. *Hebrew Bible/Old Testament: The History of Its Interpretation.* Vol 1, *From the Beginnings to the Middle Ages (until 1300), pt 1: Antiquity.* Göttingen: Vandenhoeck & Ruprecht, 1996.

Saller, Richard P. "Martial on Patronage and Literature." *Classical Quarterly* 33 (1983): 246–57.

———. *Personal Patronage under the Early Empire.* Cambridge: Cambridge University Press, 1982.

Simon, Marcel. "The Bible in the Earliest Controversies between Jews and Christians." In *The Bible in Greek Christian Antiquity,* edited by Paul M. Blowers, 49–68. Notre Dame, IN: University of Notre Dame Press, 1997.

Skeat, T. C. "The Use of Dictation in Ancient Book-Production." *Proceedings of the British Academy* 42 (1956): 179–208.

Spoerl, Kelley McCarthy. "The Schism at Antioch since Cavallera." In *Arianism after Arius: Essays on the Development of the 4th-Century Trinitarian Conflicts,* edited by Michel R. Barnes and Daniel H. Williams, 101–26. Edinburgh: T and T Clark, 1993.

Staikos, K. *The Great Libraries: From Antiquity to the Renaissance (3000 B.C. to A.D. 1600).* London: British Library; New Castle, DE: Oak Knoll Press, 2000.

Stancliffe, Clare. *St. Martin and His Hagiographer: History and Miracle in Sulpicius Severus.* Oxford Historical Monographs. Oxford: Clarendon Press, 1983.

Stemberger, Gunter. "Exegetical Contacts between Christians and Jews in the Roman Empire." In *Hebrew Bible / Old Testament: The History of Its Interpretation,* edited by Magne Sæbø, 569–86. Göttingen: Vandenhoeck & Ruprecht, 1996.

Swete, Henry Barclay, H. St J. Thackeray, and Richard Rusden Ottley. *An Introduction to the Old Testament in Greek.* 2nd ed. Cambridge: Cambridge University Press, 1914.

Talmon, Shemaryahu. "The Old Testament Text." In *The Cambridge History of the Bible,* edited by P. R. Ackroyd and C. F. Evans, 159–99. Cambridge: Cambridge University Press, 1970.

Teitler, H. C. *Notarii and exceptores.* Amsterdam: J. C. Gieben Publisher, 1985.

Thelamon, Françoise. *Païens et chrétiens au IVe siècle: L'apport de l'Histoire ecclésiastique de Rufin d'Aquilée.* Paris: Études augustiniennes, 1981.

Thierry, J. J. "The Date of the Dream of Jerome." *Vigiliae Christianae* 17 (1963): 28–40.

Thorgerson, Erika. "The *Vita Augustini* of Possidius: The Remaking of Augustine for a Post-Augustinian World." Dissertation, Princeton University, 1999.

Tov, Emanuel. *Textual Criticism of the Hebrew Bible.* Assen: Van Gorcum; Minneapolis: Fortress Press, 1992.

Trigg, Joseph W. *Origen.* London and New York: Routledge, 1998.

Trout, Denis E. "Damasus and the Invention of Early Rome." *Journal of Medieval and Renaissance Studies* 33 (2003): 517–36.

———. *Paulinus of Nola: Life, Letters, and Poems.* Berkeley: University of California Press, 1999.

Turner, E. G. *Greek Manuscripts of the Ancient World.* 2nd edition. London: Institute of Classical Studies, 1987.

———. *Greek papyri: An Introduction.* Oxford: Clarendon Press, 1968.

———. *The Typology of the Early Codex.* Philadelphia: University of Pennsylvania Press, 1977.

Vessey, Mark. "Conference and Confession: Literary Pragmatics in Augustine's *Apologia contra Hieronymum*." *Journal of Early Christian Studies* 1, no. 2 (1993): 175–213.

———. "The Forging of Orthodoxy in Latin Christian Literature: A Case Study." *Journal of Early Christian Studies* 4, no. 4 (1996): 495–513.

———. "Jerome's Origen: The Making of a Christian Literary *Persona*." *Studia Patristica* 28 (1993): 135–45.

Vogüé, Adalbert de. *Histoire littéraire du mouvement monastique dans l'antiquité.* Paris: Éditions du Cerf, 1991–.

Wermelinger, Otto. *Rom und Pelagius: Die theologische Position der römischen Bischöfe im pelagianischen Streit in den Jahren 411–432.* Stuttgart: A. Hiersemann, 1975.

White, Peter. "*Amicitia* and the Profession of Poetry in Early Imperial Rome." *Journal of Roman Studies* 68 (1978): 74–92.

———. *Promised Verse: Poets in the Society of Augustan Rome.* Cambridge, MA: Harvard University Press, 1993.

Williams, Megan. "Jerome's Biblical Criticism and the Making of Christian Scholarship." Dissertation, Princeton University, 2001.

Wilson, Nigel Guy. *Scholars of Byzantium.* Baltimore: Johns Hopkins University Press, 1983.

Wright, John. "Origen in the Scholar's Den." In *Origen of Alexandria: His World and His Legacy,* edited by Charles Kannengiesser, 48–62. Notre Dame, IN: University of Notre Dame Press, 1988.

Index